PRESENCE AND PRESENTATION

THE NEW MIDDLE AGES

BONNIE WHEELER

Series Editor

The New Middle Ages presents transdisciplinary studies of medieval cultures. It includes both scholarly monographs and essay collections.

PUBLISHED BY ST. MARTIN'S PRESS:

Women in the Medieval Islamic World: Power, Patronage, and Piety
   edited by Gavin R. G. Hambly

The Ethics of Nature in the Middle Ages: On Boccaccio's Poetaphysics
   by Gregory B. Stone

The Lost Love Letters of Heloise and Abelard:
Perceptions of Dialogue in Twelfth-Century France
   by Constant Mews and Neville Chiavaroli

PRESENCE AND PRESENTATION

WOMEN IN THE CHINESE LITERATI TRADITION

Sherry J. Mou
Editor

St. Martin's Press
New York

ISBN 0-312-21054-X

Library of Congress Cataloging-in-Publication Data

Presence and Presentation : women in the Chinese literati tradition /
    edited by Sherry J. Mou.
      p.   cm. — (The new middle ages ; 4)
    Includes bibliographical references and index.
    ISBN 0-312-21054-X
    1. Women—China—Social conditions.   2. China—History—221
B.C.–960 A.D.   I. Mou, Sherry J., 1954- .   II. Series.
HQ1767.P74   1998
305.4'0951—dc21   98-26386
                                                                                            CIP

Design by Letra Libre

First edition:
10   9   8   7   6   5   4   3   2   1

To
Professor Yan-shuan Lao and Shimu

for
his retirement

CONTENTS

Series Editor's Foreword   ix
Acknowledgments   x
Explanatory Notes   xii
Chronology of Chinese Dynasties   xiii
Introduction   xv
       Sherry J. Mou

1   The Death of a Princess: Codifying Classical
    Family Ethics in Early Medieval China   1
    Jen-der Lee

2   Women in China's Frontier Politics: *Heqin*   39
    Ning Chia

3   From Cross-Dressing Daughter to Lady Knight-Errant:
    The Origin and Evolution of Chinese Women Warriors   77
    Sufen Sophia Lai

4   Writing Virtues with Their Bodies: Rereading the
    Two Tang Histories' Biographies of Women   109
    Sherry J. Mou

5   *Ji^a^*-Entertainers in Tang Chang'an   149
    Victor Xiong

6   Smell Good and Get a Job: How Daoist
    Women Saints Were Verified and Legitimatized
    during the Tang Dynasty (618–907)   171
    Suzanne Cahill

7   Father in Heaven, Mother in Hell: Gender Politics in
    the Creation and Transformations of Mulian's Mother   187
    Sufen Sophia Lai

8 Bonds of Certain Consequence: The Personal Responses
   to Concubinage of Wang Anshi and Sima Guang   215
   Don J. Wyatt

Bibliography   239
Glossary   267
About the Contributors   291
Index   293

SERIES EDITOR'S FOREWORD

The New Middle Ages contributes to lively transdisciplinary conversations in medieval cultural studies through its scholarly monographs and essay collections. This series provides focused research in a contemprorary idiom about specific but diverse practices, expressions, and ideologies in the Middle Ages; it aims especially to recuperate the histories of medieval women.

Presence and Presentation: Women in the Chinese Literati Tradition, edited by Sherry J. Mou, is the eighth volume in this series and the very first published collection that focuses on the lives of women in medieval China. The scholars who have collaborated in this project have culled their perceptions from a wide range of carefully shaped and often highly conventional literary, historical, and religious texts. Like its predecessor volume, *Women in the Medieval Islamic World: Power, Patronage, and Piety* (edited by Gavin R. G. Hambly, 1997), this study attempts to tease information about women's lives out of writings by primarily male authors, cautiously but daringly reading these works from the position of their subject(s). The stories analyzed here provide new points of departure for thinking about women in modern as well as medieval Chinese societies. Furthermore, the authors of the studies in *Presence and Presentation: Women in the Chinese Literati Tradition* challenge what they view as a totalizing impulse in contemporary feminism: Mou and others claim that Western thinkers sometimes universalize theoretical assumptions about women and power. Both in subject and in stance, then, this collection is fresh and forceful.

Bonnie Wheeler
Southern Methodist University

ACKNOWLEDGMENTS

My gratitude goes first to Juris G. Lidaka, who first introduced me to Kalamazoo more than ten years ago and who helped me tremendously throughout the past decade. Without his moral and practical support, both in my work and in private life, this book would still be a dream. I also want to thank Wellesley College, whose generous early-leave program allowed me the luxury of time to work on this book, and whose Faculty Awards enabled me to get better software and other editorial assistance.

My colleagues in the Chinese Department also helped me in many ways. Yuan-chu Ruby Lam read through some portions of the early draft and offered invaluable suggestions. Jing-heng Sheng Ma graciously provided me with several wonderful student assistants. Martha Menne's good-humored help—especially with office supplies, mailing, and faxes—was beyond measure. Many students at Wellesley also helped at various stages of this book. Catherine Wu helped at the early stages, converting files from different programs and setting up bookkeeping details. Ngoc-Diep To, Ding Wu, and Ying Zhang helped with word-processing. Collene Frashure's, Luoluo Diao's, and Hui Men's careful proofreading spared me many embarrassments. Without their help, this book would be still in limbo.

A special thank you goes to Don J. Wyatt, who has been most generous with his advice in matters great and small, sharing his expertise and experience in history and editing. Eugene Wei-chun Chiu, Susan Mann, and Ellen Widmer also read portions of the book and offered valuable comments and suggestions. Bonnie Wheeler, the series editor, tirelessly read through the manuscript, offered both substantive and editorial suggestions, and brought invaluable comparative insights from her own scholarship in medieval European women. Alan Bradshaw, the Production Manager at St. Martin's Press, and an anonymous copyeditor patiently went through the draft and offered precious suggestions and comments. I am grateful to them all.

Finally, to Professor Yan-shuan Lao and *Shimu,* I will always be indebted for their kindness, encouragement, and exemplary teaching. Professor Lao's erudition in Chinese literature and history has been attested to by many scholars in the past; I hardly need add anything. I only want to thank him here for opening the window of Chinese history for me. Though it cannot adequately convey my gratitude for all the help I received from him, this volume will nevertheless bring Professor Lao and *Shimu* my sincerest wishes for a joyful retirement, reading Du Fu and composing poems.

Sherry J. Mou
Wellesley College
May 5, 1998

EXPLANATORY NOTES

1. In general, *pinyin* is used for romanizing quotations from Chinese texts. Chinese proper nouns and titles also follow *pinyin,* with two exceptions: (a) when the author's own spellings are known, they will be respected; and (b) the names of a few places well known to Westerners, such as Taipei, are spelled conventionally.

2. The Glossary is arranged alphabetically according to the *pinyin* of individual Chinese characters, regardless of word divisions. Thus, Shanxi (the province) will proceed Shang (the dynasty) in a list. Chinese entries in the bibliographies are also alphabetized this way.

3. Titles and names that appear in the Bibliography are not repeated in the Glossary. Nor are dynastic names, which are included in the Chronology of Chinese Dynasties.

CHRONOLOGY OF CHINESE DYNASTIES

Shang 商 (sixteenth to eleventh centuries B.C.E.)

Zhou 周 (ca. eleventh century-256 B.C.E.)
    Western Zhou 西周 (ca. eleventh century-771 B.C.E.)
    Eastern Zhou 東周 (770-256 B.C.E.)
        Spring and Autumn period 春秋 (770-453 B.C.E.)
        Warring States period 戰國 (453-256 B.C.E.)

Qin 秦 (221-207 B.C.E.)

Han 漢 (206 B.C.E. - 220 C.E.)
    Western (Former) Han 西漢 (206 B.C.E. - 8 C.E.)
    Xin 新 (9-23)
    Eastern (Later) Han 東漢 (25-220)

Three Kingdoms 三國 (220-80)
    CaoWei 曹魏 (220-65)
    Shu Han 蜀漢 (221-63)
    Wu 吳 (222-80)

Jin 晉 (265-420)
    Western Jin 西晉 (265-316)
    Eastern Jin 東晉 (317-420)

Northern Dynasties 北朝 (386-581)
    Northern Wei 北魏 (386-534)
    Eastern Wei 東魏 (534-50)
    Western Wei 西魏 (535-57)
    Northern Qi 北齊 (550-77)
    Northern Zhou 北周 (557-81)

Southern Dynasties 南朝 (420-589)
    Liu Song 劉宋 (420-79)
    Southern Qi 南齊 (479-502)
    Liang 梁 (502-57)
    Chen 陳 (557-89)

Sui 隋 (581-618)

Tang 唐 (618-907)

Five Dynasties 五代 (907-60)

Song 宋 (960-1279)
　　Northern Song 北宋 (960-1127)
　　Southern Song 南宋 (1127-1279)

Yuan 元 (1271-1368)

Ming 明 (1368-1644)

Qing 清 (1644-1911)

INTRODUCTION

Sherry J. Mou
Wellesley College

Background

The essays in this volume originated in recent presentations about medieval Chinese women at the annual International Congress on Medieval Studies.[1] The term "medieval Chinese" (*zhonggu,* literally middle
antiquity) needs some explanation. As a periodization term, it was used by
the Japanese sinologist Naitō Konan (1866–1934) in his hypothesis on
Chinese periodization, which divided Chinese history into "high antiquity" *(jōko),* "middle antiquity" *(chūko),* and "modern times" *(kinsei)—*
terms that generate vigorous debate and revision to this day. The general
consensus is that China's medieval age goes from the latter part of the Later
Han Dynasty (25–220) to the end of the Tang Dynasty (618–907),[2] a period in which Daoism and Buddhism permanently ruptured Confucianism's outlook on the world and view of life.[3] With one exception (an essay
on two Song Dynasty dignitaries), the essays collected here fall within this
time frame. All these essays study medieval Chinese women and deal with
texts or topics that have rarely, if ever, been studied; yet these texts and topics barely begin to explore the issues involved.

In the United States, the last decade has witnessed a mushrooming of
studies relating to Chinese women, to which the presence of Chinese
studies at Kalamazoo provides an interesting parallel. Sessions devoted to
Chinese studies first appeared there in the late eighties and early nineties.
Many of those early sessions were stuck in rooms next to staircases or
washrooms: dissonant sounds often joined the scholars' voices. The first session at Kalamazoo that I myself organized in 1992 was similarly marginalized: a handful of listeners, a small classroom, in one of the last sessions in
the early Sunday hours. Interesting exchanges at the end struck sparks but
could hardly sweep away the sense that we were out of place. The wind
does change, though. In 1997, one of the two sessions on Chinese women

attracted a standing-room-only crowd. The range of questions indicated that dialogue between East and West was indeed happening. Intellectual engagements have become a part of our scholarly conversation, and not merely as a token presence appended in the questions. Although Chinese and European medieval societies have been worlds apart, by studying them together comparatively, even simultaneously, we gain insight into these remote pasts and bring our present intellectual worlds closer. Such ventures also provide a measured, learned response to some current academic concerns with multiculturalism, by whose sway we must have been affected in more ways than we recognized.

Recent publications within Chinese studies on the subject of Chinese women also indicate broadening interest. Research has finally moved beyond such exotic topics as footbinding and concubinage[4] to include more fundamental inquiries into the epistemology and ontology of Chinese women's lives and histories, and new studies on the formation of Chinese womanhood, women's roles in the institutions of marriage and family, and issues relating to women's writings. Such studies focus on women's issues customarily slighted in Chinese studies, but they also complement canonical study by viewing old vistas in new perspectives, thus shifting the whole focus of the field. One ready example of such recent studies is Meng Yue and Dai Jinhua's Oedipal reinterpretation of the May Fourth Movement (1917–27) as a rare instance of patricide in a culture that worshiped the father image.[5] This new perspective inevitably questions whether, behind the advocacy of women's freedom of marriage, the male authors of the May Fourth Movement were indeed demanding their own liberation from father figures. Such a re-vision of the male authors' stance also sheds new light on why in China male scholars were traditionally the leading voices in advocating women's rights and questioning society's appropriation of women's positions.

However, most of these recent studies investigate the twentieth century or late imperial China, especially the Ming (1368–1644) and Qing (1644–1911) Dynasties.[6] Recently published studies of late imperial women further our understanding of the recent past, but they show more interest in "Japanese and Western models and in fighting for women's rights than in discussing the position of women in ancient China,"[7] as Tienchi Martin-Liao pointed out over a decade ago. A richer understanding of women in recent centuries must be grounded in historical antecedents. Thus, we situate our study of women by reexamining traditional discourse about women as well as by unearthing new materials by and about women. On both counts, one important point of departure is the literati tradition, the backbone of Chinese culture.

The Literati Tradition

"Literati" is a term applied here in the same sense as the later meaning of the term *shidaifu,* which means a social class configured by shared background in learning and in moral values, not merely by official positions (which many literati did occupy), wealth, or genealogy. The Chinese literati tradition can be roughly traced back to the Zhou Dynasty (eleventh century–256 B.C.E.). According to Hu Shi, in the Western Zhou there were two kinds of *shi,* the *Zhou shi* and the *Yin shi. Zhou shi* were mainly warriors who helped the Zhou king rule, and as a class they were at the bottom of the Zhou aristocracy.[8] *Yin shi,* also called *ru* (Confucianists),[9] the social class to which Confucius belonged, were among the descendants of the Shang Dynasty (sixteenth to eleventh centuries B.C.E.), and they were originally priests, tending to sacrificial ceremonies for the state. As the Zhou supplanted the Shang, the social position of *ru* was also supplanted by the *Zhou shi.* They used their knowledge to manage ancestral and funeral ceremonies for fellow Shang descendants. Out of professional necessity, both *Zhou shi* and *Yin shi* were not only versed in bookish learning but also capable of ritual services, music, archery, riding, and hunting.[10] In the social turmoil of the Eastern Zhou Dynasty (770–256 B.C.E.), or the Spring and Autumn and the Warring States periods, numerous feudal lords and states needed consultants and advisors, providing exceptional opportunities for all *shi* and bringing about shifts in social status. Because of their wide range of knowledge and practical function in society, *Yin shi* were respected among the top of the ruled non-Zhou.[11] With nobles moving down and commoners up, the *ru* and the *shi* further mingled, becoming the errant-gentlemen *(youshi)* of the pre-Qin period.

During the Qin and Han Dynasties (221 B.C.E.–220 C.E.), many of the errant-gentlemen were subofficials and teachers; their holding various offices *(daifu)* eventually led to the descriptive class designation *shidaifu* (literati). From the third to the sixth centuries, China entered the Era of the Great Division and split into North and South, each ruled by a series of short-lived governments. This political upheaval provided a hotbed for "the ontological mode of thinking" of Neo-Daoism and the "radical other-worldliness"[12] of the new religion Buddhism. A new religious dimension of the literati consciousness emerged that fused the this-worldly spirit of pre-Qin Confucianism with the otherworldly sentiment of Daoism and Buddhism. After the further blending of Confucianism with Buddhism under the Tang Dynasty (618–907) and through the revival of Confucianism (neo-Confucianism) in the Song Dynasty (960–1279), the literati conscience became identified with the Chinese social conscience.

No longer bound by their professional identity, the literati were found in most walks of life—they were officials, scholars, and even merchants,[13] distinguished from others by their shared sense of values, which was seasoned through similar educational formation and moral upbringing. But—and this is one problem with the accepted history of the literati tradition— women seem invisible. Where were they?

To answer this question, it is crucial to apply the category of gender to the analysis of the literati tradition[14] and to foreground women's presence in the literati tradition. Were women indeed not part of this tradition? Written records of the literati tradition allow us to ask where women stand there. Since the Sui Dynasty (581–618), Chinese books have been categorized into classics, histories, philosophers, and belles lettres (*jing shi zi ji*). By the time of the Tang Dynasty, when the civil-service examination system was established, twelve of the thirteen classics were canonized, and most were adopted by the government as basic texts for the civil-service examination.[15] Although women are not at the center of the classics, they are included in them, especially in the three classics of rites (*Li jing*) and the *Book of Poetry* (*Shi jing*). The many tomes of the official histories alone—to say nothing of the unofficial histories and the quasi-histories— provide numerous interesting perceptions about women. The philosophers also needed women in order to theorize about the operation of the universe as the exchange of the yin and the yang, as exemplified by women and men, subordinates and rulers. Finally, the literary works would not have much left were we to remove women from them.

Indeed, women are very much a part of the literati tradition; however, if we take an ahistorical, modern squint at this tradition, we see that it allotted a very specific and limited space for women. Women in the classics and the histories remain familial and passive, and the discourse of the tradition—molded not just by the Confucianists but also by the Daoists and Buddhists—often presented the feminine as a force that needed suppressive regulation. Women have always been present in the literati tradition, rarely as active agents, but plentifully as projections of male ideals and fantasies. These are the muted wives, daughters, mothers, and mothers-in-law of the classics; the pious adepts and atrocious sinners of religious literature; and, most of all, the potent presences of vernacular literature, fashioned from real life as well as from imagination. Women and their lives necessarily affect the formation and development of the literati tradition in ways more profound than have thus far been recognized.

Nor were women simply passive images filling pages of male-authored texts. In fact, many writings that explicate and promulgate regulations suppressing women came from women writers of a literati background. The best example is Ban Zhao's (49–120) "Admonitions for Women" ("Nü

jie"), a comprehensive treatise on women's behavior that was used in
women's education persistently until the 1930s. This peculiar phenomenon
is mainly a result of a gender-determined educational system. For women,
education was limited to the practical and functional purpose of better
serving their families, to which the Confucian classics were thought to be
a sufficient guide. Thus, when women's voices are heard, the tune is dis-
tinctly Confucian. When Ban Zhao, the most erudite woman historian,
wrote "Admonitions for Women," she advocated the regulation of female
behavior according to the Confucian point of view, focusing on family
roles and passive submission. Even the most renowned poetesses, such as Li
Qingzhao (1084-circa 1151) and Zhu Shuzhen (twelfth century), found
their subjects well within the Confucian confines of conjugal love and history. Literati women of later ages reflect a similar propensity, as Dorothy
Ko observes, so that even seventeenth-century Chinese literati women
"were inclined more to celebrate their role as guardians of Confucian
morality than to repudiate it."[16]

Presence and Presentation

This educational system resulted in three historical facts relevant to this
volume's inquiry into gender formation and its implications: (1) most texts
were written by men; (2) thus most, if not all, were from a male perspective inevitably including blind spots that cannot be accessed unless we
change perspective; and (3) even sympathetic works by men (such as the
male writers of the May Fourth generation) and works written by women
(such as Ban Zhao's "Admonitions for Women") should be subjected to
feminist scrutiny. In terms of dealing with our materials, we must, as Susan
Mann argues, "defamiliarize the familiar" and "rediscover the neglected
sources," so that we can "reconceptualize the organization of Chinese society in historical time."[17]

In expressing an affirmative view of the lives of medieval European
women, Alcuin Blamires compares his venture to "the obverse of a character assassination."[18] This nearly impossible job involves constructing "a
mode of discourse which aims to build a positive representation of women
in response to either specified or implicit accusations," based almost entirely
on works written by men. Thus, he warns against undue expectations of his
study on three accounts: (1) the case is not "a new feminist theory about
medieval women"; (2) it is by no means an exhaustive study of all possible
ways to look at medieval women affirmatively; and (3) this case may not
even be one that the medieval women would make themselves.[19] In the
same fashion, our study of Chinese medieval women simply presents one
aspect of the discourse on Chinese women. If at times we seem to magnify

(through isolation) women's power and glory in mostly male-crafted texts, it is because our aim is to tease out these women's own voices. And although they did not produce large bodies of written works as modern women have, women in the past were not merely oppressed and voiceless.

Nancy Armstrong suggests that "'femininity' is the primary object of feminist analysis, especially when we want to understand where various representations of women differ or converge." Armstrong wrote that the answer "does not lie in real women but in the logic of representation itself, since the culture's definition(s) of femininity will determine what a 'woman' really is, that is, the remainder that seems to resist the categories of its moment."[20] In a similar spirit, the essays collected here examine various representations of women in historical, literary, or religious accounts, and all in relation to the literati tradition. Each asks how women's presence has affected that tradition and how women are appropriated by that tradition. Two issues especially concern us: the centrality of family and the strategic, essentialist position of women's bodies.

These two themes are in fact very closely related. Epochal transformations of any social conventions described in the historical documents need to be reexamined through the lenses of women's lives, since women have been the fundamental support of most familial relations. This is not a new insight. As early as 1972, in her *Women and the Family in Rural Taiwan*, Margery Wolf coined the term "uterine family" in discussing women in Chinese family structure, in which a woman formed a "cohesive unit" centering on herself and her children.[21] Such a female-centered power structure within the institution of the family becomes visible only when we shift the focus to women, and the notion of uterine family is a useful tool not only for historical investigation, but also for literary analysis. Study of the classic Chinese novel *Honglou meng* [Dream of the red mansions] is only one example in which using the notion of uterine family as an analytical tool to dissect familial power structures yields fruitful results.

Another theme common to every essay is the inscription of the female body. Historical women's bodies help to inscribe women today; for, to rephrase Armstrong's words, what a woman *is* is defined by the cultural representation of femininity.[22] As Denise Riley noted, one does not sense her womanness all the time. Moments that remind a person of her womanness are varied and bound to specific social milieus and historical moments.[23] Yet these moments construct what culture defines as one's gender. For example, bound feet express both limitation and liberation, depending on a woman's class and family as well as on her historical era.[24] Whether or not gender is exclusively situated in one's body, acknowledging the distinctive existence of female bodies is strategically necessary in the study of women.

Such a position will not square with some current feminist theories. As Blamires maintains with medieval European women, any case exalting women that is based on medieval texts will satisfy few feminist criteria, because such a case "is a very indirect ancestor of modern feminism."[25] We seek in these essays not only to use "woman" as a tool of formal analysis to unsettle the very male-centered notion of the "literati tradition,"[26] but also to unsettle historical and unnuanced theories of sex and gender.

Representation

The essays in this book are arranged in a relatively chronological order, and they also share the two foci of the family and women's bodies. Besides exploring women's roles as laid out by the traditional family structure, the authors also reveal the influences and implications of the choices women made. We see women functioning in politics: shrewd regents and active, though not always voluntary, participants under the *heqin* policy (marriage between Chinese imperial princesses and nomadic rulers of Inner Asia). We see women being appropriated in religion: Daoist saints and epitomes of Buddhist evil. We see women being transformed in literature: from cross-dressing filial daughters to female knights-errant, and from a helpless mother to an archsinner. We see women earning livings on their own as different kinds of entertainers. Last but not least, we see women living at home as daughters, wives, widows, and mothers; here we see them not just as oppressed victims, but also as a part of the forces upholding the patriarchal system.

The two cases involving princesses—the death of one (ch. 1) and the *heqin* marriages of others (ch. 2)—can be viewed as variations of marriage and family life. The discussion of the two Tang histories' sections consisting of the biographies of women (ch. 4) summarizes the four paradigms historians assigned to women, all of which are within the confines of family: filial daughters, loyal wives, chaste widows, and sagacious mothers. An examination of the lady knight-errant (ch. 3) further supports the validity of these paradigms, for cross-dressing daughters uphold the ideal of filiality and women warriors fight for their husbands' causes. We also see career women in the anatomy of the Tang *ji*ᵃ-entertainers system (ch. 5); even though they were outside the realm of regular family life, many of the *ji*-entertainers dreamt of nothing but having families of their own. Interestingly, most women in the Daoist transformation accounts (ch. 6) were supported by their families in their religious calling. The transformation of Mulian's mother (ch. 7) in Buddhist literature exemplifies a misogynistic view of women comparable to that embodied in the story of Eve and original sin. A sense of the family's collective responsibility is visible in

legal codification (ch. 1) and in a shared class sentiment in procuring concubines to ensure posterity (ch. 8), bringing to full circle the importance
of Chinese family ethics.

But these essays are also about women's bodies and the meanings inscribed on them. The battered, pregnant body of a princess speaks at once
of the vulnerability of women (ch. 1). If the institution of marriage pros-
pered from the commodification of women's bodies, the *heqin* princesses'
political positions heightened the exchange value of women (ch. 2). On the
other hand, without political backing, the *ji*[a]-entertainers sought to increase
the commercial value of their bodies by acquiring skills such as singing,
dancing, poetry writing, and entertaining (ch. 5). The case concerning concubinage unflinchingly shows that the procuring of concubines was nothing but a commercial transaction of women (ch. 8). For women warriors,
dressing as men only enhanced their sense of being women (ch. 3). The
Daoist adepts' passage to sainthood literally depended on the well-being of
the body (ch. 6). The bodily mutilation that filial daughters, loyal wives, and
chaste widows incurred upon themselves speaks eloquently of women's ex-
asperation at their prescribed positions in the institution of the family (ch.
4). Finally, the graphic delineation of the sufferings of Mulian's mother in
Hell turns a woman's body into a teaching tablet (ch. 7). Together, these papers point out how pertinent women's presence, however defined, is to the
entire literati tradition, which values the social role of the family, whose
foundation would tumble without the support of women.

Jen-der Lee's essay on the death of a princess reads like a detective story,
peeling away one layer of implication after another to expose the complexity of the codification of family ethics in early medieval China. Her
discussion branches out into minuscule venues of social practices both
horizontally, covering the Southern as well as the Northern Dynasties, and
vertically, from the two Han Dynasties to the Tang Dynasty. What we see
is not just the codification of laws pertaining to domestic affairs but also
breaches in carrying out these laws. Although situated in the center of the
ruling class, Lee's case study weaves together several intricate threads, revealing that race, class, and gender have been issues since ancient times, not
at all just modern concerns. Furthermore, the court officials' heated
protests and debates about legal procedures beg us to recheck the general
notion that the Chinese legal system lay in the hands of the rulers. We see
literati legalists acting both for and against the interests of women. The lesson, as Jen-der Lee reminds us, is that women need to be in positions of
power in order to effect changes involving their interests.

Also about court ladies, Ning Chia's paper reexamines the historical
practice of *heqin* to expose the *heqin* women's point of view on: their his-

torical position, their role as emissaries between the two states, their political grasp, their personal feelings, and their image in Chinese cultural memory. By foregrounding *heqin* women in her discussion of frontier politics in imperial China, Chia looks at the gender politics of agents at several levels: agrarian and nomadic societies, China and Inner Asia, imperial parents and daughters, husbands and wives (of different ethnic backgrounds), and the wives themselves. Chia's paper resonates with popular literary and cultural theories in more ways than those she has included in her discussion. Issues, such as distinctive life styles (the agrarian versus the nomadic) and ethnicity (the Han versus the Huns and other tribal peoples), are dealt with only in relation to gender and politics, because of the focus of her discussion. Nevertheless, her explication of the *heqin* women's families as a part of politics between the two states redefines the feminists' saying that "the personal is the political": In the *heqin* context, the familial is the political.

In Sufen Lai's images of cross-dressing daughters and women-warrior wives, we see another appropriation of family ethics. These seemingly unconventional women, who perform most "unwomanly" actions on battlefields and in revenge cases, turn out to promote the most basic literati ethics of loyalty, filiality, integrity, and righteousness *(zhong xiao jie yi)*. They lit up the popular stage and filled the pages of vernacular literature to become some of the most efficient preachers of literati morality.

My paper on the two Tang histories' biographies of women raises other questions about women's presence in the literati tradition. If women's education did not include the study of official histories, the biographies of women compiled in these histories must have had men in mind as their audience. The "biographies of women" sections in Chinese official histories, a tradition about women written by men, therefore instructed the literati scholars in what was expected of Confucian womanhood. The men then projected these expectations onto the behavior of their daughters, wives, and mothers. What the biographies recorded was by and large wish fulfillment. Thus, in tracing the theme of suicide and death in these biographies, one finds that, however a woman dies, the causes are invariably filiality, chastity, or loyalty. Were these issues indeed these women's primary concerns? Did their actions indeed constitute passive submission to convention? Or were their actions silent protests against a tradition that did not adequately value their presence?

In comparison, Victor Xiong's paper presents a more straightforward assessment of women as recorded by a literati scholar and a frequenter of the entertainment quarter. The lives of the ji^a-entertainers were recounted and interpreted in a matter-of-fact fashion, revealing both classist and gendered undertones. The fate of the ji^a-entertainers is symbolic of medieval women's position. Many literati scholars' association with ladies of the red-light district was an important part of their lives, partly because of intense personal involvement and not least because the red-light district was located within the capital city. Nevertheless, these ladies of the red-light district remained a vignette in history.

Suzanne Cahill's paper focuses on Daoist women saints. Cahill discusses how these women's transformations link lineage and bureaucracy, two important Confucian themes, to community worship and individual salvation. She bases her analysis on historical and literary accounts of several Daoist holy women of the Tang Dynasty. The ritualistic details for the care and disposition of their bodies attest to the women's ordinariness and sainthood simultaneously. Most of these women's close ties with their families also put them in interesting contrast to male religious figures, for whom families are often ornaments to their religious achievements. These accounts of women adepts reconcile their religious sentiments with other literati values, finding no conflict between their religious callings and their family lives.

Sufen Lai's study of the Mulian story, especially with regard to the transformation of the mother figure, reflects a similar situation. Following Stephen F. Teiser's comprehensive study of the Ghost Festival in medieval China, Lai's paper illustrates how the simple Indian Buddhist salvation story of a monk saving his mother from Hell grew into elaborate Chinese religious versions in the "transformation texts" (bianwen) and "precious scrolls" (baojuan) genres. This process exemplifies the assimilation of Buddhism, Confucianism, and Daoism by medieval China. The addition of the father figure adroitly heightens the theme of filial piety, already underlined by Mulian's endurance of a legendary ordeal to save his mother. The subsequent secularization of the story through the integration of Chinese historical settings and Daoist heavenly hierarchy further unites the Mulian legend with Chinese culture. In all these intricate developments, Lai sees Mulian's mother, in both gendered and cultural terms, as a representation of "collective otherness": the other world and the other gender.

Don J. Wyatt's paper looks the literati tradition straight in the eye, examining two of the most prominent Confucian literati scholars (Sima Guang and Wang Anshi), who were also seasoned politicians, historians, and literary figures. Wyatt describes a society that ranked family relations so far above gender relations that the wives of these two Song scholar-politicians tried to procure concubines for them, even though the husbands themselves publicly endorsed but privately rejected concubinage. A monolithic association of the oppression of Chinese women with concubinage is problematic at best; gender politics is far too complicated to be formulated simply as men's oppression of women. The two wives' active

participation in the process of getting their husbands appropriate concubines also suggests a class consciousness separating wives and concubines,
not more personal sentiments among equals such as jealousy. Wyatt urges
compassion for decent literati men and women. Wrought separately in the
same world bound by sets of seemingly rational rules, women and men
nevertheless found certain rules personally unpalatable.

Besides opening new windows for our queries about medieval Chinese
women, these essays also provide crucial reflections of our own lives. Many
issues these women confronted have their contemporary counterparts. The
marital violence that resulted in the death of a princess is repeated every
day in many families. The undervaluation of the *heqin* princesses' contributions persists in the undervaluation of volunteer work done today by
women, without which society could hardly function. Common women
had as their models wives and daughters who go to extremes to express
culturally coded virtues or to promote their famous husbands. Career
women were phenomenal, but the family remains an important part of the
discourse of female careerists. Only a harmonious coexistence of career
and family, such as that displayed by the Daoist adepts and the cross-
dressing daughters and wives, could win cultural approval. The female entertainers' yearning for an ordinary family reinforces the extraordinary
value of family that culture places in women's lives. The triangular relationship among wife, husband, and concubine in a family repeats itself in
forms other than romantic love. Finally, a mother suffers more and more
for the sake of her son's achievement.

If the essays in this collection lean more to the side of textual analysis
than to that of theory, it is because we still know too little about Chinese
women before the Song Dynasty and because a "historicization of dis-
courses on [these] women" would be precarious at best even with sufficient
understanding of what is in the extant texts, to borrow Blamires' comments
on the study of European medieval women.[27] In this first volume devoted
to medieval Chinese women, we offer different ways to look at familiar and
unfamiliar texts, and what we hope to achieve is the extraction of female
intentions, if not voices, from these mostly male perspectives.

Are we smarter than women of the past? Hardly. Their silence on many
issues of today may also lead us to see how they negotiated with themselves
and with oppressive forces (in the forms of institutions as well as of men
and other women) socially, politically, and personally. If the essays in the current collection appear to exaggerate women's power or their ability to as-
sert their power, this is the result of our wish to portray our subjects as
active agents rather than as passive objects. In the absence of legal or other
structures that might have strengthened their position, these women

formed their own strategies for coping and living their lives. Although we must derive our understanding of them from men's words, we cannot dismiss these women as silent participants in history with no subjectivity at all.

Notes

1. From 1992 to 1998, the themes, moving from general to specific, were "Women and Chinese Classics" in 1992; "Death and Rebirth of Women in Medieval China: Histories and Fiction" in 1996; "Biographies of Chinese Women" (Session I: Court Ladies and Woman Warriors—The Pernicious and the Heroic, and Session II: Nuns and Courtesans—The Religious and the Monstrous) in 1997; and "Cities and Daily Life in Medieval China" in 1998.

2. For the Naitō hypothesis, see Hisayuki Miyakawa, "An Outline of the Naitō Hypothesis and Its Effects on Japanese Studies," *The Far Eastern Quarterly* 14.4 (August 1955): 533–52. Mao Han-guang defines "medieval age" as the period between the Jian'an reign (196–220) of the Han Dynasty and the Tianyou reign (904–6) of the Tang Dynasty, in *Zhongguo zhonggu shehui shi lun* [A discussion of Chinese medieval social history] (Taipei: Lianjing chuban shiye gongsi, 1988), pp. iv–v. Albert E. Dien views the late Han Dynasty and the Six Dynasties (220–589) as "early medieval" in *State and Society in Early Medieval China* (Stanford: Stanford University Press, 1990).

3. Yü Ying-shih sees this period as one of the three major breakthroughs in the Chinese intellectual tradition. The other two are Confucius's time, when several schools of thought (such as the Confucian, the Mohist, and the Daoist) emerged from the primeval cultural tradition, and the neo-Confucianism of the Song Dynasty. See Yü Ying-shih, "Intellectual Breakthroughs in the T'ang-Sung Transition," in *The Power of Culture, Studies in Chinese Cultural History,* eds. Willard J. Peterson, Andrew H. Plaks, and Ying-shih Yü (Hong Kong: The Chinese University Press, 1994), p. 158.

4. This is not to say that studies of concubinage and footbinding are obsolete; in fact, both are still very popular research topics. However, study of these practices has become more sophisticated, and the focus has shifted from looking at them as curious emblems of Chinese backwardness to treating them as pieces of a much larger mosaic of imperial Chinese society. Two examples are Dorothy Ko's discussions of footbinding as a sign of social status and an important factor in mapping out women's space during the Ming and Qing Dynasties and Don Wyatt's case study of concubinage (in this volume) from ethical standpoints other than gender relations. See Dorothy Ko, *Teachers of the Inner Chambers: Women and Culture in Seventeenth-Century China* (Stanford: Stanford University Press, 1994), pp. 147–51; and her "The Body as Attire: The Shifting Meanings of Footbind-

ing in Seventeenth-Century China," in *Journal of Women's History* 8.4 (Winter 1997): 8–27.

5. Meng Yue and Dai Jinhua, *Fu chu lishi dibiao: Zhongguo xiandai nüxing wenxue yanjiu* [Voices emerging into the foreground of history: a study of contemporary Chinese women's literature] (Taipei: Shibao wenhua, 1993), ch. 1, sec. 1, "Shi fu shidai" [The age of patricide], pp. 52–64.

6. See, for example, among books published in America alone, Chow; Gilmartin et al.; Honig and Hershatter; Ko; Lily Xiao Hong Lee; Yuning Li; McMahon; T'ien; Watson and Ebrey; Widmer and Chang; and Yenna Wu. The exception is Patricia Buckley Ebrey's study of women in the Song Dynasty (960–1279), *The Inner Quarters: Marriage and the Lives of Chinese Women in the Sung Period* (Berkeley: University of California Press, 1993).

7. Tienchi Martin-Liao, "Traditional Handbooks of Women's Education," in *Women and Literature in China,* eds. Anna Gerstlacher et al. (Bochum, Germany: Studienverlag Brockmeyer, 1985), p. 165.

8. For a discussion of the origin and rise of the *Zhou shi,* see Cho-yun Hsu, *Ancient China in Transition: An Analysis of Social Mobility, 722–222 B.C.* (Stanford: Stanford University Press, 1965), pp. 7–8 and 34–7.

9. As a profession, *ru* existed long before Confucius. As a school, the term Rujia (the *ru* school) first appeared in *Qi lue* [Seven summaries] by Liu Xin (ca. 46 B.C.E.–25 C.E.). It should be noted that Rujia does not base the value of the entire school on Confucius the way Confucianism does, although his distinguished position in the *ru* school is unquestionable. Hu Shi's appropriation of Confucius's relation to Ruism is most judicious: "Confucius is the leader who revived the Ruism, not its founder." See Hu Shi, "Shuo Ru" [On Ru], 1934, in *Hu Shi wencun* [Collected writings of Hu Shi] (Taipei: Yuandong tushu gongsi, 1968), p. 37.

   Although "Confucianism" is generally used to describe the school of *ru* (often translated as "literati" as well), it is in fact a Western appropriation of Ruism (Rujia) at best. According to the *Oxford English Dictionary,* Confucius is a Latinized form of *K'ung Fu-tzu,* "K'ung the Master," and the name was first used in 1687 by four Roman Catholic missionaries who published a translation of three of the Chinese classics at Paris. The term Confucianism refers to "the doctrines or system of Confucius and his followers" and was first used in 1862.

10. See Hu, pp. 15–17.

11. Gu Jiegang believes that the earliest *shi* were all knights-errant *(wushi)* and that the literati *shi (wenshi)* were derived from the knights-errant. See Gu Jiegang, "Wushi yu wenshi zhi tuihua" [The metamorphosis of the knight-errant and the literati], in *Shilin zashi chu bian* [The first compilation of miscellaneous topics on history] (Beijing: Zhonghua shuju, 1963), pp. 85–91. Yü Ying-shih disputes this position in "Gudai zhishi jieceng de xingqi yu fazhan" [The rise and development of the intellectual class of

antiquity], which is the first chapter of *Shi yu Zhongguo wenhua* [Literati and Chinese culture] (Shanghai: Shanghai renmin chubanshe, 1987). See especially pp. 9–26.

12. Yü Ying-shih was specifically referring to the transition in intellectual history from Confucianism to neo-Daoism and Buddhism during the third and the fourth centuries. See his "Intellectual Breakthroughs," p. 158.

13. See ch. 4, "Handai xunli yu wenhua chuanbo" [The subofficial functionaries of the Han Dynasty and the spreading of culture], and ch. 8, "Zhongguo jinshi zongjiao lunli yu shangren jingshen" [The religious ethics and the merchant spirit of China's modern times], in Yü Ying-shih's *Shi yu Zhongguo wenhua.*

14. See, for example, Joan Scott, "Gender: A Useful Category of Historical Analysis," in her *Gender and the Politics of History* (New York: Columbia University Press, 1988), pp. 28–55.

15. *Mencius [Mengzi]* was added to the classics during the Song period.

16. Ko, *Teachers of the Inner Chambers,* p. 9.

17. Susan Mann, "What Can Feminist Theory Do for the Study of Chinese History? A Brief Review of Scholarship in the U.S.," in *Jindai Zhongguo funü shi yanjiu* [Research on women in modern Chinese history] 1 (June 1993): 241–60.

18. Alcuin Blamires, *The Case for Women in Medieval Culture* (Oxford: Clarendon Press, 1997), p. 9.

19. Ibid.

20. Nancy Armstrong, "Postface, Chinese Women in a Comparative Perspective: A Response," in *Writing Women in Late Imperial China,* eds. Ellen Widmer and Kang-I Sun Chang (Stanford: Stanford University Press, 1997), pp. 420–1.

21. See Margery Wolf, *Women and the Family in Rural Taiwan* (Stanford: Stanford University Press, 1972), pp. 32–41. Susan Mann praises this work as the first "pathbreaking work exploring the relationship between gender and power in Chinese society." See Mann, p. 242.

22. Armstrong, pp. 420–1.

23. Denise Riley, *"Am I That Name?" Feminism and the Category of "Women" in History* (Minneapolis: University of Minnesota, 1988), pp. 96–101.

24. See Ko, "The Body as Attire."

25. Blamires, p. 11.

26. I am extending Rey Chow's suggestion that "the use of 'woman' needs to become a tool of formal analysis that would unsettle the very notion of 'tradition' itself," on p. 52 of her *Woman and Chinese Modernity: The Politics of Reading Between West and East* (Minnesota: University of Minnesota Press, 1991).

27. Blamires, p. 18.

CHAPTER ONE

THE DEATH OF A PRINCESS: CODIFYING CLASSICAL FAMILY ETHICS IN EARLY MEDIEVAL CHINA

Jen-der Lee

Institute of History and Philology, Academia Sinica

> *Women's involvement in legal cases, whether as victims, criminals, or arbitrators, shows that the road to Confucianization in early medieval China was bumpy, especially in the Northern Dynasties.*

Introduction

Marriage and family ethics are often believed to play an effective role in stabilizing a society. Thus, the codification of such ethics readily attracts the attention of ruling authorities. In western Europe, biblical teaching on marriage and family was interpreted and taught by the twelfth-century canonists, not only to direct people toward a more sacred life but also to increase the secular power of the Catholic Church, which was engaged in a contest with the feudal lords. The Church was not powerful either as a political entity or as a social force in the early Middle Ages. The monastic reform in the tenth and eleventh centuries, however, built up a cult of celibacy within clerical circles and freshened up the tainted image of the papacy. Through the Church courts, then, the Church established its power to regulate the marriage customs of the laity and to give spiritual justifications for marital ethics.[1] In China, it was the Confucian Classics that provided such ethics, and the state, instead of any religious organization, was the institution that undertook the task of enforcing those marital and familial norms.

Since the last century, traditional Chinese society has been perceived as almost monolithically Confucian, and the state, with a legal mechanism at its disposal, has often been seen as a willing participant in the "inevitable" development of Confucianization. However, like the Catholic Church before the Cluniac reform, the state (or better, states) in early medieval China was not yet sufficiently powerful to carry out its will. During the period of disunion between the fall of the Han Dynasty (206 B.C.E.–222 C.E.) and the reunification of the Sui (581–618), the state was divided and without encompassing power. (See Appendix I for Chinese dynasties till the seventh century.) Moreover, ethnic diversities, struggles for political survival, and differences in social structure all contributed to discrepancies in ethical values both among states and within a government. The issue was not only whether the ruling authorities intended to Confucianize society through the codification of classical ethics, but also, first, which aspects of those marital and familial ethics were integrated into the law; second, in what way the codification was carried out; and, third, who the ruling authorities were.

With regard to the first issue—which marital and familial ethics were integrated into the law—the codification of classical ethics in Chinese history was most vividly demonstrated in the application of *wufu,* the five degrees of mourning, to revising the law and making verdicts.[2] The "Sangfu" [Mourning] chapter of *Yi li* [The book of ceremonies], which contains a discussion of the five degrees of mourning (see Appendix II), established the duration and clothing (mostly flax) for mourning a family member. The duration of mourning, ranging from three months to three years, and flax clothing of five different qualities and shapes, were assigned to each family member, corresponding to his or her relation with the deceased in terms of closeness and status. The mourning-obligation system thus exemplified the scope and composition of the patriarchal family.[3] As shown in Appendix II, the mourning obligations were fashioned around the male members of the family. According to the "Sangfu" chapter, while a man stayed in his natal family with his relations to other members uninterrupted, a woman's mourning obligations changed with her marital status. When she married out of her natal family and into her husband's, her mourning obligations for her natal family members were reduced, while those for her husband's family were given priority.[4] As the *Yi li* put it, a father was the "heaven" to his child; the husband, the "heaven" to his wife. Since a person could not have two heavens, a woman's "heaven"—her greatest mourning obligation—was transferred from her father to her husband. The key points are that a woman's family identity shifted after her marriage, and that she was inferior to her husband in his family.[5]

As for the second issue, the implementation of these ethical standards, imperial decrees, and officials' memorials were often cited to demonstrate progress in the codification of Confucian ethics.[6] For instance, early in the Western Jin period (265–317), it was decreed that the five degrees of mourning should be employed as a principle for legal decisions[7]; that is to say, graded penalties would be meted out by justices to show and to ensure the definition of the hierarchy within a family should its members become involved in legal cases. However, careful investigation suggests that the application of the five degrees of mourning in verdicts varied among cases in different regimes due to factors including court politics, pleas from powerful aristocrats, possible nomadic influence, and personal characteristics of different rulers, which were all related to the third issue, the makeup of the ruling authority.

This article examines a case in the sixth century to trace progress and regress in the codification of Confucian ethics by the state. This disastrous case involved Grand Princess Lanling of the Northern Wei Dynasty (386–534), founded by the Tuoba clan of the nomadic Xianbei people, and her husband Liu Hui, son of an imperial clansman from the Liu-Song Dynasty of the South (420–79) who had surrendered to the northern rulers. Their violent marriage ended with a miscarriage and the death of the princess. The story of her death provides valuable insights into the relationship among state, family, and ethics in early medieval China. The case involved sex crimes, marital violence, concealment, and collective responsibilities among family members—all important aspects of the more general problem of the codification of classical ethics. To reach a verdict, court officials cited statutes and precedents from earlier periods, exemplifying how the Northern Wei both continued and deviated from the legal practices of their predecessors in the Han and subsequent dynasties.

In this article, we will first reconstruct the case of Princess Lanling, based on the "Biography of Liu Hui" and the "Monograph of Law" in the *Wei shu* [The history of the (Northern) Wei Dynasty],[8] and then examine the arguments of Cui Zuan, the most important official involved. Subsequently, we will investigate three elements in codifying the classical family ethics displayed by this case: (1) sex crimes; (2) marital violence; and (3) familism, which includes the issues of concealment and collective responsibility *(lianzuo)*. Along with the analysis, related statutes and cases will be cited to demonstrate the rationale of the contending arguments. Finally, we will discuss the positions and backgrounds of the participants not only to show various influential components of the ruling body—a nomadic woman ruler versus her legal bureaucrats—but also to underline the complexity of the Confucianization of Chinese society.

The Marriage of Grand Princess Lanling and Liu Hui

Grand Princess Lanling married Liu Hui at the turn of the sixth century. The princess is said to have been so jealous that she once killed a maid impregnated by Liu Hui. Still furious, the princess aborted and mutilated the unborn child, stuffed the maid with straw, and showed her naked to Liu Hui. Appalled and angered by the princess's behavior, Liu Hui determined to ignore her after this incident. The situation was reported to Empress Dowager Ling (reigned 516–28), the princess's sister-in-law and regent of the Northern Wei government at that time. After an investigation, Liu Hui was deprived of his noble title and was divorced, some ten years after his marriage to the princess. The reason given was that they no longer had "reason to be husband and wife."[9]

One year later, however, probably at the princess's request, a powerful eunuch and an imperial clansman who had handled the divorce investigation asked the Empress Dowager for the reunion of the princess and Liu Hui. The Empress Dowager was reluctant to grant the request at first, fearing that the princess would not mend her ways. After repeated petitions from the two, the Empress Dowager finally granted the request, escorted the princess out of the imperial palace personally, and asked her to exercise more discretion in the future.[10]

In 519 or 520, when the princess was pregnant, Liu Hui committed adultery with commoner Zhang's sister Zhang Rongfei and commoner Chen's sister Chen Huimeng.[11] History says that the princess changed her tactics and at first held her temper; however, agitated by her female relatives, she started fighting with Liu Hui again. Liu Hui pushed her out of bed, beat her, and stamped on her. She suffered a miscarriage and later died. In the meantime, Liu Hui had fled.[12] A reward, equaling an earlier one for a rebel, was offered for his arrest.[13] During the period between the princess's miscarriage and her death, when Liu Hui was still in hiding, the court fell into serious debate over the charges and verdicts for the two adulterous women and their brothers.[14] Bureaucrats challenged imperial decrees that favored severe punishments.

The Department of Chancellery *(menxia)* proposed that both Liu Hui and the two adulteresses be sentenced to death; the women's brothers should be banished to the borderland since they knew of the situation and did not prevent it from happening.[15] An imperial decree approved the proposal but reduced the women's death penalty to beating and head-shaving *(kunbian fugong)*[16] followed by palace slavery. Cui Zuan, then director of the three dukes *(sangong langzhong)* in the Department of State Affairs *(shangshu sheng),* did not agree with the verdict.[17] His argument consisted of four major points, including the verdicts for the three parties involved and a contention over the division of bureaucratic power.

The first point addressed the verdict for Liu Hui—whether his death sentence was appropriate according to various law codes. Cui Zuan claimed that the law was the foundation of government and should not be affected or altered by emotion or affinity. Liu Hui had not committed treason, and it was wrong to treat him as if he had. His crime, Cui Zuan tried to convince the imperial authority, was killing his unborn child. Cui Zuan cited the "Law of Assault" *(Doulü)* of the Northern Wei, saying that one who killed one's grandchild or child by beating would be sentenced to four years' labor, while one who killed one's grandchild or child with a weapon such as a knife would be sentenced to five years' labor. If one killed with love or hatred in mind, the penalty would be one degree more severe. He then argued that, even though the princess was prestigious, her aborted child was still Liu Hui's flesh, and thus his penalty should have been decided accordingly.[18]

Although historical records do not explain why Liu Hui was treated as a traitor, the way Cui Zuan argued for him provides some hints. Treason law since the Han Dynasty considered a person who killed an imperial family member a traitor.[19] That the imperial authority applied this precedent to Liu Hui suggests that it considered the aborted child an imperial family member. This runs against the idea of the patriarchal family defined in the *Yi li*. When Cui Zuan suggested a verdict based on the "Law of Assault," he was actually arguing for the recognition of the patriarchal family as described in the Confucian Classics. If the unborn child was perceived as Liu Hui's child instead of the princess's flesh, Liu Hui should not have been treated as a traitor who had killed an imperial family member. Instead, he should have been charged with killing his child.[20]

Second, Cui Zuan argued that, although the imperial decree showed mercy and reduced the two adulterous women's penalty, the punishment was still too harsh for their deeds. If they were considered Liu Hui's accessories, their sentence should have been postponed until he was captured. Cui Zuan cited a statute of 511 that maintained that the verdict for a principal criminal should be given before that for the accessories if the penalty involved banishment and execution *(xing)*.[21] Besides, Cui Zuan argued, what Zhang Rongfei and Chen Huimeng had committed was adultery; if they were caught at the scene of the crime with clear evidence, then they should have been convicted and punished as adulteresses. In no way should they be sentenced to slavery.[22] Cui Zuan did not quote any law code on the penalty for adultery, but his colleague, You Zhao, then right vice director *(you puye)* in the Department of State Affairs, came to his support and called for the labor penalty for the women.

Cui Zuan's third point focused on the innocence of the two brothers and the unfair application of collective responsibilities in their sentence. According to Zhang's testimony, his sister Rongfei was already married and had two daughters. Since the *Yi li* held that the husband was a married woman's heaven, Cui Zuan argued, her husband instead of her brother should have been responsible if she committed a crime. Cui Zuan referred to an important legal revision on collective responsibility from the Cao-Wei (220–65) and Western Jin periods; this revision mandated that a maiden be punished for her parents' treacherous crime and a wife for her husband's.[23] Moreover, Cui Zuan contended, the law allowed concealment among *jiqin,* family members with one year's mourning obligation, even if they had committed only ordinary crimes. The government should not have required siblings, also defined as *jiqin,* to testify about scandalous behavior such as adultery—not to mention that there was no collective responsibility in adultery cases anyway. Therefore, Cui Zuan asserted, the court should not punish the brothers because of its resentment against Liu Hui.[24]

What Cui Zuan referred to here were the two most important items in the Confucian ethical code: the right of concealment among family members, and the collective responsibility of the family as a whole. Both practices were based on the scope of the patriarchal family as defined by the five degrees of mourning prescribed in the *Yi li*. The statute on concealment was codified in the middle of the first century B.C.E. under the Han Dynasty. The treason case that stirred debates on women's collective responsibility took place near the end of the Cao-Wei rule and finally led to a modification of relevant laws in the beginning of the Western Jin period. Cui Zuan's reference to them indicates that the once-nomadic Xianbei continued the law of its Han predecessors and illustrates Cui's own efforts to integrate Confucian family ethics into legal decisions.

The fourth aspect of Cui Zuan's argument concerned the division of duties and power in government. He stated directly that officials of the Department of Chancellery belonged to the imperial palace; their job was to report cases and memorials, not to decide verdicts.[25] Who then was to decide the verdict? Cui Zuan did not make this explicit. But there is good reason to believe that the Department of State Affairs should have been the office in charge, especially since all disagreements came from officials of that department.

Yuan Xiuyi, imperial secretary *(shangshu)* of the Department of State Affairs, agreed with Cui Zuan's argument on the innocence of the brothers and cited the *Spring and Autumn Annals (Chunqiu)* to prove the cessation of connections between a married woman and her natal family. Since her natal family would not be accountable for any crimes committed by her, her brother should not have been charged and punished.[26] You Zhao, mentioned earlier, not only agreed with Cui Zuan's objections, but also emphasized that it was not the business of the Department of Chancellery to investigate felonies and propose verdicts. He therefore suggested that the court put the appropriate office in charge and retry the case.[27]

These proposals were not appreciated by the imperial authority. The imperial decree following the discussions confirmed the earlier verdicts. It explained that such a heavy reward was offered because Liu Hui's crime could not be pardoned and he had to be arrested. The decree claimed that the two women had indulged their passions and confused Liu Hui's mind by adultery, which caused the disastrous miscarriage of the princess. "If [they are] not executed, how can [the court] punish and purge [others in the future]?" questioned the decree. Though the decree acknowledged the validity of the bureaucrats' legal arguments on collective responsibility, it still accused the two brothers of failing to prevent the crime and concealing it after the fact. The wording of the decree affirmed the brothers' role in introducing their sisters to Liu Hui and suggested the importance of a harsh penalty as a warning to potential criminals, thus rationalizing the severe punishment meted out to the two brothers.[28]

With regard to the division of duties in government, the imperial court stated bluntly that it had the right to put the Chancellery in charge because, first, this was not an ordinary case, and, second, there had been imperial prisons since ancient times and not all cases were to be decided by judicial bureaucrats. The decree then accused the Department of State Affairs of misleading the populace by "going against righteousness." Cui Zuan was therefore deprived of his official position while the other two officials who had raised objections were deprived of their salaries for a period of time.[29]

Princess Lanling died from the miscarriage after the punishment was meted out. The *Wei shu* states that the Empress Dowager was so sad that she not only attended the funeral, crying wholeheartedly, but also accompanied the funeral procession personally several miles out of the capital. Later she told one of her officials that she could not help but cry in excess because the princess tolerated Liu Hui and never spoke up although she was insulted by him more than once. She said, according to the *Wei shu,* "There was no such [woman] in the past, nor is there any such today. That is why I feel so sorry." Liu Hui was later captured but was pardoned due to an amnesty right before his execution. He regained his noble and official title in 522 but died, presumably from natural causes, the following year.[30]

This case easily attracts a historian's attention. Inspired by today's historiography, we see in the story a rare opportunity to exercise our newly acquired sensitivity to issues of class, ethnicity, and gender. The match was an intermarriage between a nomadic princess and the son of an ethnic Han who had surrendered to the nomads. The debates occurred between the imperial regent, a nomadic woman ruler who wanted to avenge her sister-in-law, and her legal bureaucrats, who were either of Han ethnic origin or Confucian educational background. The case concerned not only members of the imperial family but also commoners, and the debates mainly concerned the latter's verdicts. In part because of its complexity, this case serves as a valuable example for discussing the codification of Confucian ethics in early medieval China. In addition, it includes almost every aspect of criminal law and litigation in which a traditional Chinese woman could be involved: sex crimes, marital violence, and issues of legal familism such as concealment and collective responsibility.[31] A closer look at each of these three aspects shows that not only did the codification of Confucian ethics advance and backslide, but also women and marriage-related issues were often important checkpoints of such development. Furthermore, the imperial intervention of a Northern Wei female regent congregated in one case social, class, and gender issues—cruxes in contemporary discourse as well.

Sex Crimes and Their Punishment

Although Liu Hui, Zhang Rongfei, and Chen Huimeng all committed adultery and were sentenced to death, Liu Hui was not charged or pursued as an adulterer. Instead, he was accused of treason for killing an imperial family member. Similarly, when Cui Zuan opposed the original verdict by the Chancellery and argued for a lighter penalty for Liu Hui, he did not base his argument on Liu Hui's crime as an adulterer but on the definition of treason. It was not that the Xianbei imperial authority did not punish sex crimes such as adultery, but that a punishment for adultery would not be severe enough. Given the statement Cui Zuan made about Liu Hui's killing his own flesh and the "Law of Assault," one suspects that Cui Zuan was proposing a four- or five-year labor penalty for Liu Hui. This could have been a more severe punishment than any Liu Hui might have received for adultery only.[32]

Legal penalization of sex criminals, both adulterers and fornicators, was an established tradition since the early imperial period. It is often assumed that women were punished more severely than men for sex crimes, but historical evidence suggests that generational taboos and incestuous conduct were more critical factors than gender in deciding the verdicts. We will examine the penalty for adulterous men first before turning to that for women.

Under the Han, a man who committed adultery could be punished by a monetary fine, deprivation of his noble title (if he had one), or manual labor service for three years. If his accomplice was one of his senior relatives, such as a wife or concubine of his father or paternal uncle, he could be put to death.[33] The Jin court carried on the Han spirit. According to Jin law, one who committed fornication with a widow would be sentenced to three years' penalty, while one who committed adultery with his paternal uncle's wife would be sentenced to *qishi* (execution in the marketplace).[34] The Southern Dynasties (420–589) adhered to the Jin codes, making few revisions, and one can be certain that they also punished sex criminals although no detailed statutes and cases are available.[35]

There is no law book left from the Northern Wei to show the penalty for an adulterous man. Cases mentioned in the dynastic history, *Wei shu,* indicate that sex criminals were punished much more severely in the early years of the nomadic Xianbei rule than in later years. Tribal laws executed men and women who "had intercourse outside propriety."[36] At least six times after the establishment of the Northern Wei Dynasty in 386, the Xianbei imperial authority decreed the revision of the law.[37] Although no specific information on changing the punishment was left in historical records, later penalties for adultery must have been more lenient for both aristocrats and commoners.

Due to the nature of the historical documents, extant relevant cases are mostly about aristocratic men. These cases suggest that unless the crime involved sedition, which often required more-severe punishment, imperial clansmen and officials, whether committing adultery with aristocratic or common women, were only deprived of their official titles when their conduct was uncovered, often by the husband of the accomplice.[38] If their partners were widows, the result for these adulterous men ranged from marriage to the woman to simply being despised by their contemporaries.[39] Sometimes it seems as if adultery did not attract much attention if the man was not involved in other, more complicated criminal cases. Recorded stories suggest that adulterous imperial clansmen could be impeached, beaten, or executed only if they were also liable for administrative corruption or treason.[40]

With regard to women, Cui Zuan's protest obviously does not consider the reduction from the death penalty for the two adulteresses fair enough, and it also suggests that adultery was not perceived as a heinous crime for women either. Although some Han Dynasty legal documents mention the death penalty for adulterous women (harsher than the penalty for men), there is no indication of such a penalty being carried out in Han times or later.[41] In most of the adultery cases recorded in the *Wei shu,* which mainly involve the aristocracy, there was no mention of the penalty for the woman. In some of the cases the adultery may have been tolerated either by the legal authority or by the husbands.[42] Some women were forced to marry their lovers.[43]

However, some adulterous women were killed not by legal verdict but by their husbands, who often paid the price later. *Wei shu* records an official, Wei Rong, who killed his wife Ms. Li because he suspected her of an extramarital affair with an imperial clansman. He later committed suicide for fear that his crime would be uncovered.[44] A certain aristocrat who had married an imperial princess was suspected of murdering her to avenge her notorious penchant for adultery. Though no charge was pressed while the princess's brother was on the throne, the man was deprived of his noble title and barred from all official posts when Empress Dowager Ling, the princess's sister-in-law, came to power.[45]

By and large, though sex crimes were considered destructive of family ethics and marital stability, neither men nor women would be sentenced to death simply for adultery should they be brought to court. With regard to the scope of and hierarchy within a patriarchal family, the overall picture suggests a selective application of classical ethics in the codification process.

First of all, though women in the late imperial period were supposed to be penalized more harshly than men for sexual misconduct, these cases have not shown such a practice among the aristocracy in the early medieval period.[46] How a commoner who committed adultery would be penalized is not clear. Nevertheless, based on the arguments of Cui Zuan and You Zhao, one can assume sentences of hard labor. According to the Jin code cited above, fornication with a widow warranted a sentence of three years' labor. The Tang code *(Tang lü)* of the seventh century made it even more explicit that men and women were to be penalized equally: one and a half years for fornicators, and two for adulterers.[47]

Second, intergenerational sex and incestuous behavior, which might have been punished with decapitation under the Han, did not seem to have been a serious concern under the Northern Wei. Some of the adultery cases actually happened between close relatives. For instance, Ms. Zheng, who lived in Empress Dowager Ling's time, committed adultery with the nephew of her husband. She was neither divorced nor penalized. No word was given on the punishment of the nephew, whose conduct would have brought execution had he lived in the Western Jin period.[48] Also in Empress Dowager Ling's time an imperial clansman was impeached for adultery with his paternal first cousin's wife. We have no evidence of the verdict, but one suspects that he was at least deprived of his noble title. Whatever the original verdict, he was pardoned during an amnesty and then appointed to an official post. The fact that his accomplice was the wife of his paternal first cousin, a relative with a one-year mourning obligation, seemed to have been insignificant in the legal process.[49]

Finally, it is interesting that in the Northern Wei period, the adultery of a wife did not justify murder as it did under murder law in later periods.[50] Since the early imperial period legal authority penalized violence among family members, but in later periods the penalties given were graded according to the hierarchical relations of those involved.[51] As a result, the verdicts for marital violence cases let us determine if the law considered a woman inferior to her husband. Let us now look at cases that explicate this aspect in the codification of classical family ethics.

Marital Violence and the
Status of Women in the Family

Under the Han Dynasty, husbands and wives do not seem to have been punished differently for violence, and it is not until the Tang Dynasty (618–907) that we see graded punishments.[52] This suggests that the codification of husbands' and wives' relative status took place in the period between the Han and the Tang, when Liu Hui's case happened. Court discussion on Liu Hui's case did not mention the penalty for marital violence. Although Cui Zuan attempted to shift the focus of the debate on Liu Hui's sentence to child-killing, the imperial decree apparently did not follow his line of argument. It seems as if the court did not emphasize any specific action on the part of Liu Hui, but perceived his crimes as a whole, from adultery to the beating of the princess that caused the miscarriage. Given the remarks made by Empress Dowager Ling in grieving the princess's death, one suspects that the dowager's chief concern was the injury Liu Hui inflicted on the pregnant princess, not the injury to the unborn child.[53] Lacking codes and statutes from the period of disunion, we do not know for sure how husbands and wives were treated by law in instances of marital violence at that time. But judging from punishments meted out in cases of sex crimes during similar periods, we may conclude that the court would not argue along that line since a husband's beating

his wife may not have been perceived as a heinous crime and the punishment therefore would not be sufficiently severe.

Based on extant cases, it seems that men injured their wives for various
reasons and received various punishments for their deeds. If the beating resulted in death, brutal husbands could be executed by law. One man in the
fourth century beat and eventually killed his wife when he had a relapse
into madness. Although some officials argued for a lighter penalty based on
his lack of intent, he was sentenced to death.[54] In the time of Emperor
Xiaowen (r. 471–99) of the Northern Wei, a man beat his wife for drinking liquor and killed her by accident. He was first sentenced to death by a
local official, but his son's appeal moved the minister who reported the case
to the throne, and the emperor reduced the penalty to exile.[55] Adultery
cases cited above, in which murderous husbands killed themselves, also
confirm that a man who slew his wife could face the death penalty regardless of the reasons for his action. Sometimes, imperial intervention
might mean that violent husbands could be sentenced to death for lesser
crimes. One official in the third century ordered his servant to beat his
wife because he believed she was having an affair with the reigning emperor. The wife sued the husband, and he was later executed.[56]

Other times, violent husbands got off lightly or were even set free, especially if the connection between the beating and the death were not as-
certained.[57] An official in the third century hit the stomach of his pregnant
wife with a sword handle when she candidly analyzed his personality. One
account says that the blow caused her miscarriage and death, but no one
filed any accusation, apparently due to the difficulty in establishing the
case.[58] Basically, two elements that would lead to punishment in such a
case were absent: first, a confirmation of the connection between the beating and the death, and second, a qualified person to file the accusation.

The verification of the causality between the beating and the death was
further complicated by a standard legal practice called "protecting the innocent" *(baogu),* which granted a grace period of a certain number of days
to be specified by law to observe the beaten party. If the victim suffered
serious injury or even death within that period, the offender would then
be charged.[59] For instance, the Tang law commanded that one who hurt
others with hands or legs would be charged with injury if the victim suffered serious damage, such as a miscarriage, within ten days.[60] Under such
conditions, a husband who beat his wife and caused a miscarriage would
not be pardoned. However, the law required the injured wife to bring
charges personally; only when the beating resulted in her death could
someone else file an accusation against the husband. As a result, most abuses
probably remained undiscovered. To add insult to injury, even when death

did result, the children of the offender were not permitted to file an accusation, for laws from the Qin Dynasty (221–206 B.C.E.) prohibited family
inferiors, such as children and slaves, from accusing superiors, such as parents and masters.[61] Therefore, throughout early medieval China, a son
could not expose his father's violence against his mother, though he might
be the only or most important witness.

When mothers were the offenders, however, the situation differed depending on who was injured or killed and on different interpretations of
family ethics between the South and the North. First of all, women's acts
of violence often came from jealousy and usually were aimed at their rivals instead of their husbands: some women killed or tortured their husbands' concubines and maids. Grand Princess Lanling's mutilation of the
maid impregnated by Liu Hui is only one example. Moreover, although
laws had prohibited killing maids and slaves since the Han Dynasty, it is
likely that most violence of this kind remained hidden due to the legal
procedure required to establish a case,[62] which often let the offenders
maneuver around the law. However, if the woman's attack was aimed at
her husband, there was a good chance her deeds would be exposed. The
following two cases, focusing directly on injury to husbands, show both
the consequences involving the wives and the children and the different
interpretation of Confucian ethics by the Southern and the Northern
Dynasties.

In the Liu-Song South, a certain Tang Ci died from vomiting toxic
worms after he attended a banquet. Before he died, he told his wife Ms.
Zhang to dissect his body afterwards so that the reason for his death could
be revealed. Ms. Zhang did so and was charged by the local official with
cruelty; her son Tang Fu was also accused since he did not stop her. But
the local official could not decide on a verdict right away because this case
happened just before a general amnesty.[63] The case was presented to the
court along with pertinent information: the Liu-Song law ruled that
(1) one who ruined a corpse would be sentenced to a four years' penalty;
(2) a wife who injured her husband would be sentenced to five years' punishment; and (3) a son who was not filial to his parents (buxiao) would be
sentenced to qishi (execution in the marketplace).

In the court discussion, some officials tried to argue for Ms. Zhang and
her son by pointing out their obedience to Tang Ci's will and their lack of
intent to hurt. But others argued that if the law considered that merely to
remove a corpse from the road, which was much less injurious to the
corpse than to dissect it, was "to go against moderation and rupture reason" (budao), then to dissect a corpse would be worthy of even greater
punishment. There could have been a lighter penalty in this case if other

codes were applied or if the amnesty were considered. However, in the final verdict Ms. Zhang was charged with *budao,* a crime with an impious and heinous connotation, and Tang Fu with being unfilial.[64] Both crimes warranted the death penalty.[65] The case shows that a southern woman who injured her husband would be punished more severely than the culprit in an ordinary injury case, a spirit not seen in the Han documents but firmly integrated into the Tang code. The final verdict suggests that harsher punishment was applied in order to make clear the superiority of husband over wife, which was ordained in the *Yi li.* Moreover, the charge of being unfilial made against Tang Fu in this case and his final execution also reveal the dilemma a child would have to face.

In the North, however, legal debates indicate a more lenient treatment of a child who concealed his mother's violence. At the beginning of the Eastern Wei Dynasty (534–50), a new set of laws was proclaimed, presumably to confirm the legal practices of the preceding Northern Wei Dynasty.[66] According to the law, a son should not report his mother to the government if she killed his father; one who reported his own mother to the authorities would be executed. Court official Dou Yuan disagreed with the law and sent a memorial to the throne. His argument was based on the idea that a wife and mother occupied a status inferior to that of a husband and father in legal matters:

> If one's father kills one's mother, it is a husband killing a wife. Since a mother holds an inferior status in the family, it is right for the son not to report the homicide. But it is not right for a son to conceal the crime if his mother kills his father. . . . If he conceals such a crime, he demonstrates that he only knows his mother but not his father. This is the attitude of the wild men; such behavior is close to that of a beast. . . . A father is the heaven for both a mother and a son. When she kills her husband, she destroys the heaven for both of them. This is a crime that cannot be pardoned. The moment she commits the killing, the affection between mother and son is severed. Therefore, the son should not conceal the crime in the name of the mother and son relationship.[67]

The emperor sent his memorial to the Department of State Affairs for discussion. Feng Junyi, then gentleman of the three dukes, disapproved, arguing that

> A person receives flesh and care from both parents and has the same affection for both of them. Now [Dou Yuan's] presumptuous distinction between superiority and inferiority is hard to endure and bears no historical precedent. If one's mother kills one's father and is executed after one's report, then

her death is caused by her child. There is no country that does not have mothers. Where can this child go?[68]

In response to the Department of State Affairs, Dou Yuan cited examples and prescriptions from classics such as the *Yi li* to prove that he was arguing on a historical foundation. However, no further response was heard from the imperial court, and the matter stopped at this point, suggesting that Feng Junyi's opinions were accepted and Dou Yuan's were dismissed.[69]

Since this account of Dou Yuan's legal thinking was included in the "Biographies of Good Officials" in the standard northern histories, perhaps both Wei Shou, the author of *Wei shu,* and Li Yanshou, the author of *Bei shi,* considered Dou's ideas laudable. However, such ideas were probably not in accord with contemporary perceptions of family relations or with legal practices in the Northern Dynasties. The Tang code explicitly prescribed that a son was to report homicide within the family only if his father was killed by his father's legal wife *(dimu),* his foster mother *(cimu),* or his stepmother *(jimu).*[70] That no word was given concerning the killing of one's father by one's birth mother indicates the continuance of the Northern Wei legal practices: on the assumption that he should love both parents equally, a son was supposed to treat them equally, at least in the area of concealment.

We can make several observations based on our discussion of these often-fragmentary cases related to marital violence. First, while men usually directed their violence against their wives, women usually assaulted rivals for their husbands' affection. Second, when death resulted, it was difficult to build injury cases unless the husbands were the victims. Third, should a case be established, penalties differed due to varied factors, such as personal relations or noble status, and were not necessarily related to the status of husband and wife in the family. However, we can be certain of two points in terms of the codification of Confucian ethics. First, while there is no indication that in Han times graded punishment was given to husband and wife in cases of marital violence, the Southern Dynasties nevertheless penalized offending wives more severely than offenders in regular violence cases. Second, though most family violence was hard to expose due to the legal procedures required to establish a case, the law of the Northern Dynasties, after ardent debate, still allowed a son to conceal his mother's violence against his father.

Concealment actually correlated with collective responsibility in legal practice. Those who were allowed to conceal a crime such as marital violence would not be punished later when the crime was uncovered. However, those who were expected to uncover a crime such as high treason would later be punished collectively if they did not report it. To decide who would or would not be exempt from responsibility was therefore to demonstrate the scope of and the hierarchy within the family. We will now turn to the issue of legal familism, the third aspect in the codification of classical ethics, to investigate the family identity of women.

Legal Familism and the Family Identity of Women

In his objection to the charge brought against the two brothers, Cui Zuan cited a statute—apparently a continuation of a Western Han practice—to affirm the brothers' right to conceal the crime. In 66 B.C.E., Emperor Xuandi (r. 73–49 B.C.E.) decreed that whoever concealed his parents or grandparents would be pardoned, as would a wife concealing her husband, while whoever concealed his sons, grandsons, or wife would be tried in front of the emperor if the case involved the death penalty.[71] According to the mourning obligations that represented degrees of relations, one had to pay one to three years' mourning to these family members. Relatives with a one-year mourning obligation *(jiqin)* therefore became the outer limit of concealment.[72] Dou Yuan's argument on a mother's legal inferiority and the eventual dismissal of this argument show that concealment between parents and children was allowed throughout the Northern Dynasties.

Other than grandparents and grandchildren, *jiqin* also included brothers (see Appendix II). The scope of concealment allowed in the Han code may have been extended in the post-Han periods. When Cui Zuan defended the two brothers, he cited the law and claimed that *jiqin* could conceal one another in ordinary cases, not to mention in scandalous cases such as adultery. He also dismissed the verdict that the two brothers should have been punished on the basis of collective responsibility, not only because the law did not require such punishment for adultery cases but also because members of a married woman's natal family bore no such responsibility for her.

Since the preimperial period, collective responsibility had been an important method for deterring people from committing crimes and for discovering hidden criminal liabilities. The practice underwent some alterations under the Han due to new ideological thinking and sociopolitical circumstances, but it never disappeared and was inherited by subsequent dynasties.[73] While arguing that the two brothers had no responsibility for their adulterous sisters, Cui Zuan also referred to the high treason case of Guanqiu Jian in the Cao-Wei period (220–65), which eventually led to the revision of law under the early Western Jin.

When Guanqiu Jian was executed for treachery, his married and pregnant granddaughter was awaiting execution in keeping with the principle of collective responsibility. Her mother filed a plea for mercy and brought the issue of a woman's collective responsibility into question. A court discussion was proposed in favor of not punishing the married daughter of the offender.[74] One of the arguments ran thus:

> A woman has the obligation to follow three men in her life and not to arbitrarily seek her own way.[75] If she is married, her mourning period for her parents will be reduced; therefore, it is clear that her affection for them should be different from that of a maiden. However, according to the law, when a parent commits a crime, a married daughter will be punished; when the husband's family is executed, the wife will also be put to death. She has to endure penalty from both sides. Once a woman is married, she is the wife of another surname; if she gives birth to a child, she is the mother of another family. A man cannot be executed for connections to both families. This neither shows pity for weakness of a woman nor does it clarify the law.[76]

The official in charge therefore suggested that a maiden should be responsible only for charges against her parents, while a married woman should be penalized only for her husband's family. The emperor accordingly decreed a change in the law. When the newly established Jin Dynasty proclaimed its revised law code in 267, both divorced mothers and married daughters were exempted from the collective responsibility of their previous families. The revised Jin code also stated explicitly that "future verdicts will be decided based on the principle of the five degrees of mourning in order to enforce the [Confucian] ethical teaching."[77]

This principle must have been an integral part of Northern Wei legal ideas by the sixth century since Cui Zuan cited it when he came to the brothers' defense. However, the principle, in its original spirit and later application, meant that women were not only collectively executed for treachery crimes committed by their male family members, but also punished for various misdeeds done by their husbands.[78] Interestingly, it was often when the officials in charge pitied women for their "weakness in nature" that the government began discussions on legal revision.

At the turn of the fourth century, the execution of Ms. Xie, arrested for her father's treason one day before her wedding, induced a discussion on reducing the penalty for women in cases of high treason.[79] In 307, family execution was abolished by the Jin court. Although it was revived in 325, women in the family would have their death penalties reduced.[80] The Southern Dynasties continued this practice of reductions: according to the Southern Liang code, one who committed high treason would be decapitated; his father, sons, and brothers would be executed; and his mother, wife, concubines, and other female family members would be sentenced to official slavery rather than collective execution.[81]

Such a reduction was also visible in the Northern Dynasties. In the early fourth century, before the Tuoba clan established the northern empire, harsh laws were applied to facilitate the clan's rule: a traitor's family members, both men and women, would be decapitated. In 431, however, in a revision of law decreed by the new emperor,[82] one who was convicted of treason would be cut asunder at the waist, and family members registered in the same household *(tongji)* would be put to death, but boys under fourteen were to be castrated, and women were to be put into official slavery.[83]

A woman's collective responsibility for her husband did not stop at treason, nor was official slavery the only penalty. Near the end of the Eastern Han Dynasty, the government executed women whose husbands evaded conscription.[84] In the Northern Wei, if a subofficial clerk *(li)* escaped after criminal conduct, his wife and children would be banished to the borderland.[85] Women who were arrested because their husbands were runaways could only contest their marital status if they wanted to escape the harshest penalty.

Sympathetic officials who pleaded for these women often based their arguments on the Confucian Classics on marriage. In some cases, argument was made on the Confucian principles that defined a "wife" in a patriarchal household. In other cases, it was made on the basis of women's three followings *(sancong)*. For instance, one official managed to save a woman's life by showing the lack of complete Confucian rites in her wedding; since her marital status was not yet confirmed, she could not be punished collectively for her husband.[86] In another case, one official freed a widow from conscription for a crime committed by her husband's relatives by claiming that the one she should have followed was her son.[87] Whatever the situation, the family identity of women was expressed through marriage, and in verdicts concerning concealment and collective responsibilities we see gradual conformity to Confucian family ethics throughout the Six Dynasties.

It was according to these precedents that Cui Zuan argued for the two brothers' innocence and defined the nature of Liu Hui's crime. Since a woman's family identity changed upon her marriage, the people responsible for her, Cui Zuan maintained, should also change. If a married woman identified herself with her husband's family, then what Liu Hui committed was not the murder of an imperial family member, but the murder of his own flesh. However, the Northern Wei imperial court did not follow Cui Zuan's argument. Instead, the final verdict in Liu Hui's case showed the tension within the ruling class between the imperial power, represented by a nomadic woman ruler, and the legal bureaucrats, mostly of Confucian educational background.

A Woman Ruler versus Her Legal Bureaucrats

Many factors were present in Liu Hui's case; some had more influence in the final outcome than others.[88] Two factors, however, cannot be overlooked: imperial interference in deciding the verdict and the gendered nature of such interference.

Though often perceived as a driving force in implementing Confucian ethics, the ruling authorities in various dynasties in fact applied classical ideals highly selectively. For instance, when promoting classical values, Chinese governments since the early imperial period endeavored to suppress the custom of revenge, which was sanctioned in the classics, so that governmental power over people's lives would not be undermined.[89] Guanqiu Jian's case, cited earlier, demonstrates that the law was revised to conform to Confucian ethics in response to pleas from powerful families and not because of imperial intervention. In fact, imperial power was often exerted when such codification ran contrary to the interests of the ruling house. In Liu Hui's case, Cui Zuan's argument based on classical marital ethics was not appreciated, and the imperial power used the Department of Chancellery to express its disagreement forcefully.

Under the Northern Wei, the chancellery was supposed to serve as a channel through which the Secretariat (zhongshu sheng) submitted proposals to the throne and imperial pronouncements were put in final form before being transmitted to the Department of State Affairs for implementation.[90] That is why its duty was considered only as "presentation and delivery" by Cui Zuan and You Zhao.[91] However, as the executive agency closest to the imperial power, the chancellery in practice often contended for influence in policy decisions. Cui Zuan and You Zhao, both from the Department of State Affairs, which carried on general administrative business, including litigation, protested against imperial interference as exhibited by the verdict of the chancellery. Their arguments grew out of the idea of the division of governmental power and their background of legal studies.

Cui Zuan came from the celebrated Boling Cui family, which produced several important legal bureaucrats for the Northern Wei.[92] Cui Zuan himself became noted for his brilliant opinions as a prosecutor before he was appointed director of the three dukes in the Department of State Affairs.[93] You Zhao came from the Guangping You family, which was also notable for its legal heritage.[94] You Zhao served as chief minister for law enforcement (tingwei shaoqing) during Emperor Xuanwu's reign and became right vice director in the Department of State Affairs before Cui Zuan argued for Liu Hui's case.[95]

Legal studies had been carried on in certain families since the Eastern Han. Though encountering setbacks toward the fall of the Han Dynasty, legal learning appears to have been preserved through family tradition throughout the unstable Six Dynasties.[96] In addition to the Boling Cui and the Guangping You, the Qinghe Cui and the Bohai Feng families were among the most distinguished in the Northern Dynasties.[97] One of the best-known kinsmen from the Feng family was Feng Junyi, mentioned earlier, who argued on the basis of the impartiality and consistency of the law against Dou Yuan's proposal for ranking one's father above one's mother.[98]

All these families from Shandong maintained the legacy of legislation from Han times throughout the Six Dynasties and contributed to the unified Sui and Tang Dynasties as well.[99] When Cui Zuan and You Zhao argued in Liu Hui's case, they were actually protesting against imperial interference as members of their family's profession. The only other person who also argued in Liu Hui's case, but who did not mention the division of power in government or protest against imperial interference, was the imperial secretary Yuan Xiuyi. Yuan Xiuyi, however, cited stories from Confucian texts that demonstrated the changed relationship between a woman and her natal family after her marriage. Since he was an imperial clansman of nomadic Xianbei ethnicity, his argument confirmed the sinification of the Tuoba ruling authority at that time.

Although the sinification movement of the Northern Wei was not full-fledged until Emperor Xiaowen (471–99) was on the throne,[100] the Xianbei government actually had maintained some aspects of the Han legacy in its rule over the northern territory from earlier days. Legal revisions undertaken since the establishment of the Northern Wei suggest tremendous dependence on the conventional wisdom of the Han and subsequent dynasties. Remarks by various legal bureaucrats cited above were full of quotations and interpretations of Confucian Classics. The codification of Confucian ethics appears to have been adopted by the Northern Wei. However, Liu Hui's case, occurring decades after the sinification movement, illustrated again the unpredictability of imperial attitudes in the process of Confucianization.

Imperial interference this time came from a woman ruler whose already-unusual non-Han ethnic background was further complicated by a gendered attitude. Modern scholars argue over whether women rulers are more favorable toward their female subjects, and carefully scrutinize women rulers for feminist sensitivities. Take Wu Zetian (r. 684–705), the only female emperor in Chinese history, for example. A recent study[101] suggests that, although notorious for her ruthlessness towards competitors, Wu nevertheless revealed her "proto-feminist sentiments" through institu-

tional modifications and public performances. The most significant indication of such sentiments for our subject was that Wu increased the mourning period for a deceased mother from one to three years, whether or not
the father was alive at the time. Since the scope of and the hierarchy within
a patriarchal family were demonstrated by the system of mourning obligations, to disregard that system challenged Confucian family ethics. In view
of this, Empress Dowager Ling's words and deeds will most likely cause
one to assume some feminist sentiment. The many cases cited above, in
which adulterous women were pardoned and murderous husbands were
punished in Empress Dowager Ling's reign, seem to substantiate such an
assumption. We see a gendered attitude most vividly in the case of Grand
Princess Ji'nan (see note 45) and Prince Runan (see note 53). While the
princess's brother, the reigning emperor Xuanwu, never desired to avenge
his sister's death by imperial interference, the succeeding regent Empress
Dowager Ling punished the princess's murderous husband without hesita-
tion. In Prince Runan's case, in order to protect beaten royal wives, Empress Dowager Ling went even further to punish her violent male in-laws,
whose family she should have identified with.

Male and female rulers seem to have also shown different attitudes toward jealous women. While Emperor Ming (r. 466–72) of the Liu-Song
Dynasty repeatedly reprimanded jealous princesses and official wives,[102]
Empress Dowager Ling was determined to condemn violent and unfaith-
ful husbands. Her marveling at how Lanling tolerated Liu Hui indicates
contemporary sentiments on marital egalitarianism in the North.[103] The
original verdict—that Liu Hui was a traitor who killed an imperial family
member—suggests that the court considered the unborn child mainly as
the princess's flesh and ignored the classical instruction on the shift of a
woman's family identity upon her marriage. However, the fact that Empress Dowager Ling harshly punished female commoners such as Zhang
Rongfei and Chen Huimeng raises suspicions concerning the "quality" of
her feminist sentiment. Yet, given the comparisons presented above, suffice
it to say that Empress Dowager Ling's interference in Liu Hui's case reveals
a certain kind of gender awareness, although not without class prejudice.

Conclusion

As stated in the beginning, the codification of marriage and family ethics
often attracts the attention of ruling authorities. We have a case in another society in which a religious institution applied such a codification not only to
exercise social control but also to empower itself in contention with the lay
authorities. Studies of medieval Europe show that the papacy's promotion of

sexual and marital ethics increased its power, on the one hand, and helped separate jurisdiction between clerical and secular authorities, on the other. In China, however, it was the state, rather than a Buddhist or Daoist organization, that undertook such responsibility. And the state in early medieval China was facing competing ethics as well as authorities in and around itself.

When Ch'ü T'ung-tsu wrote *Law and Society in Traditional China* in 1965 to describe the Confucianized legal system, he rightly started his book by introducing the scope of a patriarchal family based on the five degrees of mourning and included a section discussing the legal position of a wife in that family. With evidence collected mainly from the late imperial period, Ch'ü concluded that a wife had a legal status dramatically inferior to that of her husband as a result of the codification of classical Confucian ethics.[104] Later research, with more information from the early imperial period, has enriched these arguments and revised this general view by showing the workings of a "pre-Confucian" society in Han times.[105] To date, the earliest complete extant law book is the Tang code, which forms the basis of Ch'ü's argument about early imperial China. The development of law between the Han and the Tang, in which the codification of Confucian ethics presumably occurred, not to mention women's legal status in that period, remains obscure to us due to the insufficient and scattered nature of the source material. Chen Yinke, in a remarkable display of erudition and ingenuity, successfully traced the origins of the Tang code from earlier periods, but Chen's research focused mainly on the heritage of legal studies and the construction of legal systems, without getting into the details of law codes, legal cases, and their verdicts.[106]

This article uses Liu Hui's case in the early sixth century as an example and a point of departure not only to examine the codification of Confucian values but also to substantiate the inheritance of legal practices between the Han and the Tang. Several points can be made here.

First of all, in addition to Chen Yinke's efforts in reviewing the heritage of legal institutions, actual accounts of crimes and the arguments and judgments they inspired reveal much about the content of legal learning in early medieval China. The five degrees of mourning, which showed the scope of a patriarchal family and demonstrated the Confucian ideals of marital hierarchy, were mentioned constantly and implemented in various verdicts. Cui Zuan's reference to concealment among *jiqin* and women's collective responsibility indicates the Xianbei inheritance of the law of the Han, Cao-Wei, and Jin Dynasties and adds important evidence to Chen Yinke's work on the origins and inheritance of the Sui-Tang legal systems.

Second, it seems that the codification of classical family ethics in legal revisions was not necessarily due to the rulers' original intention to Confucianize, and that conflict of interest within government bodies occurred from time to time. Guanqiu Jian's case in the Cao-Wei period shows that Confucian principles were raised in legal arguments and integrated into statutes sometimes because of the personal interests of the powerful. In view of this, it is not surprising to see that the codification of Confucian ethics suffered setbacks once in a while; it was not favored wholeheartedly by the imperial authority when running contrary to imperial interests. Liu Hui's case is only one example.

Third, using women's involvement in criminal cases as an indicator, one can easily perceive that the road to Confucianization was bumpy, especially in the Northern Dynasties. For instance, the punishment for sex crimes varied in different cases under different regimes, not only because of the aristocratic status of those involved but also because of the lack of Confucian propriety at the time. Adulterers and fornicators in the Northern Dynasties, regardless of their gender and generation, seem to have been penalized relatively lightly in most cases.

As for marital violence, it seems that murderous conduct between husband and wife tended to be punished severely. However, extant cases imply some regional differences. While a southern wife would be penalized more harshly than offenders in ordinary cases, a northern husband would be executed for killing his wife by accident. Moreover, a southern son would be decapitated for not reporting his mother's dissection of his father's remains, even for medical reasons. A northern son was, however, allowed by law not to disclose his mother's murder of his father.

It appears that Confucian family ethics were applied more in cases concerned with concealment and collective responsibilities than in cases of sex crimes and marital violence. At least in the North, the five degrees of mourning were used more often to define a woman's family identity than to define her status as inferior to that of her husband within that patriarchal family. Dou Yuan's argument and its dismissal demonstrate that the Confucian ideal of the husband's superiority and the wife's inferiority was not yet successfully incorporated into legal practices in the North till the end of the Six Dynasties in the latter half of the sixth century.

Finally, the issue of women rulers provides a useful insight for scholars of women's history. Inspired by historical events, we learn that, when we discuss women's legal positions, we need to examine not only women's places in laws and cases, but also women's accessibility to legal agents and their influence in making laws. Although there are constant debates over the feminist quality of powerful women, it appears that women need to be in power to change their lot. This is perhaps a lesson history could teach to sisters of our time.

APPENDIX I

CHINESE DYNASTIES FROM QIN TO TANG

221 B.C.E.   Qin

206 B.C.E.   Western Han

8 C.E.   Xin (Wang Mang)

23   Eastern Han

220

Six Dynasties

222 — 221 Shu Han   220 Cao-Wei

Wu   263   265

280   Western Jin

304

The Three Kingdoms

317   Eastern Jin   Sixteen Kingdoms   386

420 Liu-Song   439

479 Southern Qi   Northern Wei

The Southern Dynasties

502 Liang

535 Western Wei   Eeastern Wei 534

557 Chen   557 Northern Zhou   Northern Qi 550

589   581

The Northern Dynasties

Sui

618   Tang

907

APPENDIX II: MOURNING OBLIGATIONS

great great grandfather
(*zicui* 齊衰 3 months)

great grandfather
(*zicui* 齊衰 3 mos.)

clan great
grandfather

grandfather
(*ji* 期 1 year)

xiaogong
小功 5 mos.

sima
緦麻

father
(*zhancui*
斬衰 3 years)

paternal
uncle
(*ji* 期
1 year)

xiaogong
小功

sima
緦麻

wife x *ego*
(1 year)

brothers
(*ji* 期
1 year)

paternal
cousins
(*dagong*
大功 9 mos.)

xiaogong
小功

sima
緦麻

sons by
concubine
(*ji* 期
1 year)

oldest son
by wife
(*zhancui*
斬衰 3 years)

sons of
bros. (*ji* 期
1 year)

sons of
cousin
(*xiaogong*
小功 5 mos.)

sima 緦麻
(3 mos.)

dagong
大功
9 mos.

oldest
grandson
(*ji* 期 1 year)

grandsons
of bros.
(*xiaogong*
小功
5 mos.)

grandsons
of cousin
(*sima* 緦麻
3 mos.)

great grandson
(*sima* 緦麻 3 mos.)

great grandsons
of bros. (*sima*
緦麻 3 mos.)

great great grandson
(*sima* 緦麻 3 mos.)

Note: Time spans in parentheses are ego's obligations to his relatives. This table is
based on "Sangfu" in *Yi li*. It defines the scope of a family and its relatives in
the classics, and exemplifies the patrilineal nature of such a family.

INTENT, MISTAKE OF FACT, AND ACTUAL ACCIDENT

	Dynasty				
	Zhou	**Han**	**Jin**	**Tang**	
Sources	*Zhou li* 周禮	Zheng Xuan's Commentary 鄭玄注	Zhang Fei's (Chang Fei) Preface to Chin (Jin) law 張裴晉律序	*Tang Code* 唐律	Wallacker's translation
Intent		*yi* 意	*gu* 故	*gu* 故	
Mistake of Fact	*bushi* 不識	*bushen* 不審	*shi* 失	*wu* 誤	slipup, physical error
Actual Accident	*guoshi* 過失	*wu* 誤	*guoshi* 過失	*guoshi* 過失	trespassory *[sic]*

Notes

1. For the Roman, Frankish, and biblical influences on medieval marriage, see Christopher Brooke, *The Medieval Idea of Marriage* (Oxford: Oxford University Press, 1989). For the struggle between the Church and the Frankish monarchy, and the building up of papal authority, see Brian Tierney, *The Crisis of Church and State 1150–1300,* part I, "The First Thousand Years" (Toronto: University of Toronto Press, 1988). For the monastic reform and its influence, see Geoffrey Barraclough, *The Medieval Papacy* (New York: W. W. Norton & Company, 1979). For canon law on Christian marriage, see Charles Donahue, Jr., "The Canon Law on the Formation of Marriage and Social Practice in the Later Middle Ages," *Journal of Family History* 18 (Summer 1983): 144–58. For the Catholic Church's assumption of power through the institution of marriage, see Georges Duby, *The Knight, the Lady and the Priest,* trans. Barbara Bray (New York: Pantheon Books, 1983), pp. 282–4.

2. See Ch'ü T'ung-tsu, *Law and Society in Traditional China* (1961; repr. Paris: Mouton, 1965), ch. I, "Family and *Tsu.*"

3. See the chapter "Sangfu" [Mourning] in *Yi li* [The book of ceremonies], in *Shisan jing zhushu* (1821; repr. Taipei: Yiwen Yinshuguan, 1981). For the definition and the scope of the family, see Tu Cheng-sheng, *Gudai shehui yu guojia* [Society and state in ancient China], part five, "Lizhi jiazu yu lunli" [Rites, lineage, and ethics] (Taipei: Yunchen wenhua chubanshe, 1992), pp. 729–876; for a detailed discussion and the implications of the mourning system for relations among family members, see Jen-der Lee, "Xi Han lüling zhong de jiating lunli guan" [Ethical ideas in law of the Western Han Dynasty], *Zhongguo lishi xuehui shixue jikan* 19 (1987): 2–11.

4. For instance, she would pay three years of mourning to her father if a maiden, but only one if married. Her biggest mourning obligation, three years, would be paid to her husband.

5. This is illustrated by the fact that her son could only pay one year of mourning to her if her husband was still alive when she died. Only if her husband died before her could her son pay her three years. Even then, her son's mourning clothes for her would not be as coarse as those he wore for his father. For detailed regulations among various family members, see the "Sangfu" chapter in the *Yi li.*

6. For examples, see Zhu Zongbin, "Luelun Jin lü rujia hua" [On the Confucianization of the Jin law], *Zhongguo shi yanjiu* 2.26 (1985): 101–24.

7. *Jin shu* [The history of the Jin Dynasty], by Fang Xuanling (Beijing: Zhonghua shuju, 1974), ch. 30, p. 927.

8. Liu Hui's biography is attached to his father's in ch. 59 of *Wei shu* [The history of the (Northern) Wei Dynasty], by Wei Shou (Beijing: Zhonghua shuju, 1974); see also ch. 111, "Monograph of Law."

9. Grand Princess Lanling was married when her brother, Empress Dowager Ling's husband, reigned. Empress Dowager Ling was in power during the

whole of her son's reign (516–28), except for one interruption (520–4), which was the result of a coup. See *Wei shu,* ch. 59, pp. 1311–2.

10. *Wei shu,* ch. 59, p.1312.

11. The sources disagree over precisely when the crime was committed. Liu Hui's biography in *Wei shu* says that he committed adultery early in the Zhengguang era (520–4), but the "Monograph of Law" in *Wei shu* records that the case happened in the Shengui era (518–9). See *Wei shu,* ch. 59, p. 1312; and ch. 111, p. 2886.

12. *Wei shu,* ch. 59, p. 1312.

13. Ibid., ch. 111, p. 2886. For this earlier treason case, see ch. 9, p. 229; and ch. 58, p. 1292.

14. Ibid., ch. 111, p. 2886.

15. Cui Zuan's memorial indicates that the two brothers' families may have also been banished to Dunhuang with them. See *Wei shu,* ch. 111, p. 2886. For the English translations of the official titles, see Charles O. Hucker, *A Dictionary of Official Titles in Imperial China* (Stanford: Stanford University Press, 1985).

16. The "Biography of Liu Hui" states that the two women were beaten with bamboo sticks *(chi).* See *Wei shu,* ch. 59, p. 1312.

17. *Wei shu,* ch. 111, p. 2886.

18. Ibid.

19. Wang Chien-wen, "Xi Han lüling yu guojia zhengdang xing—yi lüling zhong de 'budao' wei zhongxin" [Western Han law codes and the legitimacy of the state—a study of the "crimes of depravity"], *Xin shixue* 3.3 (1992): 1–36. Also see Jen-der Lee, "Family Execution and Collective Responsibilities in Han Law: Its Change of Nature and Significance," unpublished manuscript.

20. *Wei shu,* ch. 111, p. 2886.

21. Ibid. In legal documents, *xing* could mean banishment and execution; it could also mean any punishment under the five-year labor penalty. It is understood here as banishment and execution.

22. *Wei shu,* ch. 111, pp. 2886–7.

23. Ibid., p. 2887.

24. Ibid.

25. Ibid., p. 2886.

26. Ibid., p. 2887.

27. Ibid. There is no record available to show the specific penalty for fornication and adultery in the Northern Wei Dynasty. But the Tang code, issued with annotations in 653, required one-and-a-half-years' labor for fornication and two years' for adultery. See *Tang lü shuyi* [Annotations on the Tang code], by Zhangsun Wuji (died 689) (Taipei: Hongwenguan chubanshe, 1986), ch. 26, "Zalü" [Miscellaneous codes], p. 493; and Wallace Johnson, trans., *Specific Articles,* vol. 2 of *The T'ang Code* (Princeton: Princeton University Press, 1997), ch. 26, "Miscellaneous Articles" ("Zalü"), p. 474.

28. *Wei shu,* ch. 111, pp. 2887–8.
29. Ibid.
30. *Wei shu,* ch. 59, p.1312.
31. Due to the fragmentary nature of the material, we do not know their cat-egories in the law of the Northern Wei. The *Tang lü shuyi* included sex crimes in the "Miscellaneous Articles" and categorized marital violence and legal responsibilities of the family under "Assault and Accusations" ("Dousong"), all with specific regulations and penalties.
32. It was a well-established tradition since the preimperial period that verdicts would be decided according to the state of mind of the criminals when they committed a crime. Although Liu Hui did not kill the unborn baby on purpose, he could still have killed it due to his hatred toward the princess. Cui Zuan did not mention whether Liu Hui should have been charged with *yi* (intent) or not. But it looks as if he was trying to find a middle ground between Liu Hui's execution as a traitor and a very light penalty simply as an adulterer, with which the imperial authority would certainly disagree. For definitions of various mind-sets in different dynas-ties, see Appendix III, "Intent, Mistake of Fact, and Actual Accident."
33. See Jen-der Lee, "Xi Han lüling."
34. *Jin shu,* ch. 30, p. 927.
35. Cheng Shude, *Jiu chao lü kao* [A study of Chinese law of nine dynasties (from the Han to the Sui)], ch. 13, "Nan-Bei chao zhu lü kao xu" [Preface to the law codes of the Southern Dynasties] (Shanghai: The Commercial Press, 1927).
36. *Wei shu,* ch. 111, p. 2873.
37. At least six revisions of the law were made during the one hundred and fifty years of Xianbei rule: 428–31, 451, 453–65, 466–70, 481, and 504. See *Wei shu,* ch. 111, pp. 2874–80. Also see Chen Yinke, "Sui Tang zhidu yuanyuan luelun gao" [On the origins of the institutions in the Sui and Tang Dynasties], part four, "Xinglü" [Law and penalty], in *Chen Yinke xi-ansheng lunwen ji* [Collected essays of Mr. Chen Yinke] (1944; repr. Taipei: Jiusi chubanshe, 1977), pp. 94–109.
38. For instance, Yuan Shen, prince of Guangyang in Empress Dowager Ling's time, was accused by Yuan Hui, prince of Chengyang, of committing adul-tery with his wife Ms. Yu. After a discussion among imperial clansmen, Yuan Shen was deprived of his official title and sent back to his principal-ity. See *Wei shu,* ch. 18, p. 429. The other case involved a male official and a female commoner. Dou Sengyan was accused by a commoner named Jia Miao of committing adultery with his wife; Dou Sengyan was also de-prived of his official title. See *Wei shu,* ch. 46, p. 1036.
39. For instance, after Pei Xun's affair with the widowed grand princess Taiyuan came to light, he was ordered by the emperor to marry her. See *Wei shu,* ch. 45, p. 1022. Lu Zhengsi committed adultery with the widow of his brother and was impeached. There is no mention of further punishment except

being despised by his contemporaries. See *Wei shu,* ch. 47, p. 1053. Zheng Yanzu committed adultery with his cousin and "showed no sense of guilt although his contemporaries felt shame for him." See *Wei shu,* ch. 56, p. 1242.

40. See the cases of Yuan Gan and Yuan Xiang in *Wei shu,* ch. 21, pp. 543, 561–3.

41. Jen-der Lee, "Xi Han lüling."

42. Ms. Yu (mentioned earlier in Yuan Shen's case) seems to have avoided legal penalties. See also the case of Ms. Zheng, discussed later, in *Wei shu,* ch. 47, p. 1062.

43. The widowed grand princess Taiyuan, mentioned earlier, was married to her accomplice Pei Xun by Emperor Xiaoming (r. 516–28), probably by suggestion of the regent, Empress Dowager Ling. The *Wei shu* also records that Princess Taiyuan bore a son, Yu Yan, from her adulterous affair with Yu Xianye. Yan was given several official posts by Emperor Xiaojing (r. 534–50). Given the time span, this Princess Taiyuan must have been the same person as the Princess Taiyuan in Empress Dowager Ling's time. See *Wei shu,* ch. 26, p. 658; ch. 33, p. 1022.

44. Wei Rong thought his wife had an affair with Yuan Jingzhe, prince of Zhangwu. See *Wei shu,* ch. 45, p. 1015.

45. This was the case of Grand Princess Ji'nan and her husband, Lu Daoqian. See *Wei shu,* ch. 47, p. 1051.

46. See Ch'ü Tung-tsu, p. 110. For recent studies on women's status in late imperial law, see Paul S. Ropp, "The Status of Women in Late Imperial China: Evidence from Letters, Laws and Literature," paper presented at the American Historical Association, Washington D.C., December 26–9, 1987; also Paola Paderni, "I Thought I Would Have Some Happy Days: Women Eloping in Eighteenth-Century China," *Late Imperial China* 16.1 (1995): 1–32.

47. See *Tang lü shuyi,* ch. 26, "Zalü," p. 493; and Johnson, trans., *Specific Articles,* vol. 2 of *The T'ang Code,* ch. 26, "Miscellaneous Articles," p.473.

48. See *Wei shu,* ch. 47, p. 1061.

49. This was Yuan Qin, who was impeached by Feng Hui, a legal bureaucrat from the Bohai Feng family. See *Wei shu,* ch. 12, p. 443, and ch. 32, p. 762. Also see note 97 below.

50. See Ch'ü T'ung-tsu's discussion on the position of a wife in *Law and Society in Traditional China,* pp. 102–10.

51. For instance, parents who either injured or killed their children were often punished less severely than those who assaulted strangers, while children who assaulted their parents would definitely be punished more sternly for being unfilial. For Han practice, see Jen-der Lee, "Xi Han lüling," pp. 14–21. For related statutes and cases in the period during the Northern and Southern dynasties, see Jen-der Lee, "Han Sui zhijian de 'shengzi buju' wenti" [Infanticide and child abandonment from Han to Sui], *The Bulletin of the Institute of History and Philology, Academia Sinica* 66.3 (1995): 747–812.

52. The *T'ang Code* prescribed that one who injured his wife would be sentenced to "being caned eighty strokes," two degrees less than one who injured a stranger, who would receive one hundred strokes. A woman who injured her husband, however, would be sentenced to one year's labor, one degree more than a woman who injured a stranger. If the injury resulted in death, the offenders would be sentenced to death regardless of their status in the family. See *Tang lü shuyi*, ch. 22, "Doulü," pp. 409–10; and Johnson, trans., *Specific Articles*, vol. 2 of *The T'ang Code*, ch. 22, "Assaults and Accusations," pp. 358–61.

53. Another relevant incident involves an order Empress Dowager Ling made concerning Prince Runan, who constantly assaulted his wife and concubines after he decided to cultivate immortality through vegetarianism and homosexuality. When Empress Dowager Ling found out, she ordered that whenever a princess was ill for over one hundred days, the case had to be reported to the imperial court, and that any prince who beat his wife would be demoted. See *Wei shu*, ch. 22, p. 593.

54. Zu Taizhi, "Yi Qian Geng shaqi shi" [On Qian Geng's killing his wife], in *Quan Jin wen* [Comprehensive collection of literature from the Jin Dynasty], ch. 138, p. 12a., in *Quan shanggu sandai Qin-Han Sanguo liuchao wen* [Comprehensive collection of literature from ancient times to the Six Dynasties], comp. Yan Kejun (1894; repr. Beijing: Zhonghua shuju, 1958).

55. This was Zhangsun Lü's case. See *Wei shu*, ch. 77, p.1882.

56. This is Liu Yan's case in the Shu Han period (222–80). During this time, it was a regular ceremony for officials' wives and mothers to go to the imperial palace to offer congratulations on the occasion of certain festivals. Liu Yan's wife Ms. Hu went to one of these ceremonies and was kept in the palace for a month by special order of the empress dowager. This made Liu Yan suspect that she was having an extramarital affair. After Liu Yan's execution, however, the congratulatory ceremonies were abolished. Since it was unusual for a man to be executed for simply beating his wife, it is reasonable to believe that there was imperial interference in the verdict. See *Sanguo zhi* [The history of the Three Kingdoms], by Chen Shou (Beijing: Zhonghua shuju, 1959), ch. 40, p. 1002.

57. *Nan shi* [The history of the Southern Dynasties] records the case of Liu Rong, an aristocrat in the fifth century who injured his wife with a knife, probably in a fight, and was only deprived of his noble title. See *Nan shi* by Li Yanshou (Beijing: Zhonghua shuju, 1975), ch. 15, p. 428.

58. See Yu Huan, *Wei lue,* cited in *Sanguo zhi,* ch. 9, p. 290.

59. For the grace period from ancient times to the Han period, see Cheng Shude, *Jiu chao lü kao,* ch. 4, p. 28.

60. There was also a twenty-day "protecting the innocent" grace period for beatings with instruments like sticks; a thirty-day one for those who injured others with knives, hot water, or fire; and a fifty-day one for those who broke others' limbs and bones. See *Tang lü shuyi*, ch. 22, "Doulü," pp

388–9; and Wallace Johnson, trans., *Specific Articles*, vol. 2 of *The T'ang Code*, ch. 22, "Assaults and Accusations," pp. 333–4.

61. See A.F.P. Hulsewé, *Remnants of Qin Law* (Leiden: E. J. Brill, 1985), p. 148.

62. Both Zhangsun Zhi's case in the Northern Wei period and Hu Changcan's case in the Northern Qi period (550–77) indicate little legal interference in cases involving the killing of maids within a family. Zhangsun Zhi, a general-official near the end of the Northern Wei period, had an affair with Ms. Luo, then murdered her husband and married her. The *Wei shu* states that Luo was very jealous because she was some ten years older than Zhi. Even though she prevented him from taking concubines and killed at least four of his servants, he still "loved and respected" her very much. Neither accusation nor legal interference was ever mentioned. See *Wei shu*, ch. 25, p. 649. Hu Changcan of the Northern Qi period was known for his lust. His wife Ms. Wang once killed one of his maids. Hu Changcan was very angry with her and refused to see her for three years. But there is no legal activity indicated in this case either. See *Bei shi* [The history of the Northern Dynasties], by Li Yanshou (Beijing: Zhonghua shuju, 1974), ch. 80, p. 2691.

63. *Song shu* [The history of the (Liu) Song Dynasty], by Shen Yue (Beijing: Zhonghua shuju, 1974), ch. 81, p. 2080.

64. *Song shu*, ch. 81, p. 2080.

65. In his "Preface to the Jin Law," Zhang Fei (Chang Fei) interpreted *budao* as "to go against moderation and rupture reason" (*nijie jueli*); since the Han period it was often preceded by *dani* (great rebellion) to designate treason cases; it was also one of the Ten Abominations in the Tang code. In the Jin law, *budao* was a more serious crime than *bujing* (disrespect), which was defined as "to fall short in rites and to reject moderation." Since *bujing* criminals were to be sentenced to execution in the marketplace by the Jin code, there is no doubt that Ms. Zhang would have been executed even though there is no specific information about her penalty. For discussion on *budao* in Han times, see Oba Osamu, *Shin Kan hōseishi no kenkyū* [Study on the legal history of the Qin and Han Dynasties] (Tokyo: Sobunsha, 1982), pp. 151–64. For *budao* and *bujing* in the Jin law, see *Jin shu*, ch. 30, p. 928. Translation by Benjamin E. Wallacker, "Chang Fei's [Zhang Fei's] Preface to the Chin Code of Law," *T'oung Pao* 72.4–5 (1986): 229–68. For the Ten Admonitions in the Tang code, see *Tang lü shuyi*, ch. 1, "Mingli," pp. 6–15; and Wallace Johnson, trans., *General Principles*, vol. 1 of *The T'ang Code*, ch. 1, "General Principles," pp. 61–83.

66. Both the Eastern Wei and the early Northern Qi followed Northern Wei law. Not until 564, when legal scholars finished the modification, did the Northern Qi government issue a new set of dynastic laws. See *Sui shu* [The history of the Sui Dynasty], by Wei Zheng (580–643) et al. (Beijing: Zhonghua shuju, 1973), ch. 25, pp. 704–6. For discussion of the modification of law in the Northern Dynasties, see Chen Yinke, "Sui Tang zhidu," part four, "Xinglü."

67. *Wei shu,* ch. 88, pp. 1909–10; *Bei shi,* ch. 86, pp. 2871–2.

68. *Wei shu,* ch. 88, p. 1910; *Bei shi,* ch. 86, pp. 2871–2.

69. *Wei shu,* ch. 88, pp. 1911–2; *Bei shi,* ch. 86, pp. 2871–2.

70. *Tang lü shuyi,* ch. 22, "Dousong," pp. 409–10; Johnson, trans., *Specific Articles,* vol. 2 of *The T'ang Code,* ch. 22, "Assault and Accusations," pp. 358–61. For the definition of the three mothers in the Tang law, see *Tang lü shuyi,* ch. 1, "Mingli," p. 259, and Johnson, trans., *General Principles,* vol. 1 of *The T'ang Code,* ch. 1, "General Principles," pp. 136–7.

71. *Han shu* [The history of the Former Han Dynasty], by Ban Gu (Beijing: Zhonghua shuju, 1962), ch. 8, p. 251.

72. See Appendix II for the mourning obligations.

73. For example, the application of *dani budao* (high treason and crimes of depravity) changed throughout the Former and Later Han Dynasties. First, owing to ideological reasons such as ethical ideas and cosmological thinking, family relations of a criminal sentenced to death would have been exiled to the borderland after Emperor Zhaodi (r. 86–74 B.C.E.) of the Former Han Dynasty. Second, due to the growing influence of powerful families from the beginning of the Eastern Han period, the range of collective responsibilities among family members also grew. While only one's parents, wife, and children would be responsible under the Western Han, relatives within the five degrees of mourning would also be punished under the Eastern Han. Third, since powerful families and intellectual families became synonymous and more influential in the political field, the punishment of exclusion from governmental service became more common and forceful under the Eastern Han. See Jen-der Lee, "Xi Han lüling," pp. 34–9; also Jen-der Lee, "Family Execution."

74. When Guanqiu Jian was executed for high treason in 255, his son Guanqiu Dian and Dian's wife Ms. Xun should also have been sentenced to death in accordance with the principle of collective responsibility. But Xun Yi, Ms. Xun's paternal male third cousin, had a marriage alliance with Sima Shi, then regent, and pleaded with the emperor, who let Ms. Xun divorce Dian to save her own life. Ms. Xun's daughter, Jian's granddaughter, Guanqiu Zhi, already married and pregnant, was under arrest and awaiting execution because of her collective responsibility for her natal family. Ms. Xun asked the Metropolitan Commandant (*sili jiaowei*) He Zeng for mercy and said she would become an official slave to save her daughter from the death penalty. He Zeng pitied her and told his assistant magistrate (*zhubu*) Cheng Xian to propose the court discussion cited here. For details, see *Jin shu,* ch. 30, p. 926. The principle that a divorced wife would not be collectively punished for crimes of her ex-husband and his family, on which basis Ms. Xun was spared, was codified by the end of the Former Han Dynasty. See *Han shu,* ch. 81, p. 3355.

75. This is the *sancong,* the women's three followings, also prescribed in the "Sangfu" chapter of the *Yi li.* It demanded that a woman follow her father

before she got married, her husband after she got married, and her son
when she was widowed.

76. *Jin shu,* ch. 30, p. 926.

77. Ibid., p. 927.

78. Under the Eastern Jin, a female shaman was sentenced to slavery for her
husband's involvement in a robbery. See *Nan shi,* ch. 14, p. 386.

79. In 300, one day before Ms. Xie was to marry into the Pei family, her father, Xie Jie, was accused of treason and given the sentence of family execution. The Pei attempted to save Ms. Xie's life, perhaps by faking the
wedding date, on the basis of the code of exemption of the "married
daughter." But Ms. Xie refused and said that there was no point living
on alone when her family was destroyed. She then died in accordance
with the law of collective responsibility. Later the imperial court began
to discuss reducing collective execution of women. See *Jin shu,* ch. 60,
p. 1633.

80. *Jin shu,* ch. 5, p. 116; ch. 6, p. 163

81. *Sui shu,* ch. 25, p. 699.

82. It was Emperor Taiwu (r. 424–51) of the Northern Wei who ordered a program, headed by Cui Hao, then Minister of Education (*situ*), to revise the
law code. See *Wei shu,* ch. 111, p. 2873.

83. *Wei shu,* ch. 111, p. 2874. The Northern Wei may have applied family execution also to nontreason cases prior to 474. Emperor Xiaowen issued a
decree in 474 to stop household execution (*menfang zhi zhu*) in nontreason cases and to punish only the person who committed the crime. See
Wei shu, ch. 111, p. 2876.

84. *Sanguo zhi,* ch. 22, p. 650.

85. *Wei shu,* ch. 64, pp. 1422–3.

86. For instance, Ms. Bai in the third century was sentenced to *qishi* only
several days after her wedding because her husband had fled to avoid
the military draft—this was even before he had formally received her.
Only after the local assistant magistrate Lu Yu argued the case in her
favor was her punishment reduced from the death penalty. Lu Yu referred to two principles. First, the classical rites required the bride to
be presented in the ancestor temple five days after the wedding so that
she could be established as a "wife" (*fu*) in the household. If she died
within those five days, she would be returned to her natal family for
burial. Second, legal precedent suggested that accomplices should be
punished less severely than the principal criminals and that it was better to release a suspect than to kill an innocent person. Lu Yu apparently cited the first principle to show that Ms. Bai was not yet a fully
received member of her husband's family, and intended to apply the
second one, which was also quoted by Cui Zuan when he pleaded for
the two adulteresses, to propose a lighter punishment for Ms. Bai. See
Sanguo zhi, ch. 22, p. 650.

87. In a Liu-Song case, a widow was first sentenced for the robbery committed by the sons of her husband's brother, who were her relatives of one-year's mourning obligation (*jiqin*). Since Liu-Song law required that *jiqin* of convicted robbers must be conscripted, she was to be penalized, and her sons, who had only nine-months' mourning obligation for their robber cousins, would be drafted together with their mother into military service, both due to the law of collective responsibility. She was pardoned only after the official in charge argued in her favor, on the basis of the principle of a woman's "three followings" (*sancong*), which was also prescribed in the *Yi li:* since her husband was already dead when the crime was committed, she was supposed to follow the way of her sons; in no way should she have been collectively responsible for her nephew's criminal deeds. See *Song shu,* ch. 64, p. 1704.

88. One could suspect that Liu Hui's southern origin may have caused antipathy from the Xianbei imperial house, but extant historical documents do not confirm this suspicion. Whether the fact that Liu Hui was from the South made him inferior in the northern court and in this case is hard to determine. The wording in the verdict never mentions his southern background, and the biography of Liu Hui and his father shows no sign of discrimination. It could be that Empress Dowager Ling's anger towards Liu Hui was more the result of her feelings for her sister-in-law than of Liu Hui's southern origins. For Liu Hui's origins, see *Wei shu,* ch. 59, pp. 1307–12.

89. See Jen-der Lee, "Conflicts and Compromise between Legal Authority and Ethical Ideas: From the Perspectives of Revenge in Han Times," *Journal of Social Sciences and Philosophy* 1.1 (1988): 359–408.

90. For the development of the Secretariat, Chancellery, and Department of State Affairs, see Yen Keng-wang, "Bei Wei shangshu zhidu kao" [On the system of shangshu of the Northern Wei], *The Bulletin of the Institute of History and Philology, Academia Sinica* 18 (1948): 252–360; and Zheng Qinren, *Bei Wei guanliao jigou yanjiu xubian* [Second study on the bureaucratic system of the Northern Wei] (Taipei: Daohe chubanshe, 1995), pp. 5–10.

91. *Wei shu,* ch. 111, pp. 2886, 2887.

92. Cui Ting participated in legal revision in Emperor Xiaowen's reign (471–99) when Empress Dowager Wenming was the regent (466–7, 476–90). He was highly commended by Li Chong, then imperial secretary and leader of the government transformation movement, and was once rewarded by the emperor with eight hundred bolts of cloth, eight hundred bushels of grain, two horses, and two oxen for his contribution. His brother Cui Zhen was appointed chief minister for law enforcement at the beginning of Emperor Xuanwu's reign (500–15) and was praised for his keen investigation as well as fair judgment. Cui Xiaofen, Cui Ting's son, was also known for his capability in legal judgment and served as chamberlain for law enforcement (*tingwei*) at the beginning of Emperor Xiaoming's reign

(516–28). Cui Zuan was Cui Xiaofen's kinsman. For the Cui family and their legal contribution, see *Wei shu*, ch. 57, pp. 1264–72. For the Boling Cui family and its history, see Patricia Buckley Ebrey, *Aristocratic Families of Early Imperial China: A Case Study of the Po-ling Ts'ui Family* (Cambridge: Cambridge University Press, 1978). Boling is close to Anping city in present-day Shandong province. See Tan Qixiang, *Zhongguo lishi ditu ji* [The historical atlas of China], vol. 4 (Shanghai: Cartographic Publishing House, 1982).

93. *Wei shu,* ch. 57, p. 1275.

94. You Zhao's father, You Minggen, was in charge of the Department of State Affairs in Emperor Xiaowen's reign and participated in legal revision. The *Wei shu* states that he was so diligent in his legal profession that the emperor once rewarded him with one thousand bolts of cloth and one thousand *hu* of grain. In 451 You Minggen's paternal cousin You Ya was appointed by Emperor Taiwu (r. 423–52) to revise the law codes to better fit the Tuoba's rule in China. For You Minggen's legal profession, see *Wei shu*, ch. 55, p.1215. For You Ya's legal contribution, see *Wei shu*, ch. 54, p. 1195; ch. 111, p. 2875. For discussion of the legal tradition of the You family and its significance in revising Northern Wei law in line with Han legal tradition, see Chen Yinke, "Sui Tang zhidu." Guangping is close to Handan in present-day Shandong province. See Tan, *Zhongguo lishi ditu ji*, vol. 4.

95. *Wei shu,* ch. 55, pp. 1216–7.

96. Legal studies may have encountered some setbacks at the end of the Eastern Han period, when the government recruitment system placed more emphasis on literary ability than on administrative and legal knowledge. It is said that legal knowledge was so lost among the scholars in the central government that the Cao-Wei Dynasty had to establish erudites (*boshi*) for legal learning (*lü boshi*) to preserve such knowledge and train legal officials for the government. For the development of legal learning under the Eastern Han, see Hsing Yi-tien, "Qin Han de lüling xue—jian lun Cao-Wei lü boshi de chuxian" [The rise and decline of law-learning in Qin Han officialdom—an explanation of the emergence of the Erudites of law in the early third century], *The Bulletin of the Institute of History and Philology, Academia Sinica* 54.4 (1983): 51–101.

97. Cui Hong and his son Cui Hao of the Qinghe Cui family led the legal revisions in the reigns of Emperor Daowu (389–409) and Emperor Taiwu, respectively. See *Wei shu*, ch. 111, p. 2874. Feng Hui of the Bohai Feng family was praised by his contemporaries for impeaching imperial clansman Yuan Qin for adultery under the rule of Empress Dowager Ling. See *Wei shu,* ch. 32, pp. 760–3; also see note 49 above. His kinswoman Ms. Feng, who married into the Qinghe Cui family, was so renowned for her knowledge of legal precedents that she was recorded in the "Biographies of Women" in *Wei shu*. See *Wei shu*, ch. 92, p. 1978. Qinghe is near Linqing county, and Bohai is near Dongguang county in present-day Shandong province. For their locations, see Tan, *Zhongguo lishi ditu ji,* vol. 4.

98. Feng Junyi was actually in command of the legal revision around 534, which resulted in the proclamation of a new law for the succeeding Northern Qi Dynasty (550–77). See *Bei Qi shu* [The history of the Northern Qi], by Li Baiyao (Beijing: Zhonghua shuju, 1972), ch. 43, p. 573; and *Wei shu,* ch. 98, pp. 1908–12.

99. Chen Yinke's study of the origins of the legal system of the Sui and Tang Dynasties argues this point in detail. See Chen Yinke, "Sui Tang zhidu."

100. A recent study by Kang Le suggests that Empress Dowager Wenming, who was regent in most of Xiaowen's time, was actually the mastermind of this movement. For her efforts in transforming the government and the impact of the sinification movement on the Xianbei imperial clansmen, see Kang Le, *Cong xijiao dao nanjiao* [From the west suburb to the south suburb] (Taipei: Daohe chubanshe, 1995), part two, "Empress Dowager Wenming," pp. 111–64.

101. See Chen Jo-shui, "Empress Wu and Proto-Feminist Sentiments in Tang China," in *Imperial Rulership and Cultural Change in Traditional China,* eds. Frederick Brandauer and Chun-chieh Huang (Seattle: University of Washington Press, 1995), pp. 77–116.

102. Emperor Ming (r. 466–72) of the Liu-Song not only interfered in marriage issues personally, but also intended to promote female tolerance by circulating "antijealousy" literature. After executing an official's wife, Emperor Ming told one of his officials to write a book named *The Stories of Jealous Wives,* presumably to show their miserable fate and to warn other women. Before a certain aristocrat was about to marry an imperial daughter, the emperor asked an official to compose an article in the name of the aristocrat. In this article, he was supposed to decline the marriage proposal because of other aristocrats' painful experiences in marrying jealous princesses. For Emperor Ming's actions, see *Song shu,* ch. 41, pp. 1290–2; for different attitudes toward jealous women in the North and the South, see Jen-der Lee, "Jealousy in the Six Dynasties: Crime in the South and Virtue in the North," unpublished manuscript.

103. For the sentiment of marital egalitarianism under the Northern Dynasties, see Jen-der Lee, "Women and Marriage in China during the Period of Disunion," Ph.D. diss., University of Washington, 1992, ch. 4, "Conflict and Termination of Marriage"; also, Jen-der Lee, "The Life of Women in the Six Dynasties," *Journal of Women and Gender Studies* 4 (1993): 47–80.

104. Ch'ü Tung-tsu, chs. I–II.

105. Jack Dull, "Marriage and Divorce in Han China: A Glimpse at 'Pre-Confucian' Society," in *Chinese Family Law and Social Change,* ed. David C. Buxbaum (Seattle: University of Washington Press, 1978), pp. 23–74.

106. See Chen Yinke, "Sui Tang zhidu," part four, "Xinglü," in *Chen Yinke xiansheng lunwen ji.*

CHAPTER TWO

WOMEN IN CHINA'S
FRONTIER POLITICS: *HEQIN*

Ning Chia
Central College

> In China's frontier politics, the heqin women performed powerful roles in a
> male-dominated world. They offer us a unique opportunity to examine gen-
> der, race, and politics.

Although intermarriage between Chinese imperial princesses and
powerful nomadic rulers of Inner Asia was long an institutionalized
part of frontier politics, these women have not been acknowledged as a
category in the analysis of China's frontier politics.[1] This intermarriage was
strategically designed by the imperial court of China from the Han (206
B.C.E.–8 C.E. and 25–220) to the Tang (618–907) Dynasties under the
name of *heqin,* literally "harmony" *(he)* and "intimacy" *(qin),* often translated as the "appeasement policy"[2] and "harmonious kinship."[3] This intermarriage also served the Inner Asian powers as a strategic method to
maintain a peaceful relationship with China and to increase their prestige
and wealth. An examination of how women actually brought the *heqin*
policy into effect can lead to a new perspective in the study of China's
frontier politics.

Such a perspective will also contribute to the general study of Chinese women, which has become a vigorous field since the mid-1980s, although women in *heqin* intermarriage have not been included. To
reconstruct these women's lives and to rediscover their contribution will
add to the "new body of women's studies research" that has highlighted

gender as a category of analysis and aimed at opening new ways of pre-senting an awareness of women's lives. Constructed in order to give gen-der a place in historical and cultural change, this research makes women part of the discussion in all social, cultural, and political issues and makes gender relationships a legitimate object of inquiry.[4] Such a reconstruc-tion of the female role in China's frontier politics will show that in this specific political arena, women in a male-dominated world actually served a powerful function that men could not. Women should thus be credited as active participants in China's frontier politics as much as the male decision-makers who designed and determined these women's marital fates.

Women's political representation can be approached from four angles. First, for over seven hundred years in the united Chinese dynasties from the Han to the Tang, women directly participated in *heqin* intermarriage. This participation incorporated these women's marital and family lives completely into politics, and they therefore upheld an important frontier institution in imperial China. Second, working for both her father (the Chinese emperor) or natal family (China) and her husband (the Inner Asian ruler) or marital family (an Inner Asian power), a *heqin* woman was empowered to stand between two states that had long been in military confrontation, and her marriage was arranged to create a family-type medium by which the two states could form a bilateral relationship. Since *heqin* was always a peace settlement between the two states, the weaker the imperial court of China, the more urgent a *heqin,* and the more powerful the women in changing the fate of the imperial family. Even China's sinocentrism could often be applied to Inner Asians only in terms of a family relationship through the marital bond, by which women established a relative-like connection between rival political men. Third, women's feelings in these political marriages, their lives in the Inner Asian households, and their personal sacrifices in political causes should be included as part of our understanding of frontier poli-tics. Although the surviving stories of these women from limited histor-ical records and their extant poems seem to leave us merely their sorrow and tragedy, a unique female value can still be discovered amid their grief and pathos. Finally, even though the women in *heqin* intermarriage be-long to a small, countable group in comparison to the uncountable women in all of Chinese society, their experience nevertheless represents a special part of human life in our inquiry into gender, women, and pol-itics. This special experience has impacted Chinese historical memory, in which these women have perpetually remained the symbol of female beauty and virtue.

Heqin Women in Sight:
Intermarriage in Chinese History

Heqin, which based peace on a marital relationship, has been viewed as one of the three important contact mechanisms (together with tribute and the frontier market) in Chinese-Inner Asian relationships.[5] The first heqin arrangement was signed as an armistice agreement in 198 B.C.E. by Emperor Gaozu (reigned 206–195 B.C.E.) of the Western Han Dynasty (206 B.C.E. - 8 C.E.) and Medu chanyu (died 174 B.C.E.)[6] of the Xiongnu.[7] Following this agreement, not only the Western Han, but also the Eastern Han (25–220 C.E.), the Sui (581–618), and the Tang (618–907) Dynasties all committed themselves to utilizing heqin intermarriage as an important component in frontier policy. Since the non-Chinese dynasties—the Mongol Yuan (1271–1368) and the Manchu Qing (1644–1911)—did not need the Han and non-Han marriage to solve the frontier problem, the only dynasties that did not practice heqin policy were the Qin (221–207 B.C.E.), the Northern and Southern Song (960–1279), and the Ming (1368–1644). By this account, during over two thousand years of imperial history (221 B.C.E. - 1911 C.E.), four among the eight united dynasties relied on heqin to improve relationships with nomadic Inner Asia, as the table below shows. In other words, China's heqin policy was sustained by women's necessary participation in one-third of imperial history or one half of the united Chinese dynasties.

Han Gaozu's heqin policy initiated an alternating pattern of peace and war in China's frontier policy-making. The Shi ji [Records of the Grand Historian], the Han shu [The history of the Former Han Dynasty], and the Jiu Tang shu [The (old) history of the Tang Dynasty] all show that in

Heqin in Imperial Dynasties under Chinese Rule

United Dynasties under Chinese Rule	Heqin
Quin 221–206 B.C.E.	No
Former (Western) Han 206 B.C.E.–8 C.E.	Yes
Later (Eastern) Han 25–220	Yes
Sui 581–618	Yes
Tang 618–907	Yes
Northern Song 960–1127	No
Southern Song 1127–1279	No
Ming 1368–1644	No

China's frontier politics, civilian Confucian officials always insisted on the *heqin* for peace, while military officials insisted on subjugation for defense.[8] Sima Guang's *Zizhi tong jian* [Comprehensive mirror for aid in government] offers more details about the vacillation of imperial policy between these two alternatives. In 622, Tang emperor Gaozu (r. 618–26) asked his officials: "[Since] the [East] Tujue invaded us first and then came [to us] looking for peace, which will be good for us, peace or war?" One official argued that "war will deepen the hatred and is not as beneficial to us as peace," but another official insisted that "making peace without a fight will show our weakness, [the Tujue] will come back [fighting against us] next year. . . . after we win the fight and then make peace, we can show [them] both grace and [military] strength." Emperor Gaozu accepted the war proposal. Two years later, however, when Emperor Gaozu discussed West Tujue's request for intermarriage and asked for one of the two choices, he accepted the peace proposal.[9] Emperor Taizong (r. 627–49) once discussed with his court officials how "the Xueyantuo were strong in the north of Gobi. Today there are only two ways to defend ourselves against them: sending troops to destroy them or arranging a marriage to appease them. How should we make our choice?" After Fang Xuanling answered, "I believe the *heqin* choice is superior," the emperor stated, "I am the parent of people, if [I can give] people profit, how should [I only] love a daughter [instead]." He then arranged Princess Xinxing's marriage with the Tujue ruler.[10] These historical records implicitly show that frontier peace in certain periods of imperial China was achieved mainly by women's engagement in *heqin* intermarriage, and that those women became the symbol of peace.

Although *heqin* intermarriage hardly ever effected a long-term peace, the temporary peace it brought was still highly valued by both sides. The *heqin* policy, even though frequently practiced, was never a priority in the policy of the Chinese imperial court. It was instead a forced reaction to China's military weakness. The *Shi ji* records that once one of the two sides became weak or both became exhausted in war, *heqin* became the way to stop war and to keep in contact.[11] During the Han and the Tang Dynasties, *heqin* intermarriage was often the major or even the only means to achieve peace. As soon as Chinese and Inner Asian military strength became comparable, however, *heqin* agreements became ineffective. The capability and duration of a *heqin* intermarriage, as Lin Gan has argued, always depended upon the power balance between the two sides.[12] We can therefore conclude that the relationship between Inner Asian powers and China was either war by refusal of a marriage alliance or peace as result of a marriage alliance. If war and peace were the only two options, it has been argued, peace was much more worthwhile a policy for the people on both sides.[13] Thomas Barfield has pointed out that "the Ho-chin [*heqin*] policy did accomplish its primary goal of avoiding continuous frontier warfare which would have imposed a heavy burden on the Han treasury."[14] The same was also true of other dynasties. In this reasoning, one reality should not slip away from our attention: it was the *heqin* women who devoted their lives to the cause of peace.

Heqin intermarriage was also used by the Chinese court and the Inner Asian powers as a diplomatic means for making military alliances against a common enemy. In the relatively simple defense structure of the Han, which faced only one major threat in Inner Asia—the Xiongnu—Emperor Wudi (r. 140–87 B.C.E.), who first favored military action over *heqin* in dealing with the Xiongnu, still had to utilize *heqin* in the northwest in order to win support from the enemies of the Xiongnu in Central Asia.[15] The Tang faced several strong powers (the Tujue, Tibet, Uyghur, Xueyan-tuo, Tuyuhun, and others), all in confrontation with China at either the same or different times. The Tang court had to develop the *heqin* policy diplomatically as a means of strategic control over different Inner Asian powers. In this use of intermarriage, the Tang could employ one Inner Asian power to attack another or even obtain military support from an Inner Asian power for internal security. For example, by intermarriage the Tang employed and rewarded the Uyghurs and the Türgis for military as-sistance against rebellions inside China or against rival Inner Asian powers, such as Tibet, for a period of time. It has been specifically noted that the Tang-Uyghur intermarriages served the Tang in putting down internal re-bellions.[16] During Emperor Suzong's reign (756–61), for example, the Uyghur *khaghan* Dengli (r. 759–80) married a Tang princess. He once asked to meet his father-in-law, Huai'en, a member of the imperial clan. At the meeting, Huai'en's advice that the *khaghan* should not betray the Tang emperor's trust influenced Dengli, and he sent an envoy to the Tang court expressing his offer of military support in the Tang's war against the rebel Shi Chaoyi.[17]

As long as China was stronger, the Inner Asian powers tried to make marriage alliances with China in order to raise their prestige among the other powers and in the eyes of their own people. If the marriage proposal was refused, the ruler's followers and his subordinate Inner Asian peoples would rebel.[18] One such example is recorded in *Zizhi tong jian*. In 628, a *khaghan* of the West Tujue came to the Tang asking for intermarriage, but the Tang did not grant it. As a result, the nations subordinate to this *khaghan* rebelled against him.[19] No matter how either side, China or an Inner Asian power, used *heqin* intermarriage for political purposes, the *heqin* women were the diplomatic medium that, through the marriage tie, set the course of history. They often were a source of stability and prestige for a power, worked for establishing an equal status between the two sides, and led the Inner Asian leaders to associate themselves politically with the Chinese court.

Since the frontier issues were always related to China's domestic stability and prosperity, the *heqin* policy was not limited only to China's frontier security. *Han shu* commented that Emperor Zhaodi (r. 86–74 B.C.E.) restored Han strength by reducing taxes, practicing a laissez-faire policy, and reopening the door for Han-Xiongnu intermarriage; China then lived in prosperity.[20] The significance of the *heqin* intermarriage to Chinese life can also be found in a negative example in Henry Serruys' study of Sino-Mongolian relations in the Ming Dynasty. The Ming relationship with the Mongols was, according to Serruys, "completely different from relations of the Han and the Tang . . . the Ming never sent Chinese princesses to become the consorts of Mongol rulers, not even the most powerful ones or those on the best of terms with the Ming Court. . . . one of the reasons behind the Oyirad invasion of 1449 was the refusal to send a Chinese princess to Esen-tayisi."[21]

The ideal *heqin* agreement required a woman of status, such as an emperor's daughter or sister. In reality, however, the Chinese court often met this requirement in other ways. Lin Enxian graded *heqin* women into five levels: (1) daughters or sisters of emperors; (2) emperors' nieces; (3) women from the imperial household; (4) nieces of members in the imperial household; and (5) palace women (selected by the imperial court for the emperor but without a marital title), daughters of important court officials, and selected common women.[22]

Under the Western Han, fourteen intermarriages were recorded. Five were arranged before Emperor Wudi's time with the Xiongnu: two for Medu *chanyu* (d. 174 B.C.E.), one for Laoshang *chanyu* (d. 161 B.C.E.), and two for Junchen *chanyu* (d. 126 B.C.E.). After the middle of Emperor Wudi's reign, the strategic concern moved to the northwest area. Then two princesses were married to the Wusun *kunmi*,[23] one to the Guizi King, and two palace women to the Wusun noble and the Shanshan ruler. The actual arrangements for *heqin* intermarriages were more than fourteen because after Emperor Yuandi (r. 48–33 B.C.E.), there was no need to use marriage for military alliance; the Han court just granted palace women to the Xiongnu Huhanye *chanyu* without making a clear record of these women in the historical materials.[24] During the time of Wang Mang (r. 8–23 C.E.), two intermarriages with Xiongnu were recorded.[25] During the Eastern Han period, because of the successful intermarriage between the Xiongnu Huhanye *chanyu* and the Western Han woman Wang Zhaojun in 33 B.C.E., the Xiongnu *chanyu* came to the Eastern Han for one *heqin* after another in the years 51, 52, 63, 65, and 104, in order "to restore the friendship of Huhanye."[26]

After the three intermarriages during the Sui Dynasty,[27] *heqin* intermarriages during the Tang increased to twenty-seven. In the Early Tang period, five princesses were married to Tujue (Turk) *khaghans* and the other two to the Tuyuhun. In the Middle Tang period, thirteen women married Xi, Khitan, Tuchishi, and Ningyuanguo rulers, with seven of these marrying Xi and Khitan. The Late Tang saw the Chinese court arranging seven intermarriages with the Huihe (Uyghur).[28]

Comparing the Han with the Tang—the two major dynasties practicing *heqin*–policy—more Han princesses were not blood daughters of the emperor but either daughters of his relatives or just palace women. More Tang princesses, however, were blood daughters of the emperors. For example, four among the seven *heqin* women of the Late Tang period were blood daughters of Tang emperors.[29] This suggests the increasing significance of *heqin* intermarriage in the Tang Dynasty. Furthermore, Han intermarriage was simply a one-way arrangement: Chinese women only married out, with no Inner Asian women marrying in. Intermarriage between the Tang court and the Tujue saw the possibility of a two-way arrangement. A Tujue khan asked the Chinese court to let her daughter marry a Chinese prince, and the Chinese court agreed. But this solitary case of two-way intermarriage was finally not effected because the two sides fell to war again.[30] It has been acknowledged that by the marriage of Inner Asian rulers with Tang princesses, together with such other efforts as "the bestowal of the Tang imperial surname, with the implication of their incorporation into the imperial family's system of kinship; and by the education of their future rulers in China as 'hostage princes,' usually serving long terms as officers in the imperial guards . . . the larger and more powerful border peoples and their paramount leaders were inducted even further into the Tang order."[31]

To sum up this historical review of the *heqin* policy, a small group of *heqin* women carried the burden of China's frontier peace during the Han and the Tang eras. Whereas each woman's story in the intermarriage varied from the others' in details, their collective experience represents a female contribution to Chinese frontier politics. By their marriageable gender status (female) and political status (from the royal family or the imperial palace), they supported a frontier institution necessary for China's national security. They were also some of the very few, if not the only, Chinese before the Qing Dynasty (1644–1911) with the imperial assignment to live permanently outside the Great Wall. Since *heqin* was a political strategy not only for the Chinese court but also for the Inner Asian powers, these women participated in politics for the benefit of both sides. A women's perspective in this field of study will correct the biased treatment of *heqin* only in terms of the politics involved, the male managers, and the political consequences. The women who actually took part in this frontier institution must have a place of their own.

Hequin Women in Power: Family Behind Politics

The essence of *heqin* intermarriage was the political use of women's marriageability in forming a family alliance between two political powers. Such a use created a special pattern to relate female to male, marital life to politics, and family to state. As two individuals underwent a status change from unrelated singles to husband and wife, the two rival political entities—the Chinese Empire and the nomadic power in Inner Asia—changed from enemies into in-laws who were supposed to perform mutual obligations as part of the family alliance. In this case, the gender categories (male and female) transformed the political categories (rival and alliance). The *heqin* women represented the imperial court of China for an anticipated political cause: peace between two rival states. How the two sides of the *heqin* family (two states, in fact) responded to the intermarriage decided how long the peace between them would last. In successful cases of intermarriage, China's control of the frontier situation was actually achieved by *heqin* women's marital relationships with their Inner Asian husbands.

It was through family principles that *heqin* women gained political power in several ways. First of all, cultural understandings of the family had directed politicians to arrange intermarriages from the very beginning of the *heqin* policy. Liu Jing's proposal for the intermarriage in 198 B.C.E., the first in Chinese history, shows that due to the Confucian principles of family life in regard to descendants and sons-in-law (and brothers-in-law later), women were put at the center of intermarriage and of great political expectations. Liu Jing persuaded Emperor Gaozu that "if she [the *heqin* princess] gives birth to a son, he [that son] will be the crown prince [in line] to become the *chanyu*. . . . While Medu is alive he would be [your] son-in-law, when he dies [your] grandson would become the next *chanyu*. It is unheard of for a grandson to compete against a grandfather. Then without war [the Xiongnu] can gradually be subdued."[32] In this proposal, "the idea of descent," as Carol P. MacCormack argued, "is equated with the transmission of rights, duties, power and authority,"[33] and *heqin* women had to carry out this transmission. The Confucian morality of filial piety of children towards parents or grandparents was also involved in this proposal for political gains beyond the boundaries of the Chinese state and its culture.

Following Confucian assumptions about family, the *heqin* in-law relationship throughout all the dynasties practicing *heqin* always designated the Chinese emperor as of the elder generation, which indicated his superiority and authority over the younger generation—now the Inner Asian in-laws. The *heqin* policy, therefore, converted gender relations into generational relations and put Inner Asians into the generational hierarchy of the Chinese: marriage to the Chinese emperor's daughter reduced the nomadic ruler to the Chinese emperor's son-in-law (or younger brother-in-law or nephew, in some cases). Although later the Chinese court was not able, as expected, to rely on any *heqin* women's descendants or relatives to work for long-term frontier peace, Chinese cultural norms concerning family significantly initiated and bolstered the *heqin* policy in China's frontier politics.

Second, regarding the control of power in family life, the *heqin* women belonged to a very unusual female group in imperial China. While most Chinese women's lives were traditionally tied to the interests of family alliances, the *heqin* women's were tied to the fate of the whole Chinese Empire and the related Inner Asian power. As most Chinese women did not have a strong position in their own marriage alliances, a *heqin* woman needed to be a power operator by herself in an alien society. She had to work for her father's family and nation and at the same time for her husband's. Though she was required to be submissive within the marriage arrangement, she was to be highly creative in political affairs after the marriage. Also, Inner Asian societies allowed the *heqin* women to perform an active role in politics. They were well integrated into their marital families and received a personal share of the husbands' patrimony apart from that given to male offspring, and widows rarely left the husbands' families to remarry.[34] As Inner Asian rulers' wives, they were not excluded from political power, for Inner Asian societies gave married women equal family status. Thus, the *heqin* women could influence their husbands' decisions in many ways.

Princess Xieyou (120–49 B.C.E.) of the Western Han, for example, played such a role. In 73 B.C.E., she presented an emergency letter to Emperor Xuandi (r. 73–49 B.C.E.) on behalf of her husband (the Wusun ruler), reporting a Xiongnu attack on the Wusun. She delivered the request of the Wusun ruler for military cooperation with the Han against the Xiongnu—a message that the Han welcomed. The Wusun ruler approached this cooperation as a way to "save the Han princess." This letter led to combined Han-Wusun military action that defeated the Xiongnu and caused their decisive decline.[35] In the Tang period, the princess Little Ningguo—granddaughter of Emperor Xuanzong (r. 712–56), who lived in Uyghur territory for thirty-three years (758-791) and finally died there—was admired by the Tang court, which said that "She indeed assists [the court] with merit and helps the application of [the court's] policy of conciliation."[36]

Even with the extreme shortage of historical records about how these *heqin* women really advised their husbands in policy-making toward China, we still have reason to believe that they did more than we can know. One indication is found in *Sui shu* when the Sui court instructed Princess Dayi, rather than her husband Landu Khaghan of the Tujue, to send Tujue troops to act in military cooperation with the Sui.[37] When "the party to control the peace was the Inner Asian powers but not China,"[38] a Chinese woman in the intermarriage could do even more to avoid further conflict. Thomas J. Barfield has commented that since the tribal leaders of Inner Asia were often guided by their Chinese wives in making alliances with the reigning Chinese dynasty, "tribal politics revolved around such marriage exchanges."[39]

The discovery of *heqin* women in China's exercise of sinocentric ideology brings to light an untouched, but meaningful, topic. Many examples illustrate that imperial sinocentrism was often achieved not by the political or military methods of the Chinese court, but by the family ties that *heqin* women's intermarriage created. Sinocentrism, which assumed the cultural and political supremacy of the Chinese over all other peoples, has dominated Chinese relationships with surrounding non-Chinese as the main principle guiding the Chinese court in its relationship to the other powers.[40] However, other studies have found that this sinocentric principle often was not practical in Chinese-nomadic relationships[41] and was never accepted by Inner Asian leaders, who thought, in turn, that they were equal or even superior to the Chinese court.[42] In this ideological and cultural confrontation, the *heqin* intermarriage provided the possibility of peaceful contact between the two sides, despite disagreement over sinocentric principles.

In the example of the Han emperor Gaozu's intermarriage policy, which sought to make the powerful Xiongnu *chanyu* a son-in-law in order to bring peace, the family method for achieving the political goal was explained from a sinocentric viewpoint by Chinese scholar-officials. According to the Han historical records, the goal of letting the "barbarians" submit themselves as Han vassals *(chengchen)*, which also meant being an inner and subordinate part of China *(neifu)*, could often be reached by claiming them as younger brothers[-in-law] *(chengdi)* or sons-in-law *(chengxu)*. *Hou Han shu* stated that "Xiongnu related with Han by relations of [in-law] brothers . . . [which means] to submit as the Han vassals *[chengchen]* generation after generation."[43] The later Han emperors and emperors of other dynasties continued to rely on the in-law relationship to lead Inner Asian "barbarian" rulers to accepting sinocentric notions. After Emperor Gaozu's application of intermarriage to turn back the Xiongnu invasion by creating a brother-in-law relationship,[44] Emperor Wendi (r. 179–157 B.C.E.) kept the term "brothers" to communicate with the Xiongnu for the purpose of keeping the border peace.[45] In an edict concerning *heqin* with the Xiongnu, he claimed *heqin* would "create a tie of brothers."[46] During Emperor Wudi's time, both the Han court and the Wusun claimed the intermarriage between them would "create a tie of elder and younger brothers [who would] then fight against Xiongnu together."[47]

During the Sui Dynasty, when a defeated Tujue *khaghan* of the Sui presented a letter to the Sui emperor asking for peace, he used the words: "The emperor is [my] wife's father, the emperor is therefore [my] father. [I] am the husband of [your] daughter, I am therefore [your] son-in-law. Although we live in two different places, we have the same love toward each other."[48] When a Chinese official, Zhangsun Sheng, presented Ishbara Khagan with an imperial decree from Emperor Wendi, Ishbara, regarding himself as equal and even superior to the Chinese court, refused to stand up and bow at the presentation of Princess Dayi as his wife. Sheng said that "Both the [lords] of the Tujue and the Sui are the Sons of Heaven of the Great Kingdoms. You, the *khaghan,* refused to stand up, how can I disagree? But the *khatun* [the princess] is the daughter of the emperor; therefore, you the *khaghan* are the son-in-law of the Great Sui. How can [you] refuse to honor the father-in-law?" Ishbara accepted this rationale and said, "I have to bow to the father-in-law. I shall obey."[49]

The same situation can be found in the Tang Dynasty. In 758, the Tang emperor Suzong (r. 256–61) arranged for his youngest daughter Princess Ningguo to be the wife of Pijiajie Khaghan. When the imperial official brought the princess to his tent, Pijiajie arrogantly treated the imperial official, a cousin of the emperor, in a way that indicated the Uyghur state was superior to the Tang. He complained that "I and your Heavenly Khaghan [the Chinese emperor] are equals as masters of each nation, there should be a courtesy between master and his subject, so why you do not bow to me with that courtesy?" The Tang official answered that "the previous intermarriages between our two nations were all arranged with a princess in the imperial clan. But now our Son of Heaven gives you his own daughter because of your meritorious service for the Tang. His grace is so mighty, how can you, the son-in-law of the Son of Heaven [the Tang emperor], ignore your father-in-law and not go down from your chair to receive his entitlement respectfully?" These words affected Pijiajie. He changed immediately and followed the instructions of the Tang official. The next day he made the Tang princess his principal wife.[50]

In another case, when the Tang court and the Tibetan power were negotiating peace, the Tang emperor sent a diplomatic envoy to visit the Tang princess Jincheng (d. 739), who had married the Tibetan ruler. The two sides developed a harmonious discussion for peace by recognizing the uncle (the Chinese emperor)–nephew (the Tibetan king) relationship.[51] As the result of the intermarriage between the Tang princess Wencheng (d. 680) and the Tibetan king Songtsan-gambo (ca. 617–50) in 641 and later that of Princess Jincheng to Tri-de Tsug-ten in 710, a treaty between Tibet and China was carved on a stone tablet erected in front of the Dazhao Temple in Lhasa in 823. Both the Tibetan and the Chinese versions of the treaty described how Tibet and the Tang were "in a relationship of nephew and uncle" that would "never change." However, the Tibetan text shows that the Tibetan king and the Chinese emperor "conferred together for the alliance of their kingdoms," while the Chinese text shows that "they discussed national affairs as in the same nation."[52] The *Xizang zhi* [Gazetteers of Tibet] states that the intermarriage started the formal relationship between the Tang and Tibet. This relationship is further politically described as Tibetan *neifu* (subordination) to the Chinese empire. Tied by this intermarriage, the Chinese and Tibetan nations defined the border between them and established a friendly alliance.[53] *Weizang tongzhi* [The chronicle gazetteer of Tibet] recorded that the Tibetan king very carefully observed an uncle-nephew etiquette with regards to the Tang official after his marriage to the princess Wencheng.[54]

Furthermore, the terms *brother-in-law* and *son-in-law* were often used in Tang-Tujue and Tang-Tuyuhun relationships.[55] These historical cases suggest that *heqin* intermarriage worked to avoid ideological conflicts between China and Inner Asia. The in-law relationship between the Chinese emperor and the Inner Asian ruler established a contact pattern that could meet Inner Asians' economic needs from China without touching the issue of superiority, and at the same time satisfied Chinese sinocentrism without offending the Inner Asian ruler. Thus, the family model symbolized the state relationship, and family terms were frequently used in cross-state communications.

Not only by the Chinese court, but also by the Inner Asians, the family terms established by the *heqin* intermarriage were employed for political goals, especially when the Inner Asians moved into China. The Xiongnu Huhanye *chanyu* (d. 33 B.C.E.), who married the Han palace woman Wang Zhaojun, claimed to be the brother(-in-law) of the Han emperor and asked for another intermarriage.[56] This episode of later years served the Xiongnu in legitimizing their entry into China during the internal chaos in Wang Mang's time.[57] The Xiongnu attacked Wang Mang's army in the name of the Han emperor's brother in-law and attempted to establish a new Chinese emperor with the Han family name—Liu.[58]

With knowledge of these historical events, anthropological studies of the family as a human institution and of family-related issues such as gender, sexuality, marriage, and kinship can assist our inquiry into why and how these *heqin* women gained power in the intermarriage. First, gender and sexual issues can help us inquire into women's empowerment. The sociologist Fei Xiaotong has commented that Chinese princesses who married the nomadic rulers of Inner Asia can be viewed as the creative force of female sexuality.[59] Nancy Chodorow argued, "every society is organized by a 'sex/gender system'" that "consists in a set of arrangements by which the biological raw material of human sex and procreation is shaped by human, social intervention and satisfied in a conventional manner."[60] "In the maps of social reality drawn by Freud and Lévi-Strauss," Gayle Rubin asserted, "there is a deep recognition of the place of sexuality in society, and of the profound differences between the social experience of men and women."[61] The *heqin* intermarriage was the typical case of "human and social intervention" in gender-/sex-based marital life. The "deep recognition" of women's sexual and familial roles originated in the specific political relationship between China and Inner Asia. In this highly politicized family relationship, the *heqin* woman's life was, and could only be, shaped by political accountability, even from the male marriage managers who did not consciously mean it at all. This political accountability is in sharp contrast to the unaccountability of women elsewhere in Chinese politics and social life. Michel Foucault's study of the history of sexuality can explain this reality: gender can become "the basis of relations" and sexuality can work "as an especially dense transfer point for relations of power." In social and political use, "Relations of sex gave rise, in every society, to a development of alliance: a system of marriage, of fixation and development of kinship ties, of transmission of names and possessions."[62] *Heqin* intermarriage, more than any other marital examples in either Chinese or Inner Asian societies, highlights the fact that "sex is ultimately a political and therefore a social fact," and society can determine "the way gender is construed."[63]

Women's role in marriage, family, and kinship becomes the next point of inquiry into women's empowerment in the *heqin* intermarriage. E. E. Evans-Prichard has argued for women's status as "defined fundamentally through the tie of marriage."[64] Jane F. Collier and Michelle Z. Rosaldo have argued furthermore that "marriage organizes obligations" and "such obligations shape political life."[65] Kinship systems "rest upon marriage," according to Gayle Rubin, and therefore "transform males and females into 'men' and 'women,' each an incomplete half which can only find wholeness when united with the other."[66] So the special status of *heqin* women is created by human institutions of marriage, family, and kinship. Through these institutions, the *heqin* women were manipulated by the men of their natal family into creating a symbolic family and kinship across the frontiers; the women were thus transformed from powerless daughters with no control over even their own lives to empowered Inner Asian family/clan members with high political expectations in the two states' relationships. After the intermarriage, the *heqin* women not only strongly identified themselves with the natal family-state (China), but also had to identify themselves, to a certain degree, with their marital family/kinship (Inner Asia). They were endowed with political obligations that stood in complicated cross-state relationships. The symbolic frontier family created a symbolic frontier order, in which two gender-divided individuals stood for two nations and the marital union symbolized the union of the agrarian power (China) and the nomadic power (Inner Asia). In this frontier order, "there is a clear connection between systems of representation and the way males and females are brought into the social order as sexual and social beings."[67] Even though women were under male control in their personal lives, their gender and sexual roles, determined by the nature of the human family system and imperial China's *heqin* policy, brought them to a position of political representation through the marriage-family-state connection.

Such a study of women's role in regard to power and control in the *heqin* intermarriage lets us reconsider the general theory of the "exchange of women" between men. Anthropological research has adequately studied this exchange, that, as the "essence of kinship systems," directs the political and economic relationship between two social groups.[68] In these studies, the exchange of women between two groups is reciprocal. The *heqin* intermarriage, on the other hand, was a one-way exchange: women were sent only from one group (China) to the other (Inner Asia), and the women-taking group returned only a promise of peace to the women-giving group. By the operation of cultural and family principles in social and political hierarchy, China did not accept any women from Inner Asia. It is in regard to this type of exchange of women that we discuss the issue of women's power and control, which was quite "irregular" in the light of what anthropology has told us about the "exchange of women," in which "men have certain rights in their female kin, and . . . women do not have the same rights either to themselves or to their male kin. In this sense, the exchange of women is a profound perception of a system in which women do not have full rights to themselves."[69] However, although the *heqin* women completely lacked power and control in their natal family, they did not lack them in their marital family. Their control of the marital family, in turn, increased the power of their natal family's control of the frontiers. Thus, beneath the politics at China's Inner Asian frontier, a "hidden structure" on a "far more complex level of what men and women actually do," as Carol P. MacCormack put in her conclusion to her African studies,[70] was in fact working in the *heqin* policy, and this "hidden structure" was the family/kinship structure based on the marital union of two human beings of different genders and sexes; in this union the female could gain power from the marital family. The fact that *heqin* women significantly upheld this "hidden structure" to support Chinese–Inner Asian frontier order has not been duly recognized in either premodern or modern times.

Last, as a result of the intermarriage, the use of family terms and patterns of communication based on family relationships between China and Inner Asian powers is as Claude Lévi-Strauss described: "from marriage to language one passes from low- to high-speed communication," which in *heqin* means ineffective (political language) and effective (family language) communication. The *heqin* women served as a "person to symbol" or a "value to sign" when the relationship "[reached] a certain degree of complexity"[71] among gender-/sex-divided individuals, a culturally designed marriage and family institution, and confrontation between the agrarian and nomadic states. Based on the "complex pattern of male and female interaction,"[72] only the terms of marriage and family—and not political terms—could work for political needs. Women in *heqin* intermarriage changed the communications between the two sides from state-to-state language (in which the political status of the Xiongnu under the Chinese tribute system was "outer vassal") into family-to-family language (in which the Xiongnu became China's "brotherly state").[73] In this pattern of communication, the Chinese cultural hierarchy was denied by the Inner Asians, but the family hierarchy was often accepted, and the Chinese court generally equated this family order with sinocentric political and cultural order.

In accordance with the statement that "economic and political analyses are incomplete if they do not consider women, marriage, and sexuality,"[74] it is impossible for anyone to leave *heqin* women out of an account of the political scene when faced with the question of who implemented China's *heqin* policy or sinocentric ideology at the imperial frontiers. The gender status as female, the sexual eligibility for marriage, the family and kinship orientation of the *heqin* policy, and the political expectations regarding the women in intermarriage were all resources and mechanisms to empower women. In other words, the power of the *heqin* princesses initially came from the basic gender/sexual division of human life and then from culturally designed human institutions of marriage, family, and kinship. Through these institutions, the power of a single *heqin* woman could become stronger when Chinese imperial power turned weaker in confrontation with the Inner Asians.[75] This is of course an "unusual" empowerment: without consciously arranging it, the male decision-makers in China gave power to the *heqin* women, albeit power without political, cultural, and public recognition. Without knowing it, the *heqin* women themselves often worked more effectively than either military efforts or ideology to protect China in military, ideological, and diplomatic crises involving Inner Asia. After the intermarriage, these women created a political sphere in which the male politicians and rulers could not negotiate alone, but had to rely greatly on *heqin* women to provide "a better means of obtaining peace"[76] and to build cooperation between China and nomadic nations.[77] A remark by a Qing poet in praising Wang Zhaojun gives a lively picture of an empowered *heqin* woman: "she just brought a string instrument and traveled across the Great Wall all by herself alone . . . the Han family [then] discussed the policy to appease the war with the 'barbarians' [the Xiongnu], [her marriage] was however stronger than sending ten-thousand troops at the border."[78]

To sum up, in China's frontier politics, resolution of conflicts between male-dominated political powers required female participation through intermarriage, and the success of the *heqin* policy depended on how dynamically women played their role as the agents of the two states united in a family life. The *heqin* women were empowered by creating family relationships between the two states, which permitted the family pattern to penetrate and even in some cases to dominate politics. If marriage and its resulting family and kinship are matters that influence an "entire social system,"[79] as Gilmartin and others have argued, then the marriages of *heqin* women and their dynamic role as representatives of their natal nation influenced the entire frontier system of China.

Heqin Women in Life: The Value in Grief

The empowerment of the *heqin* women in political causes formed a sharp contrast to these women's deep personal grief. Empowered and deprived at the same time, they underwent a very unusual life experience. In complete denial of female choice, the male decision-makers or the intermarriage-managers who implemented the *heqin* policy used women as human tools for solidifying alliances and producing progeny. Thus women were undervalued when equated with material goods the imperial court of China granted to the Inner Asian "barbarians." Further, *heqin* women's expression of feelings and suffering tells much about their view of the intermarriage, which was in many cross-cultural aspects harder than any arranged marriage within Chinese culture. Therefore, the details of these women's grief and life tragedy should be studied and related to the discussion of China's frontier politics. As we study the *heqin* women, their sorrow should not only develop sympathy toward them, but also become a resource for us to discover more about the meaning of imperial China's *heqin* policy. Their grief should not reduce their credit; rather, it should increase our estimation of their value in China's frontier politics.

A *heqin* woman was offered as a gift in a political bargain by the gift-giver (the Chinese court) in return for a peace promise from the gift-taker (the Inner Asian ruler). The gift-taker requested a Chinese woman as wife primarily as an economic bargain, for the promise of economic advantage over the gift-giver. *Heqin* women were thus always listed with other material items the Chinese emperor bestowed upon Inner Asian rulers. The Chinese terms for granting a woman to an Inner Asian ruler were no different from the terms for granting any other material goods; in Chinese documents,[80] *ci* indicates that the superior gracefully bestows gifts upon the political and cultural inferior. The intermarriage itself was also always mingled with material arrangements together with a politically equalized relationship. Emperor Gaozu's first *heqin* arrangement was accompanied by three other agreements: (1) that the Chinese court would annually give material property (silk, wine, rice, and other gifts) to the Xiongnu; (2) that the Han and the Xiongnu would become "brotherly states" with equal status; and (3) that neither side would engage in military actions along the Great Wall, which marked the border between them.[81] The *heqin* policy in later years continued with the Chinese court treating nomadic powers as equals and presenting gifts of grain that amounted to tribute.[82] Jagchid and Symons conclude that "princesses of imperial households were regarded by sedentarists simply as another form of bestowal offered to nomadic rulers in return for frontier products and security along the borders." When nomadic rulers sought to normalize their relations with China, an intermarriage proposal was sometimes "the first thing requested" in exchange for access to frontier markets or yearly payments. "Intermarriage meant dowries and wedding gifts and equally important closer relations with agrarian courts. This enabled nomadic states to obtain more easily the prized commodities of China."[83]

What was the women's reaction to the emperor's granting (ci) of them in intermarriage? Due to the disinterest of the male recorders, very little in this regard is known. However, a crucial clue can be found in a few words from the records of Emperor Gaozu's heqin process. After Gaozu accepted the suggestion to arrange for his own daughter to be the Xiongnu chanyu's bride, his wife Empress Lü cried out to him, "why do you abandon [our daughter] to the Xiongnu?"[84] "Abandon," qi in Chinese, strongly indicates the inner feelings of many Chinese women and the heqin women in particular towards marriage with a "barbarian" ruler. Chinese cultural attitudes toward Inner Asian people and their lives also point toward distress in the heqin women. In the Han and Tang historical records, Inner Asian "barbarians" were described as lacking civilized etiquette and customs, living like animals, being cruel, greedy, deceitful, and untrustworthy, and being China's worst enemies.[85] Heqin women had a very hard time living because of this cultural prejudice. The Sui shu recorded Princess Qianjin of the Sui as she met her uncle in her Tujue home: "the khaghan has a brutal nature and he will snap at you if you argue against him too much."[86] The Chinese character qi, therefore, expresses the misery felt as a result of an emperor's grant, ci. It leads us to understand how women in a heqin felt abandoned by their fathers, family members, and nation.

The undervalued heqin women, however, are not the whole story when considering women's value in the intermarriage, for these Chinese women were highly regarded by the Inner Asians. Even though the reasons for such high valuation have not been found in the historical sources, especially those in Inner Asian languages, it is attested by sufficient supportive evidence. "Gaodi ji" [The biography of Emperor Gaodi] in the Han shu shows how valuable a Chinese wife was to an Inner Asian ruler. When Emperor Gaozu, Liu Bang, was seized by the Xiongnu for seven days and was in danger of execution, his release was effected by a scheme developed by his official, Chen Ping: He sent a portrait of a Chinese beauty to Medu's principal wife and told her that if the Xiongnu did not release the Han emperor, the court would present this beauty to her husband as a bride. Medu's wife feared being abandoned if this woman were accepted, so she immediately advised Medu to release the Han emperor.[87] The wife's fear of a Chinese bride suggests that Inner Asian rulers hardly ever refused brides from China. It also suggests that Medu would probably have valued the Chinese bride highly and placed her in a position that would have threatened his principal wife's status. Since Gaozu's wife was so grieved by the news that her only daughter would have to marry a "barbarian" ruler, the emperor adopted a girl and entitled her princess of the imperial house-hold to replace his own daughter in this marriage.[88] Although Medu knew the bride was a surrogate for Gaozu's real daughter, he still accepted her as the Han royal princess in order to solidify his relations with the Han court and to obtain the dowry, gifts, and opportunity to trade that came through intermarriage.[89] This fact suggests that it was not the actual blood relation but the concept of a Chinese bride that symbolically worked for the po-litical and economic goals.

The material gifts and military assistance rendered to the Chinese court by Inner Asians in return for Chinese brides also reflect the value of Chi-nese women from an Inner Asian point of view. When the Wusun ruler sent the Han court an envoy to request an intermarriage, he brought one thou-sand horses as betrothal gifts. This request resulted in Princess Xijun's mar-riage to the Wusun ruler as his Right Wife.[90] During the Tang Dynasty, the Tibetan king Sron btsan sgampo (r. 618–49) used his great military strength to present to the Tang court a peace proposal that entailed his political mar-riage to a Chinese princess. This proposal was motivated by his knowledge that both the Tujue and the Tuyuhun had received Chinese princesses in marriage, and he had to make the same kind of alliance. After the Tang re-fused this proposal, Sron btsan sgampo put military pressure on China and threatened the Tang that "if the princess is not given [to me], I will fight deeply inside [China]." Facing threats also from the Tujue and the Khitan, the Tang had no choice but to accept this proposal. Sron btsan sgampo then sent an official with five thousand ounces of gold and several hundred pre-cious gifts to the Tang emperor Taizong to accomplish this intermarriage.[91] In 627, a West Tujue *khaghan* presented a thousand golden belts and five thousand horses to the Tang court to welcome his bride.[92] In 822, an Uyghur *khaghan* who received a *heqin* agreement from the Tang court sent twenty thousand horses, one thousand camels, and two thousand guards to the Tang capital to welcome his wife Princess Taihe, daughter of Emperor Xianzong (r. 806–20) and sister of Emperor Muzong (821–24).[93]

These costly material gifts in return for a Chinese bride indicate that, although deemed special among gifts, women were undervalued since they were considered nothing but gifts. As Gayle Rubin concluded, "the result of a gift of women is more profound than the result of other gift transac-tions, because the relationship thus established is not just one of reciproc-ity, but one of kinship. The exchange partners have become affines, and their descendants will be related by blood."[94] The ability to create a fam-ily relationship, as discussed before, determined women as a "human gift" with more ability than any material gift to achieve the goal of frontier pol-itics that came at the price of these women's sorrow. On a personal level,

not only should women's participation in frontier politics and their political functions be acknowledged, but also their sacrifice should be considered part of that politics. In this regard, personal stories take a place in
politics.

All recorded stories of *heqin* women show that they accepted the intermarriage either because of a lack of alternatives or because of their
tragic life in the imperial palace. Among recorded *heqin* women, only
two are mentioned as volunteers. One is Princess Qianjin who, coming
from the Northern Zhou royal family, volunteered to be married to the
Tujue *khaghan* in order to have revenge against the Sui emperor, Yangdi
(r. 581–604), who massacred her family and usurped the Northern
Zhou throne. The other is Wang Zhaojun, a court lady-in-waiting of the
Western Han, who used the intermarriage as a protest against her life in
the palace. Wang Zhaojun's story has touched Chinese hearts deeply, and
there are many historical records about her. Her voluntary marriage to
the Xiongnu *chanyu* came from her miserable life among the numerous
beautiful women in Emperor Yuandi's palace. Having lived there for several years, she still had not even seen the emperor. Unwilling to spend
all her life in this fashion, she resolutely presented herself to the court
as a candidate for marriage to the Xiongnu chief Huhanye, who had
come to the Han emperor asking for an intermarriage.[95] The silent
anger behind this decision is not difficult to feel. Princess Qianjin (later
named Dayi by the emperor Yangdi) volunteered to change her status
from that of a Northern Zhou princess to a Sui princess so that she
could be married to the Tujue *khaghan,* who initiated the marriage alliance. She used her influence, spurred several border incidents, and became such a threat to the Sui that Emperor Yangdi manipulated the
Tujue to have her killed.[96]

After the intermarriage was arranged, the *heqin* women lived in great
hardship due to the lifestyles in Inner Asia. The "exotic" nomadic life was
negatively presented by the Chinese, who depicted the nomads as eating
the flesh, drinking the milk, and wearing the hides of tame animals. They
did not work for a living, but they demanded from the Chinese tribute in
grain and silk.[97] The Chinese women in *heqin* intermarriage, therefore, had
to change not only their moral values but also their living habits: they went
from eating wheat or rice with vegetables to eating solely meat, from living in palaces to living in tents or camps, and from drinking tea to drinking milk. They were alone in an alien place, isolated from their relatives,
and rarely given a chance to visit home. Because of the language barrier,
they often could not communicate well, if at all, with their husbands.
Sometimes communication was impaired not just by language. Princess

Xijun, for example, was in such grief after the intermarriage that she was unable to talk with her husband, the aged Wusun ruler.[98]

The greatest cultural shock to these *heqin* women was probably the marital custom of the levirate that highlighted "the difference between the organization of steppe society and that of sedentary, agricultural China." [99] The Chinese had strongly expressed their ideological aversion to this custom of the nomadic peoples in Inner Asia. Levirate required a woman to marry a brother, uncle, nephew, or even son of another wife of the late husband. Inner Asians from the Xiongnu of the Han period to the Mongols of the Yuan period and other nomadic peoples of these times all lived according to this pattern.[100] Chinese records repeatedly reported in a contemptuous tone that the Inner Asians had the custom of "making all the stepmothers wives" and "making all the sisters-in-law wives," [101] and "when fathers died, their sons married their stepmothers in the polygamous household, and when brothers died, the remaining brothers married the widows of the dead." [102] Guided by their own cultural exclusiveness and discrimination, Chinese regarded the levirate as "bestial," [103] an outrage on marital and family morality, and as behavior just like that of "dogs or pigs." [104]

Zhong Xingshuo, an official at the Han emperor Wendi's court who later surrendered to the Xiongnu, commented on the usefulness of the levirate marriage system for the Xiongnu: the levirate helped forestall the disappearance of clan and family, which was one of the dangers of their mobile lifestyle. In other words, although the Xiongnu family life seemed chaotic to the Chinese, the levirate was essential to maintaining Xiongnu clan and family lines.[105] E. D. Phillips has also pointed out in his study of the Mongols that "the practice by which the heir took over without marriage all his father's wives except his own mother shocked the Chinese and others, but it was very common among the Altaic nomads. It gave the widows and their children security against virtual enslavement and robbery of their goods and animals." [106] According to Jennifer Holmgren's study of the levirate system of the Mongols, "The bride-price system ensured that ordinary Mongols rarely had more than one wife unless the others were inherited from a relative . . . or captured in war. . . . Thus levirate was undoubtedly a widespread institution amongst the middle and lower ranks of the society where it was a means of protecting the economic and social integrity of the family." [107]

Although the levirate was prohibited by the Han and the Tang governments and was punishable by strangulation, with the occasional practice being considered at the very least not respectable,[108] the Chinese court always instructed *heqin* women to consent to this "unacceptable" kind of marriage for political reasons. *Heqin* women thus faced a moral conflict. The Han princess Xijun is but one of the numerous examples. After she married the aged Wusun ruler in 105 B.C.E., he arranged for her to marry his grandson. She tried to refuse the marriage and wrote to the Han emperor for help. The emperor answered that she should "follow the custom of the nation, [because our court could then] ally [itself with] Wusun to destroy the Xiongnu."[109]

Another example is Xieyou, a princess of eighteen or nineteen who followed Princess Xijun to marry the Wusun ruler in 101 B.C.E. While she was on her way to Wusun territory, the waiting groom died. According to *husu* (barbarian custom), she had to become the wife of his successor, who was his son and her stepson, and later the wife of this new ruler's son, her step-grandson. During her life in Wusun territory, which lasted more than half a century, she had to marry three Wusun rulers across three generations. Her unhappiness led to her assassination of the third husband (the grandson of her first husband) at a banquet.[110] The alliance between the Han and the Wusun by her marriage, however, helped the Han establish *Xiyu duhufu* (the military office in western territory), which was viewed as a symbol of Chinese rule in Central Asia. In 51 B.C.E., when Princess Xieyou was about seventy years old, she expressed to the Han court her willingness to be buried in her hometown, and she was permitted to return to China. Her female servant Feng Liao also married a Wusun general and became a Han diplomat in Central Asia; she finished her life in Wusun territory.[111]

In the famous intermarriage between Wang Zhaojun and the powerful Xiongnu *chanyu* Huhanye in 33 B.C.E., Wang Zhaojun (his third wife) was asked to marry her stepson after he died. She wrote to the Han emperor requesting permission to refuse this marriage and return home, but the emperor urged her to "follow the barbarian custom." She then had to become the wife of the new *chanyu*.[112] This personal tragedy, however, was politically successful in bringing about a sixty-year peace between the Han and the Xiongnu.[113]

The Sui princess Yicheng lived in Tujue territory for more than twenty years and had to marry four succeeding *khaghans*.[114] The Tang princess Ningguo, the youngest daughter of the Tang emperor Suzong, became a widow less then one year after her marriage to the Uyghur *khaghan* in 757, and was asked to be buried alive with her dead husband, in accordance with Uyghur custom. Princess Ningguo refused, saying, "[you] the Uyghurs have admired Chinese custom, so [you] marry a Chinese woman as wife. If [I have to] follow your custom, why should I marry you and come here from ten thousand miles away!" Although she was permitted to refuse suicide for the dead *khaghan* and even to return to the Tang capital, she had to follow the Uyghur funeral tradition (one not practiced in her homeland), in which his relatives cut her face seven times with a knife at the memorial service, to let tears and blood flow down together.[115] After Princess Ningguo's return home, another princess from the imperial household, Little Princess Ningguo, was sent to marry the new Uyghur *khaghan* in 758. In her life in Uyghur territory, she was asked to marry five times, and her two sons were both killed in a power struggle at the Uyghur court. She died among the Uyghur in 791, thirty-three years after her first marriage.[116] Princess Xian'an, the eighth daughter of the emperor Dezong (r. 780–804), married an Uyghur *khaghan* in 787 and suffered from her husband's decline only two months later; she then became the wife of four subsequent Uyghur *khaghan*s. She lived in Uyghur territory for twenty-one years and died there in 808.[117]

Hardships in *heqin* women's lives could also come from the fact that— even after the intermarriage—tension remained between China and Inner Asia, and war could break out at any time. Many of the *heqin* women had to live in Inner Asia when China and nomadic powers engaged in war. In some cases, their lives were in danger. For example, after Princess Honghua married the Tuyuhun ruler in 640, the Tuyuhun chief minister, who favored an alliance with Tibet, planned to attack her and abduct her husband to Tibet.[118] In some cases, it was the husbands of these Chinese women who led the fighting against China. Princess Yicheng of the Sui Dynasty was thus killed when the Tang troops defeated the Tujue.[119] In other cases, a *heqin* princess was in a difficult position; for example, the Han princess Xijun, whose husband, the Wusun ruler, also married a Xiongnu woman and placed the Xiongnu woman as his Left Wife and Xijun as his Right Wife. Since the Xiongnu viewed the left as superior to the right, this reflected that the Wusun were more afraid of the Xiongnu than of the Han,[120] and the two political wives from the two enemy nations had to live in the same household. This difficulty was passed on to Princess Xieyou. Hoping the Han would protect him against the Xiongnu, the Wusun ruler had married her. Being threatened by the Xiongnu, the Wusun ruler also agreed to a Xiongnu request for him to marry a Xiongnu woman in order to make an alliance against the Han. Princess Xieyou became his second principal wife, and the Xiongnu woman was his first principle wife.[121] In all these cases, *heqin* women's private lives and treatment by their husbands and other Inner Asians are not documented but can be imagined.

Poems written by some of the *heqin* women show firsthand their extreme sadness. Princess Xijun's poem shows her sadness in its description of her living environment and complaints about the material aspects of her life—housing, food, drink, and so on. No other poem by her has been found to show the poignancy and horror of the levirate she had to face in reality, but this poem, with details of life, underlines the suffering such a lifestyle caused a Chinese woman. It was this poem that touched the heart of the Han emperor, and he sent material goods to assuage her, but still he could do nothing about her real grievance—the levirate—except ask her to comply. Xijun wrote:

> My family married me
> To the other side of the Heaven;
> And trusted me in a foreign country.
> The yurt is my house,
> And the felt is my wall.
> The meat is my food,
> And the sour milk is my drink.
> Living here [in a foreign country],
> My grief is inside my heart by longing for my native soil,
> I wish to turn into a yellow crane
> And fly back to my homeland.[122]

Wang Zhaojun's poem tells of a broken heart and eagerness to go back to her "father and mother," a metaphor for her own country and lifestyle:

> Although I have a place to settle down unwillingly,
> My mind wanders in uncertainty.
> . . . .
> Mountain peaks are piling up,
> And rivers are deep and broad.
> My dear father and mother,
> They stay too far far away.
> Oh,
> My pent-up heart is in mourning.[123]

This desolation and longing to return to the homeland is echoed by Princess Dayi, who became the wife of three Tujue rulers during the Sui period:

> Rise and fall like the dawn and night,
> The way of the world is rootless as the duckweed,
> Glory and splendor are difficult to preserve,
> Ponds and chambers will be leveled.
> At present, where is wealth and honor?

Aimlessly exhausting [myself] in painting.
Wine and drink never provide happiness,
How can music and song produce the melody?
Originally I was a child of the Royal Household,
[Now] darting around the camp of barbarians.
Seeing both success and failure,
The emotion in [my] heart is unrestrained.
It's the same from the ancient times.
I am not alone in my complaint.
The feeling of a far-married woman was
Described by the song of Ming-chun.[124]

These words from her heart, however, were detested by the Sui emperor, who granted her fewer and fewer material things, suspected her loyalty, and withdrew her title of princess. He even instructed another Tujue *khaghan,* Tuli, to murder her as a condition for granting him a Chinese bride, Princess Anyi. After a slanderous discussion between the Tuli *khaghan* and her husband, Princess Dayi was slain.[125]

The collective sorrow shown by these poems reveals that it was in such deep suffering that these women achieved great success. Politically, as Jagchid and Symons have concluded, they worked both as diplomats and as wives by guiding their husbands toward a peaceful relationship with China. Culturally, they offered a channel for the dissemination of China's way of life and culture into Inner Asia, because they usually brought imperial objects, silk, and other splendid gifts with them. Some of them were even allowed to build their own palaces in Chinese style on nomadic land. Economically, their intermarriages were closely associated with the opening of frontier markets and official channels of economic exchange through the tribute system—the crucial elements for peace or war at China's Inner Asian frontier.[126]

In the examples above, the *heqin* women unwillingly played an active role on the political stage. Each detail of their tragic lives was part of the foundation of frontier politics. The "undervalued" treatment of them offset the "irreplaceable value" they acquired in success.

Heqin Women in Chinese Memory:
Female Beauty and Virtue

After the intermarriage, women became an independent category in politics; they lived not under Chinese but Inner Asian authority, and their loyalty was the only tie (often a very strong one) between themselves and their natal nation and family. An antithesis can be found between women's unwilling and passive stance toward the intermarriage and their self-dedication and active performance in the new, alien land once they were married.

The *heqin* women have made a great impression on Chinese historical memory. Legends about the *heqin* women's private lives and feelings have always been popular in China. Despite the lack of existing portraits, they have been conceived as beauties, and their physical beauty has always been linked to their female virtue.[127] The more the traditional value of the frontier politics was given only to men, the greater the psychological impact on the *heqin* women. Their powerlessness over their own lives contrasts with their powerful engagement in politics. This impact can even be found in historical records, which remarked upon the *heqin* women briefly while recording men's political activities.

Both the *Han shu* "Yuandi ji" [Biography of Emperor Yuandi] and the *Hou Han shu* "Nan Xiongnu zhuan" [chapter on the southern Xiongnu] described Wang Zhaojun admirably in the best Chinese literary language applicable to a woman. She was a vivid young girl of seventeen, selected from southern China as one of the numerous palace women, and she volunteered to marry the Xiongnu *chanyu* out of her anger at palace life. When she appeared in the imperial court as the emperor's gift for the *chanyu*, her extreme beauty and graceful manner startled the emperor and all the court officials. Then the heartbroken emperor deeply regretted being unable to keep her in the palace because he could not break his promise to the *chanyu*.[128]

Historical sources also indicated the moral qualifications of Wang Zhaojun. Unlike the many palace women who tried to draw the emperor's attention by bribing the imperial painter whose paintings would introduce them, Wang Zhaojun detested that deception. Her confidence in her own beauty and her righteousness prevented her from using bribery to acquire the emperor's attention. Her anger came from disappointment at palace corruption.[129] This girl, from a humble peasant family and even without a title in the imperial palace, finally decided to challenge the divine emperor by leaving the palace to marry the Xiongnu *chanyu*.

In Chinese moral judgment, Wang Zhaojun was an upstanding young woman: physically her beauty infatuated the emperor the first time he set his eyes on her, and morally she was pure, clean, incorruptible, and upright. From the Western Jin Dynasty (265–316) to today, about six hundred poems have been written commending her valiant decision to marry the Xiongnu *chanyu* and help establish peace. These commendations were full of great compassion for her personal grief in this marriage. From Shi Chong's verses in the period of the Western Jin Dynasty to now, poems in different genres (*shi, ci, ge,* and *fu*), dramas, and novels about her have created a "Zhaojun study" in literature and performing art. From the period of the Yuan Dynasty to the present, at least twenty-five known operas or plays have been based on her life.[130] The latest biography represents the respectful Chinese view of this legendary young girl.[131] Throughout history she has been imagined as one of the four most elegant ancient beauties.[132]

Heqin women's female virtue can be found in another example from the limited historical documents, the Tang princess Ningguo. The record really concerned her father, Emperor Suzong, and mentioned her in only one sentence. At the sad moment of leaving to marry the Uyghur *khaghan,* she said to her father that "the matter of the country is my first consideration, I will not regret it even if I die for it." The sorrowful emperor then returned to the palace with his eyes full of tears.[133] This record shows admiration for Princess Ningguo's moral qualities from a Confucian perspective, in which personal sacrifice for the group, family, and nation is highly commended. The tears of the male—her father and the emperor—serve as further evidence of the women's sorrow and the psychological intensity of their sacrifice in intermarriage.

The public honor given to these *heqin* women for their self-sacrifice on behalf of their nation reflects their moral and political standing in Chinese historical memory. In this memory, they are perfect both physically and morally.

Conclusion

The traditionally male-centered perspective has long blinded us to women's roles in China's frontier politics. Reading historical documents and the history of *heqin* policy with a women's perspective helps us to reconstruct the historical fact that women had a special kind of power in male-dominated politics. While men (the Chinese emperors, officials, and Inner Asian rulers) dominated the process of policy-making and *heqin* arrangements, the women who engaged in this kind of political marriage often performed as the actual agents for accomplishing the political goals.

Throughout the pre-Qing imperial history of China, these *heqin* women belonged to the only group to stand inside the cross-state politics on a durable basis. They experienced one of the most complicated as well as the most confused situations possible in human life. On the one hand, they were expected to keep absolute loyalty to their natal family-nation; on the other hand, they were expected to obey their husbands, willingly or unwillingly, in an alien culture and society. They were required to serve men in both societies who were often rivals before or even after the *heqin* intermarriage. They were also required to be creative in working for the political destinies of the two sides.

The reconstruction of *heqin* women's unique lives and experiences deepens our knowledge of the role of gender in political dealings between agrarian and nomadic societies. In the various hostile and peaceful long-term relationships between China and Inner Asia, there was a need for people who, even temporarily, could cross the cultural, political, and economic barriers between the two sides. Women were chosen by men to perform this task. In such frontier politics, females belonged to a "politicized gender,"[134] which functioned powerfully through the social institutions of marriage and family.

As often happened, only through *heqin* could the Chinese court and the Inner Asian powers find a basis for peace negotiations and establish a mutual obligation to guarantee peace. Since "Marriage is a concern of both sexes,"[135] women gained a special value. After this marriage, the resulting family often served as a strong means to reach political goals: the Chinese court employed family order to work for political order, and the Inner Asian powers accepted this order by accepting their marital and family status. Women in such frontier politics should, therefore, be understood as "sexual beings" in a special political system. As Collier and Rosaldo have pointed out, "Cultural conceptions of women acknowledge their role as participants in the heterosexual relationships through which adults organize and manipulate mundane cooperative bonds."[136] Without an understanding of the role of gender in human life and of the possible political use of gender in dealings between different social groups, we would not be able to explain how women could be chosen as agents in China's frontier politics.

Heqin women's experiences can also show the male politicians' unconscious use of female power that was an important part of China's frontier politics. At the same time that politicians devaluated women by commodifying them as gifts, they also placed women at the center of politics. Even though the *heqin* women were excluded from politics by Confucian ideology, they were in essence positioned at a high level, in areas where men could not play a role themselves.

Heqin women's experience is full of paradox: their impressive courage and deep sorrow, their great contribution and immense tragedy, and their loyalty to two political entities and painful isolation in personal life. Their tearful tales, however, accompanied their general success in frontier politics. It has been stated that *heqin* intermarriage was the best means of cultural communication between the Chinese Empire and the Inner Asian powers, and the best among other pre-Qing imperial policies for reducing antagonism between the agricultural Chinese and the nomadic Inner Asians. It has also been commented that the *heqin* policy contributed to today's multinational Chinese society.[137] These commendations of inter-marriage will become more appropriate and complete when we integrate the *heqin* women into our studies of frontier politics—a task that has been neglected for too long.

In historical times and in the present, different opinions concerning these *heqin* women in their political aspect can be found among peoples who were involved in the historical *heqin* relationship. For example, the Ti-betans, the Mongols, and the Uyghurs may have had viewpoints different from those of the Han-Chinese toward the Chinese princesses who mar-ried non-Chinese leaders.[138] These different perspectives are worth exam-ining in further research in order to understand the overall frontier politics in Chinese–Inner Asian relationships, yet the *heqin* women themselves should still be valued and studied for their unique human experience and prominent role in China's frontier politics, in which they had an unques-tionable, verifiable part. As long as those frontier politics remain in the Chinese people's historical memory, *heqin* women will stay alive in that memory.

Notes

1. Historically, from the Chinese point of view, Inner Asia includes Manchuria (three provinces in modern Northeast China), Mongolia, Tibet, and Chinese Central Asia (modern Xinjiang).

2. Lien-Sheng Yang uses this term in "Historical Notes on the Chinese World Order," in *The Chinese World Order*, ed. John K. Fairbank (Cambridge: Har-vard University Press, 1970), p. 29.

3. See Yü Ying-shih, "Han Foreign Relations," in *The Cambridge History of China, Volume 1: The Chin and Han Empires, 221 B.C.–A.D. 220,* eds. Denis Twitchett and Michael Loewe (Cambridge, England: Cambridge Univer-sity Press, 1986), p. 386.

4. In the Introduction to *Engendering China: Women, Culture, and the State,* the editors suggest adding "women to the social and historical picture, and highlighting gender as a category of analysis" (p. 2). They state that they "all speak to the shared project of making women visible and taking power-laden gender relationships as a legitimate object of inquiry" (p. 3). They point out that gender emphasis has "produced a new body of women's studies research since the mid-1980s" (p. 4). To continue research in this di-rection, the book aims to "search for women's agency" and "open up new ways of presenting an awareness of women's lives." See Christina K. Gilmartin, et al., eds., *Engendering China: Women, Culture, and the State* (Cambridge: Harvard University Press, 1994), pp. 2–4 and 12.

5. See Sechin Jagchid and Van Jay Symons, *Peace, War, and Trade Along the Great Wall: Nomadic-Chinese Interaction through Two Millennia* (Bloomington: Indiana University Press, 1989), pp. 22–3.

6. The ancient pronunciation for "Maodun" is "Medu." "Shanyu" as "chanyu" has not been noted in the previous English publications. Both *Shi ji* [Records of the Grand Historian], by Sima Qian (145–ca. 86 B.C.E.) (Beijing: Zhonghua shuju, 1959); and *Han shu* [The history of the Former Han Dynasty], by Ban Gu (32–92) (Beijing: Zhonghua shuju, 1962), give pronunciation guidance. See also Chen Yongling, ed., *Minzu cidian* [Encyclopedia of Chinese minorities] (Shanghai: Cishu chubanshe, 1987), pp. 734 and 791–2.

7. Ge Liang, "Han yu Xiongnu diyige heqinyue kaoshu" [The textual research of the first *heqin* agreement between the Han and the Xiongnu], *Zhongguo bianjiang shidi yanjiu* 2 (1995): 97.

8. *Shi ji*, ch. 122, "Kuli liezhuan [Zhang Tang]" [The biographies of the oppressive officials (Zhang Tang)], p. 3141; *Han shu*, ch. 49, "Xiongnu zhuan, shang," p. 3830; Lin Gan, ed., *Xiongnu shiliao huibian* [Collected historical materials on the Huns] (Beijing: Zhonghua shuju, 1988), vol. 1, pp. 105 and 272; and *Xinjiaoben jiu Tang shu fu suoyin* [The new annotated edition of the history of the Tang Dynasty with index], by Liu Xu (888–947) et al. (Taipei: Dingwen shuju, 1979), ch. 196, "Tufan, xia" [Second chapter on the Tibetans], pp. 5266–7.

9. Sima Guang, *Zizhi tong jian* [Comprehensive mirror for aid in government] (Jiulong, Hong Kong: Zhonghua shuju, 1956), chs. 190 and 191, pp. 5954 and 5995.

10. Sima Guang, *Zizhi tong jian*, ch. 196, pp. 6179–80; and Chen Peng, *Zhongguo hunyin shigao* [Manuscript of the history of marriage in China] (Beijing: Zhonghua shuju, 1990), p. 43.

11. See *Shi ji*, ch. 122, "Kuli liezhuan [Zhang Tang]"; and in Lin Gan, ed., *Xiongnu shiliao huibian*, vol. 1, p. 272.

12. Lin Gan, *Zhongguo gudai beifang minzushi xinlun* [New discussions on China's northern minority history during ancient times] (Hohhut, Mongolia: Nei Menggu renmin chubanshe, 1993), p. 96.

13. Ge Liang, p. 95.

14. Thomas J. Barfield, *The Perilous Frontier: Nomadic Empires and China* (Cambridge: Basil Blackwell, 1989), p. 54.

15. See *Han shu*, ch. 61, "Zhang Qian zhuan" [The biography of Zhang Qian]; and Lin Gan, ed., *Xiongnu shiliao*, vol. 1, p. 276.

16. Ma Dazheng and Hua Li, *Gudai Zhongguo de beibu bianjiang* [The northern frontiers in ancient Chinese history] (Hohhut, Mongolia: Nei Menggu renmin chubanshe, 1993): 138–9; and Jagchid and Symons, p. 157.

17. Sima Guang, *Zizhi tong jian*, ch. 3, p. 7133.

18. Chen Peng, pp. 44–5.

19. Sima Guang, *Zizhi tong jian*, ch. 3, p. 6060.

20. See *Han shu*, ch. 7, "Zhaodi ji" [The biography of Emperor Zhaodi]; and in Lin Gan, ed., *Xiongnu shiliao*, vol. 1, p. 346.

21. Henry Serruys, *Sino-Mongol Relations During the Ming: The Tribute System and Diplomatic Missions (1400–1600)* (Bruxelles: Insititut belge des hautes etudes chinoises, 1967), p. 18.

22. Lin Enxian, "Cong minzu zhuyi guandian kan Han-Tang zhi heqin zhengce" [Examining the *heqin* policy of the Han and the Tang from the perspective of nationalism], *Zhongguo bianzheng* 95.10 (October 1987): 11.

23. *Kunmi* is the title of the Wusun ruler, as *chanyu* is of the Xiongnu ruler.

24. Ma and Hua, p. 137; Lin Gan, ed., *Xiongnu shiliao*, vol. 1, pp. 165, 170, 201–2, 276, and 284; and Lin Enxian, "Cong minzu zhuyi," p. 19.

25. *Han shu*, ch. 99, "Wang Mang zhuan" [The biography of Wang Mang] p. 4139; *Hou Han Shu* [The history of the Later Han Dynasty], by Fan Ye (398–445) (Beijing: Zhonghua shuju, 1965), ch. 12, "Peng Chong zhuan" [The biography of Peng Chong] p. 504; and in Lin Gan, ed., *Xiongnu shiliao*, vol. 1, pp. 416 and 423.

26. *Hou Han shu*, ch. 89, "Nan Xiongnu zhuan" [Chapter on the southern Huns] pp. 2945, 2949, 2957, and 2966 cited from the *Hou Han shu;* and in Lin Gan, ed., *Xiongnu shiliao*, vol. 1, pp. 116, 119, 128, 138, 448, 450, and 454. There are also records of two separate requests in the years 65 and 87 from the Xiongnu asking the Han for an intermarriage, but the source in both cases does not mention any Chinese woman actually sent to the Xiongnu; see Lin Gan, ed., *Xiongnu shiliao*, pp. 456 and 477.

27. Jagchid and Symons, pp. 148–50.

28. The total number of the Tang intermarriages is slightly different among the following three sources: Lin Enxian, "Cong minzu zhuyi," pp. 14–7; Lin Gan, *Tujue yu Huihe lishi lunwen xuanji* [Selected theses on the history of the Turkic and Huihe peoples] (Beijing: Zhonghua shuju, 1985), vol. 2, pp. 1013–4; and Niu Zhiping, "Tangdai hunyin de kaifang fengqi" [The flexibility in marriage during the Tang Dynasty], *Lishi yanjiu* 4 (1984): 86. For stories of these *heqin* intermarriages, see Jagchid and Symons, ch. V, "Intermarriage," pp. 141–64.

29. Lin Gan states four blood daughters of emperors, and Ma and Hua record three. See Lin Gan, *Zhongguo gudai, beifang minzushi xinlun* [New discussions on China's northern minority history during ancient times] (Hohhut, Mongolia: nei Menggu renmin chubanshe, 1993), p. 117; and Ma and Hua, pp. 138–9. Lin Enxian's "Cong minzu zhuyi" lists the Han and Tang *heqin* women in detail; see pp. 10–21.

30. *Xinjiaoben jiu Tang shu*, ch. 194, "Tujue, shang" [First chapter on the Turks], p. 5170.

31. *Cambridge History of China*, Volume 6, *Alien Regimes and Border States*, eds. Herbert Franke and Denis Twitchett (Cambridge: Cambridge University Press, 1994), p. 8.

32. *Shi ji,* ch. 99, "Liu Jing zhuan," p. 2719; *Han shu,* ch. 43, "Liu Jing zhuan," p. 2122; and Lin Gan, ed., *Xiongnu shiliao,* vol. 1, pp. 164–5. For translation, see Jagchid and Symons, p. 57. In this quotation I change "Mao-tun" into "Medu" and "Shan-yu" into "chanyu."

33. Carol P. MacCormack, "Nature, Culture and Gender: a Critique," in *Nature, Culture and Gender,* eds. Carol P. MacCormack and Marilyn Strathern (New York: Cambridge University Press, 1980), p. 14.

34. Jennifer Holmgren, "Imperial Marriage in the Native Chinese and Non-Han State, Han to Ming," in *Marriage and Inequality in Chinese Society,* eds. Rubie S. Watson and Patricia Buckley Ebrey (Berkeley: University of California Press, 1991), p. 77.

35. *Han shu,* ch. 96, "Xiyu zhuan"; and Lin Gan, ed., *Xiongnu shiliao,* vol. 1, p. 351.

36. The *Quan Tang wen* [Complete Tang prose] 1,000 ch., comps. Dong Gao (1740–1818) et al. (1814; reprint, Beijing: Zhonghua shuju, 1982), ch. 49, p. 657, "Cehe Huihe gongzhu wen" [The article for the Turkic princess]; and Lin Gan, *Zhongguo gudai,* p. 118.

37. See *Sui shu* [The history of the Sui Dynasty], by Wei Zheng (Beijing: Zhonghua shuju, 1973), ch. 84, "Bei di" [The northern barbarians], p. 6.

38. Yang Lien- Sheng, "Historical Notes on the Chinese World Order," in *The Chinese World Order,* ed. John K. Fairbank, p. 30.

39. Barfield, p. 112.

40. Fairbank, "A Preliminary Framework," in his *The Chinese World Order: Traditional China's Foreign Relations* (Cambridge: Harvard University Press, 1970), pp. 1–5.

41. Morris Rossabi, ed., *China Among Equals* (Berkeley: University of California Press, 1983), pp. 18–21.

42. Lin Gan, ed., *Xiongnu shiliao,* vol. 1, pp. 14, 46, 48–9, 64, and 95. Henry Serruys pointed out that "the Altan-qan did not consider himself in any way subject to imperial approval for any decision he made in his own territories" (p. 17). Barfield pointed out that the Xiongnu *chanyu* "ranked almost equal to the Chinese emperor" and therefore was "not part of the Han administrative structure" (p. 64).

43. *Hou Han shu,* ch. 12, "Lu Fang zhuan" [The biography of Lu Fang], p. 506; and in Lin Gan, ed., *Xiongnu shiliao,* vol. 1, p. 422.

44. *Shi ji,* ch. 110, "Xiongnu liezhuan," p. 2895; *Han shu,* ch. 94, "Xiongnu zhuan, shang"; and in Lin Gan, ed., *Xiongnu shiliao,* vol. 1, pp. 12 and 43.

45. *Han shu,* ch. 94, "Xiongnu zhuan, shang," p.3756–7; and in Lin Gan, ed., *Xiongnu shiliao,* vol. 1, pp. 43–4 and 49.

46. *Han shu,* ch. 4, "Wendi ji" [The biography of Wendi], p. 134.

47. *Han shu,* ch. 66, "Xiyu zhuan, xia" [Second chapter on the western territory], pp. 3902–3.

48. *Sui Shu,* ch. 84, "Bei di," p. 4.

49. Jagchid and Symons, p. 148.

50. *Xinjiaoben jiu Tang shu,* ch. 195, "Huihe" [The Huihe people], p. 5201; and Sima Guang, *Zizhi tong jian,* ch. 3, p. 7059.

51. *Xinjiaoben jiu Tang shu,* ch. 196, "Tufan, shang" [First chapter on Tibet], pp. 5230–3.

52. For the Tibetan text, see Hugh E. Richardson, *Tibet and Its History,* 2d ed. (Boston: Shambhala, 1984), p. 259. For the two versions of Chinese text, see Wu Fengpei, ed., *Xizang zhi* [Gazetteers of Tibet] (Lhasa: Xizang yanjiu bianjibu, 1982), p. 44; and Wang Furen and Suo Wenqing, *Zangzu shiyao* [A brief history of Tibet] (Chengdu, China: Sichuan renmin chubanshe, 1982), p. 244.

53. Wu Fengpei, pp. 1–2.

54. Song Yun, *Weizang tongzhi* [The chronicle gazetteer of Tibet] (Lhasa: Xizang yanjiu bianjibu, 1982), p. 172.

55. Sima Guang, *Zizhi tong jian,* chs. 192 and 194, pp. 6049 and 6119.

56. *Han shu,* ch. 78, "Xiao Wangzhi zhuan" [The biography of Xiao Wangzhi], p. 3279; and in Lin Gan, ed., *Xiongnu shiliao,* vol. 1, p. 367.

57. *Han shu,* ch. 94, "Xiongnu zhuan, shang," p. 3829; and in Lin Gan, ed., *Xiongnu shiliao,* vol. 1, p. 105.

58. *Hou Han shu,* ch. 12, "Lu Fang zhuan," p. 506; and in Lin Gan, ed., *Xiongnu shiliao,* vol. 1, p. 422.

59. Fei Xiaotong, *Shengyu zhidu* [The reproductive system] (Tianjin, China: Tianjin renmin chubanshe, 1981), p. 50.

60. Nancy Chodorow, *The Reproduction of Mothering Psychoanalysis and the Sociology of Gender* (Berkeley: University of California Press, 1978), p. 8.

61. Gayle Rubin, "The Traffic in Women: Notes on the 'Political Economy' of Sex," in *Toward an Anthropology of Women,* ed. Rayna R. Reiter (New York: Monthly Review Press, 1975), p. 160.

62. Michel Foucault, *The History of Sexuality* (New York: Pantheon Books, 1978), vol. 1, pp. 103 and 106–7.

63. Jane F. Collier and Michelle Z. Rosaldo, "Politics and Gender in Simple Societies," in *Sexual Meanings: the Cultural Construction of Gender and Sexuality,* eds. Sherry B. Ortner and Harriet Whitehead (New York: Cambridge University Press, 1991), p. 318.

64. Quoted in Robert H. Winthrop, *Dictionary of Concepts in Cultural Anthropology* (New York: Greenwood Press, 1991), p. 134.

65. Collier and Rosaldo, p. 316.

66. Rubin, p. 179.

67. Olivia Harris, "The Power of Signs: Gender, Culture and the Wild in the Bolivian Andes," in MacCormack and Strathern, eds., p. 71.

68. Rubin, p. 171.

69. Ibid., p. 177.

70. MacCormack, p. 12.

71. Claude Lévi-Strauss, *Structural Anthropology* (New York: Basic Books, 1963), pp. 296–7.

72. MacCormack, p. 14.

73. Yü Ying-shih, "Han Foreign Relations," p. 395.

74. Rubin, p. 210.

75. "The power of a single *heqin* woman" is used because the imperial court of China usually arranged one intermarriage during a historical period.

76. Jagchid and Symons, p. 164.

77. Fei Xiaotong, p. 50.

78. Ge Liang, p. 127.

79. "Introduction" in *Engendering China: Women, Culture, and the State,* p. 5.

80. *Han shu,* ch. 94, "Xiongnu zhuan, xia" [Second chapter on the Hans]; and in Lin Gan, ed., *Xiongnu shiliao,* vol. 1, p. 82.

81. *Shi ji,* ch. 110, "Xiongnu liezhuan"; and in Lin Gan, ed., *Xiongnu shiliao,* vol. 1, p. 12; Ge, pp. 97–9; and Yü, p. 386.

82. Yang, pp. 23 and 29; and Charles O. Hucker, *China's Imperial Past* (Stanford: Stanford University Press, 1975), p. 125. About the issue of tribute at China's Inner Asian frontier, see Jagchid and Symons, ch. IV, "Tribute and Bestowals."

83. Jagchid and Symons, p. 141.

84. *Shi ji,* ch. 99, "Liu Jing zhuan," p. 2719; *Han shu,* ch. 43, "Liu Jing zhuan," p. 2122; and in Lin Gan, ed., *Xiongnu shiliao,* vol. 1, pp. 164–5.

85. Lin Gan, ed., *Xiongnu shiliao,* vol. 1, pp. 33, 42, 64, 92, 108, 151, 275, 327, 339, 381, 442, 477–8, 535, and 556; *Xinjiaoben jiu Tang shu,* ch. 194, "Tujue, shang," pp. 5161–2, ch. 196, "Tufan, shang," p. 5232, "Tufan, xia" [Second chapter on the Tibetans], p. 5267, and ch. 199 (*xia*), "Bei di," p. 5346; and Sima Guang, *Zizhi tong jian,* chs. 190 and 193, pp. 5954 and 6076.

86. *Sui shu,* ch. 84, "Bei di," p. 4.

87. *Han shu,* ch. 1, "Gaodi ji" [The biography of Emperor Gaodi], p. 63.

88. *Shi ji,* ch. 99, "Liu Jing zhuan," p. 2719; *Han shu,* ch. 43, "Liu Jing zhuan," p. 2122; and in Lin Gan, ed., *Xiongnu shiliao,* vol. 1, p. 165.

89. Jagchid and Symons, p. 142.

90. *Han shu,* ch. 96, *xia,* p. 3903; and in Lin Gan, ed., *Xiongnu shiliao,* vol. 1, pp. 281–2.

91. *Xinjiaoben jiu Tang shu,* ch. 196, "Tufan, shang" [First chapter of Tibet], p. 5221; *Xin Tang shu* [The new history of the Tang Dynasty], by Ouyang Xiu (1007–72) and Song Qi (996–1061) et al. (Beijing: Zhonghua shuju, 1975), ch. 216, "Tufan, shang" [First chapter of Tibet], p.6073; Sima Guang, *Zizhi tong jian,* ch. 3, p. 5157; and Christopher I. Beckwith, *The Tibetan Empire in Central Asia; A History of the Struggle for Great Power among Tibetans, Turks, Arabs, and Chinese during the Early Middle Ages* (Princeton: Princeton University Press, 1987), p. 24.

92. Sima Guang, *Zizhi tong jian,* ch. 192, p. 6046.

93. Lin Gan, *Zhongguo gudai,* pp. 119–220.

94. Rubin, p. 173.

95. *Hou Han shu,* ch. 89, "Nan Xiongnu zhuan," p. 2941; and in Lin Gan, ed., *Xiongnu shiliao,* vol. 1, p. 112.

96. Jagchid and Symons, p. 147–50; and Huang Jiuru, *Zhongguo nümingren liezhuan* [Book of famous Chinese women] (Shanghai: Zhonghua shuju, 1937), pp. 108–9.

97. E. D. Phillips, *The Mongols* (New York: Frederick A. Praeger, 1969), p. 23.

98. *Han shu,* ch. 96, "Xiyu zhuan," p. 3903; and in Lin Gan, ed., *Xiongnu shiliao,* vol. 1, p. 284.

99. Jennifer Holmgren, "Observations on Marriage and Inheritance Practices in Early Mongol and Yuan Society, with Particular Reference to the Levirate," *Journal of Asian History* 20:2 (1986): 127.

100. Phillips, p. 23; Su Bing and Wei Lin, *Zhongguo hunyin shi* [History of marriage in China] (Taipei: Wenjin chubanshe, 1994), pp. 82–3; Holmgren, "Imperial Marriage," pp. 77, 85, and 174; and Sun Xiao, *Zhongguo hunyin xiaoshi* [A brief history of Chinese marriage] (Beijing: Guangming ribao chubanshe, 1994), pp. 79–80.

101. *Shi ji,* ch. 99, "Liu Jing zhuan," p. 2900, and ch. 110, "Xiongnu liezhuan"; *Han shu,* ch. 94, "Xiongnu zhuan, shang," p. 3743; *Sanguo zhi* [The history of the Three Kingdoms], by Chen Shou (233–97) (Beijing: Zhonghua shuju, 1959), ch. 30, "Dong yi, fuyu" [Chapter on eastern barbarians, the Fuyu], p. 841; and in Lin Gan, ed., *Xiongnu shiliao,* vol. 1, pp. 16, 33, 164, and 561.

102. *Shi ji,* ch. 110, "Xiongnu liezhuan," p. 2879; *Han shu,* ch. 94, "Xiongnu zhuan, shang," p. 3743; and in Lin Gan, ed., *Xiongnu shiliao,* vol. 1, pp. 1 and 33. Also see Phillips, p. 23.

103. *Han shu,* ch. 94, "Xiongnu zhuan, shang," p. 3780; and in Lin Gan, ed., *Xiongnu shiliao,* vol. 1, p. 64.

104. *Shi ji,* ch. 110, "Xiongnu liezhuan," p. 2899; and in Lin Gan, ed., *Xiongnu shiliao,* vol. 1, p. 16.

105. *Shi ji,* ch. 110, "Xiongnu liezhuan," p. 2899; and in Lin Gan, ed., *Xiongnu shiliao,* vol. 1, p. 16.

106. Phillips, p. 27.

107. Holmgren, "Observations on Marriage," p. 134.

108. Su and Wei, pp. 82–3; and Evelyn S. Rawski, "Ch'ing [Qing] Imperial Marriage and Problems of Rulership," in Watson and Ebrey, eds., p. 174.

109. *Han shu,* ch. 96, "Xiyu zhuan, xia," p. 3903; and in Lin Gan, ed., *Xiongnu shiliao,* vol. 1, p. 284.

110. *Han shu,* ch. 96, "Xiyu zhuan, xia," p. 3906; Qiu Yongsheng, "Gong si Zhaojun de Xieyou gongzhu" [Princess Xieyou, who has the same merit as Zhaojun], in *Renmin ribao* [People's daily] October 9, 1987, p. 8; and Wang Zhonghan, ed., *Zhongguo minzu shi* [History of Chinese nationalities] (Beijing: Shehui kexueyuan chubanshe, 1994), p. 244.

111. *Han shu,* ch. 96, "Xiyu zhuan, xia," pp. 3907–8.

112. *Hou Han shu,* ch. 89, "Nan Xiongnu zhuan," p. 2941; and in Lin Gan, ed., *Xiongnu shiliao,* vol. 1, p. 112.

113. *Hou Han shu,* ch. 89, "Nan Xiongnu zhuan," p. 2953; and in Lin Gan, ed., *Xiongnu shiliao,* vol. 1, p. 123.

114. Yi Junzuo, *Zhongguo baimeiren tuyong* [Book of a hundred Chinese beauties] (Hong Kong: Tianfeng yinshuachang, 1958), pp. 104–6.

115. *Xinjiaoben jiu Tang shu,* ch. 195, "Huihe," pp. 5201–2; and Sima Guang, *Zizhi tong jian,* ch. 221, p. 7076.

116. *Xinjiaoben jiu Tang shu,* ch. 195, "Huihe," p. 5210; and Lin Gan, *Zhongguo gudai,* p. 118.

117. Lin Gan, *Zhongguo gudai,* pp. 118–9.

118. Sima Guang, *Zizhi tong jian,* ch. 196, p. 6167.

119. Ibid., p. 6073.

120. Lin Gan, *Zhongguo gudai,* p. 100.

121. *Shi ji,* ch. 123, "Dawan liezhuan" [Chapter on Dawan], p. 3172; *Han shu,* ch. 96, "Xiyu zhuan"; and in Lin Gan, ed., *Xiongnu shiliao,* vol. 1, pp. 283–4.

122. *Han shu,* ch. 96, "Xiyu zhuan," p. 3903; and in Lin Gan, ed., *Xiongnu shiliao,* vol. 1, p. 284. The translation is from Jagchid and Symons on p.143, with modifications.

123. Huang, *Zhongguo nümingren liezhuan* [Biographies of famous Chinese women] (Shanghai: Zhonghua shuju, 1937), pp. 20–1.

124. *Sui shu,* ch. 84, "Bei di," p. 6. The translation is from Jagchid and Symons, pp. 149–50.

125. Ibid.

126. Jagchid and Symons, pp. 141–3.

127. Yi, pp. 47–9 and 104–12; Huang, pp. 18–22.

128. *Hou Han shu,* ch. 89, "Nan Xiongnu zhuan," p. 2941; and in Lin Gan, ed., *Xiongnu shiliao,* vol. 1, p. 112.

129. *Xijing zaji* [The miscellanies of the western capital], quoted in Huang, pp. 18–9.

130. Liu Xianzhao and Wei Shiming, "Lun lishi shang he lishi wenxue zhong de Zhaojun heqin" [The discussion of the Zhaojun *heqin* in history and historical literature], in *Minzu wenshi lunji* (Beijing: Minzu chubanshe, 1985), p. 202; and Xu Xueqing, "You zao xinqu yong Zhaojun" [Making another new song for Zhaojun], *Renmin ribao,* October 22, 1987, p. 7.

131. Ning Faxin, *Yidai mingyuan Wang Zhaojun* [A heroine of her time: Wang Zhaojun] (Taipei: Hanxin wenhua shiye, 1995).

132. Qiu Yongsheng, p. 8; and Ning, p. 3.

133. Sima Guang, *Zizhi tong jian,* ch. 220, p. 7059.

134. Collier and Rosaldo, p. 278.

135. Ibid.

136. Ibid., p. 276.

137. Wu Qingxian, "Qian Han dui xiyu guojia de heqin zhengce" [The *heqin* policy toward the western territory in the Former Han Dynasty] *Zhong-*

guo *bianzheng* 114:12 (December 1992):17; and Lin Enxian, *Tujue yanjiu* [Study of the Turks] (Taipei: Shangwu yinshuguan, 1989), p. 209.

138. The discussion of these different viewpoints can be partly seen in Lin Gan's *Zhongguo gudai,* pp. 102–5. I also learned about these different viewpoints from contact with scholars in Tibetan studies at the 1994 NEH Summer Seminar "Reading the Manchu Summer Palace at Chengde" in Ann Arbor, Michigan, and directly through a CSCC research project in Hohhut, Inner Mongolia, during the Fall of 1994.

CHAPTER THREE

FROM CROSS-DRESSING DAUGHTER TO LADY KNIGHT-ERRANT: THE ORIGIN AND EVOLUTION OF CHINESE WOMEN WARRIORS

Sufen Sophia Lai
Grand Valley State University

> *The woman warrior is a literary type in Chinese literature that challenges Confucian principles concerning womanhood. From Mulan to The Thirteenth Sister, we see the appropriation of various women warriors by the Confucian ideal.*

While the Western stereotype of traditional Chinese women is of frail, subjugated women with bound feet; prominent women of Confucian filial piety and chastity; or beautiful Golden Lotus variations on the femmes fatales, most Westerners are not familiar with the fact that women warriors play a prominent part in the Chinese literary tradition, in which they are lauded as paradigms of female virtues. Among the many heroine types in Chinese literature, women soldiers, wandering lady "knights" *(xia),* and female outlaws occupy a unique position. If the knights of the Round Table were paradigms of European medieval chivalry and male excellence that inspired Western youths, the women warriors of medieval China—such as Mulan, She Saihua, Mu Guiying, and Liang Hongyu—were the Chinese paradigms of female courage and heroism for Chinese girls to emulate.

In the West, the idea of women warriors immediately evokes Amazons or Joan of Arc. In the Chinese tradition, an Amazonian kingdom can be found in the farcical *Romance of the Mirrored Flowers (Jinghua yuan)* by Li Ruzhen (1763–1830). The chapter "Women's Kingdom" satirizes bound feet and other corrupt and irrational aspects of Chinese culture and society that oppress women. However, women warriors in Chinese literature are a diverse group by no means confined to satires or myths. Unlike the Amazons or the women in Li Ruzhen's "Women's Kingdom," women warriors in Chinese literature are usually not segregated from men; rather, they make up a diverse group of heroines who transcend gender boundaries and become distinct literary types. The heroines defy the conventional expectations of a physically weak and subjugated woman confined within her father's or husband's household, but their marginality is still contained and well defined within the periphery of Confucian ideas of womanhood based on "three obediences and four virtues" *(sancong side).*[1] Even though the deeds of the women warriors are unorthodox and "unwomanly" in the canonical Confucian sense, the axioms behind the acceptance and celebration of these heroines are essentially Confucian. In other words, the existence and literary image of the women warriors are still well defined within the Confucian doctrine of the so-called *zhong xiao jie yi* (loyalty, filial piety, integrity, and righteousness).

Asian-American writer Maxine Hong Kingston's *The Woman Warrior: Memoirs of a Girlhood Among Ghosts* (1976) satirizes this paradoxical expectation of Chinese womanhood. The second chapter, "White Tigers," is a deliberate synthesis that mocks this dichotomous expectation of Chinese womanhood as farcical. Kingston presents her absurd heroine, "the female avenger" with a tattooed back, as a combination of the cross-dressing, filial Mulan and the mysterious lady knight-errant of a Tang *chuanqi* (fantastic tale). This "female avenger's" extraordinary character and deeds not only symbolize the unusual (as the title "White Tigers" suggests)[2] and irrational demands of an Asian-American girlhood, but also reflect the irrational patriarchal expectations of Chinese womanhood, which are based on the woman-warrior fantasy and Confucian virtues. Kingston's juxtaposition of traditional and modern women warriors not only exposes the unrealistic patriarchal fantasy about Chinese women warriors, but also points out how this unrealistic expectation has continued into the modern world. Kingston's memoirs reflect not just a twentieth-century Chinese-American woman's experience but every Chinese woman's dilemma in understanding her womanhood. In a sense, we may say that the women warriors in Chinese literature are all "white tigers"—powerful, deadly, and extraordinary.

Louise Edwards maintains a similar view:

[The] woman warrior . . . is treatening to patriarchal power, with its implicit preference for meek and mild women, and yet primarily instrumental in ensuring its continued existence because the deeds she performs are undeniably consolidating of the existing Confucian social and moral order. The disruptive potential encapsulated within her form makes her an enthralling fictional and dramatic figure and this, combined with her consolidating function, ensures her repeated appearance in fiction and drama at both elite and popular levels.[3]

Edwards further identifies filial piety *(xiao)* or loyalty *(zhong)* as the causative and rationalizing moral principles that guide the women warriors in assuming a fighting function in the novels *Honglou meng* and *Jinghua yuan*. On further examination, we recognize that Edwards' "rationalizing moral principles" indeed underlie most of the women warriors in Chinese literature, while we also find women warriors as "wandering knights" *(youxia)* and female outlaws operating under the principles of *yi* (righteousness) and *bao* (reciprocation).

Given Kingston's metaphor of "white tigers" and Edwards' "rationalizing moral principles," I will examine the historical reality and the literary representations and transformations of women warriors in four Chinese literary groups: (1) Mulan and her variations in poetry and drama; (2) lady knights-errant in Tang *chuanqi;* (3) female outlaws in the Ming Dynasty historical novel *Water Margins;* and (4) women generals of the Yang family and Thirteen Sister types in Ming (1368–1644) and Qing (1644–1911) romances. While the term *warrior* may be narrowly defined as someone who participates in battle, the word also carries the broader sense of a fearless hero or a gallant knight who fights for justice according to a code of honor. In this article, I extend the definition of "women warriors" to include women who possess martial skills and abide by a warrior code but are not necessarily combatants. Like Edwards, I will argue that the literary woman warrior is not so much a deliberate challenge to the bondage imposed on women as it is an attempt by male authors to reconcile their apprehension about the feminine mystique with their fascination with women's power. On the surface, women warriors may appear to be unorthodox and to defy gender boundaries, but ideologically they are still well defined within the Confucian moral codes of filial piety and loyalty, while many of them operate under the rationalizing principles of righteousness in the context of reciprocation.

Historical Records

Like most warfare in world history, warfare in Chinese history has been primarily a masculine activity; Chinese women's involvement and actual participation in war are occasional surprises in official histories and chronicles. In "Chinese Women Soldiers: A History of 5,000 Years," Li Xiaolin points out that "women actually appear in Chinese military history as early as Sun Zi's time (496–453 B.C.E.), when King Wu's palace concubines were turned into soldiers as a demonstration of the effects of discipline."[4] One hundred and eighty palace beauties were divided into two squads, with two of King Wu's favored concubines as captains. After some initial instructions, Sun Zi's two attempts to command the squads were received by the court ladies with laughter. In order to affirm the severe consequences of defying a military command, Sun Zi ordered the two captains beheaded despite King Wu's plea for their lives, and new captains were assigned. After this, the squads performed Sun Zi's commands perfectly and silently, and he then sent the following report to King Wu: "The troops are now orderly. The King may come down to inspect them; if the King wishes to deploy them even into 'water and fire' [i.e., very harsh circumstances], that is still feasible,"[5] implying that the court ladies have been transformed into fearless warriors. Sun Zi's deployment of court ladies to demonstrate his military talents suggests the strategist's belief that not gender, but training, is relevant to the creation of an excellent troop. We cannot affirm whether women indeed participated in military operations during Sun Zi's time; however, this episode implies that Chinese kings and military leaders could see women as potential warriors.

Such a view of women's military potential was eventually confirmed in 1976 by the discovery and excavation of Fuhao's majestic tomb in Anyang, Henan province, where more than a thousand ancient artifacts were discovered, pushing Chinese women's military achievement back to as early as the fourteenth century B.C.E. The wife of the Shang king Wuding (1324–1265 B.C.E.) and the first woman to appear in China's military history, Fuhao was a prominent political and military figure in her own right. Among the artifacts were four copper battle axes engraved with Fuhao's name—such axes were used by the Shang to symbolize great military authority and power. Among the many oracle bones and tortoise shell inscriptions from the Shang Dynasty (sixteenth to eleventh centuries B.C.E.), more than 250 of them bear her name. One oracle inscription—"Fuhao's three thousand gathered, and ten thousand, a great expedition"—refers to the campaign launched against the state of Qiang, in which Fuhao commanded a regular army of three thousand, with an additional force of ten thousand. The discovered inscriptions record not only the places she conquered but also her military tactics. The oracle inscriptions also show that after her death, her husband Wuding continued offering sacrifices to her and asking her spirit to guide his army to victory.[6]

Unfortunately, other women's participation remains obscure in the Confucian canon and official histories. Instead, works like Liu Xiang's *The Biographies of Women (Lienü zhuan)* advocate the education of women and in particular their virtues: (1) correct motherly deportment *(mu yi)*; (2) virtue and sagacity *(xian ming)*; (3) benignity and wisdom *(ren zhi)*; (4) purity and obedience *(zhen shun)*; (5) integrity and righteousness *(jie yi)*; and (6) reasoning and understanding *(bian tong)*. He does not consider the talents and virtues of women warriors as major paradigms of women's prominence.[7] In "Admonitions for Women" ("Nü jie"), Ban Zhao (died 116), completing her brother's *History of the Former Han Dynasty (Han shu)*, admonishes women to cultivate humility, subservience, self-abasement, and unconditional obedience, ideas later imitated and emphasized by many Confucian works written exclusively for women's education, such as the *Book of Filial Piety For Women (Nü xiaojing)*, by the wife of Chen Miao (Tang Dynasty); *The Female Analects (Nü lunyu)*, by Song Ruohua, a consort of the Tang emperor Dezong (reigned 780–804); and *Instructions of the Interior (Nei xun)*, by Empress Xu, wife of the Ming emperor Chengzu (r. 1403–24). These three books, along with Ban Zhao's "Admonitions for Women," were collected under the Qing Dynasty into a Confucian canon for women entitled *The Four Books for Women (Nü sishu)*.[8] Within this Confucian tradition, Chinese women were expected to develop strong moral character and submissiveness; the valiant spirit and eccentric behavior of Chinese women warriors are antithetical to such Confucian expectations.

The Literary Tradition

Mulan and Her Variations in Poetry and Drama

While some of the names and biographies of the well-known Chinese women warriors do indeed occupy a few lines in the official chronicles or historical annals, the unorthodox deeds and ingenuity of the women warriors have been conventionally reserved for genres like ballads, legends, and dramas, which foster the distinct literary types of Mulan, the cross-dressing, chivalrous lady knight-errant *(nü xia)*, and the lady generals of the Yang family in Chinese fiction and popular culture. Of all Chinese women warriors, the first to come to mind is always the legendary Mulan, who is for many Chinese a synonym for *jinguo yingxiong* (literally "headdressed-hero," or hero with woman's headdress). Her earliest literary representation is found in "The Ballad of Mulan," by an anonymous poet of the Northern Dynasties (386–581 C.E.).[9] At that time China was divided into two courts: the Northern Dynasties, occupied by the northern non-Han

nomad tribes, and the southern court, maintained by the Han culture. The
distinction between the two cultures is reflected in the folk poetry of the
Yuefu Collection (Yuefu shiji): northern literature prefers themes of nomadic
life, battles, and martial spirits, while southern literature generally expresses
an urban Han culture and esthetic. However, the northern culture was also
actively adopting the Han culture, which may account for the creation of
a woman warrior such as Mulan, who is a synthesis of northern and southern qualities. The lyrics of "The Ballad of Mulan," collected in the *Yuefu
Collection,* not only reflect the northern landscape and nomadic spirit, but
also convey the Confucian expectation of womanhood.

In "The Ballad of Mulan," the heroine is a filial and patriotic woman
warrior who disguises herself as a man to answer the court's draft of her
father. Although it is a short poem with only 332 characters, the ballad is
full of drama, action, emotion, and vivid sound and color, making it an en-
dearing and lasting masterpiece. Thematically, the ballad can be divided
into four sections: (1) Mulan's domestic role in contrast with her substi-
tuting for her father; (2) her transformation into a warrior and departure
for war; (3) her heroic deeds in war; and (4) her declining an official post
as reward and her return to her home and true sexual identity. On the surface, it is a very straightforward folk ballad that celebrates a daughter's filial piety and bravery; analyzed closely, however, each section reveals a
tension between the expected Confucian womanly virtues and the masculine world of warrior valor.

Very directly, at the opening of the poem, the reader is made aware of
this tension between Mulan's womanhood and her wish to join the masculine world. In the first section, by juxtaposing the absence of domestic
sound and the presence of a daughter's thinking, the anonymous poet suggests immediately the aberration of Mulan's unconventional filial devotion:

>   Click, Click, forever, click, click;
>   Mulan should be weaving at the door.
>   But you could not hear the shuttle's sound,
>   Instead you could hear only a daughter's sighs.
>   They asked the girl who she was thinking of;
>   They asked the girl what she was recollecting.
>   "Neither am I thinking of anyone,
>   Nor am I recollecting anything.
>   Last night I saw the military poster
>   The khan is summoning many troops
>   The soldier list is in twelve scrolls,
>   Each scroll includes Father's name.
>   Father has no grown-up son,

Mulan has no elder brother.
I wish to buy saddle and horse at the market,
And from now on fight in Father's place."[10]

The contrast between Mulan's character and a conventional woman's role is clearly laid out in the first two couplets: a daughter's duty and social role are to weave at home and serve her parents, but here the female role has already been abandoned at the very beginning. The conventional domestic Chinese woman was expected not to voice her thoughts or wishes; as Ban Zhao admonishes in the "Humility and Infirmity" ("Bei ruo") section of "Admonitions for Women," the custom of laying a newborn baby girl "below the bed plainly indicated that she was lowly *(bei)* and weak *(ruo),* and should regard it as her primary duty to humble herself before others."[11] As the ballad suggests, a woman's presence is supposed to be "heard" through the noise of her weaving machine, but her voice is not to be heard; Mulan's sighs are heard, not her loom. The expectation of women's qualities continues, nevertheless, since conventionally women's sighs and pensiveness are taken to mean a longing for romance; but the poet surprises the reader with Mulan's unexpected wish "to buy saddle and horse at the market" and "fight in Father's place." The opening suspense and the gradual revelation of Mulan's wish vividly dramatize the tension between her womanhood and her desire to act as a man. It is clear that in the poet's mind Mulan defies the conventional role of womanhood: she is a nonorthodox daughter who voices her wish to take on a man's role.

After Mulan's assertiveness is presented in the first section, the second section of the ballad details Mulan's unwomanly behavior in buying her warrior gear and turning from a domestic girl into an armed warrior:

In the east market she bought a gallant horse;
In the west market she bought a saddle;
In the south market she bought a bridle;
In the north market she bought a long whip.[12]

With these four short, repetitive verses, the poet indirectly portrays Mulan's transformation from girlhood into manhood: purchasing and equipping the "gallant horse" that will transport her from her domestic realm into the world of military actions and male valor. Here we do not actually see Mulan donning a warrior's outfit; instead, we are told of her buying warrior's gear. It is interesting to compare this poem's indifferent attitude towards sexual ambiguity with the condemnation of women's wearing male shoes and armor in Gan Bao's roughly contemporary *In Search of Deities (Sou shen ji)* (ca. 320).[13] We may speculate that the discrepancy between the two attitudes is a result of Confucian appropriation. Mulan's sexual ambiguity is justified and understated because of her "noble reason" for joining the war—filial duty *(xiao)*. This is a deliberate understatement of Mulan's crossing the gender boundary, since her actual dressing up as a man is not necessary information for the reader.

The contrast in sounds we saw in the first section continues in the second. Instead of hearing her parents call her, Mulan hears the sound of the wilderness and of men's actions:

> At dawn she took leave of her father and mother;
> At night she camped on the Yellow River's bank.
> She could not hear the sound of her father and mother calling;
> She only heard the splash of the Yellow River's flowing water.
> At dawn she took leave of the Yellow River,
> At night she rested at the top of Black Mountain.
> She could not hear the sound of her father and mother calling;
> She only heard the gallops of nomad horsemen in the Yan
>   Mountain.[14]

The juxtaposition of Mulan's parents calling with the splashing Yellow River and with the sounds of horses galloping makes clear the contrast involved in Mulan's dual role: absent daughter and trekking warrior. She is no longer confined within the household; instead, her horizon has expanded and her world is one of river and mountain. Her not hearing her parents call suggests that Mulan is completely cut off from her old world and is now at home with the sounds of splashing water and galloping horses. Not only has the sound of the loom stopped, but her identity as a daughter has also become muffled by the sound of nature and the actions of a warrior world.

Yang Mu maintains that the "ellipsis of battle" is a major characteristic of Chinese heroic poems[15]; that is, Chinese poetry reflects a kind of heroism that fundamentally does not glorify the martial spirit and warriorhood, and therefore scenes and details of fighting are usually omitted or indicated metaphorically in the Chinese heroic epics. Instead, the changing of seasons and natural landscapes are described to suggest the heroic deed.[16] Similarly, in the third and fourth sections of the ballad, Mulan's heroic deed is also both brief and symbolically represented. In six verses, the image of a cross-dressing woman warrior's spectacular achievement is figuratively summarized:

She goes ten thousand miles on the business of war;
She crosses passes and mountains as if flying.
Northern gusts carry the rattle of army pots;
Cold light shines on iron armor.
Generals die in a hundred battles;
Stout soldiers return after ten years.[17]

There is no Homeric, graphic description of Mulan fighting or killing enemies; instead, the poet describes the harsh "Northern gusts" and "Cold
light" of the vast battlefield, and we are told of Mulan's superhuman speed
and stoutness in surviving a harsh reality. In saying that "Generals die in a
hundred battles / Stout soldiers return after ten years," the poet wants us
to imagine that in her solitary career as a warrior Mulan not only fights as
bravely as any man, but also is a "stout soldier" whose valor is superior to
a general's.

In the last section of the ballad, the poet brings the reader back from
the battlefield to Mulan's social responsibility and gender identity. On her
return, Mulan's valor is recognized, and she is summoned to the khan's
court for decoration and reward. When the khan asks her what she wishes
to receive as recognition, Mulan answers as an unambitious woman and a
dutiful daughter: "Mulan has no use for a Minister's post. I wish to ride a
swift mount to take me back to my home." In the second section of the
ballad, Mulan needed a "gallant horse" to transport her away from her domestic environment. Now, she needs "a swift mount" to take her back to
the old confines of her parents' home. Her answer also reveals a woman's
reality, in that she "has no use for a Minister's post."

The ballad then concludes with the amazement and perplexity of
Mulan's fellow soldiers after seeing her reclaim her womanhood and with
Mulan's metaphorical statement: "Two hares running side by side close to
the ground, how can they tell if I am he or she?" It is interesting that in
"The Ballad of Mulan" Mulan's "process" for disguising herself as a male
soldier is expeditiously understated while, in contrast, on her return, her
reclaiming of her femininity is described slowly and carefully:

"I open my door to my east chamber;
I sit on my couch in the west room;
I take off my wartime gown,
And put on my old time clothes."
Facing the window, she fixes her cloud-like hair;
Hanging up a mirror, she dabs on yellow flower powder.
She goes out the door to see her comrades.[18]

To parallel the earlier step-by-step process of purchasing a gallant horse and equipment in the four markets, the poet in the last section gives Mulan her own voice to describe her steps in reassuming her womanhood: fixing her hair, hanging up a mirror, and applying makeup. Such contrasting treatments in describing Mulan's transforming herself and assuming different roles suggest that women's cross-dressing was still a taboo subject even under the Confucian premise of filial piety; therefore, her transformation into a warrior is suggested with the purchasing of a gallant horse and its necessary gear, while her return to womanhood is detailed with feminine motions, objects, and sentiments.

This short ballad about Mulan's legend has inspired many poets and dramatists. In another ballad in the *Yuefu Collection*, a propagandist and eulogistic sentiment sums up Mulan's accomplishment: "Her patriot loyalty and filial piety will remain unchanged as her immortal fame will never be diminished." This prophecy has been fulfilled; Mulan's name has come to symbolize the Chinese warrior heroine. Obviously, Mulan is a combination of the nomadic martial spirit of the northern tribal heritage and the Confucian heritage. Tang poet Wei Yuanfu imitated the style of the ballad in his poem *Mulan shi,* and Ming poet Yang Weizhen (1296–1370) wrote a poem entitled *Mulan ci.* Neither poem contributed much to the development of the Mulan character or legend, but both do use Mulan as a literary allusion for their didactic purposes. To Wei Yuanfu, all should emulate Mulan as a paradigm of patriotic loyalty *(zhong)* and filial piety *(xiao);* he concludes that Mulan's "*zhong* and *xiao* will both remain unchanged; her perennial fame will never be diminished."[19] On the other hand, Yang Weizhen uses his Mulan poem to satirize the imperial ruler, implying that if a ruler could advance the loyal and the good while controlling the "barbarian neighbors," then Mulan would not have to carry weapons but could remain a domesticated "mulberry picker."[20]

Although most scholars consider Mulan a literary creation, Mulan's name and deeds do find their way into historical archives and local gazetteers, and there are even historical sites alleged to be her hometown and burial ground. No record of her achievements appears in official records prior to the Song Dynasty. Thirty kilometers north of Huangpo County in Hubei province, there is a mountain named Mulan Shan (Mount Mulan). The archives record that Mulan's surname was Chu, and that she dressed up as a man in her father's place, served in the military for twelve years, performed great deeds, and was promoted to general. Mulan turned down an imperial offer of a government post. Then she retired from the military, reclaimed her gender identity, and stayed home to take care of her family. According to the county archives, the mountain was renamed

Mulan Shan in 1609 during the Wanli reign of the Ming Dynasty in order to commemorate its local heroine Mulan and her heroic deeds, and the Mulan palace was built on top of the mountain.[21]

According to the Shangqiu gazetteer *(zhi)* of Henan province, written under the Qing Dynasty, Mulan lived during the Sui Dynasty (589–618), and her family name was Wei. In the town of Yingguo in Shangqiu County, there was a Mulan temple alleged to have been built on Mulan's home.[22] This account of Mulan's family name and deeds was later quoted in the gazetteer of Bo County *(Bozhou zhi)*[23] and in a chapter on women *(Gui yuan dian)* in *Gujin tushu jicheng* [Synthesis of books and illustrations of ancient and modern times],[24] in which Mulan's hometown is said to be in the village of Dongwei in Bozhou County. It is important to notice that all of the above quasi-historical archives depart from the nomadic characteristics of the legend preserved in "The Ballad of Mulan." The key actors of the legend—Mulan, her parents, her fellow soldiers, and the ruler she serves—have all been sinicized. In these gazetteers, the "khan" who summons Mulan's father and rewards Mulan's deed in the original ballad is now the enemy who threatens the peace of the northern borders, while the emperor *(di)* is Mulan's monarch. In the original poetic tradition, Mulan's legend ends with her homecoming and return to womanhood. However, in these gazetteers *(zhi),* a new ending is added: after Mulan's true identity is revealed, the emperor desires to summon her into his royal harem, but Mulan rejects the imperial summons by threatening to take her own life. In one version, she is pressed further and commits suicide. Shocked by her fortitude, the emperor bequeaths her a general's title and the title of "filial and chaste" *(xiao lie),* and designates the eighth day of the fourth month as a memorial day for her death and birth.[25] This appropriation of Mulan's character is an obvious attempt to make her fit into the paradigms of the *Biographies of Women (Lienü zhuan),* in which many "staunch women" *(lienü)* use suicide to preserve their chastity.

An eccentric scholar, Ming dramatist Xu Wei (1521–93) had a nervous breakdown, failed in a suicide attempt after finishing his own eulogy, "Epitaph for Myself," and was incarcerated for seven years for accidentally killing his second wife. Nonetheless, he was a unique dramatist particularly interested in cross-dressing heroines,[26] and offers yet another alternative in his play *Female Mulan Joins the Army for Her Father (Ci Mulan ti fu congjun).* He not only assigns Mulan a different surname, Hua, but also gives Mulan's legend a fairy-tale–like happy ending. Among four of his variety plays *(zaju)* collected under the title of *The Four Shrieks of the Monkey (Si sheng yuan),* two deal with women camouflaging their gender identity in order to excel in the male-dominated world. With the titles of

the two plays, Xu Wei straightforwardly lays out his deliberate exploita-
tion of gender ambiguity: *Female Mulan Joins the Army for Her Father (Ci
Mulan ti fu congjun)* and *Female Zhuangyuan Departs from the Female to Attain the Male (Nü zhuangyuan ci huang de feng),* a play about a female
scholar, Huang Chonggu, who dresses as a man to participate in the imperial examination and wins the title *zhuangyuan* (champion of the imperial examination). Obviously Xu Wei intends to show the paradoxical
nature of these two plays in his titles. Since women are not supposed to
be involved in military enterprises, "Female Mulan" and "Joins the Army"
are clearly antithetical; by the same token, since women have no access to
imperial examinations, Female *Zhuangyuan* itself is an oxymoron according to the norms of the Confucian bureaucracy. As if using gender ambiguity to challenge the rigidity of feudalistic bureaucracy and patriarchal
tyranny, Xu Wei concludes both plays with sarcastic and almost feminist
remarks. *Female Mulan* concludes: "Who conquers the Black Mountain
Peak? Mulan, the daughter, combats in the battle for her father. How
many confusing matters are there in this world? The scripts could not dif-
ferentiate female from male." *Female Zhuangyuan* ends with the following:
"Whom does the good deed belong to in this world? Not to the boys,
but to the girls." Eccentric as he is, Xu Wei's reinterpretation of Mulan's
transgression of gender boundaries is still contained within the Confucian
expectations of a filial daughter and virtuous wife; therefore, as a Chinese
equivalent of "they lived happily ever after," at the end of these two gender plays both cross-dressing daughters are properly arranged into favorable marriages in which they are expected to play their "proper role."

The Lady Knights-Errant in Tang Chuanqi

In the first official history, *Records of the Grand Historian (Shi ji),* Sima Qian
(145–86 B.C.E.) initiates a historical genre called *lie zhuan* (biography),
through which he records the prominent deeds of people of all social
classes from feudal lords and sages to commoners. Among these biographies, the chapter entitled "Biographies of Wandering Knights" ("Youxia
liezhuan") probably had the most influence on later knight-errant fiction.
In Chinese literature, the outlaw figure, as seen in *Water Margin (Shuihu
zhuan),* and the *xia* figure, or the righteous man-at-arms as a champion of
justice, could be seen as descendants of the Grand Historian's wandering
knights. The term *xia* first appears in the "Five Vermin" ("Wu du") chapter of *Han Fei zi zhuan.*[27] The legalist philosopher Han Fei zi (ca. 280–233
B.C.E.) regarded both Confucians and *xia* as potential dangers to the sta-

bility of social institutions: "the Confucians with their learning bring confusion to the law; the knights with their military prowess violate the prohibitions."[28] He further identified *xia* culture as one of the results of a disordered state whose "swordsmen gather bands of followers about them and perform deeds of honor, making a fine name for themselves and violating the prohibitions of the five government bureaus."[29] Therefore, he condemns them, saying that people "who violate the prohibitions ought to be punished, and yet the bands of knights are able to make a living by wielding their swords in a private cause."[30] Regarding the impact of *xia* on society, Han Fei zi criticizes them in the "Six Rebellions" ("Liu fan") section: "men who wield swords, attack, and assassinate are violent and extreme people, but society regards them as upright and courageous men; bandits and men who conceal traitors should be condemned to death, but society regards them as men of honor."[31] Obviously, in this legalist's mind, *xia* culture is more a social hazard than a heroic paradigm.

According to James J. Y. Liu, the knight-errant first appeared on the Chinese historical scene during the Warring States period (403–221 B.C.E.). During this time of political instability, social unrest, and intellectual ferment, the old aristocracy had declined, so many impoverished nobles and former retainers with special talents and skills became socially displaced persons who roamed from one state to another, offering their services to feudal lords. James J. Y. Liu suggests that while thinkers of various schools (Confucian, Daoist, Moist, Legalist, etc.) were busy competing for the favor and conversion of the feudal rulers to their respective ideologies, "the knights-errant simply took justice into their own hands and did what they thought necessary to redress wrongs and help the poor and the distressed. They did not hesitate to use force, nor did they have much regard for the law. On the other hand, they usually acted on altruistic motives and were ready to die for their principles. Such was the beginning of knight-errantry in China."[32]

In his discussion of the history of *xia,* James J. Y. Liu summarizes the ideals of *xia* as altruism, justice, individual freedom, personal loyalty, courage, truthfulness and mutual faith, honor and fame, generosity, and contempt for wealth.[33] Although on the surface there seem to be some parallels between the chivalry of the European medieval knight-errant and the codes of Chinese *xia,* such as the codes of honor, righteousness, and justice, the similarity remains superficial. Like a medieval European knight and a Japanese samurai, the *xia* is usually a man of spectacular martial skill and ethical discipline. However, while the knight and samurai are idealized as paradigms of moral virtue and integrity, the *xia* held tightly to a code of justice and honor that is narrowly and personally defined. Judging from James J.Y. Liu's summary, we could almost see *xia* as Confucian paradigms or the equivalents of European knights. But Cao Zhengwen in *The History of the Chinese Knight-Errant (Zhongguo xia wenhua shi)* finds five categories: wandering knights *(youxia)*, assassins *(cike)*, princely knights *(qingxiang zi xia)*, righteous knights *(yixia)*, and bandits *(dao)*.[34] Therefore, James J.Y. Liu's list of ideals applies only partially to certain types of *xia*. The conduct and moral principles of *xia* are indeed dubious and antithetical to Confucian doctrine. As Sima Qian prefaces in "Biographies of Wandering Knights": "Although nowadays the behaviors of the wandering knights are not in line with the path of justice and righteousness, nonetheless they uphold the words they have spoken; they accomplish what they set out to do; they honor the promises they have made; they don't cherish their own bodies, but they reach out to those who are in trouble and dilemma."[35] It seems that the Grand Historian also sees the wandering knights as ambiguous characters who have admirable honesty and principles, but whose moral codes are not necessarily admirable.

In a sense, we may say that the character of *xia* is a combination of Confucian integrity and honesty, Daoist individualism, and Moist sense of righteousness, while their ideals are grounded in the concept of *bao*. In the Confucian context, a *xia* is not part of the four social ranks: intellectual, peasant, artisan, and merchant *(shi, nong, gong,* and *shang)*. In other words, a *xia* often considers himself above mundane social law, but disciplines himself with ethical values. Within his own narrow and personal code, a Chinese knight-errant might serve someone not so much for the purpose of defending justice, but rather for the sake of repaying favors he received from someone who appreciated him. Whether it is in Sima Qian's "Biographies of Wandering Knights" or in later collections of fantastic knight-errant stories, the principle of *bao* (reciprocation) is the most important ethical standard of the Chinese knight-errant. There are two aspects of *bao* in the Chinese context: *bao en* (repaying someone for mercy received) and *boa chou* (repaying someone as revenge). The codes of honor and justice upheld by the Chinese knights-errant are narrowly defined within these two contexts of *bao*.

After Sima Qian's biographical accounts of wandering knights, brief fantasy tales about knight-errants emerge in Gan Bao's *In Search of Deities* and Zhao Ye's *Spring and Autumn Annals of the Kingdoms of Wu and Yue (Wu-Yue chunqiu;* first century C.E.), and later become a main theme in the Tang *chuanqi*. It is in this genre that a Chinese woman first appears as a fearless lady knight-errant with spectacular power and martial art; the specific work is the *Spring and Autumn Annals of the Kingdoms of Wu and Yue:*

The King of Yue, Gou Jian, asked his minister Fan Li about the art of war. Fan replied that there was a maiden in Yue famous for her swordsmanship and advised the King to consult her. The King therefore sent for the maiden. On her way to see the King, she met an old man who said his name was Yuan [which in Chinese puns on the word for "ape"]. He said to her, "I hear you excel in swordsmanship. I would like to see it." She replied, "I dare not conceal anything from you. You may test me in any way you like." So the old man plucked some bamboo twigs and threw them at her, but she caught them all before they touched the ground. Thereupon the old man flew up a tree and became a white ape *(yuan)*.

When the maiden saw the King, the latter asked her about swordsmanship. She replied, "I grew up in a deep forest, in the wilderness away from men. I have not studied properly and I am unknown to the feudal lords. However, I am fond of swordsmanship and I have practiced incessantly. I did not receive it from anyone; I just suddenly got it." When the King pressed her further, she replied that the way of swordsmanship was very subtle yet easy, its meaning very obscure and profound; that it involved the principles of *yin* and *yang;* and that a good swordsman should appear perfectly calm like a fine lady, but capable of quick action like a surprised tiger. The King then gave her the title "The Maiden of Yue," and asked her to instruct his troops. No one could surpass her in swordsmanship at that time.[36]

As James J. Y. Liu points out, this story introduces the basic elements of the later chivalrous ladies of Tang *chuanqi* and Ming and Qing fiction: (1) growing up "in the wilderness away from men"; (2) possession of super- natural martial skills; and (3) operation as an individual agent (as the Maiden of Yue points out, she is "unknown to the feudal lords"). In the comprehensive classified collection of pre-Song fiction, the *Extensive Gleanings of the Reign of Great Tranquillity (Taiping guangji),* edited by Li Fang (925–96), there are twenty-four accounts of gallant knights-errant in four chapters, seven of which are accounts of chivalrous lady figures: "The Curly-Bearded Stranger" ("Qiuran ke"), "The Woman Inside a Carriage" ("Chezhong nüzi"), "Cui Shensi['s Wife]," ("Cui Shensi"), "The Mysteri- ous Girl of the Nie Family" ("Nie Yinniang"), "Red Thread"("Hong- xian"), "The Merchant's Wife"("Guren qi"), and "Lady Jing the Thirteenth" ("Jing shisan niang").[37] As Joseph S. M. Lau points out, "knight-errantry is a kind of temperament, not a social rank; the spirit of knight-errant is a kind of attitude, but not a kind of profession."[38]

These seven chivalrous ladies are unique characters in Chinese litera- ture. Some of them can jump many feet high and walk on the walls like flying birds; some wield swords and daggers and are equipped with martial skills that allow them to come and go without being noticed. They are also physically stronger than ordinary men and financially independent, and they are free to determine their own marriages. They work furtively at night, and they are described as enigmatic warriors who operate alone according to their own rules of justice.

These seven chivalrous ladies also represent various social classes and embody all five categories of *xia* mentioned earlier: Red Whisk (Hongfu) in "The Curly-Bearded Stranger" is a courtesan who acts like a wandering knight; Cui Shensi's wife and the merchant's wife are avengers and assassins; Nie Yinniang, a general's daughter and a governor's protector, may be seen both as an assassin and a princely knight; Hongxian, a maid, and Lady Jing the Thirteenth, a widowed merchant, may be seen as righteous knights; and the woman inside a carriage is the first female bandit in Chinese literature. On the surface, these chivalrous ladies seem to defy the Confucian expectation of womanhood; yet the virtues of *xiao* and *zhong* represented by Mulan still play an important role in these Tang tales and provide the main premise for some of these chivalrous ladies' unorthodox behavior. These extraordinary female knights-errant are not only loyal and dutiful, like Mulan, but also characterized by intriguing beauty, spectacular physical strength, and even supernatural ability. This Tang genre not only cultivates a new range for Chinese fiction, but also establishes a new idealized, although somewhat eccentric, image of Chinese women warriors.

It is worth noticing that the *xia* qualities in the women warriors often serve as a license for them to carry out unconventional deeds without cross-dressing to disguise their gender. Unlike Mulan, the seven chivalrous ladies from the "Gallant Knights" ("Haoxia") section of the *Taiping guangji* no longer disguise their gender before performing their chivalrous deeds, whereas in the "Story of Xie Xiao'e" ("Xie Xiao'e") by Li Gongzuo (ca.770-ca. 848), appearing in another section of *Taiping quangji,* the author makes Xie Xiao'e disguise herself as a manservant in order to investigate and avenge her father's and husband's deaths. This discrepancy between Xie Xiao'e's character as a cross-dressing daughter and the seven lady knights-errant as eccentric or mysterious women seems to indicate that the *xia* qualities of the seven chivalrous ladies already serve as a form of cross-dressing (i.e., crossing of boundaries) that distorts their womanhood; therefore, their gender does not seem to concern the authors or editors of the *Taiping guangji*. Xie Xiao'e, however, is not portrayed as a *xia* character who possesses martial skills or supernatural power; rather, she is an ordinary daughter and widow who needs to fulfill her filial and wifely duties by revenge. Li Gongzuo's rendering of her as a cross-dressing daughter reflects the patriarchal idea that an ordinary woman's unusual bravery or chivalrous deeds require her to disguise her gender identity. We may see

Xie Xiao'e's character as a sort of transitional phase between the filial Mulan and the later Thirteenth Sister (He Yufeng) in the Qing novel *A Tale of Heroic Lovers (Ernü yingxiong zhuan)*, who is not only a full-fledged lady knight-errant but also a filial daughter on a mission to avenge the injustice done to her father.

Among the seven fantasies of female knights-errant collected in the *Taiping Guangji*, "The Mysterious Girl of the Nie Family" is probably the most intriguing and representative of the chivalrous lady genre. The story is traditionally attributed to Pei Xing (flourished 880) and is written in the styles of biography and "random notes" *(biji)*, in which fictions are presented with specific historical dates and names. Like a journalistic report, it begins by identifying the heroine as "the daughter of Weibo General, Nie Feng, during the Zhenyuan period (785–804) of the Tang Dynasty." The daughter is kidnapped at the age of ten by a mysterious nun and is returned to her parents after five years of training in a remote cave. According to the girl's accounts to her parents, the mysterious nun has two other female trainees who consume no human food and can walk up along the cliffs as swiftly as if flying. The general's daughter is first given a magical pill and later trained to fly and fence and is twice sent to assassinate men who have done wrong. She is the nun's secret assassin, defending justice as her noble cause. After five years of training, Nie Yinniang returns home with supernatural powers and spectacular martial ability. She chooses a mirror maker to be her husband; after her father's death, the governor of Wei hires the couple to assassinate the hostile Governor Liu. After discovering that Governor Liu's power of divination has already anticipated their coming, they defect to become Governor Liu's protectors.[39]

While this tale about Nie Yinniang reflects the Chinese knight-errant code of *bao,* it also involves dehumanizing the heroine: she turns from a regular girl into a fearless and powerful *nüxia* (lady knight-errant). The tale's Daoist imagery of inaccessible mountain retreats and elixir-seeking, cave-dwelling recluses is common in later knight-errant romances *(wuxia xiaoshuo)*. This imagery associated with her mysterious abduction and return suggests the girl's mystical transformation from a Confucian daughter into a nonconforming chivalrous lady: she has become an unusual woman trained to carry out special missions and observe her own moral code. Her noble cause for killing may be justice, and her redirected loyalty to Governor Liu (whom she initially intends to assassinate) may also be categorized as loyalty. However, her definition of justice and loyalty seems ambiguous and narrow: she may be sincere when she carries out her mission, but her sincerity is based on the principle of reciprocation. It is to repay the nun's transforming her into a lady knight-errant that Nie

Yinniang becomes an assassin. She also decides to repay General Liu's generosity in forgiving her for her mission by transferring her loyalty to him. As a matter of fact, five out of the seven chivalrous ladies in *Taiping guangji,* such as the maiden named Red Thread (Hongxian), who is characterized with Nie Yinniang's mystique and skills, act as assassins and take justice into their own hands. These chivalrous ladies are the models for the later female knights-errant novels whose mysterious heroines operate according to their own code of justice.

Another unique quality of these women is that they quite often take the initiative in determining their marriages, as does Nie Yinniang, who chooses a mirror maker, and Red Whisk (Hongfu) in "The Curly-Bearded Stranger," who persuades Li Jing, a great strategist and gentleman, to elope with her. It is emphasized that Nie Yinniang chooses a husband who is good for nothing but polishing a mirror. It is also mentioned that her parents dare not oppose her wish; therefore, her father provides for her and her husband very generously. It seems that the author wants to highlight Nie Yinniang's oddity by stressing that her choice of an inferior spouse defies social norms. We may also read Nie Yinniang's preference for the mirror maker as symbolic of her favoring the mirror as a Daoist symbol, for in Daoism it is believed to have the magical power of reflecting a person's true nature. In this sense, Nie Yinniang may not be as eccentric as she appears. She and Red Whisk seem to be two chivalrous ladies who know what they prefer in marriage. The autonomy in marriage makes the lady knights-errant of Tang *chuanqi* markedly different from the gazetteers' and Xu Wei's Mulan. Mulan's freedom to cross-dress is allowed largely because it reinforces the Confucian values of filial piety and loyalty; such a gender transgression is curtailed at the end of the story by her arranged marriage, which places her within the Confucian expectations of a filial daughter and virtuous wife. In comparison, the lady knights-errant's deliberation of their own marriages is in line with their operating principles of *yi* (righteousness) and *bao* (reciprocation), not a step towards resuming their submissive gender roles. They are individualists who take their destinies into their own hands.

The mysterious independent character of the chivalrous ladies becomes even more pronounced in two other of the seven chivalrous tales: "Cui Shensi's Wife" and "The Merchant's Wife." As the titles suggest, these two chivalrous ladies, like other chivalrous ladies in Tang fiction, are nameless and only known as so-and-so's wife. The tale about Cui Shensi tells of a young Confucian scholar preparing for the imperial examination and befriending his neighbor, a mysterious woman of over thirty with two maidservants. Cui Shensi, the scholar, proposes marriage, but the woman rejects him because she is not from an official family. He then proposes to take her as a concubine, to which she consents. Two years later, she gives birth to a child. After being found missing by Cui Shensi, she comes home one night with a dagger in her right hand and a man's head in her left. She then reveals her history: her father was wrongly killed by the prefect, and she has waited for several years for revenge. Her mission is now completed, and she has to leave. She grants Cui Shensi her house and her two maids to support the child, goes into her bedroom to feed the baby for the last time, and leaves. Later, not hearing the baby cry for some time, Cui discovers the baby dead. It appears that she killed her child to sever all ties with the past. For a modern reader, the woman's extreme action at the end seems horrifying and inhuman, but for the Tang storyteller, her strong-willed character is so intriguing that he concludes the tale exclaiming, "not even ancient knights-errant could surpass her!"

From the representations of these lady knights-errant, I would like to suggest that the superhuman and almost inhuman qualities of the chivalrous ladies in Tang *chuanqi* reflect the authors' inability to reconcile an ideological paradox: female Confucian virtues and knight-errant temperament. Unlike Mulan, whose filial virtue and heroic deeds require her to disguise her gender, the lady knights-errant in Tang *chuanqi* retain their gender identity on the one hand, while on the other they abide by the *bao* code of *xia*, which is not necessarily compatible with Confucian expectations of womanhood. As women, they are expected to fulfill their Confucian role; as knights-errant, they are allowed to transgress the Confucian code. It is within this paradox that these dehumanized women warriors are created. Therefore, we see these chivalrous ladies as inhuman creatures that lack human emotions, femininity, and maternal qualities. In a way, we can say that the Tang storytellers created intriguing women warriors by stripping them of their womanhood.

Obviously, the mystique of these solitary female knights-errant fascinated many writers. In fact, they continued to inspire recreations and appropriations in later Chinese fiction. In the seventeenth-century collection *Strange Stories from the Leisure Studio (Liaozhai zhiyi)*, by Pu Songling (1640–1715), we see ladies such as Nie Yinniang and Cui Shensi's concubine assimilated into Confucian norms: Nie Yinniang is transformed into a righteous peasant woman, and the filial nature of Cui Shensi's concubine becomes the central theme.[40] In Qing romances such as Wen Kang's *The Lady Knight-Errant's Fantastical Adventures (Xianü qiyuan)*, we see the *xianü* figure even more domesticated.

The Female Outlaws of Water Margin

In the Ming Dynasty (1368–1644) historical novel *Water Margin* (*Shuihu zhuan,* also translated as *Outlaws of the Marsh* and *All Men Are Brothers*), we see a climactic fantasy of knight-errantry in Chinese literature. This seventy-chapter novel tells of the legendary deeds of Song Jiang and his band of 108 chivalric outlaws who flourished during the reign of Emperor Huizong (reigned 1101–25) of the Northern Song (960–1126). Most scholars believe Song Jiang to have been a historical character well known for his leadership in gang robbery, because three chapters in *The History of the Song Dynasty (Song shi)* give accounts of Song Jiang's and his thirty-six fellow bandits' rebellious deeds.[41] As some Chinese scholars, such as James J. Y. Liu and Sun Shuyu, have pointed out, *Water Margin* is an extremely macho book about bandits who rebel against government corruption and social hierarchy. Though these bandits are portrayed as Robin Hood–like knights-errant with *jianghu yiqi* (vagrant spirit of justice), their standard of justice is doubtful. Their heroism and loyalty are still confined to a personal code of honor based on friendship as brotherhood and on *bao* and *yi* in the contexts of *bao en* (repaying for mercy) and *bao chou* (revenge). As C. T. Hsia criticizes in *The Classic Chinese Novel*:

> In this world of endless adventure, the dominant symbol is the road upon which the heroes are forever traveling. . . . To the beginning reader, the heroes are at times indistinguishable from the villains in their equal proneness to violence. . . . According to [the hero's] code, a hero has to be honorable, though the concept of honor is not defined in the traditional Confucian manner. Filial piety is indeed stressed in the case of several heroes, particularly Sung Chiang [Song Jiang], Li K'uei [Li Kui], and Kung-sun Sheng [Gongsun Sheng], and loyalty to the emperor is always affirmed even though two or three violent souls are against the idea. But the code departs from Confucian teaching in its observance of the other basic human ties. It pays little attention to the conjugal relationship so long as a wife is presumed faithful . . . and it exalts the ideal of friendship to the point of usurping the language of brotherhood. This ideal not only endorses the Confucian saying often invoked in the book, "Within the four seas all men are brothers," but encourages the practice of knight-errantry insofar as it is preferable to execute justice by one's own hand rather than through the official channels.
>
> Though the heroic code endorses every Confucian virtue, it actually abolishes finer ethical distinctions by insisting that one must above all follow the dictates of friendship or *i* [*yi*].[42]

Hsia's comments poignantly summarize the tenets of the novel's ethical universe and the moral ambiguity manifested through these outlaw characters. Not only is this a very macho and patriarchal novel, it is also a very misogynist one that exploits the themes of women's evil quality and "woman as the root of trouble" *(nüren shi huoshui)*. As Hsia also points out, a crucial test is that the hero "should be above sexual temptation. Most members of the [*Water Margin's*] band are bachelors, and as for the married heroes the conjugal aspect of their life is rarely mentioned unless they are brought to trouble through their wives."[43] Therefore, women in this very macho novel are mainly portrayed as either temptations or potential threats to the outlaws' heroism.

In contrast to the outlaws, with their sexual stringency, the majority of the female characters are condemned for their debauchery, greed, adultery, prostitution, and unchaste behavior. As Sun Shuyu contends, the author consistently calls his young female characters "adulterous woman" or "worthless person," while calling older women "cunning hags." The female characters in this very macho novel are presented as belonging to one or the other of two dichotomous types: (1) the beautiful but adulterous and murderous femme fatale, such as Pan Jinlian (the Golden Lotus); and (2) the crude and ugly woman outlaw. Almost all the beautiful women in *Water Margin* are portrayed as the causes of men's fall or associated with troubles, disasters, and crimes. Out of the 108 Robin Hood - like "outlaws" or "bandits," there are three woman "outlaws" who may be considered women warriors. Of the three, only "Ten-Foot Green Hu Sanniang" (*Yizhang Qing* Hu Sanniang) is a mysterious and ambiguous beauty, while "Female Yaksha Sun Erniang" (*Mu yecha* Sun Erniang) and "Giant She-Bug Gu Dasao" (*Mu Dachong* Gu Dasao) are both ugly old hags with manly physiques and strength and a shrewd and cunning nature.

To the Ming author, ugliness was evidently one of the virtuous qualifications for the women warriors. Among the three women outlaws, only Ten-Foot Green seems to be based on a real historical character.[44] Throughout the entire novel, she is a silent character; the reader is told of her beauty and mystique through the narrator's description. As Hsia also points out, "with the prominent exception of Song Jiang and Li Kui, most of the heroes are memorable only for their pre–Liang-shan career. Once they join the band, they tend to lose their identity and become less distinguishable from one another in their uniform capacity as military commanders."[45] Such is also the case with the three women outlaws. Prior to her capture by Song Jiang's band, Ten-Foot Green is a fearless woman warrior—the first to capture Wang Ying the Dwarf Tiger—and it takes Song Jiang's band much effort to conquer her. In Chapter 47, "Ten-Foot Green Alone Captures Wang the Dwarf Tiger; Song Jiang Attacks the Village of Zhu for the Second Time," Du Xing, one of the Water Margin Outlaws, describes Ten-Foot Green's Amazonian character to Song Jiang's band: "But there is no one to fear in that village except a woman warrior who is called the Ten-Foot Green and she uses two swords that glitter like the sun and moon, and how terrible is she in her skill." Initially her terrible skill is not taken seriously, because her gender makes her a target of lust rather than a true physical threat. In the following excerpt, we have a glimpse of how women warriors are imagined in this very macho novel:

> Before [Song Jiang] had finished speaking this Wang the Dwarf Tiger, who was a lusty fellow with women, heard him say it was a female warrior and he hoped to seize her with one round of battle. So he gave a yell and he pressed his horse to the front and held his weapon in his hand and he came out to fight against her. The soldiers on both sides shouted. The woman whipped up her horse and whirled her two swords and she came to fight Wang the Dwarf Tiger.
>
> Now this woman had used her swords until she had a very perfect skill and Wang the Dwarf Tiger was above all in the use of his single weapon. They fought some ten-odd rounds and then Sung Chiang [Song Jiang] as he watched from his horse saw that Wang the Dwarf Tiger could not withstand her longer. . . . Now that Green Snake was a very tricky female and in her heart she thought, "How mannerless is this thing!" And with her two swords she thrust from above and beneath and how could Wang the Dwarf Tiger withstand her? He turned his horse about to make his escape, but the Green Snake urged on her horse and she pursued him and she put aside the sword from her right hand and stretched forth her fair woman's arm and she lifted Wang the Dwarf Tiger up from his saddle by his hair, and all the villagers crowded about and dragged him this way and that and so away.[46]

Since some of the male outlaw characters are modeled after historical figures found in Southern Song archives, some scholars believe that Ten-Foot Green is also derived from a historical figure. According to Sun Shuyu, there was a famous woman general, Madame Ma, nicknamed "Ten-Foot Green," among the rebel armies of the Southern Song Dynasty. She was the widow of Ma Nie and had married "Vagrant Zhang," Zhang Yong, who occupied thousands of acres of land and commanded an army of several hundred thousand. His army was once marshaled by Ten-Foot Green, who marched with her two emblematic flags inscribed with "The Staunch Woman of the Western Pass: The Protector of the Nation—Madame Ma" (*Guanxi zhenlienü: huguo Ma furen*).[47] Sun Shuyu believes that the Ten-Foot Green in *Water Margin* was inspired by Madame Ma. We may also see Madame Ma as the model and inspiration for the nomadic women generals of the Yang family, because her title "Guanxi zhenlienü" seems to suggest her nomadic origin. If Ten-Foot Green was indeed based on Madame Ma, she was obviously seen by the author of *Water Margin* as someone threatening to the male authority and power, and as someone to be tamed. Therefore, like the other women warriors of Chinese romances, this ruthless warrior beauty had to be subdued and conquered like a Hippolyta (queen of the Amazons) by a Theseus. Her encounter with the outlaw band seems to provide some kind of comic relief for this very macho novel, as her encounter with the outlaws takes on the flavor of "taming of the shrew":

> Whirling her swords The Green Snake gave rein to her horse and dashed at Lin Chong. Lin Chong lifted his spear and the two fought less than ten rounds when suddenly Lin Chong pretended to make a feint and he let The Green Snake come at him with her two swords. Then he stayed them fast with his spear held crosswise. The two swords glanced aside and Lin Chong seized the opportunity and stretched out his ape-like arm silently and he bent his wolf-like back and laying hold on the Green Snake he dragged her over upon his own horse. Song Jiang, seeing, gave him a shout of praise, but paying no heed Lin Chong bade the soldiers bind the woman.[48]

Besides having Ten-Foot Green dragged and tied up like an animal, the author seems to regard marriage and domestication as the ultimate subjugation of this threatening woman warrior. Therefore, in order to justify Ten-Foot Green's "membership" in the macho society of *Water Margin,* the author gives the beautiful woman warrior no other option but to accept silently Song Jiang's marriage arrangement between her and the very ugly and short Wang Ying the Dwarf Tiger, whom she once defeated and captured.

During the reign of the Mongols, the representation of heroines in Chinese literature took an interesting turn. From the end of the Song Dynasty (960–1279) to the end of the Yuan Dynasty (1280–1369, under Mongol rule), a large corpus of music drama called *zaju* (variety show) was written and produced. In 1238, the Mongol government abolished the imperial examination for the civil service, and Confucian scholars were degraded to the ninth class of subjects, lower than prostitutes (the eighth class) and only one class higher than the bottom class, beggars. Under such political oppression, nearly all Yuan dramatists turned to old stories, histories, popular legends, narrative poems, or early plays for inspiration and to disguise their political purpose of reminding Han Chinese of their terrible plight under Mongol rule. In this literary climate, the oppressed, the victimized, and the persecuted all become popular subjects for dramatists.

Therefore, instead of women warriors, we find tragic heroines like Wang Zhaojun, a lady-in-waiting of the Han emperor who was chosen to marry the Xiongnu (Hun) king as part of the *heqin* policy.[49] Instead of accepting her destiny and becoming the wife of a foreign king, she drowned herself. Another enduring heroine was Tou Ngo (in *The Injustice Done to Tou Ngo*), a virtuous woman who resisted temptation and corruption to the death. These Yuan dramatic heroines were "warriors" who symbolized the physically and socially weak and powerless Han, victimized by an oppressive dynasty. The Yuan literati used the stories of these heroines' battles against corruption as political protests, celebrating their unyielding spirit and integrity in order to defy the corrupt system.

Women Generals of the Yang Family and Thirteenth Sister (Jade Phoenix)

The absence of physically strong women warriors in Yuan literature was soon amended with the revival of narrative tales and novels in the Ming (1368–1644) and Qing (1644–1911) Dynasties. The women warriors of these novels are actually extensions of two woman warrior types discussed before: Mulan warriors and knights-errant, like the "Thirteenth Sister," who became the paradigmatic heroine of modern *wuxia xiaoshuo* and movies that are still quite often shown on TV in Hong Kong, China, and Taiwan.

The image of the Chinese woman warrior reaches its peak in the popular Song legends preserved and reincarnated in Ming novels, in which we see a superhuman woman warrior defending the Song people from invasion by the northern nomads or a wandering omnipotent daughter avenging an injustice done to her father. In the well-known Ming historical novel *The Heroic Lives of the Yang Family Generals (Yangjiafu shidai zhongyong yanyi zhizhuan)*, we read about the brave and loyal deeds of the Yang generals of the Song Dynasty (960–1279), their superior woman commander-in-chief, She Saihua, and her daughter-in-law Mu Guiying.[50] This historical novel centers around the heroism and patriotism of Yang Ye's family, who secured China's northern borders and whose protection and resistance against invasions by the northern Kitan Tartars spanned three generations. Yang Ye was a true historical hero. According to *The History of the Song Dynasty*, in 986 he fought a fierce battle with the Kitan Tartars in Shanxi province and was badly injured. He refused to surrender after being captured, and he died from a hunger strike after three days. His heroic feats and merits became popular legends and later inspired many novels and dramas of the Southern Song (1127–1279) and Ming periods.[51]

She Saihua and Mu Guiying are the results of such inspiration and fic-
tionalization. There are no historical accounts in Song, Yuan, or Ming
records of these two women generals. Some scholars argue that She Saihua is derived from the wife of Yang Ye, the daughter of a general in *The
History of the Song Dynasty*. Mu Guiying, on the other hand, is a purely fictional character. In the legends, both women are celebrated for their un-
usually independent minds, military skills, and strength, far surpassing
men's. Both are from families of foreign mountain kings, and both choose
their husbands through combat. In the Ming romances, the women warriors are better than their husbands in martial arts, but they all have a weakness for love. No longer upholding *xiao* as the guiding principle of their
warrior code, these women warriors of the Yang family are now guided by
love for and loyalty to their husbands. Therefore, these original women
warriors of the "barbarian kings" betray their fathers and defect to their
husbands' camps. The women warriors of the Yang family are shrewd non-
Han beauties tamed by their love for handsome Han Chinese and become
loyal defenders of the Chinese imperial court, battling against their own
people.

Besides the lady generals of the Yang family, another enduring character in popular Qing romance is He Yufeng (Jade Phoenix), nicknamed
Thirteenth Sister *(Shisan mei)* in *A Tale of Heroic Lovers (Ernü yingxiong
zhuan),* also called *The Lady-Knight's Fantastical Adventures (Xianü qiyuan),*
written by Wen Kang (flourished 1821–60), a Manchu official and aristocrat whose fortune declined later in his life. In this novel we see the idealization and the appropriation of the lady-knight character. The story
seems to be modeled after Pu Songling's "Xianü,"[52] which is based on two
similar stories. However, Thirteenth Sister is no longer like the mysterious
chivalrous ladies of Tang fiction; she is a full-fledged Chinese wandering
knight of the *wuxia* genre.

This forty-chapter[53] novel tells of the chivalrous lady He Yufeng [Jade
Phoenix], whose father was wrongly accused by a scheming and corrupt
aristocrat and died in prison. He Yufeng and her mother retreated to a remote rustic village, and she changed her name to Thirteenth Sister. She be-
friended a chivalrous man-at-arms and traveled from town to town waiting
for the opportunity to avenge her father's death and the injustice done to
him. In her wandering, Thirteenth Sister encountered An Ji, who was on
his way to bail out his own wrongly accused and imprisoned father. Thirteenth Sister saved An Ji from evil bandit monks who attempted to rob
him, and she also rescued Zhang Jinfeng (Golden Phoenix), who had been
kidnapped by the head monk. The two women became good friends, and
Thirteenth Sister even brokered a marriage between An Ji and Golden

Phoenix, even providing them with a crossbow to guarantee their safety.
(Some bandits the young couple encounter recognize the crossbow and es-
cort them safely to their destination.) After An Ji's father was released from
the prison, and the injustice done to Thirteenth Sister's father was avenged,
Thirteenth Sister initially planned to leave the world and became a nun.
However, she married An Ji and encouraged him to take the imperial examination. He finished third and was appointed head of the Imperial College, and then was promoted to commissioner in Mongolia. However, he
chose to take the position of a provincial examiner. As James J.Y. Liu bril-
liantly recapitulates in *The Chinese Knight-Errant:*

> *A Tale of Heroic Lovers* is reasonably well written, but has some serious faults.
> It has a carefully constructed plot, an unusual feature in this kind of fiction,
> and its language is lively and fluent. On the other hand, the characterization
> is uneven and sometimes inconsistent. The most striking example is the
> heroine: as Thirteenth Sister, she is a remarkable character full of noble and
> stern virtues of chivalry, but as Jade Phoenix, especially after her marriage,
> she is hardly recognizable as the same person. [An Ji's father] is too often
> merely the author's mouthpiece for expressing trite neo-Confucian moral
> views. An Ji is largely the conventional young gentleman, just as Golden
> Phoenix is the conventional virtuous wife and daughter.[54]

Indeed, if we understand the heroine of *A Tale of Heroic Lovers* in the context of the literary tradition of Chinese women warriors, such a dichotomous characterization of Thirteenth Sister and Jade Phoenix comes as no
surprise at all. In fact, it would have been more of an anomaly if Jade
Phoenix had remained a chivalrous character clinging to her own code
after marriage. The author's prologue encapsulates in four words the four
virtues that comprise the main theme of the romance: loyalty, filial piety,
integrity, and righteousness *(zhong xiao jie yi).* Before her marriage, Thirteenth Sister's chivalrous character and unusual deeds were defined within
the principles prescribed for knights-errant; she was allowed to transgress
the gender boundaries set up by Confucian orthodoxy. From a patriarchal
viewpoint, once her father's unjust death was avenged and her mother deceased, the heroine no longer had any acceptable reason to continue her
chivalry. Therefore, her alternatives besides marriage were a nunnery or
death, both of which she considered. We may say that the choice of marriage is a symbolic death of the woman warrior, whose domestication
transforms her back into the role dictated by Confucian doctrine.

As James J.Y. Liu notices, "the title *A Tale of Heroic Lovers* (*Ernü yingxiong zhuan*) is a deliberate paradox: *ernü,* literally 'sons and daughters,' is a
term often used with reference to lovers, while *yingxiong,* 'heroes,' is often

used as its antonym."[55] Obviously, this reflects the fact that the author's main objective in creating this romance is to reconcile the incompatibility of love and heroism, particularly chivalry as portrayed in Chinese literature. The author himself expresses this intention clearly in his prologue:

> Most people nowadays regard "lovers" and "heroes" as two different kinds of people, to "love" and to be "heroic" as two different things. They mistakenly think that those who indulge in force and like fighting are "heroes," while those who toy with rouge and powder or have a weakness for catamites are "lovers." Therefore, as soon as they open their mouths, they will say, "So-and-so lacks heroic ambitions but has a great capacity for love," or "So-and-so is shallow in love but has a strong heroic spirit." What they don't realize is that only when one has the pure nature of a hero can one fully possess a loving heart, and only when one has true love can one perform heroic deeds.[56]

It is precisely because of the element of love that women warriors in Ming and Qing romances become tamed and domesticated. As mentioned earlier, the chivalrous ladies in Tang fiction abide by the codes of reciprocity and righteousness; when it comes to *marriage,* reciprocity and righteousness are more important than *love.* These chivalrous ladies of Tang fiction are mysterious and do not conform to the gender boundaries precisely because they are not controlled by the theme of love. However, in the Ming and Qing romances, we see Thirteenth Sister and the female generals of the Yang family controlled and limited by love; Thirteenth Sister is persuaded to shed her chivalrous character by a Confucian patriarch, An Ji's father (who also happens to have been a great friend of Thirteenth Sister's deceased father), and to become a domesticated Confucian wife and daughter-in-law.

Conclusion

From the discussion of the various Chinese woman-warrior types, we can see that there is a tendency in Chinese literature to justify and contain the unorthodox deeds and mystiques of women warriors within the Confucian doctrine of *zhong xiao jie yi* (loyalty, filial piety, chastity, and righteousness). All four groups of women warriors were created, developed, and eventually confined within such a patriarchal frame. The first type, represented by Mulan, is a Confucian ideal whose unconventional courage and deeds are justified by her filial virtue and unthreatening character. The evolution and appropriation of her character and legend into a *lienü* reflect the patriarchal need to contain her within Confucian doctrine. The second group, represented by the mysterious lady knights-errant, is embodied in independent and sometimes solitary warriors who operate according to their own codes of honor and justice. Their deeds and characters defy conventional Confucian codes; therefore, within a patriarchal framework, these women are characterized by eccentric or enigmatic nonhuman qualities. The female outlaws of *Water Margin* reflect a misogynist attitude towards female beauty and strength; they reveal the male fantasy of subduing strong and beautiful women, and also show a clear distrust of women's beauty. In the fourth group, represented by the women generals of the Yang family and Thirteenth Sister, we see the Fuhao type of commander-in-chief romanticized and the lady knight-errant of the Tang *chuanqi* Confucianized. The female generals reflect the author's male fantasy of women as exotic barbarian beauties; they are independent minded and capable of overpowering men, but—no matter how strong they are—they are eventually subdued by the Han Chinese men they love, and they willingly join their husbands' military causes. Thirteenth Sister reflects the Confucian appropriation of the eccentric chivalrous ladies of the Tang *chuanqi* genre. In short, all four types of women warriors reflect a patriarchal culture that sees women's strength and potential as something to be subdued and appropriated. It is acceptable for the heroine to be a cross-dressing warrior or commander-in-chief as long as she is defined within the Confucian norm. But if she transgresses the code of Confucian female virtues, she is no longer human or womanly, but a deadly inhuman creature.

NOTES

1. According to Liu Xiang in the "Correct Deportment of Mothers" ("Mu yi") chapter of *The Biographies of Women,* the three obediences *(sancong)* are that a woman obeys her parents when she is young, her husband when she is married, and her sons when her husband dies, for "this is considered propriety *(li)*." See *Lienü zhuan* [The biographies of women]. *Sibu beiyao* ed. (Repr. Taipei: Zhonghua shuju, 1983), ch. 1, Biography 11. As specified by Ban Zhao (Pan Chao) in "Admonitions for Women" ("Nü jie"), the "four virtues" are womanly virtue *(fude)*, womanly words *(fuyan)*, womanly bearing *(furong)*, and womanly work *(fugong)*: "What is called womanly virtue need not be brilliant ability, exceptionally different from others. Womanly words need be neither clever in debate nor keen in conversation. Womanly appearance requires neither a pretty nor a perfect face and form. Womanly work need not be work done more skillfully than that of others." The translation is by Nancy Lee Swann, who translated "Nü jie" as "Lessons for Women" in her *Pan Chao* [Ban Zhao]: *Foremost Woman Scholar of China* (New York: The Century, 1932), p. 86.

2. "White tiger" is a rude way to refer to a woman; the phrase implies that she is both powerful and ominous.

3. Louise Edwards, "Women Warriors and Amazons of the Mid-Qing Texts *Jinghua yuan* and *Honglou meng*," *Modern Asian Studies* 29. 2 (1995): 231.

4. Li Xiaolin, "Chinese Women Soldiers: A History of 5,000 Years," *Social Education* 58 (February 1994): 67. The episode about the famous military strategist Sun Zi (also known as Sun Wu) training court ladies is recorded in ch. 65 "Biographies of Sun Zi and Wu Qi" of *Shi ji* [Records of the Grand Historian], by Sima Qian (145-ca. 86 B.C.E.) (Beijing: Zhonghua shuju, 1959).

5. *Shi ji,* ch. 65, pp. 2161–2.

6. Li Xiaolin, p. 70, n. 4 and n.5; see also *Zhongguo lidai mingren shengji dacidian* [Dictionary of famous Chinese people and places], "Fuhao" (Hong Kong: Sanlian shuju, 1994), p. 25.

7. Besides six chapters on virtuous women, Liu Xiang also includes a chapter on wicked women, entitled "Biographies of the Pernicious and the Depraved" ("Nie bi zhuan") that showcases women as femmes fatales who cause men's downfalls or are adulterers.

8. Sharon S. Hou, "Women's Literature," in *The Indiana Companion to Traditional Chinese Literature,* ed. William H. Nienhauser (Bloomington: Indiana University Press, 1986), pp. 177–8.

9. Two poems titled "Mulan shi" are included in ch. 25 of *Yuefu shiji* [Yuefu poetry in one hundred chapters], ed. Guo Maoqian (twelfth century), *Sibu congkan* ed.; Luo Genze in *Yuefu wenxueshi* (Taipei: Wenzhe chubanshe, 1972, pp. 151–5) argues for a Tang date for the poem and suggests that both Mulan poems collected in *Yuefu shiji* are by the Tang poet Wei Yuanfu.

10. The translation of "The Ballad of Mulan" is modified from Arthur Waley's translation quoted in Victor Mair, ed., *The Columbia Anthology of Traditional Chinese Literature* (New York: Columbia University Press, 1994), pp. 474–6.

11. Swann, p. 83.

12. Cf. Waley, in Mair, ed., *Columbia Anthology,* p. 475.

13. Gan Bao, *Sou shen ji* [In search of deities] (Taipei: Hongshi chubanshe, 1982), ch. 7 (nos. 187 and 93); see also ch. 6 (nos. 115, 130, and 145) on sexual ambiguity and transformation.

14. Cf. Waley, in Mair, ed., *Columbia Anthology,* p. 475.

15. Yang Mu, "Lun yizhong yingxiong zhuyi" in *Wenxue zhishi* [Literary knowledge] (Taipei: Hongfan shuju, 1979), p. 212.

16. Ibid., pp. 217–8.

17. Cf. Waley, in Mair, ed., *Columbia Anthology,* p. 475.

18. Ibid., p.476.

19. Wei Yuanfu in *Quan Tang shi* [Complete Tang poetry], comps. Peng Dingqiu (1645–1719) et al., 25 vols. (Beijing: Zhonghua shuju, 1960): ch. 272, p. 3055.

20. Yuan Xingpei, *Baiwange weishenmo: Zhongguo wenxue* [Millions of why: Chinese literature] (Taipei: Xiapu chubanshe, 1994), p. 101.

21. *Zhongguo lidai mingren shengji dacidian,* pp. 143–4.

22. *Shangqiu xian zhi* [Gazetteer of Shangqiu county] (Henan Province, Huabei region, no. 98) in *Zhongguo fangzhi congshu,* comp. Liu Dechang, lithographed in 1932 (Repr. Taipei: Chengwen chubanshe, 1968).

23. *Bozhou zhi* [The gazetteers of Bozhou], comp. Ren Shoushi in 1825, ch. 33, p. 38 rec.

24. *Gujin tushu jicheng* [Synthesis of books and illustrations of ancient and modern times], comps. Chen Menglei (1651– ca. 1723) et al. (1725; repr. Beijing: Zhonghua shuju, 1934), ch. 341, p. 61.

25. *Bozhou zhi,* ch. 33, p. 38 rec.

26. See Zhou Zhongming's Preface to Xu Wei's *Si sheng yuan* [The four shrieks of the monkey] (Shanghai: Shanghai guji chubanshe, 1984), pp. 1–2.

27. See Cao Zhengwen, *Zhongguo xia wenhua shi* [The history of the Chinese knight-errant] (Taipei: Yunlong chubanshe, 1997), p. 2.

28. Han Fei, "Wu du," section 49, in *Han Fei zi xuan,* ed. Wang Huanbiao (Shanghai renmin chubanshe, 1974), p. 10; the translation is from Burton Watson, *Basic Writings of Mo Tzu, Hsün Tzu, and Han Fei Tzu* (New York: Columbia University Press, 1967), p. 105.

29. Ibid., p.19; translation from Watson, p. 117.

30. Ibid., p.10; translation from Watson, p. 105.

31. Ibid., p.119; the translation is my own.

32. James J. Y. Liu, *The Chinese Knight-Errant* (Chicago: University of Chicago Press, 1967), pp. 1–2.

33. Ibid., pp. 4–6.

34. Cao Zhengwen, *Zhongguo xia wenhua shi* [The history of the Chinese knight-errant] (Taipei: Yunlong chubanshe, 1997), pp. 16–8.

35. Sima Qian, p. 3181; the translation is mine.

36. See Zhao Ye, *Xinyi Wu-Yue chunqiu* [Spring and autumn annals of the king-doms of Wu and Yue], annotated by Huang Rensheng (Taipei: Sanmin shuju, 1996), pp. 305–6. This synopsis is from James J. Y. Liu's *The Chinese Knight-Errant,* pp. 85–6.

37. *Taiping guangji* [Extensive gleanings of the reign of Great Tranquillity], comps. Li Fang (925–96) et al., 3 vols. (1755; reprint, Taipei: Xinxing shuju, 1973), chs. 193–6, pp. 751–65.

38. Joseph S. M. Lau, "Tangren xiaoshuo zhong de aiqing yu youqing" [Love and friendship in Tang fiction], *Youshi wenyi* 39.3 (March 1974): 3.

39. *Taiping guangji,* ch. 194, pp. 755–8.

40. Pu Songling (1640–1715), *Liaozhai zhiyi* [Strange stories from the Leisure Studio] (1886; reprint, Beijing: Zhongguo shudian, 1981), ch. 2, pp. 13–5.

41. The three chapters are ch. 22, "The Basic Annals of Huizong"; ch. 351, "Biography of Hou Meng"; ch. 351, "The Biography of Zhang Shuye." See Miao Tianhua, "*Shuihu zhuan* kaozheng" in *Shuihu zhuan* [Water margin, or all men are brothers], by Shi Nai'an and Luo Guanzhong (Taipei: Sanmin shuju, 1981), p. 1.

42. C. T. Hsia, *The Classic Chinese Novel* (New York: Columbia University Press, 1968), p. 86.

43. Hsia, p. 88.

44. Sun Shuyu, *Shuihu zhuan de laili xintai yu yishu* [The origin, psychology, and art of *Shuihu zhuan*] (Taipei: Shibao chubanshe, 1983), p. 11.

45. Hsia, p. 85.

46. *All Men Are Brothers (Shuihu zhuan),* trans. Pearl S. Buck (New York: John Day, 1968), pp. 863–4.

47. Sun Shuyu, p.11.

48. Buck, p. 867.

49. *Heqin* was a foreign policy that used political marriages to cement friendly relations with foreigners. Adopted first during the Han Dynasty (206 B.C.E. - 220 C.E.), it sent Han princesses or imperial concubines as brides to the Xiongnu king so that Han emperors would become the fathers-in-law of the nomadic kings. See Ning Chia paper in this collection for a detailed discussion of the *heqin* policy.

50. *Yangjiafu shidai zhongyong yanyi zhizhuan* [The heroic lives of Yang family generals], in *Guben xiaoshuo jicheng,* ed. Qinhuai moke (Shanghai: Shanghai guji chubanshe, 1990), vol. 539.

51. See Yuan Shishuo's Preface to *Yangjiafu shidai zhong yanyi zhizhuan,* pp. 1–2.

52. Pu, ch. 2, pp. 13–5.

53. From the prologue, we may assume that this romance originally had fifty-three chapters, but only forty have survived.

54. James J.Y. Liu, p. 129.

55. Ibid., p.125.

56. Ibid.

CHAPTER FOUR

WRITING VIRTUES WITH THEIR BODIES: REREADING THE TWO TANG HISTORIES' BIOGRAPHIES OF WOMEN

Sherry J. Mou
Wellesley College

> *The four paradigms—filial daughter, loyal wife, chaste widow, and sagacious mother—found in these biographies can be read as improvisational reactions to a tradition that both marginalized and prioritized women's sufferings.*

Introduction: The Tradition of the Biographies of Women

The tradition of the "biographies of women" in Chinese history goes back more than two thousand years. During the first century B.C.E., Liu Xiang (77–6 B.C.E.), a Confucian historian, collected 104 tales of distinguished women from antiquity to just before his own time and compiled the first *Biographies of Women*, or *Lie[a] nü zhuan*.[1] One of the most direct results of this collection was the addition of a section called "biographies of women" to dynastic histories. In the third official history, *History of the Later Han Dynasty (Hou Han shu)*, Fan Ye (398–445) included seventeen women in the biographies *(zhuan)* section and entitled it "Women" ("lie[a] nü").[2] This precedent set an example for later historians and endowed the practice with formal legitimacy; the "Biographies of Women" section (hereafter BoW) became a more or less regular feature in official histories.[3]

But the influence of Liu Xiang's *The Biographies of Women* goes beyond the accidental establishment of a new historical genre. Its inadvertently chosen title "Women" ("Lie^a nü") more than prepared readers for further focus on virtues, because the most common homophone of *lie^a* *(lie^b)* would eventually lead to a very different meaning. With a fire radical (four dots) added to *lie^a*, *lie^b* means "fierce fire" *(huo meng ye)* and is interchangeable with *lie^a*, according to *Explicating the Written Characters (Shuowen jiezi)*, the first comprehensive lexicon of the Chinese characters.[4] Thus, almost all phrases with *lie^b* in it have the meaning of staunch, vehement, and fierce, such as a blazing fire *(lie^b huo)*, the scorching sun *(lie^b ri)*, and martyrs *(lie^b shi)*. With women, *lie^b nü* originally means "a righteous woman with integrity and principles." Sima Qian (145-ca. 86 B.C.E.) used the term to describe Nie Rong, the sister of the famous assassin Nie Zheng; for, against the odds of being executed for revealing her relationship with the assassin, she claimed his dead body so that he would not go down in history anonymously.[5] In later times, however, "integrity and principles" came down to chastity. From Liu Xiang's *The Biographies of Women* to Fan Ye's BoW, the transformation already started. While *The Biographies of Women* has one chapter on the "pernicious and depraved" women,[6] all seventeen women in Fan Ye's BoW are what Natalie Zemon Davis called "women worthies,"[7] exemplars of women.[8] In later official histories, while the original *lie^a* in the title for the BoW section is maintained, the content shifted to that of *lie^b:* the "biographies of various women" *(Lie^a nü zhuan)* eventually became "biographies of chaste women" *(Lie^b nü zhuan)*. The gender-defined section is further confined to virtuous women, and the focus in these biographies, therefore, is not the women themselves, but their virtues. Thus, although these biographies are descriptive literature, their prescriptive intention of setting examples for posterity to emulate is built into the genre of history.

This paper examines a segment of this tradition of women's biographies: the BoW sections in the two official histories of the Tang Dynasty (618–907), written just before the neo-Confucianists of the Song Dynasty (960–1279) focused more rigidly on morality, making chastity a definitive virtue for women. Compiled by two groups of historians about a century apart, the *New History of the Tang Dynasty* (*Xin Tang Shu,* hereafter *XTS*)[9] was a conscious endeavor to improve *The Old History of the Tang Dynasty* (*Jiu Tang Shu,* hereafter *JTS*).[10] Which one is superior has been a popular topic for discussion in Chinese historiography for centuries.[11] The general consensus, as Wang Gungwu summarized in his study of the official histories, is that the *XTS* provides "better introductions" to Tang history and the *JTS* "better collections of authentic documents."[12] In a way, the two sets of biographies of women agree. Many biographies in the *JTS* are shortened in the *XTS,* but the *XTS* also includes some twenty-three new biographies. What is lost in bulk seems compensated for by the number of entries.

However, rather than comparing the two sets of biographies, this paper focuses on the presentation of these biographies. Several questions are particularly of core interest to the discussion. What are the ideals of womanhood these biographies present? How are they presented? Do these women have a voice (or voices) in these accounts? If so, how is it expressed? The discussion is divided into three parts. The first examines the two Introductions and one Eulogy (*XTS* does not have a eulogy), in which the historians present their view on womanhood and declare their standards for inclusion. Part two, the bulk of the paper, is a close reading of the biographies; I will discuss women in these biographies in terms of four distinctive paradigms: (1) filial daughter; (2) dutiful wife; (3) devoted widow; and (4) exemplary mother. This will be an examination of the characteristics, deeds, and implications in terms of behaviors each paradigm presents. Attention will also be given to the historians' interpretations of the events as well as the significance of their appropriation. The last part seeks to reinterpret these biographies, especially in terms of the layers of inconsistencies presented through the texts.

The Paradigms: Chinese Womanhood
of the Tang Dynasty (618–906)

The Rhetoric—Introductions and the Eulogy

Each BoW has an introduction *(xu)*, but only the *JTS* includes a eulogy *(zan)*. Together, these pieces reveal what the historians regarded as womanly virtues. They show in concrete terms the ideals of Chinese womanhood; in other words, what is expected of women. At the same time, they prescribe how women should behave.

> Possessing the innate quality of gentleness that is attributed to the realm of *yin,* women should abide by the principle of obeying other people. During former dynasties, writings about chaste wives and staunch women who sacrificed themselves for chastity specially elaborated on their ability to protect themselves with propriety. Once they became captives in courts of bandits, they would not let themselves be defiled by unrighteousness. They were heroic even under the edge of a bright knife, and they upheld themselves with an oath from the bottom of their hearts. They did not care if their bodies were crushed to pieces, and they deemed death as a homecoming. Even a strong man [under such conditions] might not be able to sustain his moral fortitude. Is it not virtuous to find such integrity in a beautiful girl?

Further, the wife of Liang Hong[13] followed him to a hermitage without
a word, and Gong Jiang[14] made an oath not to set foot in a second household. The way of married women and the exemplar of mothers can illumi-
nate both paintings and history. This indeed is the merit of these women.
Toward the end of the dynasty, general morality was indecent; thus virtuous
behavior was rare. We thereby symbolically touched upon respectful people
to offer them to women. We pray that the profession of writing about
women's lives would hopefully not be neglected.[15] (Introduction to the
BoW in *JTS*.)

The first sentence marks a perimeter of women's social position and reveals the philosophical foundation for womanhood. At the foundation of
the statement is the yin-yang theory that crystalized Chinese gender-rela-
tion ideals: "Yang is dominating and yin is submissive" *(Yang zun yin bei)*,
declared the Han Confucian scholar Dong Zhongshu's (ca. 179–104
B.C.E.) *Luxuriant Dew from the Spring and Autumn Annals (Chunqiu fan lu)*.[16]
Theoretically, yin and yang (literally shade and sunlight) are two phases of
a thing (such as a sun, whose light creates the two phases of shade and sunlight). No value judgment was attached to them. Gender attributes (men
as yang and women as yin) were gradually derived from this binary concept through an evolving development of cosmological (the sky is yang
and the earth is yin) and ethical (virtue is yang and punishment is yin) as-
sociations, as Sufen Lai demonstrates in her discussion of Chinese gender
politics, "Father in Heaven, Mother in Hell," in this book.[17]

Based on the "yang is dominating and yin is submissive" dichotomy,
once women are put into the position of yin, the rest of the sentence seems
fitting: gentleness is considered an innate quality of women,[18] and this innate gentleness ordains that women obey other people. We will get back
to who the "other people" might be shortly. But, in a not too subtle way,
the rest of the passage inherently requires women to contradict this gentle
submissiveness promoted in the beginning sentences by redefining a Confucian phrase for women: *shi shen,* literally "lost [one's] body" (translated as
"became captives" here). In *Mencius,* the term is used symbolically to mean
losing one's moral character.[19] However, for a woman, it is applied literally:
when a woman's body is where it does not belong, she has "lost [her]
body" irretrievably; hence the meaning of a woman being sexually violated
is derived from "lost [her] body." Sexuality becomes a synecdoche of the
definition of a woman. Consequently, when a woman's chastity is in danger, gentleness and obedience are not the correct principles of behavior.
She must defend her chastity with no regard for her physical safety and
"deem death as a homecoming" *(shi si ru gui).* This almost necessarily

means that, for a woman to "sustain her moral fortitude" *(shou jie),* she should either kill herself or die when facing the danger of sexual violation.

Ironically, while reducing womanhood to sexuality, this overzealous demand that a woman defend her own sexuality to the death opens up some space, however narrow, for her to exercise her limited will. Some biographies show that, in the name of chastity, women would defy their male relatives, be it fathers, husbands, or brothers. Similarly, this prioritizing of women's sexuality also gives them a license to disobey, casting a direct challenge to the phrase "women should abide by the principle of obeying other people" *(cong ren zhi yi)*.[20] In a sense, women assume their subjectivity in defending their chastity.

The second paragraph promotes active passivity in a positive light. The two examples (the wife of Liang Hong and Gong Jiang) depict the image of a submissive wife who abides by her husband's will with wholehearted devotion: she quietly complies when he is alive and formidably maintains widowhood after he dies. Although motherhood is implied in the phrase "the way of married women and the exemplar of mothers" *(fudao muyi),* the focus of the Introduction is clearly on women's sexuality (void of any implication of motherhood) and wifely duties.

Short and to the point, the Eulogy divides virtues along gender lines:

> To eulogize: When politics and education are prosperous and stable, men are loyal [*zhong*] and women are chaste [*zhen*]. [They apply] the code of propriety [*li*] to protect themselves, and, in preference to righteousness [*yi*], they will not continue living abjectly. The [women historians'] red brush is lustrous, the orchid boudoirs are resonant with fame. Only when "Guan ju" and the *Ya* section [of *The Book of Poetry*] correspond with each other can there be the characterization of the virtuous influences.[21] (Eulogy to the BoW in *JTS*.)

Although *zhong* and *zhen* both denote devotion, since the focus is on sexuality in the Introduction, we almost have to define the two words in the narrower sense: *zhong* means loyalty, devotion to the state, and *zhen* means chastity, devotion to one's husband. Thus, a division of virtues along gender lines is suggested, in which "loyalty to the state" *(zhong)* is assumed to be the responsibility of men and maintaining "sexual chastity" *(zhen)* to be the responsibility of women. Furthermore, two important Confucian virtues, propriety *(li)* and righteousness *(yi),* are redefined for women. The Confucian notion of *li* has two dimensions: the internal (often translated as propriety or decorum) and the external (mostly associated with rites). Confucius sees it as a person's behavioral code,[22] guiding interactions with others. The concept of *yi* as defined by Mencius is one of the four germs of human nature; with *yi*, a person knows what shame is and will act accordingly to avoid it.[23] For women, the Introduction implies, the sense of shame has much to do with where their presence is. If they are where they should not be, death becomes the natural path for them to take. Thus, as behavioral codes, *li* and *yi* serve women mainly as indications of when to renounce their lives.

Most importantly, the appeal to the poem "Guan ju" and the *ya* section of the *Shi jing* [The book of poetry] underlines the importance of the role of family. As the first poem in the *Shi jing*, "Guan ju" was conventionally interpreted as the celebration of the institution of marriage. The *ya* section refers to the odes sung at royal banquets and other state occasions. The emphasis on the close relation between the two, therefore, underscores the fundamental role family plays in the welfare of the state. Together, the Introduction and the Eulogy set the perimeter of women's space within the family, the most fundamental unit of Chinese society: they are to be submissive and gentle except when it is a matter of guarding their own sexuality.

In comparison, the Introduction for *XTS*'s BoW has a clearer sense of women's social roles, and the language is more straightforward:

> Women's behaviors are such that to their parents they should pay filiality; as married women[24] they should maintain integrity, and as mothers they should be with righteousness and kindness; that is all they have to do.
>
> Before the medieval time, the Book [of documents] recorded the actions of empresses, royal consorts, and duchesses for all under heaven to emulate. Later, the position of women historians was slighted and the teaching and regulations of women could no longer reach families. As a result, for a thousand years or so, capable women worthy of being recorded were very few. After the rise of the Tang Dynasty, it forged the culture and customs for a few hundred years. Many young women from well-known families and famous clans would abide by propriety on the verge of great calamities. Even a bright knife could not move their will. They thus contested for immortal fame with sages and martyrs. Such virtues, pure as snow and frost, were indeed precious.
>
> Now we collect those whose actions were particularly distinguished, to compile them into chapters and to trace the virtues and the felicity of fathers behaving as fathers, sons behaving as sons, husbands behaving as husbands, and wives behaving as wives.[25]

From the beginning, women are assigned distinctive familial roles: they are daughters, wives, and mothers, and they are expected to behave as such.

That a person is never an individual free of social relations and obligations is not a principle gender specific to women; after all, men are also identified as sons, husbands, and fathers. But for women, their familial roles are their social roles as well, for these roles are "all they have to do" *(zhi yi)*. On the other hand, men's social roles are what define them, and they are often identified by their social roles, such as scholars, merchants, officials, or artisans, rather than by their familial roles.

The Introduction then measures the Tang Dynasty's virtuous women against earlier women, betraying a preoccupation of its time—the concern with the powerful clans *(shi zu)*[26] that formed a social class of their own. For unlike the premedieval time, when the women to be emulated were empresses, royal consorts, and duchesses, the Tang period produced "young women from well-known families and famous clans," who would sustain their will under "bright knives." In other words, they would rather be killed than violated. As the *JTS* historians demonstrated in the Eulogy, propriety *(lijie,* a derivative of *li)* is narrowed down to mean sexual chastity for women. However, we should note that sexuality is in relation to propriety, not to husbands, because the term "young women" *(yaotiao shunü)* is modified by "well-known families and famous clans" *(wenjia lingxing),* which means basically the daughters of these families. In contrast to the *JTS* Introduction's focus on the role of the wife, the *XTS* Introduction focuses primarily on young daughters' chastity.

On a rhetorical level, the Introductions and Eulogy foretell both the major concerns and the conflicts of the biographies. Both Introductions concentrate on chastity, but treat it primarily in relation to propriety *(li),* rather than to one's husband. In terms of social roles, "married women" *(fu)* and young daughters are the main subject, underlining the importance of family in the Confucian tradition. What becomes problematic is that this prioritized position of family is appropriated by a male essentialist point of view, in which family is a constant. For a woman, the meaning of "family" expands upon marriage, as do her responsibilities; conflicts result from the fusion of two sets of responsibilities. Many biographies show how such conflicts are forced upon women and how they accommodate them.

Finally, let us consider an important point that, although beyond the scope of the current discussion, is relevant to our understanding of the materials: the historians' own moral sense. Since historians were products of their own times, with their own moral priorities, their value judgments often show traces of their own times. Considering the more rigid focus on morality of the dynasties in power when the *XTS* was compiled, especially the Song, the seeming preoccupation with women's chastity and the constrictions put into the rhetoric of the Introductions and the Eulogy should

be read as a reflection of the morality of the historians' own times as well
as that of the Tang Dynasty.

The Examples—the Biographies

A comparison of the correspondence, addition, and elimination of biographies between the two BoWs is found in Appendix I. For the current study, a biography that appears in both is considered as one case, and
fifty-three cases altogether are collected in the two BoWs. The *JTS* collected twenty-six biographies, and four more are attached to other biographies (2, 15, 19, and 26),[27] making a total of thirty cases. Three
biographies (*JTS* 4, 16, and 25) are omitted from the *JTS,* and twenty-
three new ones are added, making a total of forty-seven biographies covering fifty cases (*XTS* 26 has one attached case, and *XTS* 30 has two) in
the *XTS*. The number of biographies in *XTS* increased almost by forty
percent from the *JTS*.

Although the Introduction of *XTS*'s BoW listed three roles for
women—daughters, married women, and mothers—the biographies show
that married women are further categorized into wives and widows, each
with somewhat different responsibilities. Furthermore, although the Introduction specifically associated daughters with filiality, wives and widows
with chastity, and mothers with righteousness and kindness, the biographies show that each role indeed displays more than the one assigned
virtue (two assigned virtues in the case of a mother). More specifically, filiality, loyalty, and chastity are the three most distinguished virtues in all
three roles, with the exception of the mother figures, whose dominant
traits are maternal love *(ci)* and sagacity, a seasoned wisdom. A closer reading of the biographies also indicates that for daughters filiality is the primary virtue, for wives loyalty, for widows chastity, and for mothers sagacity.
Thus, my discussion of the biographies will proceed by following these
four paradigms: (1) filial daughter; (2) dutiful wife; (3) devoted widow; and
4) exemplary mother. Appendix II shows the paradigms, virtues, and expressions found in the two BoWs.

Most women in these biographies, as in real life, collapse two or three
roles together at various points in their lives. A wife does not stop being a
daughter until her parents die, nor does a mother cease being a wife unless her husband dies. Some biographies show that the duties of filiality
may even call from the world beyond and demand that a daughter avenge
her father's murder. As a result, virtues valued in one role may contradict
those valued in another. Since not all such contradictions can be resolved,
how did women deal with them? More importantly, how did the histori-

ans assess these contradictions? These questions will also be examined in the following discussion.

Filial Daughter

Almost all Confucian Classics address filiality in one way or another,[28] but more emphatically, in the opening chapter of the *Xiao jing* [The classic of filiality], filiality is defined as "the root of all virtues and the birthplace of all other teaching" *(fu xiao de zhi ben ye jiao zhi suo you sheng ye).*[29] The filial daughter paradigm supports this statement. Eighteen out of the fifty-three cases feature filiality as their main theme. Whether they are married or not, women in these biographies place the welfare of their parents ahead of all other concerns. The expressions of filiality include caring for and serving parents while they are alive, observing mourning rituals after they die, avenging their murders when necessary, and guarding chastity in the name of the family. In all these actions, gender is not a central concern, if it is a concern at all, and other social functions are often sacrificed. Some married daughters leave their husbands and children and go back to their natal families to care for their parents. Yet with few exceptions, such cases, which often seem to breach the code of propriety as prescribed in the *Li ji,* meet official recognition or even imperial recognition.

With the exception of revenge, the case of Xiahou Suijin (9/9) shows all the expressions of filiality possible for a daughter:

> Liu Ji's wife [from the family of the] Xiahou was from Zuocheng of the Huazhou, and her courtesy name was Suijin. Her father Changyun was the Aide *(cheng)*[30] [to the magistrate] of Yancheng. He went blind after she was married with two daughters. She requested a divorce from her husband and returned to take care of her sick father. And she also became renowned in her filiality in serving her stepmother. After five years her father died.[31] She was so devastated that she could hardly sustain herself. She let her hair down, walked barefoot, carried dirt to build the tomb, constructed a hut next to the tomb, and lived there with only one meal a day for three years.
>
> An imperial edict was issued to award her twenty pieces of cloth and ten *dan*[32] of grain, and to decorate the door of her family with insignia. Later, when her daughters mourned her death, they followed their mother's example. The officials again awarded them grain and silk, and had their door decorated with insignia.[33]

Much of what Xiahou Suijin performed after her father's demise were mourning rituals prescribed in *Li ji.*[34] Several other cases share the same details, phrased slightly differently with regard to mourning rituals. For example, seven out of the nine biographies[35] with mourning ceremonies feature daughters who performed *lumu,* the ritual of building a hut next to the tomb and living there for years. Five of them planted pine and cypress tress at the graveyard.[36]

Three other women went to frontiers to bring back their fathers' and other relatives' bodies (11/12, 26/35, and 26a/40) before they built huts next to the tombs and lived there for a long while. The highly repetitive descriptions of mourning rituals illustrate a close observance of prescriptions in the *Li ji.* Either these women indeed internalized these values from the *Li ji* and acted on them accordingly, or the historians just edited in such details in accordance with the prescriptions in the *Li ji.* Ironically, the very passage in which *lumu* is defined in the *Li ji* also indicates that married women should not have to live in the hut *(furen bu ju lu).*[37] Although one may read these daughters' performance of duties usually expected of sons as subversive because they insisted on making their own contribution and gaining recognition within the clan, what finally gives these women's sacrifices value is imperial recognition. All three cases end with the emperors sending edicts to honor the family with an arch or at least with imperial insignia to decorate their doors, amounting to imperial encouragement of actions against both common sense and the classical prescriptions for propriety.

Three new cases introduced in the *XTS* (17, 32, and 24) include details of mourning rituals that far exceed normalcy. One eight-year-old girl (*XTS* 17) set her father's coffin up in the hall and paid respect to it twice every day for ten years. When she was fifteen[38] and her mother wanted to arrange a marriage for her, she cut her hair off in protest and pleaded to be allowed to serve her mother until the end of her life. When her mother died, she mourned most pitifully and prepared funeral items all by herself. Afterwards, she built a hut next to the tomb, let her hair down, carried dirt barefoot to finish the tomb, and planted several hundred pine trees. Her actions were reported to the emperor, who in turn sent down an edict to erect an honorific arch in front of the family's door to commemorate her action. This short account indicates that the whole purpose of Ms. Li's life was to be a filial daughter. The extensive mourning period contradicts the rules of propriety prescribed in the *Li ji,* which specify that a mourning period should not exceed three years.[39] Yet, like the heroines' actions in the *lumu* cases discussed above, in the following passage Li Miaofa's actions were met with imperial commendation.

The case of Li Miaofa (*XTS* 32) reads like a reflection of her confused and unsteady times, when the An Lushan Rebellion (755–63) forced the emperor to leave the capital and shook the foundation of the dynasty. Relocated by the turmoil of the rebellion, Li was married and had children when she heard that her father passed away.

She wanted to take the fastest way to go back for the funeral, but her son would not let her go. So she cut off one breast and left. When she arrived home, her father was already buried. She cried deplorably and pleaded to open her father's grave to look at him, but the clansmen would not allow it. She grabbed a knife and stabbed her chest, so they complied. Upon seeing the coffin, she licked the dust off it and cleaned it with her hair. Afterwards, she built a hut on the left side of the tomb and planted many pine and cypress trees, which attracted many extraordinary birds. Later, her mother was ill and often could not eat. Miaofa would also not even look at a knife and chopsticks. After her mother died, she wrote with her own blood on her mother's arm before she was buried. She then lived in a hut next to the tomb for the rest of her life.[40]

This account, with its eerie details told in a matter-of-fact fashion, blurs the boundary between fiction and history. Li's gruesome actions, such as cutting off her breast and licking the dust off the coffin lid, defy common sense, for they have no obvious purpose and serve no practical function except expressing a nearly deranged mind. Much as with hagiographical accounts, readers are supposed to suspend their disbelief. We are to look only at the daughter's filial intent. Similarly, in *XTS* 24 the suicide of the fourteen-year-old Rao E seems pointless: starving herself to death in lament cannot bring her drowned father back to life. More importantly, such excessive display of sadness in the name of filiality is clearly discouraged in the Classics.[41]

One case that seems reasonable and appropriate, however, is omitted in the *XTS,* possibly because of the Buddhist influence it displayed. The Daoist nun Li Xuanzhen (*JTS* 25) was a direct descendant of Emperor Taizong (reigned 627–49).[42] Because her great-great grandfather was exiled to the far South, the family was there for five generations. Xuanzhen appealed to the throne to let her bring four coffins back to the capital for burial in the imperial cemetery and to enter their spirits into the ancestral temple.[43] Her appeal was granted, and her filiality was specially noted in the edict.

Since mourning and funeral rituals were an important part of ancestor worship, in which married daughters' presence was limited, the emphasis on such rituals in these biographies amounts to these women's reassertion of their position in the clan. Whatever the practice in reality, the rhetoric expressed in these biographies shows a bond between women and their natal families, one strong enough to compel many of them to sever their marital ties. This strong sentiment of filiality is further affirmed by two other types of expression: a conscious choice of death over life for the sake of the father and blood revenge for the murder of one's father.

According to Ch'ü T'ung-tsu, although blood revenge was never allowed by law, it was condoned by *li* (propriety), for familial sentiment fully
justified it.[44] Three daughters (6/7, 7/13, and *XTS* 36) schemed for years
to avenge the murders of their fathers and husbands (*XTS* 36). The cases
of Wei Wuji (6/7) and Ms. Jia (7/13) demonstrate how both law and *li* are
consumed by the rhetoric of filiality. After years of scheming, both killed
the murderers of their fathers, both were exonerated, and one was even rewarded by the emperor.

Another revenge case comes from a Tang fantastic story *(chuanqi)*.[45] The
historians' decision to include this story as a real-life event brings the relationship between history and fiction yet another step closer. The plot, as
with many other fantasy stories, includes such elements as knights-errant,
dreams, and detective work *(gong'an)*. Interestingly, it is the protagonist's
role as a daughter that is underlined most in the BoW. Xie Xiao'e and her
husband, a young knight-errant, went to do business with her father just a
little over a year after they were married. Both men were killed by robbers, and Xiao'e fell into the river, hurt her head and leg, and was saved by
some people. She became determined to find the murderers and begged
her way around. She dreamed of her father and husband, who told her the
names of the two murderers in riddles,[46] which she later found someone
to solve for her. She dressed up as a man and learned the whereabouts of
the murderers from hired hands and servants. Then she got herself hired as
a servant in one of the murderers' households and confirmed their crime
when she found her father's and husband's clothes in the house. One day,
the two murderers were drunk; Xiao'e closed the windows, took out her
sword, and cut one murderer's head off. She cried out, and neighbors came
to her rescue, catching the other murderer and members of the gang. The
officials admired her staunchness and decided not to press charges. After
she returned home, many men proposed to her, but she rejected them all.
She cut her hair and followed the Buddhist path, wearing only coarse
clothes and eating unpolished rice for the rest of her life.

This intricate story tells how far the historians would go in promoting
filiality in married daughters. Whether history imitates literature or literature imitates history, what is important is the effect of the story and the
lessons it teaches. Regardless of the fantastic details that challenge credibil-
ity, the story is recorded as history to teach and promote filiality and
widow chastity.

In her discussion of the changing patterns of the biographies of
women, Jennifer Holmgren speculates that blood revenge, especially when
carried out by women, might have received particular official patronage in
periods that stressed martial values, such as times "of foreign conquest, po-

litical instability, or fragmentation of the empire."[47] While this speculation might have a valid foundation, these three cases do not seem related directly to the political situation. Although Xie Xiao'e's case (*XTS* 36) can be read as an indication of a disturbed time, with bandits robbing and killing the innocent, the other two cases are murders committed among acquaintances (6/7) and clan members (7/13), events that could have happened in any age. As Ch'ü T'ung-tsu concluded in his discussion of blood revenge, the sympathy and thoughts of the general populace were usually on the side of the avengers, and such attitudes reflect "a conflict between *li* [propriety] and the law."[48] More specifically, in almost all the cases quoted in Ch'ü and Holmgren, the daughters were avenging the death of at least one parent.[49] Thus, the appeal of the revenge theme in the two Tang BoWs lies in its capacity to evoke family values, especially filiality.[50]

Three other cases (2/2, 18/25, and *XTS* 29) can be read as variations on the filiality theme, for although loyalty and chastity are foregrounded in these biographies, the women clearly had the names of their natal families in mind. The best example is the case of Ms. Wang (2/2), whose powerful natal family rebelled against the Sui court and declared itself an independent state. Wang's husband Yang Qing was a royal scion of the Sui, and their marriage was a political move on the part of the Wangs to win Yang Qing's support. When Yang Qing wanted to shift his allegiance to another camp, Ms. Wang did not want to betray her natal family and asked to be sent back to them. Yang did not listen, so Ms. Wang killed herself by drinking poison. Similarly, the seven-year-old Gao Meimei (*XTS* 29) was put to death along with her mother and brother by her father's adversary. Pitying Meimei's tender age, her mother pleaded for clemency, but Meimei declined and expressed her desire to die with her family, who chose to be killed "as a result of their loyalty and righteousness" to the state (*wo jia yi zhongyi zhu*), instead of surrendering. In both cases, filial sentiment is expressed in the name of loyalty to one's family, and for Ms. Wang her natal family takes precedence over marriage.

The only case concerning chastity in this category drives home several points about women's sexuality. The teenage Dou sisters (18/25) valiantly threw themselves down a ravine to avoid being raped by bandits. Touched by their chastity and staunchness, the local metropolitan governor (*jingzhao*) reported the case to the throne, and the emperor decreed an honorific arch, insignia on the family door, perpetual exemption of the family from labor service, and an official funeral ceremony for the two girls. In this very unusual way the two women's sexuality is commodified into material value for their families. The case shows that a woman's sexuality is, as Catharine A. MacKinnon so forcefully put it, "that which is most one's own, yet most taken away."[51] Before marriage, a woman's sexuality is the property of her natal family. Any shame brought to it brings shame to the family name, and defending it with one's life adds honor to the family. The emperor's edict exemplifies in a very literal sense the commodification of women's sexuality. The influence of such official patronage of a damaging act would affect women immensely in later times. By the time of the Qing Dynasty (1644–1911), widow suicide to maintain chastity had become a cult. Some women were forced to perform it in public, so that the family left behind could benefit from the material awards an official bequeathed in honoring the chaste deed.[52]

Finally, in half of the biographies (nine out of eighteen) featuring filial daughters, the daughters are also wives and widows, indicating the possibility of tension between the women's two families. Their decisions to serve the interest of their parents were often made at the expense of their service to in-laws, husbands, children, and sometimes the marriages themselves. The emperors' and local officials' recognitions of their actions usually do not mention the daughters' other family roles—such as wife, mother, and daughter-in-law—at least in what is quoted in their biographies. Yet, their decisions could not be reached easily. Either such concerns never occurred to the historians or they were deemed unimportant by them. In the BoW Introductions, the Eulogy, and the biographies themselves, the historians' silence in addressing the real-life dilemmas these women faced indicates an inadequate appropriation of womanhood from a male essentialist perspective.

Dutiful Wife

The *JTS* Introduction uses the term "the way of [married] women" *(fudao)*, and the *XTS* Introduction mentions "the teaching of [married] women" *(fuxun)*, but neither details what the two words mean. Three works help us decode exactly what is the way of married women: *Li ji*, Liu Xiang's *Biographies of Women*, and Ban Zhao's "Admonitions for Women" ("Nü jie").[53] *Li ji* prescribes a code of behavior for people in general, covering all social values and familial roles. Liu Xiang's *Biographies of Women* was the first systematic attempt to address the issue of womanhood in Confucian tradition; as such, it did not yet have a gendered vocabulary, and most ideals were expressed in much the same way as for the self-discipline of a *junzi*, a Confucian gentleman. Building upon Liu Xiang's initiative toward a construction of womanhood and gleaning through other classics, especially those of the Han yin-yang theory, we can readily discern how Ban Zhao's "Admonitions for Women" comprises, in the words of Sunming Wong, "a necessary complement to the Confucian canons which had failed to give adequate and systematic instruction concerning feminine ethics."[54]

In the chapter "Regulations of the Interior" ("Nei ze") in *Li ji,* a wife's duty is discussed primarily in terms of her relationship to her parents-in-law.[55] In Liu Xiang's *Biographies of Women,* the concerns of wives start shifting from parents-in-law to husbands. Wives actively assist their husbands, taking initiatives in helping them make decisions outside of family issues. In a way, both works are concerned with a larger picture of the entire family, and, as such, women's roles are appropriated in terms of the welfare of the clan, not just of husbands.

It is in Ban Zhao's "Admonitions for Women" that the paradigm of a tacit wife single-mindedly devoted to her husband is clearly defined, and its definition is often cited by later Confucian moralists. What Dong Zhongshu and other Han Confucianists meted out in theory was that men are yang and women are yin, and their idea that "yang is dominating, and yin is submissive" was translated into a concrete manual of behavior in "Admonitions for Women." The seven chapter titles give a good idea of what is expected of a wife: "Humility," "Husband and Wife," "Respect and Caution," "Womanly Qualifications," "Wholehearted Devotion [to the husband]," "Implicit Obedience [to the parents-in-law]," and "Harmony with Younger Brothers- and Sisters-in-law."[56] Unlike the "Regulations of the Interior" in *Li ji,* in which the parents-in-law are the primary concern, "Admonitions for Women" discusses a wife's duty to her in-laws in terms of winning her husband's approval, shifting emphasis from parents-in-law to husbands. According to "Regulations of the Interior," if a son likes his wife very much, but his parents do not, he should divorce her.[57] However, in "Admonitions for Women," the advice is that "In order for a wife to gain the love of her husband, she must win for herself the love of her parents-in-law. To win for herself the love of her parents-in-law, she must secure for herself the good will of her younger brothers- and sisters-in-law."[58] Between these two works lies Liu Xiang's *Biographies of Women,* which embraces the paradigm of wife as a "learned instructress," to use Jennifer Holmgren's term.[59] The biographies in the two Tang BoWs on dutiful wives support the paradigms established in all three works.

Of the eighteen cases included in this section, only two (8/8 and *XTS* 46) foreground the duties of daughters-in-law to their parents-in-law. One wife (8/8) protected her mother-in-law from several dozen intruding robbers when the rest of the family ran away. As a result, she herself was flogged nearly to death by the robbers. In the other case (*XTS* 46), the parents-in-law were only in the background. The wife of Zhou Di willingly sacrificed her own life to sustain her parents-in-law in a war-infested world in which the food shortage was so severe that people were sold as food. She volunteered to be sold so that Zhou Di could help the rest of his family survive. The biography ends with his going back to the market-place only to find that his wife's head was already on the chopping board.

Without political crises, loyalty would not be an issue. Cases with loyal wives show times full of rebels and bandits, who affected people's lives directly. For men in official posts, their loyalty to their states is on trial; for women who cross paths with enemies, their loyalty to their husbands is on trial. This does not mean women do not shoulder responsibility to the state, but that their loyalty to the state was mediated through their husbands and became a part of their wifely duty. Three wives helped their husbands in rather unusual ways: two (15/30a and 15a/30b) led militias against nomadic invaders and saved their prefectures from captivity; the third (XTS 30), "the staunch wife of the Yang [clan]," scolded her husband, the prefect, for not setting an example by fighting to the death to guard his prefecture. Thus encouraged, her husband organized a militia and eventually repulsed the invading enemy, all with his wife's help.

Five other wives (21/33, 23/38, and XTS 21, 43, and 47) encouraged their husbands to make loyal choices at pivotal moments, and, with one exception, all gave up their own lives, some in gruesome ways. Li Tuan's wife (21/33) was captured by her husband's commander Wu Yuanji, whose rebellion sent Li Tuan, a loyalist, to surrender to a nearby loyalist commander. In revenge, Wu Yuanji tied Li Tuan's wife to a tree and sliced her flesh off as food. But until her death she kept calling for Li Tuan to serve well his new commander, who was loyal to the government. Similarly, Ms. Xiao (23/38) held on to her husband when the rebels were taking him away. She would not let go, and as a result the rebels cut off her arm and then killed her husband. She died that same night. The other three cases are variations of these two, focusing on the wives' loyalty to their husbands and through their husbands, their loyalty to the state.

In these wives' staunch display of loyalty, the issue of chastity is often dissolved, since their deaths preempt them as chaste wives. On the other hand, one loyalty case in the JTS is omitted in the XTS selection, most probably because of the issue of chastity. During the unstable beginning years of the Tang Dynasty, Ms. Wang (JTS 4) was forced to marry her captor; thereupon she took advantage of his drunkenness to cut off his head and bring it back to her prefecture, thus causing the invading troop to be dispersed. Emperor Gaozu (r. 618–26) not only awarded her with the title "Consort of Righteousness Upholding" ("Chongyi furen"), but also forgave her husband's crime in surrendering to the enemy. Ironically, her extraordinary courage and achievement did not pass the chastity judgment of the historian's brush; she was violated once again by the historians of the *XTS* when they eradicated her from history altogether.

Many wives take drastic measures to express their chastity or abstain from normal life. Two wives (1/1 and *XTS* 31) display great self-restraint while their husbands are in exile. Pei Shuying's (1/1) father successfully appealed to the emperor to grant her a divorce from her husband, who was to go into exile. When her father wanted to marry her a second time, she cut off her hair in protest. Her husband was pardoned and returned to the capital over ten years later, and they got back together after he divorced a second wife, whom he had wedded while in exile. Ms. Dong (*XTS* 31) displayed the same kind of steadfastness in maintaining her chastity. Before her husband went into exile in the South, he told her to remarry, since it was uncertain whether he would come back alive. Instead of replying, Ms. Dong took out some string, tied her hair, and sealed it with heavy silk. She then asked her husband to put his signet on it and told him that her hair would be untied only by his hands. When he returned from exile some twenty years later, the silk and his signet were the same as before. She removed the silk, and when she went to wash her hair, it all fell off.

Other wives take drastic measures such as mutilation or suicide or even incur death to guard their chastity. Ms. Lu (*XTS* 3), the wife of the famed minister Fang Xuanling, gouged out an eye to show her steadfast vow of widowhood after her husband (a nobody at the time) was critically ill and instructed her not to remain a widow after his death. Three other wives (20/27, *XTS* 41, and *XTS* 42), all young and beautiful, shared similar fates. They were all caught by enemies who tried to force sex upon them; not yielding, all resorted to death to maintain their chastity. After reprimanding their enemies relentlessly, two were killed gruesomely, one having her heart cut out by the bandits as food, while the third drowned herself after being kidnapped by pirates.

Whether one of these wives is serving in-laws or maintaining loyalty to the state or guarding her chastity, what is prized is her degendered role. Although daughters-in-law were expected to serve their parents-in-law in specific ways, the biographies that foreground this theme (8/8 and *XTS* 46) detail incidents not specific to daughters-in-law. In fact, physically guarding a mother-in-law's safety (8/8) and volunteering to be sold for food (*XTS* 46) to support the rest of the family might seem deeds more expected of sons than of daughters-in-law. Similarly, although in the *JTS* Eulogy the historians associate loyalty with men and chastity with women, the loyalty cases indicate that loyalty to the state is promoted in women as well. Furthermore, the methods women used for maintaining their chastity also demonstrate that degenderization is the ideal. If a woman's body is the site of her sexuality, mutilating a part of it literally reduces, if it does not destroy, her sexuality. When such a measure is not feasible, suicide is the next resort. Thus, ironically, what seems to be praise of "womanly" devotion in these biographies turns out to be praise of "manly" actions by which women transcend their gender.

Devoted Widow

As an extension of a dutiful wife, a devoted widow carries on all the same responsibilities in her widowhood, serving in-laws and remaining loyal to her husband. However, with the husband gone, the expressions of wifely devotion change. Nine out of the eleven cases center on either widow remarriage or sexual assault, making widow chastity the number one issue. In five biographies (10/11, 14/15, 19a/26a, and *XTS* 20 and 44), five widows facing imminent sexual assault or pressure to remarry resort to either self- or incurred mutilation to remain chaste. Ms. Shangguan (10/11) cut off her nose and ear when her brother and sister tried to talk her into remarrying.[60] Ms. Wei (14/15) cut off her own fingers when rebels tried to force her to play the zither; not complying, she eventually provoked them to kill her. Similarly, to avoid being raped by bandits Ms. Pei (19a/26a) berated them to no end and aroused their anger so much that they dismembered her. Although pretending to submit to some pirates' sexual demands, Yuying (*XTS* 20) took advantage of their momentary trust to drown herself, after scolding them for killing her husband. Not yielding to an enemy's demand for sex, Ms. Lu (*XTS* 44) died after one of her arms was cut off.

To a lesser degree, cutting off one's hair has the same implication as mutilation, a point detailed later. Symbolically, hair becomes the locus of sexuality. One widow (*XTS* 19) cut her hair off and neglected her appearance in order to discourage a romantic dream from recurring. When pressed by her brothers to marry her widowed brother-in-law, another (17/18) escaped from her natal family in the middle of the night through a latrine; she then cut off her hair and became a nun.

Others lived to shoulder responsibilities left by their husbands, taking care of in-laws and children. One widow (3/5) took care of her in-laws, and another (5/6) took care of her only son and killed herself when he died at eighteen. This second case is almost tailor-made to back up the fate of women as described in the Introduction to the *XTS*: "Women's behaviors are such that to their parents, they should be filial; as wives, they should be chaste; as mothers, they should be righteous and kind; that is all they have to do." In the biography, Xiangzi was a filial daughter, a devoted wife, and a benevolent mother. Married at fifteen and widowed soon after her son was born, Xiangzi resisted remarriage plans made by her brother and sister-in-law. Later, when both her mother and son died, she told her relatives, "My mother died, and so has my son. There is no reason for me to continue living."[61] She starved herself to death.

One widow (24/39) avenged her husband's wrongful death. Like the biography of Xie Xiao'e (*XTS* 36), this widow's case reads like fiction, with crime, suspense, and retribution all woven together:

> Heng Fanghou's wife was from the Cheng clan. During the Taihe years [827–35], Fanghou was the administrative supervisor *(lushi canjun)* of Yongzhou. [His superior] The Bandit-suppression Commissioner *(zhaotao shi)* Dong Changling's governing was not appropriate, and Fanghou argued with him several times. Changling was furious, so he wanted to arrest Fanghou and put him in jail. [Fanghou] excused himself for illness, but [Changling] would not allow it. So [Fanghou] had a death report sent to Dong, while lying in a coffin [to give some truth to the statement]. Knowing [Fanghou was faking death], Dong ordered the coffin nailed securely. Fanghou was shut in for a long time, so he scratched the coffin hard with bare hand and died after all his fingernails broke. [Fanghou's wife] Cheng was afraid that she would also be killed, so she dared not cry. Changling did not take the matter to heart and provided for substantial funeral arrangements.
>
> After the funeral, Cheng went to the capital on foot and reported to the right office of transmission *(you yintai)* her husband's wrongful death. She cut her ear off in front of the office and related her deep grievance. The censorate *(yushi tai)* investigated vigorously and found evidence [to support Cheng's accusation], and Changling was indicted. Emperor Wenzong [r. 827–40] conferred upon Cheng the title of "District Mistress of Wuchang" ("Wuchang xianjun") and awarded one of her sons the ninth rank of the regular official *(jiupin zhengyuan guan)*.[62]

What distinguishes Ms. Cheng's revenge and the revenge of the filial daughters is their display of determination through self-mutilation. Short of a blood tie, a wife emphatically demonstrates that there is one in essence with her own flesh and blood. Since her body is an indication of her determination, an irreversible mutilation demonstrates her ultimate resolution. As the site of both her sexuality and her will, the body offered a woman a space to write her own script, one that would be heeded and tended to.

To sum up, a devoted widow took care of parents-in-law and children, especially sons. If her husband died suspiciously, she avenged him. Most importantly, she remained chaste and defended her chastity with her own life if necessary. In cases where she fell into the hands of bandits or enemies, a suicide or incurred death was almost certain. Remarriage was out of the question, and this resulted in tension when the natal family of the widow tried to arrange a second marriage, usually for her sake. However, as shown in at least three biographies (5/6, 10/11, and 17/18), the pressure for widow chastity came mostly from an internalized moral value rather than from a social dictate. In each biography, the widow's elder brothers and sisters were the ones who tried to persuade her to remarry, and not only was remarriage permitted, it was condoned by law.[63] Several studies have shown that up until the period of the Yuan Dynasty (1271–1368) widow remarriage was practiced quite commonly among all social classes.[64] If these widows' lives seem unbearable, we can take consolation in the fact that their cases were not the norm and that they were recorded precisely because of that fact.

Exemplary Mother

The role of mothers is noted in both Introductions; the *JTS* Introduction uses the term "exemplars of mothers" *(mu yi)*, and the *XTS* says that mothers should be righteous and kind *(mu ye yi er ci)*. The word *exemplars (yi)* refers both to a person's appearance and behavior. With the call for righteousness and kindness, what is emphasized in this paradigm of the exemplary mother is her capacity to care for and to teach her children. This mother-instructress[65] image can be traced back directly to Liu Xiang's *Biographies of Women,* in which he elevated the role of mothers primarily by placing the biographies of exemplary mothers in the first chapter.[66] Further, for Liu Xiang, the magnitude of maternal instruction started from pregnancy and extended into the sons' adulthood,[67] including their marriages and, as Jennifer Holmgren appropriately put it, "matters external to the home and family,"[68] such as career-related decisions. Although this does not preclude expressions of motherly love in a general sense, it does indicate a cultural appropriation of motherhood that drew heavily upon Confucianism's emphasis on learning and moral cultivation. As a result, Chinese motherhood differs from most other cultures in its stress on teaching, not on maternal affection.

Images of the caring mother and the mother-instructress are both present in the biographies, as the phrase "righteous and kind" indicates. The former provides tender care, and the latter offers moral and practical guidance. However, a caring mother does not have to be a biological mother. In fact, in the two cases of caring mothers found here, the caregivers are not the biological mothers. This indicates, as John Carmi Parsons and Bonnie Wheeler maintain,

That literal, utterly and appropriately *essentialized* womanly status of "mother" does not necessarily apply to the practice of "mothering." . . . Maternity is a biological fact, rooted in the female body through birth, yoked to breast-nurture through infancy. But mothering is an activity. As an activity, mothering is culturally constructed, "grounded in specific historical and cultural practices." [69]

Thus, since the two cases of motherly care involve a nanny and a sister as *motherers,* it is more appropriate to discuss them in terms of loyalty and filiality.

The first case (2a/4) is about a nanny called Wang Lanying who selflessly cared for her three-year-old master Dugu Shiren during the war-infested last years of the Sui Dynasty. Shiren's father was executed for treason, and he was spared because of his tender age. To continue tending Shiren, Wang Lanying volunteered to have her head shaved and an iron clasp clapped to her head, penalties meted out to criminals. Since the wars had made many starving and homeless, Lanying begged for food and gave it all to Shiren, eating earth and drinking water herself. Her deeds touched even the first emperor of the Tang Dynasty, Emperor Gaozu, who awarded her handsomely and specially commended her benevolence and kindness *(ci hui)*. The other case (13/14) tells how Wang Azu, a young widow without child, took care of her sister for twenty years. When her sister died, she buried her with all the proper rites. It is possible to categorize this biography as a filial daughter case since Azu was serving her elder sister as if the sister were her mother. In reality, however, what Azu was offering to the elderly sister was material care. It is also interesting to note that although Azu did not remarry, the phrase "therefore could not bear to marry [again]" *(nai bu ren jia)* indicates that it was her prerogative, rather than an internalization of the ideal of widow chastity, that stopped her from remarrying.

Of the four cases in which the mothers show exceptional sagacity, only one biography (*XTS* 22)[70] clearly noted the mother's own education.[71] This means that the mother-instructress was not always learned herself and that book knowledge was not the core of her instruction. Rather, what is emphasized in the mother-instructress is her ability to provide moral guidance; for a properly laid sense of morality will later enable a child to embark on any other kind of cultivation of the self, whether bookish study or self-discipline.[72] Dong Changling's mother, Ms. Yang, epitomizes this widowed mother-instructress paradigm with both verbal and behavioral instruction. Widowed young, she raised Dong to become an administrator *(zhang shi)*. Later, she was held hostage by a rebel general. Yet she admonished Dong secretly not to be bothered by the thought of her being a hostage, maintaining that he should strive to be a loyal vassal of the state.[73] Sometimes, if sons strayed from moral behavior, such as being useful and loyal vassals of the state, mothers would sever their relationships with them, as did Li Yu's mother (*XTS* 16) and "the righteous wife of Jin" (*XTS* 28).

Without exception, all sagacious mothers are widows who discipline their sons in preparation for a distinguished career that will bring honor to the family. Safely degendered because of their widowhood and advanced age, and reasonably empowered because of cultural reverence to generation and to the notion of filiality, exemplary mothers generally do not have to resort to violent measures like mutilation in their confrontations with their children. In fact, widowhood in advanced age becomes a virtue in itself, involving at the same time stoicism, staunchness, resourcefulness, loyalty, and chastity. In this sense, these exemplary mothers are establishing what would gradually become a full-fledged foundation of Confucian motherhood: a widowed mother strictly disciplining her sons in preparation for a distinguished career that will bring honor to both the family and to herself.

Interpreting the Inconsistencies: The Undercurrents in the Biographies

To conclude, women in the two Tang BoWs are to be explained and defined with reference to their families.[74] Filial daughters avenged their fathers' deaths, took care of the surviving relatives, and observed mourning rituals. Loyal wives advanced their husbands' careers, attended to in-laws, and maintained marital faithfulness. Chaste widows took care of their children and in-laws, avenged their husbands' deaths, and most importantly guarded their sexuality. Exemplary mothers cared for the young and instructed them with both words and deeds. Thus, at least on the surface, these biographies present what the historians mapped out for women's lives in four stages that are not necessarily linear:

I. As a daughter:
    A. she is known for her filiality as a child;
    B. she avenges her father's death;
    C. when her honor is threatened, she commits suicide; and
    D. she remains filial to her parents even after her marriage, and will sever her marital relation to serve them or die of excessive sadness over their deaths.

II. As a wife:
   A. she serves her parents-in-law with great filiality and reverence;
   B. she urges her husband to be a loyal vassal to the state; and
   C. she guards her chastity with her own life.
III. As a widow:
   A. she takes care of surviving in-laws and children;
   B. she avenges her husband's death; and
   C. she commits suicide or mutilates herself when faced with sexual affronts or remarriage.
IV. As a widowed mother:
   A. she admonishes sons, from childhood into adulthood, to be loyal vassals and severs her relationship with them if they do not listen.

Problems resulted when the supposedly steady discourse of family became elusive, forcing women to make a choice between their natal and marital families and thus exposing the illusion of any specific family as a steady field of discourse for women. Since widowed mothers with grown-up sons are the only ones with a relatively anchored position in the discourse of family, the paradigm of exemplary mothers does not need enforcement. That is why in comparison to Liu Xiang's *The Biographies of Women,* in which motherhood is exalted above all other categories, the BoW sections do not prioritize motherhood; rather, the main focus is on the paradigms of daughters, wives, and widows. Their biographies provide scripts and provisions for women to deal with situations that lie ahead on their roads to Confucian motherhood, which in a sense was already instituted in the pantheon of Confucian sagehood.

From this point of view, we can see why the same virtues of filiality, loyalty, and chastity are extolled repeatedly in all three paradigms, with each emphasizing one of them: for a daughter, filiality is the most important paradigm; for a wife, loyalty; and for a widow, chastity. However, the ways these virtues are expressed vary. For a daughter, filiality is expressed much the same way as expected of a son, namely through observing mourning rituals, caring and providing for parents, and, when the situation requires it, avenging the wrongful death of a father. For a wife, loyalty to her husband and to the state is the crown virtue; however, her devotion to the state is mediated through her husband, which means that her loyal actions are usually carried out from the standpoint of a wife-assistant. Filiality is expanded to include serving in-laws, and sexual chastity is expressed in such determined manners as abstinence, mutilation, and suicide. But it is with a widow that chastity becomes the major issue of life; most resort to mutilation and death to counter sexual assaults or remarriage, and the meaning of their entire life seems condensed to the preservation of chastity. Finally, when the sexuality of a widowed mother with grown-up sons is no longer an issue, it is only through her sons' achievement that her capacity for wisdom will be acknowledged.

There are many ways we can read these biographies. First, we can read them as countercurrents that constantly challenge the flow of the mainstream, similar to what Gayatri Chakravorty Spivak termed the "Subaltern consciousness."[75] Women in these biographies, reaching out to us through the brushes of male historians, which have been dipped in the ink of Confucianism, present meanings through narrative inconsistencies, moral contradictions, and textual cracks. Take for instance the issue of obedience, a virtue several women were said to possess. Of the four cases in which the word *obedience* or *obedient (shun)* is used to describe the propensities or attitudes of the women (1/1, 5/6, 8/8, and 12/10),[76] two (1/1 and 5/6) show the women exactly the opposite in the biographies—both disobeyed their elder relatives in the name of chastity, for both would not be remarried by their well-intentioned relatives. These women's abiding by the code of chastity simultaneously displays and refutes the spirit of obedience. Without a narrative voice of their own, they reveal by their actions the inherent contradictions in the culturally imposed notions of chastity, obedience, and filiality. When Pei Shuying (1/1) was told by her husband upon separation that her father would probably marry her to someone else, she responded, "A husband is the sky. How can one turn her back to the sky? [I would] rather die with no other [thought]" *(fu tian ye ke bei hu yuan si wu ta).*[77] While the rhetoric on following one's husband is in line with what is expected of a wife, it also provides Pei Shuying with a license to disobey her father.

However, this is not to say that "husband as a wife's sky" was a constant discourse and irreducibly steady. For wives did turn their backs on their "sky" and return to their fathers in the name of filiality, as in the cases of Xiahou Suijin (9/9) and Li Miaofa (*XTS* 32). Similarly, women in many biographies maneuvered with limited choices in refusing to follow what was expected of them; they had to use the rhetoric of either filiality or chastity. Narrative inconsistencies resulting from the attribution of a specific virtue (obedience) to someone whose behavior steadfastly runs counter to that very virtue show the inherent moral contradictions that eluded the historians' own comprehension. That women could upon different occasions claim the urgency of one virtue—be it filiality, chastity, or wifely devotion—at the expense of other virtues also shows the tension resulting from moral contradictions among these virtues.

Some biographies also reveal textual cracks that invite different readings. For example, many biographies list "wife" as women's primary identification, but the biographies warrant no place for their husbands except in the beginning to identify the woman, such as in "Yu Minzhi's Wife, née Zhang" (12/10) and "Lu Fu's wife, née Li" (19/26). Such designation of identities creates a paradox that simultaneously belittles and inflates the role of a husband. On the one hand, without any action, a man enters history by virtue of being someone's husband; on the other hand, wifely devotion is trivialized and overshadowed by other relations in a woman's life.

Another way to read the implication of these biographies is through the interpretation of one recurring theme: bodily mutilation.[78] Compared to the BoWs in early official histories, the two Tang BoWs present a surge of mutilation cases. While only four cases of bodily mutilation are found in the eighty-four biographies from all previous official histories,[79] twelve of the fifty-three cases in the two Tang BoWs include self- or incurred mutilation.[80] If we include three cases that contain details of mutilating enemies and eight that entail hair-cutting, the percentage is even higher. With the exception of the exemplary mother, bodily mutilation is a recurring theme in all the paradigms. And of the twenty-three mutilation cases, including hair-cutting,[81] eleven are for chastity, eight for filiality, and four for loyalty. Three of the four loyalty cases also border on chastity, since mutilation was performed by wives who were grieving or avenging their husbands.[82] Thus, to a great degree, bodily mutilation should be discussed in terms of filiality and chastity.

But, as the title of Qiu Zhonglin's essay points out, mutilating one's body in the name of filiality constitutes a paradox: unfilial filiality *(bu xiao zhi xiao)*. According to the first chapter of *Xiao jing* [The classic of filiality], our "flesh, hair, and skin are given by [our] parents and therefore [we] dare not damage them. This is the beginning of filiality" *(shenti fa fu shou zhi fumu bugan huishang xiao zhi shi ye).*[83] Thus, according to *Xiao jing,* people should do everything possible to keep themselves from being hurt. It is therefore ironic that many daughters expressed filiality in the most unfilial fashion by mutilating their own bodies. Yet, through mutilation and death, these women subverted the very system that marginalized them and to which they were the peripheral "other;" their often-unexplainable behavior reflected the incoherent ideals mapped out for them by the center. Expressing filiality with the ultimate unfilial act of damaging the body, these women were rewriting the script of the male discourse (the classics) with their mutilated bodies. What the Confucian Classics stress with regard to filiality is altered from its very core.

The mutilation cases invoked in defense of chastity further help us interpret the codification of the chastity of Chinese womanhood. As discussed earlier, the body is the site of a woman's sexuality both physically and rhetorically. To mutilate a part of the body is to affirm her subjectivity to it. This assertion by denial spoke eloquently of women's desire for a different rhetoric concerning womanly virtues (including their sexuality) and for a different expression for Confucian womanhood than the incoherent and inconsistent appropriation women thus far were allotted. Their meanings seeping through the brushes of male historians, women articulated themselves through their bodies. With a nose, an ear, or an eye, a woman translates her chastity; with a torn arm or severed fingers, she writes about her steadfastness; with a cut-off heart or pieces of flesh, she discloses her loyalty; finally, many a daughter scrawls out her filiality with her own life. Indeed, mutilating one's body becomes an ultimate gesture of rewriting the male text.

Yet this is not to say that these women were their own agents in any historical sense. As Spivak said of the "Subaltern," since they "cannot appear without the thought of the 'élite' [the male historians in the case of the BoWs], the generalization [of a collective consciousness] is by definition incomplete."[84] Similarly, in the BoWs, women's effort in countering the dominating official Confucian discourse was fragmented, and a coherent script of their own was always in the making and could never have been completed. For the assertion of life in the form of bodily mutilation or self-deprecation is the introduction of a lesser life: no ear, nose, or fingers, and certainly no head chopped off can grow back. Most importantly, a voiceless announcement would not be heard, and an interpretation of it would sooner be assimilated into the dominant discourse. Thus, while the mutilated female body rewrote the script of the classics, it simultaneously helped internalize and affirm the very values it tried to deflate and depreciate. It is in this sense that the most basic Confucian values—such as devotion *(zhen)*,[85] integrity *(jie)*, and filiality *(xiao)*—became oppressive tools for Chinese women.

Still, to borrow once again Spivak's comment on one subaltern story, "used as a teaching tool," these biographies "can deconstruct those ideas even in their natural habitat."[86] For the bodies of these women are the locus of discourse and center of change. However damaging to themselves and seemingly ineffectual at the time, these women, through their bodies, wrote out their grievance without a pen, protested injustice without a voice, and sowed seeds of change without a hand. It is in this sense that these biographies are meaningful, less for outlining how Tang Dynasty women lived either qualitatively or quantitatively, but more for presenting the ideals that the Chinese Confucianists would have liked to see in women, and, perhaps more importantly, for the reaction and resistance women improvised in response.

APPENDIX I
COMPARISON BETWEEN THE TWO TANG HISTORIES'S BIOGRAPHIES OF WOMEN

Legend: BoW: Biographies of Women; *JTS (Jiu Tang shu): The Old History of the Tang Dynasty; XTS (Xin Tang shu): The New History of the Tang Dynasty*; * the subject mutilated others

BoW		NAME		MUTILATIONS	
JTS	XTS			JTS	XTS
1	1	Pei Shuying	李德武妻裴淑英	hair	hair
2	2	Wang, Ms.	楊慶妻王		
2a	4	Wang Lanying	獨孤師仁姆王蘭英	hair	hair
3	5	Li, Ms.	楊三安妻李		
4		Wang, Ms.	魏衡妻王氏	* beheads enemy	
5	6	Jing Xiangzi	樊會仁母敬		
6	7	Wei Wuji	衛孝女無忌		
7	13	Jia, Ms.	賈孝女	* enemy's heart & liver	* enemy's heart & liver
8	8	Lu, Ms.	鄭義宗妻盧		
9	9	Xiahou Suijin	劉寂妻夏侯碎金		
10	11	Shangguan, Ms.	楚王靈龜妃上官	nose & ear	[wants to cut off nose & 1 ear]
11	12	Wang, Ms.	楊紹宗妻王		
12	10	Zhang, Ms.	于敏直妻張		
13	14	Wang Azu	李氏妻王阿足		
14	15	Wei, Ms.	樊彥琛妻魏	fingers	fingers
15	30a	Xi, Ms.	鄒保英妻奚氏		
15a	30b	Gao, Ms.	古玄應妻高氏		
16		Wei, Ms.	宋庭瑜妻魏氏		
17	18	Lu, Ms.	崔繪妻盧	[becomes a nun]	hair
18	25	the Dou sisters	竇伯女仲女		
19	26	Li Shi	盧甫妻李		
19a	26a	Pei, Ms.	王泛妻裴氏	dissected by enemy	dissected by enemy
20	27	Bo, Ms.	鄒待微妻薄		

21	33	Li Tuan's wife	李湍妻	pieces to death	pieces to death
22	34	Yang, Ms.	董昌齡母楊		
23	38	Xiao, Ms.	韋雍妻蕭	1 arm	1 arm
24	39	Cheng, Ms.	衡方厚妻程	1 ear	1 ear
25		Li Xuanzhen	女道士李玄眞		
26	35	Wang Hezi	王孝女和子	hair	hair
26a	40	Zheng, Ms.	鄭孝女	hair	hair
	3	Lu, Ms.	房玄齡妻盧		1 eye
	16	Li Yu's mother	李畬佘母		
	17	Li, Ms.	汴女李		hair
	19	Li, Ms.	堅貞節婦李		hair
	20	Yuying	符鳳妻玉英		
	21	Qin, Ms.	高睿妻秦		
	22	Wei, Ms.	王琳妻韋		
	23	Xu, Ms.	盧惟清妻徐		
	24	Rao E	饒娥		
	28	Ms. Jin	金節婦		
	29	Gao Meimei	高愍女		
	30	Yang, Ms.	楊烈婦		
	31	Dong, Ms.	賈直言妻董		ties hair for 20 years
	32	Li Miaofa	李孝女妙法		1 breast; spears heart
	36	Xie Xiao'e	段居貞妻謝		* beheads enemy
	37	Xiao, Ms.	楊含妻蕭		
	41	Cui, Ms.	李廷節妻崔		heart cut out & eaten
	42	Feng Xu	殷保晦妻封絢		
	43	Dou, Ms.	竇烈婦		
	44	Lu, Ms.	李拯妻盧		1 arm
	45	Zhao, Ms.	山陽女趙		1 ear
	46	Zhou Di's wife	周迪妻		head
	47	Wang, Ms.	朱延壽妻王		

PARADIGMS, VIRTUES, AND EXPRESSIONS IN THE BOWS IN THE TWO TANG HISTORIES

PARADIGMS	VIRTUES	EXPRESSIONS		BoW	
				main theme	subtheme
FILIAL DAUGHTER (18 cases)	Filiality	Mourning / Funeral Rites	JTS	9, 11, 26, 26a /[+] 25,	
			XTS	(9)(12)(35)(40)/(17)(24)(32)(37)	
		Revenge	JTS	6, 7 /	
			XTS	(7)(13) / (36)	
		Others	JTS	12, 19 /	1, 5, 13
			XTS	(10)(26) / (45)	(1)(6)(14)
	Loyalty	Suicide	JTS	2 /	
			XTS	(2) / (29)	
	Chastity	Suicide	JTS	18 /	
			XTS	(25) /	
DUTIFUL WIFE (18 cases)	Filiality	Serving in-laws	JTS	8 /	10
			XTS	(8) / (46)	(11)
	Loyalty	Military Exploits	JTS	15, 15a /	
			XTS	(30a)(30b) /	
		Assisting Husband	JTS	21, 23 / 4, 16	
			XTS	(33)(38) / (21)(30)(43)(47)	(36)
	Chastity	Suicide Mutilation Abstinence	JTS	1, 20 /	
			XTS	(1)(27) / (3)(31)(41)(42)	
DEVOTED WIDOW (11 cases)	Filiality	Serving in-laws	JTS	3 /	
			XTS	(5) /	
	Loyalty	Revenge	JTS	24 /	
			XTS	(39) /	
	Chastity	Mutilation	JTS	10, 14, 19a /	
			XTS	(11)(15)(26a) / (20)(44)	
		Others	JTS	5, 17 /	
			XTS	(6)(18) / (19)(23)	(22)
EXEMPLARY MOTHER (6 cases)	Maternal Love	Caring	JTS	2a, 13 /	5
			XTS	(4)(14) /	(6)
	Sagacity	Teaching	JTS	22 /	2
			XTS	(34) / (16)(22)(28)	(2)(30)

+ Biographies listed before the slash correspond to the ones in the other history; biographies listed following the slash do not have correspondence in the other history.

Notes

The earliest version of this paper was given at the Symposium on Life and Death in Imperial China at Brigham Young University, February 8–10, 1996. I want to thank Professor Gary S. Williams and several participants for their comments on some initial ideas. A short version was presented at the Thirty-Third International Congress on Medieval Studies at Western Michigan University, May 7–10, 1998. Professor Yuan-chu Ruby Lam read portions of early drafts and offered invaluable suggestions. Juris Lidaka read through many later versions with great patience, forcing me to rethink many points from angles outside my own discipline. My sincerest gratitude to all of them. Any remaining errors are of course my own.

1. Whether or not Liu Xiang's *The Biographies of Women* is the first of its kind, it is the earliest extant one by all known accounts. The edition used here is *Sibu beiyao,* reprinted by Zhonghua shuju in Taipei in 1983. Chinese homophones pivotal to the discussion are designated with superscripts a and b. See the discussion below and the Glossary for clarification. For a more specific discussion of Liu Xiang's *The Biographies of Women,* see Zhang Jing, "Lieᵃ nü zhuan yu qi zuozhe" [*The Biographies of Women* and its author] in *Zhongguo funü shi lunwen ji* [Collection of Chinese women's history], eds. Li Yu-ning and Zhang Yufa (Taipei: Shangwu yinshuguan, 1981), pp. 50–60; Marina H. Sung, "The Chinese Lieh-nü Tradition," in *Women in China* eds. Richard W. Guisso and Stanley Johannesen (Lewiston, NY: Philo, 1981), p. 63; and Sherry J. Mou, "Gentlemen's Prescriptions for Women's Lives: Liu Hsiang's [Liu Xiang's] *The Biographies of Women* and Its Influence on the 'Biographies of Women' Chapters in Early Chinese Dynastic Histories," Ph.D. diss., The Ohio State University, 1994, pp. 25–76.
2. *Hou Han shu* [The history of the Later Han Dynasty], by Fan Ye (398–445) (Beijing: Zhonghua shuju, 1965).
3. Of the twenty-five official histories, thirteen have BoW sections. However, while this practice insured that women were represented in the histories, it also confined ordinary women to just the BoW sections. I use the term "ordinary women" as opposed to empresses, imperial consorts, and other female members of the imperial families; for most official histories have separate sections on empresses and consorts ("Hou fei zhuan").
4. See Xu Shen (30–124), *Shuowen jiezi* [Explicating the written characters] (Shanghai: Shanghai guji chubanshe, 1981), p. 180 *(lieᵃ)* and p. 480 *(lieᵇ)*. For more-recent definitions of the two characters, see *Ci yuan* [The origins of words] (Beijing: Shangwu yinshuguan, 1984), 4 vols., where *lieᵃ*, with regard to people, means "lines," "opposing," and "numerous," and *lieᵇ* means "staunch," "ruthlessly," "fragrant," "achievement," "lustrous," "burning," and "lines." Since Chinese is not inflected, a Chinese character can be used for different parts of speech, depending on the syntax.

5. *Shi ji* [Records of the Grand Historian], by Sima Qian (Beijing: Zhonghua shuju, 1959), ch. 86, p. 2526.
6. See Liu Xiang, ch. 7, "Biographies of the Pernicious and the Depraved" ("Nie bi zhuan"). The chapter includes sixteen women in fifteen biographies; all but one were royal consorts. Although the chapter title is not gender specific, along with the biographies it evokes the image of an evil concubine, which found its way to modern Chinese history in women such as Empress Dowager Cixi and Jiang Qing, the wife of Chairman Mao.
7. See Natalie Zemon Davis, "Women's History in Transition: The European Case," *Feminist Studies* 3, nos. 3–4 (Spring/Summer 1976): 83–103.
8. Even with the inclusion of all "women worthies," Fan Ye was faulted by later historians for his selections. Among the seventeen women was Cai Yan, the extremely learned daughter of a Confucian scholar, Cai Yong (132–92). Cai Yan was kidnapped by nomads, spent twelve years with them, and had two sons by the nomadic chieftain before she was ransomed back by her father's good friend Cao Cao (155–220) and married to a third husband. Her intricate life has been the subject of many literary works and paintings throughout Chinese history. Dore J. Levy studies the transformation of the image of Cai Yan (Ts'ai Yen) in Chinese poetry and painting in "Transforming Archetypes in Chinese Poetry and Painting: The Case of Ts'ai Yen," *Asia Major*, 3d series, 6.2 (1993): 147–68. Maxine Hong Kingston brought Cai Yan's story to the Western audience in her book *The Woman Warrior*, which ends with the image of Cai Yan in a barbarian land, trying to communicate with her child, who speaks only the foreign tongue. See *The Woman Warrior, Memoirs of a Girlhood among Ghosts* (New York: Vintage Books, 1975): 241–3.

The most critical comments on Fan Ye's inclusion of Cai Yan are from the Tang Dynasty historian Liu Zhiji (661–721), who says that, although "exceptionally talented in learning, [Cai Yan] lacked in integrity" *(wenci youyu jie gai buzu),* for she had been "insulted" by her kidnappers in the court of the nomad. For Liu Zhiji, Cai Yan's becoming the spouse of the nomadic chieftan underlines her lack of integrity—no woman should serve more than one husband. See Liu Zhiji, *Shitong* [Historical perspectives], ch. 8. The edition of *Shitong* used is the one annotated by Pu Qilong (1679–1761), *Shitong tongshi* [Comprehensive explanations of the historical perspectives] (Taipei: Shijie shuju, 1980), p. 114.
9. *Xin Tang shu* [The new history of the Tang Dynasty], by Ouyang Xiu (1007–72), Song Qi (996–1061), et al. (Beijing: Zhonghua shuju, 1975).
10. *Jiu Tang shu* [The old history of the Tang Dynasty], by Liu Xu (888–947) et al. (Beijing: Zhonghua shuju, 1975).
11. See, for example, Wang Mingsheng's (1722–98) *Shiqi shi shangque* [A critical study of the seventeen dynastic histories], 2 vols. (Beijing: Shangwu yinshuguan, 1964), chs. 69–92.

12. Wang Gungwu, "Some Comments on the Later Standard Histories," in *Essays on the Sources for Chinese History,* eds. Donald D. Leslie, Colin Mackerras, and Wang Gungwu (Columbia: University of South Carolina Press, 1973), p. 62.

13. The biography of the wife of Liang Hong appears in a supplementary chapter to Liu Xiang's *The Biographies of Women.* See Liu Xiang, ch. 8, 10a–10b. The chapter is obviously added by a later scholar, since it contains biographies of women after Liu Xiang's time.

14. Gong Jiang's story is from the *Shi jing* [The book of poetry], ch. 4, in *Shisan jing zhushu* [The thirteen classics with annotations and notes] (1821 ed.; repr. Taipei: Yiwen yinshuguan, 1981), p. 109.

15. *JTS,* p. 5138.

16. See Dong Zhongshu, *Chunqiu fan lu* [Luxuriant dew from the *Spring and Autumn Annals*], ch. 43, pp. 289–91. For the relationship between the yin-yang theory and women's position in China, see Pao Chia-lin, "Yin-yang xueshuo yu funü diwei" [The yin-yang theory and the position of women], in Pao Chia-lin, ed., *Zhongguo funü shi lunji, xuji,* pp. 37–54. I am grateful to Yuan-chu Ruby Lam for drawing my attention to the significance of the derivation of "gentleness" from the concept of yin.

17. For a detailed discussion of the development of the yin-yang theory from its topographical nature through its association with cosmology and sociopolitical ethics to its ultimate integration into a theological system from antiquity to modern times, see Xu Fuguan, *Zhongguo renxing lun shi* [Treatises on Chinese human nature] (Taizhong, Taiwan: Donghai daxue chubanshe, 1963).

18. This assumption contradicts Simone de Beauvoir's famous motto that a woman is not born, but rather becomes, a woman; see *The Second Sex* (1949; New York: Vintage Books, 1974), p. 301. Nancy Chodorow takes this stand further and contends convincingly that the "feminine personality" is basically the result of women mothering; in other words, of socialization. She believes that the role of mother is the most essential element in the genderization of both men and women. See *The Reproduction of Mothering: Psychoanalysis and the Sociology of Gender* (Berkeley: University of California Press, 1978). Chodorow talks about how "relational abilities and preoccupations have been extended in women's development and curtailed in men's" (p. 169).

19. See *Mengzi* in *Shisan jing zhushu,* ch. 7, p. 135; *Mencius,* trans. D. C. Lau (1970; repr. New York: Penguin, 1984): IV.A.19, p. 125.

20. The term is derived from "three obediences" *(sancong)* in *Yi li* [The book of ceremonies] in the context of women's funeral clothing. Since women generally did not hold official positions, they dressed in accordance with the rank of their fathers before marriage, their husbands after marriage, and their sons after their husbands died. See *Yi li* in *Shisan jing zhushu,* ch. 30, p. 359. However, the term is soon redefined as a code of behavior,

rather than simply a code of clothing. Another classic, *Li ji* [The book of rites], which is generally an explanation of *Yi li*, already interprets the "three obediences" as codes of behavior. See *Li ji* in *Shisan jing zhushu*, ch. 26, p. 506. Thus, the meaning of the term is transformed to "obey her father before marriage, her husband after marriage, and her son after her husband dies."

21. *JTS*, p. 5152.

22. For example, in *Lun yu* [The Analects], 8.2, Confucius says, "Unless people possess *li*, in being respectful they will wear themselves out, in being careful they will become timid, in having courage they will become unruly, and in being forthright they will become intolerant." The *Lun yu* used here is the *Shisan jing zhushu* edition; see p. 70. The translation is based on D. C. Lau's *The Analects* (New York: Dorset, 1986), p. 92.

23. The other three germs are benevolence (*ren*), rites (*li*), and wisdom (*zhi*). See *Mengzi* [Mencius] in *Shisan jing zhushu*, ch. 3c, pp. 65–6.

24. I translate *fu* as "married women" here, instead of as "wives," because *fu* includes both wives and widows; widows' chastity is particularly relevant in the biographies. See discussion below. Elsewhere, *fu* is generally translated as "wives."

25. *XTS*, p. 5816.

26. Mao Han-guang lists sixty powerful clan families, which produced most scholar officials during the Tang Dynasty. See *Zhongguo zhonggu shehui shi lun* [A discussion of China's medieval social history] (Taipei: Lianjing chuban shiye gongsi, 1988), pp. 55–9. More than half of the women and their husbands in the two BoWs are from these sixty families.

27. For easy reference, numbers are assigned to the biographies according to the order in which they appear in the BoWs; the attached biographies are designated with letters after the numbers. Biographies that appear in both histories will be noted by a parenthesis with the *JTS* number appearing first, followed by a slash and then the number in the *XTS*, such as (5/6).

28. Confucius discusses filiality with many disciples in *Lun yu*; see, for example, chs. 1–2. The three books on *li* (decorum and propriety)—*Yi li* [The book of ceremonies], *Zhou li* [The book of rites of the Zhou Dynasty], and *Li ji* [The book of rites]—also describe how people should serve their elders, especially parents; see for example, *Li ji*, ch. 1.

29. See *Xiao jing* [The classic of filiality] in *Shisan jing zhushu*, p. 10.

30. All official titles follow the translations in Charles O. Hucker, *A Dictionary of Official Titles in Imperial China* (Stanford: Stanford University Press, 1985).

31. The *JTS* stated fifteen years. No explanation is offered by the *XTS* historians for the change, which also mentions two daughters and the fact that the daughters later repeated their mother's filial acts.

32. A *dan* is ten bushels.

33. *XTS*, p. 5819.

34. See *Li ji*, ch. 34, "Concerning Mourning" ("Wen sang") for baring feet (p. 946); ch. 34, "Rushing to the Funeral" ("Ben sang") for letting down hair (p. 910); ch. 22, "The Grand Record of Mourning" ("Sang da ji") for building a mourning hut (p. 782); and ch. 49, "The Four Principles of Mourning" ("Sangfu sizhi") for adding earth to a tomb (p. 1033).

35. They are 9/9, 11/12, 26/35, 26a/40, and three more in the *XTS*—17, 32, and 37.

36. The phrases used in the five biographies are also formulaic. Ms. Li (*XTS* 17) "planted several hundred pine trees" *(shi song shu bai)*, another Ms. Li (*XTS* 32) "planted pine and cypress trees all by herself" *(shou zhi song bo)*, Ms. Wang (26/35) "planted pine and cypress trees" *(zhi song bo)*, Ms. Zheng (26a/40) "planted a forest of pine and cypress trees" *(shou shu song bo cheng lin)*, and Ms. Xiao (*XTS* 37) "planted pine and cypress trees" *(shi song bo)*.

37. This is to distinguish the closeness of relationship between the dead and the mourners, which, as discussed in Jen-der Lee's paper in this collection, is one indication of the unequal spirit between the genders. See *Li ji*, ch. 45, "Sang da ji," pp. 782–3.

38. The Chinese term *ji ji*, literally "reaching hair-tying," refers specifically to girls who were fifteen, the age when their hair was long enough to be held (tied) up with a hairpin. It is a euphemism for marriageable age.

39. See *Li ji*, ch. 49, "Sangfu sizhi," p. 1033.

40. *XTS*, p. 5826.

41. For example, see Lau, trans., *The Analects*, p. 67; *Lun yu*, ch. 3, p. 26.

42. Li Xuanzhen's great-great grandfather, Li Zhen (Prince Yue), was the eighth son of Emperor Taizong, not the sixth son as the biography indicates. His biography is in the *JTS*, ch. 76.

43. "Entering a spirit into the ancestral temple of a dead person" *(fu)* is one of the last steps of the burial ritual and an important part of ancestral worship. See *Li ji*, ch. 15, "Sangfu xiao ji" [The lesser record on funerals], pp. 592–3.

44. See Ch'ü T'ung-tsu, *Law and Society in Traditional China* (1961; repr. Paris: Mouton, 1965), pp. 78–87.

45. Written by Li Gongzuo (ca. 770-ca. 848), Xie Xiao'e's story is considered one of the first detective stories in Chinese literature. The story is collected in *Taiping guangji* [Extensive gleanings of the reign of Great Tranquillity], comps. Li Fang (925–96) et al., 3 vols. (1755; repr. Taipei: Xinxing shuju, 1973), ch. 491, pp. 1882–5. Also see "Li Kung-tso [Li Gongzuo]" in *The Indiana Companion to Traditional Chinese Literature*, ed. William H. Nienhauser, Jr., 2d ed. (Taipei: SMC Publishing, 1986), p. 542.

    The *Taiping guangji* (in chs. 270–1) has ten more biographies on women also found in the two BoWs. However, since this study focuses on the biographies received as history, a study of these biographies and their sources will be left out here. *Quan Tang wen* [Complete Tang prose] 1,000 ch., comp. Dong Gao (1740–1818) et al., 11 vols. (1814; repr. Beijing:

Zhonghua shuju, 1982) also collected these essays on women whose lives are recorded in the BoWs: Li Hua's "Ai jiefu fu" [Eulogy lamenting a chaste wife] (20/27), in ch. 314, p. 3189; Liu Zongyuan's "Rao E bei" [Epitaph of Rao E] (*XTS* 24), in ch. 587, p. 5931; Li Ao's "Gao Min nü bei" [Epitaph for the daughter of Gao Min] (*XTS* 29), in ch. 638, pp. 6445–6; also Li Ao's "Yang liefu zhuan" [Biography of the staunch wife, née Yang] (*XTS* 30), in ch. 640, pp. 6465–6; and Pi Rixiu's "Zhao nü zhuan" [Biography of the daughter of the Zhao] (*XTS* 45), in ch. 799, p. 8391.

46. The riddle was also collected in *Quan Tang shi* [Complete Tang poetry], comps. Peng Dingqiu (1645–1719) et al., 25 vols. (Beijing: Zhonghua shuju, 1960), ch. 877, p. 9940.

47. See Holmgren, "Women's Biographies in the *Wei-shu:* A Study of the Moral Attitudes and Social Background Found in Women's Biographies in the Dynastic History of the Northern Wei," Ph.D. diss., Australian National University, Canberra, 1979, pp. 241–3.

48. Ch'ü, p. 87.

49. One man beheaded the murderer of his friend's father to appease the friend, who expressed his deathbed regret that he was unable to avenge his father's murder. Besides displaying the importance of friendship, one of the "five human relationships" *(wulun),* the case can also be read as a variation of the filial son. See Ch'ü, p. 79.

50. Holmgren suggests a similar conclusion for the BoW of the Wei and Northern Qi periods; see Holmgren, "Women's Biographies," p. 242.

51. Catharine A. MacKinnon, "Feminism, Marxism, Method, and the State: An Agenda for Theory," in *The Signs Reader: Women, Gender and Scholarship,* eds. Elizabeth Abel and Emily K. Abel (Chicago: University of Chicago Press, 1983), p. 227.

52. See, for example, T'ien Ju-k'ang's discussions of the cult of female marital chastity during the Qing Dynasty in his *Male Anxiety and Female Chastity: A Comparative Study of Chinese Ethical Values in Ming-Ch'ing Times* (Leiden: E.J. Brill, 1988), pp. 126–48.

53. Ban Zhao's "Nü jie" is included in her biography in *Hou Han shu,* pp. 2786–93.

54. Sun-ming Wong, "Confucian Ideal and Reality: Transformation of the In-stitution of Marriage in T'ang China (A.D. 618–907)," Ph.D. diss., University of Washington, 1979, p. 45.

55. See *Li ji,* ch. 12, "Nei ze" [Regulations of the interior], especially pp. 518–22. It should be noted that besides describing how daughters-in-law should serve their parents-in-law, the chapter also details how sons should serve their parents, and how parents-in-law should treat their daughters-in-law.

56. The translation is based on Nancy Lee Swann's *Pan Chao* [Ban Zhao]: *Fore-most Woman Scholar of China* (New York: The Century, 1932), pp. 82–90.

57. *Li ji,* ch. 12, "Nei ze," p. 521.
58. Swann, trans., p. 88.
59. Holmgren, "Women's Biographies," pp. 178–81.
60. The two BoWs differ on whether she did succeed in cutting off her nose and ear. According to the *JTS,* she "grabbed a knife and cut off her nose and ear to make a vow . . . and died soon afterwards" *(ju jiang dao jiebi ge'er yi zi shi . . . xun zu)* (p. 5143). The *XTS* records the mutilation as a gesture and also does not say that she died afterwards: she "wanted to cut off her nose and ear, so the others dared not to force her anymore" *(jiang zi yi er zhong sui bugan qiang)* (p. 5819). It is fair to conclude that at least she had made a strong gesture of self-mutilation, even if she did not succeed.
61. *XTS,* p. 5818.
62. *XTS,* p. 5829.
63. According to the Tang code, only a widow's parents and grandparents could force her to remarry. See *Tang lü shuyi* [Annotations on the Tang code] by Zhangsun Wuji (died 689) (Taipei: Hongwenguan chubanshe, 1986), ch. 14, "Hu hun." See also discussions of remarriage during the Tang Dynasty in Xiang Shuyun's *Tang dai hunyin fa yu hunyin shitai* [The marriage law and the reality of marriage of the Tang Dynasty] (Taipei: Shangwu yinshuguan, 1991), pp. 190–209; and Dong Jiazun's "Cong Han dao Song guafu zaijia xisu kao" [A study on widow remarriage from the Han to the Song Dynasties] in *Zhongguo funü shi lunji* [Collection of Chinese women's history], ed. Pao Chia-lin (Taipei: Daoxiang chubanshe, 1979), pp. 152–8. Both works also list over twenty princesses of the Tang royal family who remarried, some more than once.
64. See, for example, Patricia Buckley Ebrey's study of the Song Dynasty (960–1279) in *The Inner Quarters: Marriage and the Lives of Chinese Women in the Sung Period* (Berkeley: University of California Press, 1993), especially pp. 204–6; and Nie Chongqi's "Nüzi zaijia wenti zhi lishi de yanbian" [The historical evolution of women's remarriage] in Pao Chia-lin, ed., pp. 128–38. Jennifer Holmgren's "The Economic Foundations of Virtue" points out that under certain social sectors and conditions, widow remarriage was encouraged, although not necessarily a desired practice from women's point of view; see Holmgren's *Marriage, Kinship and Power in Northern China* (Norfork, England: Ashgate Publishing, 1995), II, pp. 1–27.
65. Jennifer Holmgren coined the term in her discussion of the BoW of the *Wei shu.* She sees the mother-instructress as a part of the "Learned Instructress" motif in the development of biographies of women in the official history. See Holmgren, "Women's Biographies," pp. 178–81. Holmgren listed the "Learned Instructress" as one of the major themes found in her study of the BoW in *Wei shu;* the other ten are Devoted Wife, Chaste Widow, Wife-Mother Relations, Revenge, Sexual Chastity, Frugality, Self-Mutilation, Suicide, Military Exploits, and Filial Piety. See her "Women's Biographies," ch. 6, pp. 178–202.

66. However, Liu Xiang does not limit the image of educated and talented women to mothers only. The second chapter of *Biographies of Women*, "Biographies of the Capable and Intelligent" ("Xianming zhuan"), features capable and intelligent wives who advised their husbands not only in household decisions but also in political matters. See Mou, pp. 40–4.

67. In one biography (Liu Xiang, ch. 1.6, pp. 7–8), prenatal instruction is discussed in great detail. The translation is from Albert Richard O'Hara, *The Position of Woman in Early China According to the Lieh Nü Chuan "The Biographies of Chinese Women"* (Taipei: Mei Ya Publications, 1971), pp. 23–4.

T'ai Jen [Tairen] was capable in prenatal instruction. In ancient times, a woman with child did not lie on her side as she slept; neither would she sit sidewise nor stand on one foot. She would not eat dishes having harmful flavors; if the food was cut awry, she would not eat it; if the mat was not placed straight, she would not sit on it. She did not let her eyes gaze on lewd sights nor let her ears listen to depraved sounds. At night she ordered the blind musicians to chant poetry. She used right reason to adjust affairs, and thus gave birth to children of correct physical form who excelled others in talent and virtue. For this reason a woman with child should be careful about things that affect her. If she is affected by good things, the child will be good; if she is affected by evil things, the child will be evil. Men resemble the natural order because their mothers were influenced by that order. For that reason their features and sounds correspond to it.

See also Anne Behnke Kinney's "Dyed Silk: Han Notions of the Moral Development of Children," in *Chinese Views of Childhood,* ed. Anne Behnke Kinney (Honolulu: University of Hawai'i Press, 1995), pp. 26–32, in which she discusses "fetal instruction" *(taijiao)* and the notions of "gradual" *(jian)* and "transformation" *(hua).*

It should be noted that all except two biographies in the first chapter of Liu Xiang's *Biographies of Women* focus on the relationship between mothers and sons. The other two (7. "A Maiden of Wei, Ding Jiang" and 8. "The Governess of the Lady of Qi") celebrate the relationships between a mother-in-law and a daughter-in-law and between a young woman and her governess. The mother-daughter relationship in the classics is one of the least-discussed topics.

68. Holmgren, "Women's Biographies," p. 180.

69. John Carmi Parsons and Bonnie Wheeler, eds., *Medieval Mothering* (New York: Garland Publishing, 1996), p. x.

70. Ms. Wei's biography also has a subtheme on a devoted widow. When her family wanted to remarry her, she resisted sternly, would not listen to music, confined herself in one room, and often fasted for the entire day. See *XTS,* pp. 5822–3.

71. The *JTS* listed five literate women (1, 8, 16, 22, and 25) and the *XTS* six (1, 8, 16, 22, 42, and 44), but only one of these women (22/34) is noted for her role as a mother-instructress. Only three (*JTS* 22; *XTS* 16 and 22) of the eleven feature the exemplary mother as the main theme. Li Yu's mother (*XTS* 16) is said to be "sagacious" *(yuan shi)*, which could be understood as meaning learned, but could also mean knowledgeable in a general sense.

72. See also Kinney, pp. 31–2.

73. Incidentally, Ms.Yang's son Dong Changling, portrayed in 22/34 as a filial son and loyal vassal, appears in another biography (24/39) as an obstinate and somewhat cruel commander later in his life, causing the cruel death of a subordinate. See the section on "Devoted Widow" for the discussion of the revenge of Ms. Cheng, the wife, on behalf of her husband's wrongful death.

74. This frame, taken from Simone de Beauvoir, marks a fundamental difference between Chinese and womanhood and the Western womanhood de Beauvoir describes in her *The Second Sex*. Her argument anchors women in marriage: "The celibate woman is to be explained and defined with reference to marriage, whether she is frustrated, rebellious, or even indifferent in regard to that institution" (p. 475). In comparison, women in the BoWs were anchored in families—both their natal families and their husbands' families.

75. For Gayatri Chakravorty Spivak, the "Subaltern consciousness," situated in the voicelessly oppressed, is articulated through the writings of the Subaltern studies group, an elite circle of scholars reading and interpreting colonial Indian contexts. The irony is that those who formed the "Subaltern consciousness" do not have a voice to speak for themselves, and the elite Subaltern group that tries to speak for them can speak only with a learned tongue—English in the case of Subaltern historians. I shun a direct application of Subalternism, because the Confucian tradition is only minimally comparable to colonialism. Although we can view women in traditional Confucian society the same way we do colonized natives, those who occupied the position of the imperialists—the men in the Confucian context—remain a floating entity, for the powerful husbands and fathers in some scenes are the voiceless and subjugated sons and vassals in others.

Nevertheless, in the BoWs, (1) women, (2) the male historians who inscribed and interpreted these women, and (3) Confucian virtues are parallel to the Subaltern (1) Indian peasants, (2) Subaltern historians, and (3) English, the language they learned from the imperialists. See Spivak's "Subaltern Studies: Deconstructing Historiography," in *In Other Worlds: Essays in Cultural Politics* (New York: Routledge, 1988), pp. 197–221.

76. There are some discrepancies between the two BoWs. *JTS* 8 did not have the word "obedience," but the same biography in *XTS* 8 did; similarly, *JTS*

12 used "obedient," but *XTS* 10, the same biography, did not. Here, a close textual comparison between the two BoWs should yield a more interesting interpretation.

77. The quotation is from *XTS,* p. 5816. For "a husband being the sky of the wife," see *Yi li,* ch. 30, "The Principles of Mourning" ("Sangfu"), p. 359.

78. My discussion here is more on the rhetorical aspect of mutilation. For a more behavioral and sociological discussion, especially in regard to the specific act of *gegu* (cutting a piece of flesh), see Qiu Zhonglin's "Bu xiao zhi xiao Tang yilai gegu liaoqin xianxiang de shehui shi chutan" [The unfilial filiality, a preliminary investigation into the social history of the phenomena of "cutting a piece of flesh to heal one's parents" since the Tang Dynasty], *Xin shixue* 6.1 (March 1995):49–94; and T'ien Ju-k'ang, pp. 149–61.

79. They are *Jin shu* [The history of the Jin Dynasty], "The Married Woman of Shan" ("Shan furen"), pp. 2520–1; *Wei shu* [The history of the (Northern) Wei Dynasty], "The Wife of Wei Pu, Ms. Fang" ("Wei Pu qi Fang shi"), pp. 1979–80; *Sui shu* [The history of the Sui Dynasty], "Princess Huayang's (Kai's) Consort" ("Huayang wang Kai fei"), p. 1800; and *Sui shu,* "The Wife of Han Ji" ("Han Ji qi"), p. 1806. All three histories are the Zhonghua shuju punctuated editions.

80. See last two columns of Appendix I for cases with mutilations.

81. It should be noted that in traditional China, hair, like other parts of the body inherited from one's parents, should not be cut randomly. Hair cutting was an important cultural issue and a sign of political protest in Chinese history as late as this century, shortly after the demise of the Qing Dynasty in 1911. See Michael R. Godley's "The End of the Queue: Hair as Symbol in Chinese History," *East Asian History* 8 (December 1994): 53–72.

82. The four cases are *JTS* 4, 21, 23, and 24. The only exception is the case of Wang Lanying (*JTS* 4), the nanny who faithfully took care of her young master.

83. *Xiao jing,* in *Shisan jing zhushu,* ch. 1, p.11.

84. Spivak, p. 203.

85. Here, I am talking about *zhen* (devotion or virtue) in its gender-neutral interpretation, which broadly embraces loyalty and truthfulness to one's ideals. However, when applied to women, *zhen* is narrowly understood to mean chastity. Even compound terms with *zhen,* such as *jianzhen* (of firm virtue) in "Jianzhen jiefu Li" (*XTS* 19, "The Chaste Wife of Firm Virtue, Ms. Li"), imply a woman's chastity.

86. See her "A Literary Representation of the Subaltern: A Woman's Text from the Third World," in *In Other Worlds,* pp. 245–6.

CHAPTER FIVE

JI^A-ENTERTAINERS[1] IN TANG CHANG'AN

Victor Xiong
Western Michigan University

This article studies the best-known red-light district of ninth-century China in the capital city, Chang'an, with a focus on the lives and careers of its female entertainers.

Introduction

The thriving female entertainment business and its corollary, prostitution, in the capital city of Chang'an (present-day Xi'an) during the Tang Dynasty (618–907) has been well documented, thanks to the *Beili zhi* [Record of the Northern Quarters], a random collection of anecdotes written by a Late-Tang client, Sun Qi.[2] Beili, or the Northern Quarters, refers to the red-light district of Chang'an. His book records his personal encounters with the area's female entertainers, known as *ji^a*, and stories he collected about them. In all likelihood, the *Beili zhi* was completed around 885, and the coverage is essentially limited to the reigns of Emperors Xuan^azong (reigned 846–59), Yizong (r. 859–73) and Xizong (r. 873–88).[3]

In Tang times, three terms are most often associated with female entertainers. *Ji^a* is the most common term. Although in modern usage it is mostly identified with *prostitute,* its definition under the Tang is different: like geisha, the *ji^a* were trained in a variety of entertainment skills, including singing, dancing, playing musical instruments, drinking, companionship, and reciting poetry.[4] Prostitution was involved, but it was by no means the main calling of the *ji^a*. Due to these historical attributes, I will refer to them as "*ji^a*-entertainers."[5]

The second term is *chang*[a]-prostitute, a derivative of the bisexual term *chang*[b]-entertainer.[6] In Tang times it referred to those females, often poorly trained in entertainment skills, who provided sex for cash. It is believed that the earliest datable appearance of the term *chang*[a]-prostitute is found in the "Story of Yang Chang"[7] by Fang Qianli, a *jinshi*-degree holder of the Late-Tang period,[8] according to whom "A *chang*[a] offers sex for service, and will do so only for a profit."[9] The third term is *ji*[b]-courtesan, which is often associated with the exotic dancers of Central Asia. It seems that the *ji*[b]-courtesans were more respectable.[10]

In the following pages, I will deal with neither *chang*[a]-prostitutes nor *ji*[b]-courtesans, not only because they occur less frequently in Tang sources, but also because they are extraneous to the central theme of the present study, *ji*[a]-entertainers.

Ji[a]-entertainers

In terms of functionality, Tang *ji*[a]-entertainers can be roughly classified as court entertainers *(gongji*[a]*)*, official entertainers *(guanji*[a]*)*, army entertainers *(yingji*[a]*)*, home entertainers *(jiaji*[a]*)*, and Northern Quarters entertainers *(Beiliji*[a]*)*.[11]

Court entertainers were employed on a permanent basis for imperial entertainment. In spite of their low social station, these entertainers usually confined their service to stage performances. In the capital, Chang'an, they were initially housed in the Pear Gardens *(liyuan)*, which were located in the Palace City *(gongcheng)*.[12] (Map 1 in the Appendix gives a rough city plan of Tang Chang'an.) Emperor Xuanzong (r. 712–56), the "brilliant emperor," relocated them to the Left and Right Departments of Stage Performances *(zuoyou jiaofang)*[13] in Changle and Guangzhai Wards *(fang)*.[14] There were two major classes of court entertainers: insiders *(neiren)*[15] and court persons *(gongren)*. An insider was supposedly a free woman, while a court person was legally a bond servant *(jianli)*, who often had been forced into bondage to punish a spouse or father convicted of serious crimes. The insider wore at her waist a metal fish token (a decorative status symbol) that set her visually apart from the court person.[16] Freedom of movement was quite limited even for an insider. Quartered in the compounds of the Department of State Performances, she was allowed to receive a visiting close relative, usually her mother, twice a month. Only a privileged few called "the ten" *(shijia)*, who enjoyed special favor from the emperor, were able to visit family members regularly at home.[17] On stage they sang, danced, and played instrumental music. A major difference between court entertainers (both insiders and court persons) and other *ji^a*-entertainers was their relative detachment from prostitution.[18]

Both official entertainers *(guanji^a)* and army entertainers *(yingji^a)* served government employees. Official entertainers, as suggested by the name, were owned by civilian governments and provided entertainment on official occasions. Some official entertainers also provided long-term companionship to high-ranking government officials and accompanied them to their new assignments or, upon their retirements, to their homes.[19] The army entertainer was the counterpart of the official entertainer in the barracks. Although the tradition of keeping entertainers in the army dates back to the Han Dynasty (206 B.C.E. - 220 C.E.), information on Tang army entertainers is scanty.[20]

Home entertainers *(jiaji^a)* were privately owned by their masters, a common practice for ranking officials and royal relatives, the number varying from one to over a hundred, depending on the wealth and power of the master.[21] In social status, the home entertainer ranked below the concubine but above the maid. The best-known home entertainers were perhaps those owned by Bo Juyi (772–846), whose poetry, as in the short passage below, made two of his private entertainers proverbial—Fan Su, a gifted singer with a small mouth, and Xiaoman, a talented dancer with a slender waist:

> A cherry,
> The lips of Fan Su.
> A willow tree,
> The waist of Xiaoman.[22]

When an owner became infatuated with his home entertainer, he often kept her for long-term service. Such an arrangement could be interrupted if a more powerful person requested a transfer of ownership. The prose-writer Liu Yuxi (772–842) once kept a favorite entertainer noted for her beauty. Li Fengji, an autocratic chief minister, contrived to lure her out of Liu's place by inviting all court officials and their entertainers to a state banquet held in his mansion, and then kept her against Liu's will.[23] If an owner thus lost custody of his prized possession, attempts to continue the old relationship could be costly, as is illustrated by the case of Qiao Zhizhi, who lived during Wu Zetian's reign (684–705) and was a left bureau director *(zuosi langzhong)* and a man of letters.[24] Qiao chose to stay unmarried on account of his favorite entertainer, Yaoniang. Still, he had to release ownership of her at the request of Wu Yansi, a relative of Wu Zetian. Qiao fell ill with sorrow and frustration. He wrote a nostalgic and reproachful poem and sent it to her in secret. On reading it, a mortified Yaoniang drowned herself in a well.[25] Wu had Qiao tortured and executed on trumped-up charges.[26]

The last category of Tang ji^a-entertainers is the *Beiliji^a*, professional providers of companionship, artistic entertainment, and sex in exchange for profit. Compared with other categories of ji^a-entertainers, they were more commercialized, professional, and promiscuous. It was their services that kept attracting clients to the red-light district of Chang'an.

Beili and Pingkang li

Beili (Northern Quarters) was traditionally associated with pleasure-seeking. In the *Shi ji* [Records of the Grand Historian], the Han historian Sima Qian gives an account of the overindulgence of the last king of the Shang Dynasty, in which he also talks about Beili:

> King Zhou . . . liked wine and amorous music, and indulged in woman-izing, showing particular favor to Da Ji (his concubine), whose requests [he] inevitably granted. Consequently, Master Juan was ordered to create new amorous harmonies, the dances of *Beili* and pompous music.[27] (My emphasis.)

In Tang times, Beili became synonymous with Pingkang li, a residential area in the capital best known for its entertainment businesses and organized prostitution. As one of the standard wards of Chang'an, Pingkang li was located immediately west of the Eastern Market and southeast of the Imperial City. It was divided into four equal-sized sections, with parts of its northeast and southeast sections constituting the red-light district.[28] Maps 1 and 2 in the Appendix give the approximate locations and outline of Beili (Pingkang li) in Chang'an.

The red-light district in Pingkang li was established earlier than Sun Qi made his records. The Kaiyuan chapter of the *Kaiyuan Tianbao yishi* [Anec-dotes of the Kaiyuan and Tianbao eras] observes:

> There was Pingkang fang in Chang'an, where ji^a-entertainers lived. Chival-rous young men often gathered there. Moreover, each year, the new *jinshi*, upon receiving their degrees, would visit the place, carrying with them red paper for writing poems. This ward was referred to by its contemporaries as the fountain of romance.[29]

This indicates that during the Kaiyuan period (713–41) Pingkang li was already the established center of female entertainment.

When did Pingkang li start to be identified as Beili, or the Northern Quarters? According to Ishida Mikinosuke, the early Tang poets Luo Bin-wang (died 684) and Lu Zhaolin made references to Beili in their poems; thus, the entertainment business in Pingkang li should be datable at least to the same period. However, although these poets did write about entertainers, judging by the context, it is more likely that they used the term *Beili* in a generic sense to mean some "northern residential quarters." Extant records show that "Beili" had not been used to refer to the entertainment section of Pingkang li until late Tang times, when Sun Qi in his *Beili zhi* called the *ji*ᵃ-entertainers of Pingkang li "the entertainers of the Northern Quarters" *(Beili zhi ji*ᵃ).[30]

Beili Ji*ᵃ*-entertainers

A major difference between the Beili *ji*ᵃ-entertainers and other types lies in organization and patronage. The Beili *ji*ᵃ-entertainers primarily worked in private businesses, unlike court entertainers, military/army entertainers, or official/civil entertainers. They were also different from the privately owned home entertainers in that an "adoptive mother," or madam *(jiamu)*—not a master—served as their owner.

Some of the madams had been entertainers themselves, as in the cases of Wang Tuan'er and Yang Miao'er, who had passed their prime and retired from active service.[31] The madams did not have husbands themselves. Those whose attractiveness had not completely faded often had as their masters provincial generals from various liaison offices in the capital.[32] Occasionally, the madam had a male partner, known as the adoptive father *(jiafu)*.[33]

Frequently, young girls were forced into the profession by circumstances beyond their control. They were adopted in their childhood *(gaiyu)* or preyed upon by hooligans *(butiao zhi tu)*[34] when they were in the employ of poverty-stricken households in inferior neighborhoods. Some of them came from fairly respectable families. Once in Beili, the new recruits were soon set to practice their skills, mainly in poetry-recitals and singing.[35]

The experience of Funiang (*zi* [courtesy name]: Yizhi) was quite typical. As a child of decent family background, she often went to learn needlework and poetry in the house of her neighbor, a court musician. She was then seduced by a man who brought her to Chang'an, left her in a house of pleasure in Pingkang li, and disappeared. At first she was treated kindly. As time went by, she was forced to entertain clients despite her young age, with little chance of freedom. Most of these girls lost their surnames upon adoption and took on the names of their madams. Funiang's original surname was also unknown, and we only know that her madam was Wang Tuan'er.[36]

To venture out of the district on their own to solicit clients was difficult at best, except when Buddhist preaching sessions were held at the Baotang Monastery (Baotang si, or the monastery of Protecting the Tang) to the South in the same ward. This normally took place three times a month, on the eighth, eighteenth, and twenty-eighth. The ji^a-entertainers would pay their madams one thousand coins each to get permission to look for potential clients at the monastery, where their presence attracted a very large congregation of scholars. With the madam's consent, an entertainer could go out with a client outside of the district. She would often find herself in the position of a humble servant, and the money she earned would go into the pocket of the madam.[37]

Judging from the very scanty information on the *Beili zhi*, we can identify three types of ji^a-entertainers working for a madam. The first type had no Department of Stage Performances registration *(wei xi jiaofang ji)* and was redeemable at a relatively low price.[38] The second was registered with the Department of Stage Performances *(ji shu jiaofang)*, which was in charge of court entertainers as well. However, in spite of their registration, the Beili ji^a-entertainers lived in Pingkang li.[39] These registered ji^a-entertainers were also known as beverage entertainers *(yinji^a)* and often entertained at court banquets or feasts held by new recipients of the *jinshi* degree.[40] Once registered, ji^a-entertainers carried a much higher price tag for redemption.[41] The third type of ji^a-entertainers was subjected to a special arrangement known as exclusive purchase *(maiduan)*, whereby a client entered into a more or less exclusive relationship with the entertainer by paying the madam a high price, usually one thousand coins per day. However, an exclusive purchase contract did not exempt an entertainer from being summoned for performances at official functions.[42]

Profiles of *Beili Ji*ᵃ-entertainers and Their Clientele Base

The Beili ji^a-entertainers were not only valued for their physical attractiveness, but were also especially prized for their skills and cultivation.[43] Seventeen entertainers are given a biographical description in the *Beili zhi* (page references are to des Rotours; the emphases on physical appearances are mine):

I. Chu'er (*zi:* Runniang): *the best[-looking]* of Sanqu (the entertainer section of Pingkang li), eloquent, intelligent, and good at writing poetry (p. 80).

II. Funiang (*zi:* Yizhi): clear-headed, *shapely,* and capable of elegant conversation (p. 123).

III. Gui'er: *plain-looking,* but good at entertaining visitors (p. 118).

IV. Lai'er (*zi:* Fengxian): *plain-looking,* no longer young, but eloquent and humorous, thus able to charm almost everyone (p. 109); enticed clients by quickness and subtlety (p. 117).

V. Liu Tainiang: *moderately pretty,*[44] popular with Qujiang visitors (pp. 154–6).

VI. Tianshui Xian'ge (*zi:* Jiangzhen): *plain-looking,* good-tempered, good at singing and poetry-recitals, well liked by gentlemen (pp. 72–3).

VII. Wang Lianlian (*zi:* Zhaorong): *moderately pretty*[45] (pp. 152–3).

VIII. Wang Susu: good at teasing; has spacious rooms; serves food and wine well; poetic (p. 149).

IX. Xiaofu (*zi:* Nengzhi): *devoid of grace,* but intelligent (p. 126).

X. Xiaorun (*zi:* Zimei): well-known; intimate with Cui Yin (pp. 119–20).

XI. Yaniang: stands out from the crowd; frivolous, injurious (p. 98).

XII. Yan Lingbin: well-mannered, good at writing poetry, popular with the gentlemen of the time; likes to solicit poems from scholar clients (p. 101).

XIII. Ying'er: *plain,* awkward at teasing; often irritates clients with coarse expressions (p. 118).

XIV. Yong'er (*zi:* Qiqing): amiable (more so than Lai'er) but without other talents; favored by Xiao Gou (p. 117).

XV. Yu Luozhen: *pretty,* intelligent (p. 140); promiscuous, spendthrift (p. 144); concubine of Yu Cong (chief minister) (p. 140); had sexual relations with Yu Cong's nephew Yu Zhuo; expelled by Princess Shangde (Cong's wife) (p. 144).

XVI. Zhang Zhuzhu: quick and intelligent, musical (p. 156).

XVII. Zheng Juju: good at reciting drinking rules, learned, *plain-looking,*[46] classy, good at making humorous conversation; sought by court officials (pp. 87–8).

Clearly, Sun Qi noted briefly physical characteristics of only eleven of these entertainers. Only two (1. Chu'er and 15. Yu Luozhen) are given extremely positive remarks. Three are described in somewhat flattering terms (2. Funiang [shapely], 5. Liu Tainiang, and 7. Wang Lianlian [moderately pretty]). The rest (3. Gui'er, 4. Lai'er, 6. Tianshui Xian'ge, 9. Xiaofu, 13. Ying'er, and 17. Zheng Juju) are portrayed in such negative terms as "plain-looking" or "devoid of grace."

As Edward Schafer has observed, "sheer sexual allure does not account for the admiration" the literati had for the entertainers.[47] Such epithets as *yao* (enchanting), *miao* (marvelous), and *xian* (sylphid), were often used to define the demimonde of Tang. For a lady of entertainment, lack of natural beauty could be more than made up for by grace, cultivation, and skills. Lai'er and Zheng Juju attracted clients by their humorous conversations. Tianshui Xian'ge held a special charm by virtue of her legendary mastery of poetry.[48]

The entertainers displayed a passionate love for poetry. Not only did they recite popular poems to entertain clients, they also solicited poems from scholarly clients and attempted to impress their favorite ones with their own poetic criticisms. They themselves liked to write poems, which varied in quality. Some of them were unsophisticated in their use of poetic devices, as shown in the quatrain composed by Funiang in response to a piece dedicated to her by Sun Qi himself:

> How hard I have pleaded with you to respond to my poem.
> Chanting your poem, I am thrilled with its freshness.
> Although not exactly a prose-poem of Sima Xiangru's,
> It should be worth a pound or two of gold.[49]

Not all entertainers' poems were mediocre. Zhao Luanluan, a *ji*[a]-entertainer of Pingkang li, whose life we know little about, wrote poems marked by perfect rhyming skills and elegant language, unencumbered by pedantic allusions. Her name does not appear in Sun Qi's *Beili zhi,* but in one of her poems she talks about having seen the mouth of Fan Su of the Bo [Juyi] family, which points to the Middle-Tang period as her time of activity. She chose such sensual subjects as chignons, willowy eyebrows, the scented mouth, delicate fingers, and soft breasts as her sources of inspiration, as in "Delicate Fingers" ("Xianzhi"):[50]

> Like delicate, soft jade,[51] and freshly peeled spring onions,
> They are ever draped in verdant sleeves of scented gauze.
> Yesterday, when they plucked the strings of the lute,
> Their fingernails were coated in vivid scarlet.

There is a plethora of Tang poetry either written on or dedicated to *ji*[a]-entertainers. Among Tang scholars, especially *jinshi*-degree holders and candidates, a visit with an entertainer was not only acceptable but also fashionable.[52] According to Kishibe Shigeo, the clientele base of the Beili *ji*[a]-entertainers was primarily scholars and officials: of the forty clients recorded in the *Beili zhi,* twenty were *jinshi* or advanced degree candidates, and eighteen were government officials, while only two were rich merchants.[53] Perhaps because the frequenters of Beili were usually of comparatively high social, educational, or economic status, they often found themselves in a rather subdued atmosphere at a house of pleasure, where the main activities were wine-drinking, singing, and poetry-recitals.

Precariousness of Life in Beili

The semblance of urbanity and the façade of merrymaking, however, cannot conceal the precarious nature of the *ji^*-entertainer's life in Beili. Maltreatment, as revealed in the *Beili zhi,* was fairly common. Young girls selected for the business had to undergo extremely demanding training in entertainment skills. Slackness was often punished by incessant whippings by their madams.[54]

On the other hand, it is probably true that grown-up entertainers working for madams were in better control of the situation. The *Beili zhi* does not record a single incident in which an adult entertainer suffered physically at the hands of her madam. The best of them were able to please their clients with humor and eloquence. Aggressive behavior on the part of the *ji^*-entertainer, although not appreciated, could go unpunished, such as in the case of Yaniang, known for her frivolous character, who badly scratched the faces of scholar clients teasing her, but who went unpunished.[55] The garrulous Lai'er, who worked for the madam Yang Miao'er, once bragged to her clients about the talent of her favorite lover, Zhao Guangyuan, a degree candidate. When Zhao failed to pass the exam, young men from the Southern Office *(Nanyuan)*[56] poked fun at Lai'er, who lashed out at them with an acerbic poem that mocked their immaturity.[57] On another occasion, Lai'er blamed her madam for underpaying her and cursed her profusely. The madam was reduced to tears when she talked about it later.[58]

In spite of the appearance of self-assertion, many Beili *ji^*-entertainers have tragic stories in the *Beili zhi.* Those *ji^*-entertainers bound by an exclusive purchase contract were more likely to be abused by their clients. Under this kind of contract, the client virtually took over ownership of the entertainer, who was no longer permitted to see other clients so long as the contract lasted.[59] Such arrangements often took place against the will of the entertainer. One example was Chu'er, who served on a long-term basis Guo Duan, metropolitan police officer *(buzei guan)* of Wannian County,[60] and a descendent of Guo Ziyi.[61] Whenever Guo Duan caught Chu'er trying to contact her old clients, he would severely beat her. Once in Qujiang (Serpentine River) Park, a jealous Guo Duan dragged Chu'er into the crossroads and whipped her dozens of times. Being a police officer of Chang'an and Wannian Counties (i.e., urban Chang'an), Guo had in his employ quite a few hooligans and was thus feared by the local people.[62] Guo Duan's violent temper certainly played a part in the physical abuse of Chu'er. Yet it was the exclusive nature of the service contract that predisposed Guo Duan to become possessive, and his power and Chu'er's vulnerable position allowed him to abuse her continually. Chu'er, after becoming an exclusive purchase *ji^a*-entertainer, wrote to her previous lover, Zheng Guangye, thus:

> [I] must have wronged [someone] in a former life,
> Not knowing the cause of my sufferings in this world.[63]

The case of Funiang shows the fear of a *ji^a*-entertainer for exclusive purchase. In desperation, she turned to Sun Qi for help and expressed her innermost feelings in a quatrain:

> Suffering from sorrow each day, [I] don't plan ahead.
> Nor do I want to pour out my feelings to a common fellow.
> Unlike spilled water [I] can still be reclaimed,
> [I] am only asking if my immortal man is interested.[64]

Having been rejected by Sun Qi, she was forced to work under an exclusive purchase contract. And this led her to describe herself as a "lotus bogged down in the mud" *(nilian ji mo)*[65] in another poem.

The most-tragic character is found in Yan Lingbin, a *ji^a*-entertainer noted for her grace and good manners. When she was worn down by a fatal disease, she begged some of her clients to write her elegies. On the day of Yan Lingbin's death, her madam found these elegies among her belongings and threw them out. One of her admirers picked them up and sang them in a mournful tune at her funeral. Not long after, they became popular in Chang'an. Tainted by trite imagery, these elegies nevertheless offer us a rare insight into the life of a once-popular *ji^a*-entertainer in her last days:

> Ailing in late spring, [she] had another drink [with me],
> It was a most heartbreaking evening.
> Life is a dream that ends at break of day,
> Few are the days of a flower in bloom.
> A lonely simurgh[66] looks into the mirror to no purpose,

A [male] swallow without a mate has no wish to return to [the nest under] the roof.[67]
How can [I] repay her kindness?
With a bitter heart, I offer a cup of wine [to her spirit].[68]

Apart from personal tragedies of the *ji*-entertainers, the *Beili zhi* also provides occasional glimpses into the violent side of Beili, which threatened the lives of the clients. Wang Shi, commander of the imperial insignia guard *(jinwu)*,[69] narrowly escaped murder when he was drinking in a room. A drunkard broke in, and Wang hid under a bed. A third man came in, cut off the drunkard's head, and asked, "Would you like to run us in again?" believing he had killed Wang. In another case, Linghu Gao, an erudite *(boshi)*, witnessed the murder and burial of a drunkard by a madam and her *ji*-entertainer. When he was in the company of the *ji*-entertainer the following night, he revealed his knowledge of the incident, and she nearly strangled him. The next morning, Linghu reported the case to the prefect of the metropolitan area *(da jingyin)*, who sent his men to arrest the *ji*-entertainer and her madam, who had already escaped.[70] In view of these untoward happenings, Sun Qi describes Beili as a "place of unexpected danger" *(buce zhi di)*. Though these incidents took place before the Dazhong (847–59) period, Sun Qi asked rhetorically how he could know that such things were not happening in his own time, suggesting that Beili remained dangerous.[71]

Redemption

Economic dependence and low social status often led a Beili *ji*-entertainer to seek redemption (release from her obligation to the madam) either on her own or with outside help. Funiang is a case in point. When Sun Qi got himself into an intimate relationship with her, she begged him to redeem her. Her estimated cost of redemption was around one to two hundred taels of gold. Sun Qi declined her request politely, claiming it was inappropriate for a degree candidate like him to take an entertainer as his concubine. She was then taken into custody by the attendant-in-ordinary Wei Zeng[72] and by the son of Chief Minister Wei Zhou. The money paid into the house on account of Funiang was estimated to be in excess of one thousand taels of gold. When her brothers came to bail her out, Funiang dismissed the suggestion as impossible. Instead, she sent the brothers away with several hundred taels of gold. By then, the price for her redemption must have gone up significantly, and it was quite likely that she had become registered with the Department of Stage Performances. Due to social barriers, Funiang did not achieve her goal, redemption, yet the possibility was there.[73]

For most *ji^a*-entertainers of Beili, the successful departure of their colleague Yu Luozhen from Pingkang li may have looked like extremely good fortune. With beauty and grace, she struck the fancy of Chief Minister Yu Cong, who married the daughter of Emperor Xuan^azong (r. 846–59) and took Yu Luozhen as a concubine.[74] However, Yu Cong also kept a number of other concubines *(ying)*. There was probably a major age difference as well between Yu Luozhen and her new master. Yu Luozhen's affair with Yu Cong's nephew Yu Zhuo led to her expulsion from Yu Cong's house and her eventual return to Pingkang li.[75]

A successful case of self-redemption is recorded in "The Story of Li Wa," a fantastic tale *(chuanqi)* written by Bai Xingjian (d. 826). Although it is a literary account, its realistic descriptions shed much light on the life of *ji^a*-entertainers. Li Wa, a pretty *ji^a*-entertainer living in Pingkang li, was active during the Tianbao (742–56) period. Under the patronage of her madam, Li became a favorite with many high-ranking officials and their sons. Having served her madam for twenty years, she bought back her freedom with her own savings in order to take care of her erstwhile lover, a failed degree candidate reduced to begging. Two years later, her lover took first place in the state examination, and married Li Wa officially with his father's blessings. She was ennobled as the duchess of Qian *(Qian guo furen)* in recognition of her altruistic spirit.[76]

Conclusion

The rich variety of *ji^a*-entertainers under the Tang testified to the unprecedented thriving of its entertainment business. Among the five types of *ji^a*-entertainers dealt with in this study are the court entertainers *(gongji^a)*, who were professionally trained stage performers for court entertainment. Official entertainers *(guanji^a)* and army entertainers *(yingji^a)* were officially owned entertainers, affiliated with either a local civil government or a military command. Official entertainers often lived with their clients (army officers or government officials) and provided long-term service. Home entertainers *(jiaji^a)* also lived with their clients, but they were privately owned; their clients served simultaneously as their masters. Finally, "Beili *ji^a*-entertainers" refers to those entertainers who lived and worked in Pingkang li. They offered services on demand and were controlled and owned by madams in houses of pleasure.

Thanks to the *Beili zhi* by Sun Qi, we have access to a detailed account of organized Beili *ji^a*-entertainers, who entertained their clients, typically well-educated and sophisticated scholars or officials, in houses owned by "adoptive mothers," or madams, who often were retired or semiactive. The entertainers were appreciated not only for their physical attractiveness, but also for their character, humor, conversational skills, and literary talent. A Beili *ji*ᵃ-entertainer at work was often a drinking companion, a fellow conversationalist, and a poetess.

In spite of the façade of civility, life in Pingkang li was sometimes fraught with unexpected danger. Young recruits, who had to go through rigid training in entertainment skills, were routinely lashed. If an entertainer was contracted through exclusive purchase *(maiduan)* to serve a single client for an extensive period of time, she would become more vulnerable to physical abuse. She would no longer be allowed to see other clients for financial or romantic reasons. A sense of depression is often found in the poems of those entertainers who felt hopelessly trapped. Those who wanted to end their careers could do so by self-redemption or redemption through outside help, although they often had to face enormous social and financial barriers.

Like their predecessors, the *ji*ᵃ-entertainers examined were primarily engaged in the business of entertaining male clients. Although prostitution had always been associated with the female entertainment business, it seems to have played a relatively minor role in that business prior to the Tang Dynasty. Based on extant sources, it is in the Tang capital of Chang'an that a full-fledged red-light district, located in Pingkang li, took root for the first time in Chinese history; in Pingkang li organized prostitution under the cover of entertainment was concentrated in a relatively small urban area. Thus organized prostitution came of age in China.[77]

A number of factors may have contributed to such a unique development. First are the less-than-exemplary sexual practices of the ruling house of the Tang. In studying the femmes fatales of the Tang Dynasty, the Qing historian Zhao Yi (1727–1814) castigates the Tang sovereigns for their overindulgence in sensual pleasure.[78] The Southern-Song neo-Confucian philosopher Zhu Xi (1130–1200) attributes their unrestrained sexual practices to their non-Chinese roots: "The Tang [ruling house] originated from the Yi and Di barbarians, and consequently did not regard bedroom indecency as out of the ordinary."[79] While it is no easy task to determine the level of foreign influence on the mores of Tang sovereigns and its impact on society at large, lax moral standards at court may have contributed to a sexually permissive atmosphere.

Second, as the largest city in the world, with a population often in excess of one million and with a thriving economy, Chang'an offered an increasingly urbanized environment conducive to the entertainment business as a whole and providing fertile ground for organized prostitution and the growth of the first red-light district on record.[80]

Finally, the presence of a large number of young and middle-aged males, often provincials untrammeled by familial ties and with considerable means at their disposal, made up the clientele base crucial for the continued flourishing of the entertainment business and organized prostitution. It is no coincidence that Pingkang li bordered on the main commercial center on the east (Eastern Market), and Chongren fang on the north, where the largest population of candidates for state examinations was concentrated.[81]

APPENDIX

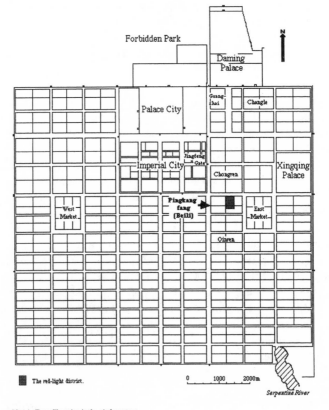

Map 1. Tang Chang'an in the ninth century.
Based on "Tang Chang'an cheng fuyuan tu" in
Tang liangjing chengfang kao.

Imperial City

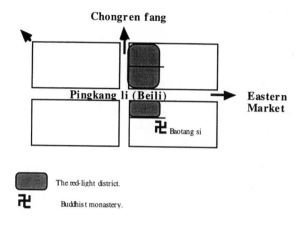

Map 2. Pingkang li (Beili) and the red-light district.
Based on Song Dexi, p. 80.

Notes

1. Chinese homophones pivotal to the discussion are designated with superscripts a and b.

2. As the most important source on Tang *ji*ᵃ-entertainers, *Beili zhi* has three
easily accessible editions: the *Gujin shuohai* (the best), the *Tangren shuohui,*
and the *Shuofu* (severely truncated but of great textual value). The *Gujin
shuohai* edition was the basis for the *Congshu jicheng* edition (titled *Sun neihan Beili zhi*) and the 1957 Shanghai edition, used here because of its easy
accessibility and its superior modern punctuation: *Beili zhi* [Record of the
Northern Quarters], by Sun Qi (Tang Dynasty), in *Beili zhi, Jiaofang ji,
Qinglou ji* (Shanghai: Gudian wenxue chubanshe, 1957). There have been
two Western translations of Sun's work. The most detailed study of Tang
*ji*ᵃ-entertainers in Chinese is Liao Meiyun's *Tang ji yanjiu* [A study of Tang
ji-entertainers] (Taipei: Xuesheng shuju, 1995). In English, Howard Levy
published an introductory article and a translation "The Gay Quarters of
Chang'an," *Orient/West* 7–9 (1962–4), primarily based on Ishida Mikinosuke's *Zōtei Chōan no haru* [Spring of Chang'an (the revised and enlarged edition) (Tokyo: Heibonsha, 1967). I do not use Levy's translation

in this article. A French translation, by Robert des Rotours, *Courtisanes chinoises à la fin des T'ang* [Chinese courtesans at the end of the Tang], Bibliothèque de l'Institut des Hautes Etudes Chinoises, vol. 22 (Paris: Presses Universitaires de France, 1968), is cited here along with Sun Qi's *Beili zhi*.

3. For the completion date of the work, see des Rotours, p. 16, which extends the beginning of the coverage to 789, on the basis of an anecdotal account of Hu Zheng appended to the *Beili zhi*. A similar account is found in the *Tang zhiyan* [Tidbits from the Tang], by Wang Dingbao (Five Dynasties) (Shanghai: Shanghai guji chubanshe, 1978), ch. 3, pp. 30–1. Hu was a classmate of Pei Du (765–839), who received his *jinshi* degree in 789. The event recorded is believed to have taken place a little after 789. The problem is that the record has nothing to do with the Beili *ji*^{a}-entertainers themselves. It is possible that this account is an interpolation.

4. For etymological studies of the term *ji*^{a}, see Wang Shunu, *Zhongguo changji shi* [A history of prostitutes in China] (1934; repr. Shanghai: Shanghai shudian, 1992), pp. 2–4; and Song Dexi, "Tangdai de jinü" [Prostitutes of the Tang Dynasty], in *Zhongguo funü shi lunji, xuji*, ed. Pao Chia-lin (Taipei: Daoxiang chubanshe, 1991), pp. 67–70.

5. Although Schafer uses "geisha" to translate *ji*^{a}, I prefer to use "*ji*^{a}-entertainer," which is composed of the transliteration *ji*^{a} and a generic translation, "entertainer." Cf. Edward Schafer, "Notes on T'ang Geisha," part 1, "Typology," *Schafer Sinological Papers* 2 (1984): 2.

6. Schafer suggests "gleemaiden" as the translation of *chang*^{a}-prostitute, in "Notes on T'ang Geisha," part 1, p. 2.

7. Song Dexi, p. 68.

8. *Xin Tang shu* [The new history of the Tang Dynasty], by Ouyang Xiu (1007–72), Song Qi (996–1061), et al. (Beijing: Zhonghua shuju, 1975): ch. 58, p. 1485.

9. *Taiping guangji* [Extensive gleanings of the reign of Great Tranquillity], comps. Li Fang (925–96) et al., 3 vols. (1755; repr. Taipei: Xinxing shuju, 1973), ch. 491, p. 1884.

10. Schafer, "Notes on T'ang Geisha," part 1, pp. 2–3.

11. Song Dexi sums up recent efforts at classifying Tang female entertainers by Ishida Mikinosuke, Kishibe Shigeo, and Fu Lecheng. See Fu Lecheng, "Tangren de shenghuo" [Life under the Tang], in his *Han-Tang shi lunji* (Taipei: Lianjing chuban shiye gongsi, 1977), pp. 134–5; and Kishibe Shigeo, "Chōan hokuri no seikaku to katsudō" [Character and activity of the Northern Quarters in Chang'an], *Rekishi to bunka* 4 of *Rekishigaku kenkyū hōkoku* 7 (1959), and his "Tōdai gikan no soshiki" [Organization of brothels in the Tang Dynasty], in *Tōkyō daigaku kyōyō gakubu jinbun kagakuka kiyō* 5, *Kodai kenkyū* 2 (1955). Song suggests that, in addition to the first four types, a fifth type of unofficial entertainers, or *minji*^{a}, should be added. However, the term *minji*^{a} is never used in Tang sources. Here I use instead the term *Beiliji*^{a}, which is found in the preface of Sun Qi's *Beili zhi*. See

Beili zhi 1; des Rotours, p. 69; Ishida Mikinosuke, pp. 101–3; cf. Song Dexi, p. 75.

12. Ren Bantang, *Tang xinong* [Tang theater], 2 vols. (Shanghai: Shanghai guji chubanshe, 1984), pp. 1119–29. The Palace City, the first official residence of the reigning emperor and his court under the Tang, was located in north central Chang'an.

13. Ren Bantang has completed an exhaustive study of the *Jiaofang ji,* which is the single most important extant source on the Department of Stage Performances. See *Jiaofang ji* [Record of the Department of Stage Performances], by Cui Lingqin (Tang Dynasty), *Jiaofang ji qianding,* edited and annotated by Ren Bantang (Shanghai: Shanghai Zhonghua shuju, 1962).

14. Besides the Palace City, the Imperial City *(huangcheng)* to the south, and the two markets, Tang Chang'an was comprised of around 110 enclosed residential wards known officially as *fang,* and unofficially as *li.* See Appendix, Map 1.

15. One passage in the *Jiaofang ji* suggests that some insiders *(neiren)* were cliquish and had an unconventional attitude toward sex. The women organized themselves into coteries of a dozen or so and called one another "sworn brothers" *(xianghuo xiongdi).* When a man from the court dated one of the sworn "brothers," her colleagues would talk about "doing it the Turkish way" and "sharing the 'wife.'" The "wife" referred to the man from the court. See *Jiaofang ji,* pp. 50–1; Ishida Mikinosuke, pp. 101–2.

16. *Jiaofang ji,* pp. 14–25. Fish tokens *(yufu)* were official status symbols made of jade, gold, silver, or bronze, usually kept in a fish token pouch *(yudai).* See *Xin Tang shu,* ch. 24, p. 525.

17. Later, the number became much enlarged, but the name "the ten" persisted.

18. Wang Tongling, "Tang-Song shidai jinü kao" [An examination of Tang-Song prostitutes], *Shixue nianbao* 1 (1929): 30.

19. Ibid., pp. 26–7.

20. See Wang Shunu, pp. 41–3, and Song Dexi, p. 77.

21. Ishida Mikinosuke, p.103.

22. "A willow tree" is a translation of the expression *yangliu* (poplar and willow trees). See *Taiping guangji* ch. 198, pp. 772–3.

23. Ibid., ch. 273, p. 1054.

24. See *Quan Tang shi* [Complete Tang poetry], comps. Peng Dingqiu (1645–1719) et al., 25 vols. (Beijing: Zhonghua shuju, 1960), ch. 81, pp. 873–8. On a translation of Qiao's poem on *jiᵃ*-entertainers titled "Tongque jiᵃ," see Schafer, "Notes on T'ang Geisha," part 2, "The Masks and Arts of T'ang Courtesans," p. 10.

25. *Taiping guangji,* ch. 274, p. 1056.

26. *Jiu Tang shu* [The old history of the Tang Dynasty], by Liu Xu (888–947) et al. (Beijing: Zhonghua shuju, 1975), ch. 190, *zhong,* p. 5012.

27. Robert des Rotours quotes another translation of the same passage, p. 50. See *Shi ji* [Records of the Grand Historian], by Sima Qian (145-ca. 86

B.C.E.) (Beijing: Zhonghua shuju, 1959), ch. 3, p. 105; and Song Dexi, p.79.

28. See des Rotours, pp. 24–5; and cf. Song Dexi, pp. 80–1.

29. See *Kaiyuan Tianbao yishi* [Anecdotes of the Kaiyuan and Tianbao eras], by Wang Renyu (Five Dynasties), in *Congshu jicheng*, ch. 1, p. 10.

30. For a criticism of Ishida's view, see Song Dexi, p. 79.

31. For the cases of Wang Tuan'er and Yang Miao'er, see *Beili zhi*, pp. 31–3; and des Rotours, pp. 108–9, 119.

32. Robert des Rotours, p. 67.

33. *Beili zhi*, pp. 26, 36.

34. Robert des Rotours (p. 65) translates *gaiyu* as "élevées comme mendiantes." I suspect that the correct translation should be simply "adoptées." For example, see *qi san chu yu gaiyang* in *Xin Wudai shi* [The new history of the Five Dynasties], by Ouyang Xiu (1007–72) et al. (Beijing: Zhonghua shuju, 1974), ch. 36, p. 385. *Butiao zhi tu* is translated by des Rotours as "gens sans profession." Cf. des Rotours, p.65.

35. *Beili zhi*, p.25; des Rotours, pp. 65–6.

36. *Beili zhi*, p. 33.

37. *Beili zhi*, p. 26; des Rotours, pp. 69–71.

38. The price tag was *yi er bai jin*, which des Rotours translates as "cent ou deux cents piéces d'or." In Tang times, gold varied in monetary form. Katō Shigeshi in his classic study on Tang-Song gold and silver regards the expression *jin* as a reference to the weight unit *liang*, which roughly corresponds to "tael." See Katō Shigeshi, *Tang-Song shidai zhi jinyin yanjiu* [Studies of Tang-Song gold and silver], a Chinese translation of his *Tō-Sō jidai no kingin no kenkyū* (1924; repr. Taipei: Xinwenfeng chubanshe, 1974), pp. 31, 35, 41.

39. Kishibe Shigeo hypothesizes that the *jiaofang* (Department of Stage) here is a euphemism for "brothels": *kyōbō to iu no ga gikan no kashō de atte,* pointing to the unlikelihood of having a *jiaofang* registration and a Pingkang li residence simultaneously. However, the *Beili zhi* contains evidence of such a practice. For example, when Funiang said: "I am lucky enough not to have been registered with the *jiaofang*," this implies that a Beili entertainer could be registered with it (des Rotours, p. 134). This is in keeping with the claim in the preface of the *Beili zhi* that these entertainers all lived in Pingkang li (des Rotours, pp. 53–4, 135; cf. Kishibe Shigeo, "Chōan hokuri," pp. 43–4, note 13).

40. *Beili zhi* Preface; des Rotours, p. 54. These *yinji*[a] differed from their namesakes at various local levels. See des Rotours, p. 68.

41. Robert des Rotours, p. 134.

42. Ibid., pp. 70, 135.

43. Wang Shunu, p. 76; Song Dexi, pp. 94–5.

44. *Cuyou rongse* (moderately pretty) is translated as "dans l'ensemble jolie" by des Rotours (p. 154).

45. *Weiyou fengmao* (moderately pretty) is rendered "avait un visage charmant" by des Rotours (p. 152), passing over *wei* (moderately).

46. Robert des Rotours translates *chongbo feimao zhe, dan fu liupin* as "elles [Zheng Juju and Jiangzhen] reprendre les gens impolis grâce à leur situation exceptionnelle," regarding *bo^a* (erudite) as a loan word for *bo^b* (to refute). *Feimao zhe* should refer to Zheng Juju herself as someone "learned but inferior in looks," instead of "les gens impolis." See *Peiwen yunfu* [A comprehensive rhyming dictionary], comps. Zhang Yushu (1642–1711) et al. (Shanghai: Shanghai guji chubanshe, 1983), ch. 99, *xia*, p. 3858.2 *chongbo*; cf. des Rotours, pp. 87–8.

47. Schafer, "Notes on T'ang Geisha," part 2, p. 3.

48. *Beili zhi*, pp. 26–7.

49. *Beili zhi*, pp. 32–3; *Quan Tang shi*, ch. 802, p. 9026. Robert des Rotours (p. 132) reads *ruo* (if) for *ku* (difficult, bitter).

50. See *Quan Tang shi*, ch. 802, pp. 9032–3.

51. *Yu* in Tang times should refer to nephrite, which is known in modern Chinese as *ruanyu* as distinguished from jadeite. On Tang Dynasty jade, see Schafer, *The Golden Peaches of Samarkand: A Study of T'ang Exotics* (Berkeley: University of California Press, 1963), pp. 223–7.

52. Song Dexi, pp. 70–2.

53. Kishebe Shigeo, "Chōan hokuri," pp. 42–3.

54. *Beili zhi*, p. 25; des Rotours, pp. 65–6.

55. Robert des Rotours, pp. 98–9.

56. Nanyuan, left unidentified in des Rotours (p. 111), was a section of the Bureau of Appointments under the Court of Personnel (*libu*), in charge of appointments of officials. See Charles O. Hucker, *A Dictionary of Official Titles in Imperial China* (Stanford: Stanford University Press, 1985), p. 342.

57. Robert des Rotours, pp. 111–2.

58. The translation of *fuyi er qu* as "jeta tous ses vêtements et s'enfuit" by des Rotours is wrong. *Fuyi* implies "a flick of one's clothes" just as *fuxiu er qu* means "to leave with a flick of sleeves." Cf. des Rotours, p. 117.

59. Robert des Rotours, pp. 70, 135.

60. Robert des Rotours translates *Wei Wannian xian buzei guan Guo Duan suo na* as "elle fut *achetée comme concubine* par Kouo Touan commissaire préosé à l'arrestation des voleurs (pou-tsei kouan) de la sous-préfecture de Wannien" (my emphasis) on p. 80. *Na* is interpreted in terms of *naqie* (accepting a concubine), though concubines were secondary wives and enjoyed certain legal privileges that set them apart from the entertainers.

61. *Beili zhi* refers to Guo Duan as "one of the descendants of Qinren [*fang*]" (*Qinren zhu yisun*). Qinren fang was known for Guo Ziyi's mansion, which occupied one quarter of the entire ward. This passage is rendered by des Rotours as "Kouo Touan appartenait à une famille qui vivait dans le quartier de Ts'in-jen [Qinren]," which is imprecise. See *Tang liangjing chengfang kao* [A study of the two Tang capitals, their cities and wards], by Xu

Song (Qing Dynasty) (Beijing: Zhonghua shuju, 1985), ch. 3, p. 61. Cf. des Rotours, p. 81.

62. *Beili zhi,* pp. 27–8; des Rotours, pp. 85–7.

63. Robert des Rotours, pp. 83–4.

64. "Immortal man" is a euphemism for client. Cf. des Rotours, p. 133.

65. Robert des Rotours, p. 137.

66. The simurgh (*luan*) is a roosterlike divine bird with a plumage symbolic of the five colors and a voice in harmony with the five notes. According to one legend, once a *luan* bird was captured and refused to sing for three years; when he saw his own image in a mirror, he gave a desperate cry and died. The *luan*-bird looking at himself in the mirror was often used as a metaphor for lonely widowhood. For a definition of *luan,* see "Dianlue" in *Yiwen leiju* [A categorized collection of literary writing], comp. Ouyang Xun (557–641) (1965; repr. Shanghai: Shanghai guji chubanshe, 1982), ch. 90, p. 1560; for the legend see "Luanniao shi xu" [Preface to the *luan*-bird poem], by Fan Tai, in *Yiwen leiju,* ch. 90, p. 1560. My translation of *luan* as "simurgh" follows Schafer's *The Divine Woman* (San Francisco: North Point Press, 1980), p. 144.

67. The paired "simurgh and phoenix" (*luanfeng*) and "swallow and its companion" (*yanlü*) are used in literary Chinese to denote harmonious relationships between husband and wife.

68. *Beili zhi,* pp. 30–1; des Rotours, pp. 104–5. According to des Rotours' version, on the last line, *dian* (offer a cup of wine [to the dead]) is replaced by *zun* (to venerate), a character that shares the same radical. See des Rotours, p. 105.

69. On the obscure origin of the term, see Hucker, *A Dictionary,* p. 168. On Wang Shi's position at the time of the incident, see des Rotours, p. 178.

70. *Beili zhi,* pp. 41–2; des Rotours, pp. 180–1.

71. Robert des Rotours, pp. 176–9.

72. *Changshi* (attendant-in-ordinary) is a high-ranking officer of a princely affairs administration. See Hucker, *A Dictionary,* p. 115. The verb used here is *qu,* which normally means "to marry somebody as one's wife." Here it is obviously used loosely to mean "to accept somebody as one's bedmate." See des Rotours, p. 139.

73. *Beili zhi,* pp. 33–5; des Rotours, pp. 138–9.

74. His title *zuokui* (left mastermind) is a popular reference to *zuo puye* (vice director of the left), a chief-ministerial post. See Hucker, *A Dictionary,* p. 523.

75. *Beili zhi,* pp. 35–6; des Rotours, pp. 140–8.

76. Her title *guo furen* (duchess) was one of nobility conferred on wives of dukes during the Tang Dynasty. See Hucker, *A Dictionary,* p. 297. The story is recorded in *Taiping guangji,* ch. 484, pp. 1858–61, and translated by Glen Dudbridge, *The Tale of Li Wa, Study and Critical Edition of a Chinese Story from the Ninth Century* (London: Ithaca Press, 1983).

77. On the evolution of the female entertainment business and prostitution prior to and during Tang times, see Wang Shunu, pp. 9–102.

78. *Nian'ershi zhaji* [Notes on the twenty-two histories], by Zhao Yi (1727–1814), ch. 19, p. 375, in the *Congshu jicheng* edition.

79. *Zhuzi yulei* 116.3, as quoted in Chen Yinke, *Tangdai zhengzhi shi shulun gao* [A preliminary study of the political history of the Tang Dynasty] (1957; repr. Shanghai: Shanghai guji chubanshe, 1982), p. 1.

80. Seo Tatsuhiko has done a number of studies on the prosperity of Tang Chang'an. See "Tōdai Chōan no sakariba" [Downtown area of Tang Chang'an], *Shiryū* 27 (1986):1–59 and 30 (1989):37–91; and "Tōdai kōhanki no Chōan to denki shōsetsu" [Chang'an in the latter half of the Tang and *chuanqi* tales], in *Hino Kaisaburō hakushi shōju kinen ronshū* (Fukuoka, Japan: Chūgoku shoten, 1987).

81. To take exams, the candidates went east from Chongren fang to enter the Imperial City through the Jingfeng Gate. See *Tang liangjing chengfang kao*, ch. 3, p. 53.

CHAPTER SIX

SMELL GOOD AND GET A JOB:
HOW DAOIST WOMEN SAINTS
WERE VERIFIED AND LEGITIMATIZED
DURING THE TANG DYNASTY (618–907)

Suzanne Cahill
University of California at San Diego

> *Medieval Daoists authenticated sainthood by the body's remaining intact after death and legitimated it by including the saint in the religious lineage and celestial bureaucracy.*

Introduction

Daoism, the major native religion of China, encompasses a wide range of both popular and elite beliefs and practices. It already had a long history before the Tang Dynasty. Daoist ideas go back to a core of nature mysticism embodied in the fourth or third century B.C.E. classics known as the "Scripture of the Way and Its Power" ("Daode jing") and the *Zhuangzi,* named for its attributive author. In the following centuries, during periods of social crisis and change, the Daoist religion, faced with competition from the proselytizing foreign faith of Buddhism, took institutional form, developing deities, heavens, clergy, temples, sacred texts, rituals, and devoted followers. It fostered belief in the perfectibility of humans through faith, good works, asceticism, and meditation, leading to individual immortality. During the fourth and fifth centuries C.E., two great schools of Daoism emerged and continued into the Tang period. The Supreme Clear Realm *(Shangqing)* tradition, which took its name from the highest Daoist heaven, emphasized individual salvation through ascetic practices and found favor with the Chinese imperial and official elites. The other school, known as the Numinous Treasure *(Lingbao)* after its scriptures, focused upon collective rituals and the community and found a broad following. In the Tang period, these schools began to come together.

The goal of medieval Chinese Daoists was individual immortality: evading death and decomposition, ascending to heaven, and obtaining a position in the celestial bureaucracy. Adepts accomplished these goals through practices designed to protect and nourish the immortal embryo within each person until that embryo, mature at last, could assume its rightful place in the Daoist heavens. While ordinary people died at the end of their lives, the Daoist adept was transformed into a perfected immortal. Tang biographies and poetry reveal that women as well as men aspired to transcendence and practiced the self-cultivation required to overcome death.

This paper uses transformation narratives contained in hagiographical accounts of Daoist holy women compiled by the Daoist master and court official Du Guangting (850–933), together with biographical materials from a collection of anecdotes recorded by Huangfu Mei (flourished 880), to examine the way in which medieval Chinese people thought about death and sanctity for women. These transformation narratives can tell us about Daoist sainthood in medieval China. [1]

How did one get to be a saint in Tang Dynasty China? In particular, what is the mechanism for sainthood in the Daoist religion? How is sanctity verified and legitimatized? How are claims to sainthood established? In China as elsewhere, saints serve as focal points for spiritual and social life and even the identity of a community, and as conduits to the divine on behalf of the community. As elsewhere in the world, verification of sanctity is important, and various means of verification are employed. Also, as elsewhere, Chinese Daoists seek to legitimize their saints by associating them with central cultural institutions; yet there is something special in the Chinese case.

In the West, the Catholic Church establishes sainthood by using systems that parallel structures central to medieval Western states. [2] The most important of these systems is law, doubly determined by religious and secular history in the West to be good. According to medieval Western thought, law was first given to humans by the deity of the Hebrew Bible in the Ten Commandments, and was also created by free male citizens as the greatest contribution of classical Athens. Legal structures grant legitimacy to the church's process of canonization.

Chinese Daoists also seek to legitimize their saints, but legal systems cannot provide a structure for them to use. Ever since pivotal debates during the fourth century B.C.E. between the followers of Confucius *(Rujia)* and the Legalist school *(Fajia),* law in China has traditionally been seen as bad, a sign of human imperfection. If humans were inherently good, the Confucians argued, we would not need laws to make us do the right thing. If we need laws to order our society, the Legalists claimed, then we must be inherently selfish and chaotic. Law in China is a necessary evil, rather than a system that grants value by association. The medieval Chinese Daoists found legitimatizing structures within their own society to incorporate or co-opt. In particular, they employed two institutions central to Chinese culture that are also two of China's most ancient obsessions: lineage and bureaucracy. Nothing is more important to the Chinese than lineage and family, and nothing is more admirable to them than the imperial bureaucracy. Surely all order must follow that of the Chinese family and state. Daoist schools traced their lines of succession through generations of teachers back to divine masters. The Daoist heavens, with their hierarchies of celestial officials, are modeled on the Chinese imperial system. Daoist saints need to be placed in the right lineage, and they need to be incorporated into a bureaucracy.

The following discussion considers the death narratives (or better: "transformation narratives," since their followers believed they did not die) of several women Daoists of the Tang Dynasty who were incorporated into the heavenly bureaucracy, and one who was not. We will examine these transformation narratives of female Daoist practitioners to show how each departure follows from the life that precedes it, how circumstances surrounding the departure are used to verify sanctity, and how claims to sanctity are established through placement in a divine lineage and the granting of an office in the celestial imperium.

Sources

The most important source for this paper is the "Records of the Assembled Transcendents of the Fortified Walled City" ("Yongcheng jixian lu"), a set of hagiographical accounts of the lives of Daoist female saints by the Shangqing Daoist Master and Tang courtier Du Guangting. The last date in the text is 885; it was completed and offered to the throne around 910. Through a critical reading of his preface, together with remarks scattered throughout his biographies, we can characterize Du Guangting's point of view in this work. As a Daoist Master, Du has several goals. He wishes to preserve stories of holy women who were otherwise ignored in the written record. He intends to demonstrate the sanctity of his subjects and link them to the Shangqing lineage, glorifying his own school. Writing during the period of destruction and chaos at the end of the Tang Dynasty, he attempts to demonstrate the efficacy of his faith as a means of personal salvation. As a court official, he writes to praise the last Tang rulers and their successor Wang Jian in order to obtain royal patronage, and to request official titles for the most recent of these saints. [3]

Our other source, although contemporary with Du's collection of holy biographies, presents a vivid contrast. The *Little Tablets [By the Fellow] from Three Rivers (Sanshui xiaodu)*, also finished around 910, is a short collection of anecdotes by the minor Late-Tang official Huangfu Mei, probably intended for circulation among a small group of literati and their families. Believed to have been based on contemporary events, it preserves several powerful stories, among them the violent and tragic tale of Yu Xuanji (844–68). Where the hagiographer Du Guangting presents his subjects in a positive light, designed to convince us of their sanctity, the storyteller Huangfu Mei entertains and instructs us with the weaknesses and failures of his central character. His Yu Xuanji is a classic negative model, warning the reader of what happens to a woman who exercises freedom of choice concerning her own sexuality, religious vocation, and intellectual life. [4] Now we turn to the transformation narratives and the bearing they have on sainthood.

Transformation and Sainthood

Rather than die at the end of their lives, Daoist transcendents undergo a transformation that enables them to ascend to the heavens. The Daoist heavens are numerous, diverse, and complex. They vary according to the author or school. Roughly speaking, for the Shangqing school, there were three major heavens in the celestial vault above the earth. These were, in descending order, the Supreme Clear Realm (*Shangqing,* from which the school takes its name), the Jade Clear Realm *(Yuqing),* and the Grand Clear Realm *(Taiqing).* Along with the three principle Clear Realms where the great gods of Daoism dwell, there are several other auspicious regions that may also be called heavens. These include grotto heavens *(dongtian)* under the earth, microcosmic paradises complete in every way. Grotto heavens connect holy mountains through secret underground caverns; they provide the faithful with a safe refuge during the periodic cataclysms that mark the end of a world age. Immortals may dwell in any of these fortunate locations and may pass freely between different realms.

Du Guangting's female subjects use a variety of successful strategies for attaining immortality. Du describes their religious practices and the results they obtain. The end of each life is determined by the practices the subject carries out while alive: the nature of her departure is determined by the quality of her life. As a result, there is also a hierarchy of departures. The most accomplished saints ascend in broad daylight with great fanfare in the presence of witnesses. Next come those who undergo a secret process known as "liberation by means of the corpse" *(shijie)*, in which they appear to die and leave a body behind for burial, while their real selves depart to join the heavenly bureaucracy. [5] Du Guangting outlines this hierarchy of departures in his account of Ms. Wang:

> The highest class of those who attain the Way ascends to heaven in broad daylight. Their form and bones fly up together to fill vacancies as realized officials. Members of the next class shed their skins like cicadas. They also soar and rise with their form and bones, their flesh and material substance climbing up to heaven. In both of these cases, they become heavenly transcendents; they do not dwell in the mountains and marchmounts.[6]

The lowest transcendents depart this life to take up official positions in grotto heavens beneath holy mountains here on earth; there they await the end of the world cycle to unite with the celestial imperium.

In contrast to successful adepts, most ordinary mortals simply die at the end of a normal life span. Daoists call such people "walking corpses" *(xing-shi)*; they are going nowhere but the grave after this life. People who have committed great sins fare even worse; they are destined to fates like that of Yu Xuanji. She provided a spectacularly negative example after her life was cut short by execution. Her dismembered body could not receive proper sacrifice because it could not be returned whole to the ground. What is more, she died before she could bear a son to honor her and tend her spirit after death. According to folk beliefs of both Daoists and Buddhists, she will wander forever as a hungry ghost. The following section translates actual transformation stories.

Transformation Narratives: Each Departure Follows from the Life That Precedes It

Du Guangting records two women who achieved the highest form of transformation available to any Daoist adept, male or female—the ascension to heaven in broad daylight. Du narrates five cases of liberation which occurred after the body had been a corpse for some time, and four of the lower sort of immortal who departs at the end of earthly existence. Du's stories share several features and are full of concrete physical detail. The adept in question has often predicted her own departure. Her departure upward is often accompanied by heavenly clouds, by divine vehicles such as cranes, and by auspicious fragrances. Huangfu Mei's story of Yu Xuanji's tragic death presents a marked contrast in outcome, but Huangfu also tends to dwell on physical details and manner of leaving. In all cases, the final manner of departure results from the life led. After examining all the stories, we will consider what they mean in terms of Daoist sanctification. We will begin with the two who ascended straight to heaven in the light of day, Wang Fajin and Bian Dongxuan.

For Du Guangting, Wang Fajin represents the embodiment of the Lingbao tradition, which emphasizes ritual and community. An accomplished female ascetic and liturgical expert, Wang Fajin saved humankind from destruction when she transmitted an essential Daoist rite of confession and thanksgiving from the Supreme Thearch in the Jade Capital. At the end of her life span, Du tells us, "in the eleventh year of the Heavenly Treasure reign period [752] . . . cloud cranes welcomed Fajin and she ascended to heaven." [7]

Du Guangting's second case of direct ascent is that of Bian Dongxuan. For the author, Dongxuan embodies his own Shangqing school, which centered upon techniques for individual salvation. Bian was an ascetic and visionary nun who starved herself while providing food for others. A divine elixir hastened her transcendent journey in 713:

> With that [the old herbalist, a deity in disguise] opened his bag and showed her two or three dippers of drug pellets that were blue-black in color and about the size of paulownia seeds. He ordered her to feel around for them inside the bag herself. Following her own whim, Dongxuan grasped three pellets from his drug bag. The old gent said: "If you ingest this cinnabar elixir, it will transform your intestines and exchange your blood. After exactly fifteen days you will ascend to heaven. This is a drug of the middle grade."
>
> Then again he brought out a box about as big as a coin from inside the flap of his robe and took out a little bit of a drug that had the appearance of peach gum. Its fragrance was also like that of peaches. The old gent himself drew water from the well to blend with this peach gum, then ordered her to swallow the pill. The old gent delightedly told her: " . . . The Grand Supreme One has given a command ordering me to summon you . . . After seven days you will be able to ascend to heaven. . . ."
>
> [Crowds gather to witness her departure.] She soared up bodily to the top of the storied building. A strange fragrance overflowed, while extraordinary clouds scattered, filling the whole prefecture. . . . Dongxuan notified the masses: "On the morning of the Middle Primordial Day [the fifteenth of the seventh month], I will definitely ascend to heaven. You may come and take leave of me."

The masses then brought about a great fast meeting. On the fifteenth day of the seventh month, from the hours of seven to nine AM, heavenly music filled the void. Dense and impenetrable purple clouds wound around the storied buildings of the belvedere. The masses of the people saw Dongxuan ascend, with standards and pennants spread out and arrayed. She departed straight to the south. The Grand Protector and the flock of officials memorialized the throne about what they had perceived that day between the hours of seven and eleven AM.

[At the same time,] the Brilliant Illustrious One of the Great Tang Dynasty [reigned 712–56], dwelling at ease in his basilica, suddenly sensed a strange fragrance as variegated purple vapors filled the courtyard. There were four blue lads leading a woman Daoist scholar whose age might have been about sixteen or seventeen. She approached and said: "Your handmaiden is the woman Daoist scholar Bian Dongxuan from Youzhou. Today I have attained the Way and am ascending to heaven. I have come to say farewell to Your Majesty [literally, you below the stairs]." Her words finished, she slowly departed. [8]

Du Guangting records five cases during the Tang Dynasty of liberation by means of the corpse. This is the second-highest means of ascent to the Daoist heavens, in Du Guangting's hierarchy of paths to immortality. The first case is Ms. Wang, an eighth- century householder and initiate who fasted and meditated. Ms. Wang spoke to her daughters as her end drew near:

"When I die, do not use a coffin. You can make me a screen of cedarwood. Convey my corpse into the wilds. After a time, you may depute someone to examine it."

That night she died. The people of her household prepared her for burial as she had instructed; everything was as agreed upon. They set her up in a grove of the hunting park, reclining as if in bed. There were no changes or alterations [in her corpse]. Twenty years later thieves pushed open her interment and abandoned her body on an earthen mound. During the [following] winter months, people suddenly heard the sound of lightning and thunder coming from beside her screen. Her whole household, startled and considering it strange, rushed forward to look. When they arrived there and lifted out her corpse, her body was as light as an empty husk. Her flesh, nails, and hair were all complete—but on the right side of her rib cage, a scar more than a foot long had split open. Afterwards, she was reburied [with rites appropriate to] a Lady of the Southern Marchmount. [9]

Hua Gu, the "Flower Maiden," achieved liberation by means of the corpse because of her good works and contributions to the cult of Lady Wei Huacun, a major goddess of the Shangqing school. Hua Gu restored shrines sacred to Lady Wei Huacun. The Flower Maiden predicted her own death and made special requests for the treatment of her corpse:

> In the ninth year of the Opened Prime reign period [721] . . . when the Maiden was about to ascend to transformation, she said to her disciples: "My transcendent journey becomes urgent; I cannot stay here any longer. After my body is transformed, do not nail my coffin shut, but just cover it with crimson netted gauze."
>
> The next day she came to an end without even being sick. Her flesh and muscle were fragrant and pure, her form and breath warm and genial. A strange fragrance filled the courtyard and halls. Her disciples followed her orders and did not nail her coffin shut, simply covering it with crimson netted gauze. Suddenly they all heard lightning and thunder strike. There was a hole about as big as a hen's egg in the gauze, and in the coffin were only her shroud and some wooden chips. In the ceiling of the room was a hole big enough for a person to pass through. At the base of the coffin they made an offering of a gourd, which after several days sprouted creepers and grew two fruits like peaches. Each time the anniversary of her death came around, wind and clouds would grow thick and suddenly enter right inside the room. [10]

Du Guangting tells us that Lu Meiniang, also called the Divine Maiden, also accomplished liberation by means of the corpse. Lu was an ascetic with long green eyebrows and miraculous weaving skills who achieved transcendence sometime around 820:

> For a long time she did not eat. Divine people regularly descended to meet her. One morning she was transformed into a feathered transcendent. Fragrant vapors filled her apartment. When they lifted her coffin to begin her burial, it felt light. So they removed its cover, finding only her old shoes. From time to time, people see her riding over the sea on a purple cloud. [11]

According to Du, Wang Fengxian, an ascetic and meditator who became a great teacher of Daoist texts and techniques, achieved liberation in the same manner:

> At the beginning of the Radiant Opening reign period [885], she moved up to Mount Qianqing in the region of Hangzhou. The people built a flowery cottage beneath the mountains for her to dwell in. After over a year, she was transformed without ever getting sick. She was forty-eight years old. There were the auspicious tokens of cloud cranes and a strange fragrance. This tallied precisely with the period of fifty years mentioned by the heavenly one [an earlier prediction]. In addition, she had not eaten for thirty years. She

had a youth's complexion and snowy flesh, as if she had remained a virgin. If not through the work of gold and cinnabar elixirs and gold fluid, how could she have reached this point? Also her spirits had frequently wandered to the borders of heaven, and she could sit upright for a whole month. Sometimes she had descended to inspect the affairs of earthly bureaus or stygian passes, or sat and looked at the eight extremities; many times she had spoken about it with people who possessed the Way. People in this world do not recognize that all her accomplishments were on account of sitting in forgetfulness. She is now Companion of the Primal Ruler of the Southern Pole and Divine Mother of the Eastern Tumulus. [12]

Xue Xuantong, the last entry in Du Guangting's records, was a householder who fasted, meditated, and took elixirs. She provides our final example of liberation by means of the corpse:

The next year [882], in the second month, Xuantong washed her hair and face, then took the tidbit of elixir that the Primal Ruler of the Purple Void had given her. Two transcendent women secretly descended to her room, urging her to proceed to the heights of Marchmount Song (Song Yue). On the fourteenth day of that month, she manifested symptoms, and in a single evening it was finished. At her private residence, thirty-six wingspans of transcendent cranes gathered on top of her room. Xuantong's form and substance were light and warm; her appearance was like that of a living person. The centers of her cheeks looked as if they were smoking, and there was a dot of radiant light that after a good long time transformed itself into purple vapor. When she had washed her hair and face, her dark hair had increased in thickness and grown several feet in length.

On the night of the fifteenth day, clouds of variegated colors filled her room, and suddenly people heard the sounds of thunder and lightning shaking and crashing. Her coffin lid flew up inside the courtyard; her corpse had disappeared, leaving behind only her empty burial garments and quilt. Strange fragrances arose. The cloud cranes stayed ten days before departing.[13]

Du Guangting records four cases of the lower sort of immortal who simply departs. One day, the adept in question disappears and is seen no more. We are left to assume that she has attained transcendence.

Gou Xiangu was a hermit and defender of the faith. As her time draws near, she tells her disciple, a former Prime Minister: "'After the present time, all within the Four Seas will run into many difficulties; I cannot dwell much longer among humans. I will perform divinations, then retreat to Nine Uncertainties Mountain.' Then one morning she departed." [14] Another lower transcendent is the magician Xu Xiangu, who simply disappears. [15] Then there is Yang Pingzhi, wife of a banished immortal. After a lecture on the structure of the grotto heavens' bureaucracy, "within ten days, husband and wife departed together." [16]

The banished immortal Huang Guanfu provides our last example of a lower immortal who simply disappears. She leaves her parents twice. First she commits suicide by drowning to avoid marriage and comes back as a statue; later, after revealing that she is a banished immortal, she leaves again:

> When she reached marriageable age, her parents wanted her to marry. Suddenly she said to her father and mother: "There is something extremely strange in the River by the head of the gate." . . . Then she threw herself into the River. After a good long time passed and she did not emerge, her father and mother dredged the River and obtained a wooden statue, like those carved of the heavenly honored ones in the olden days. Its gilding and painted colors were already mottled. Its form and appearance were no different from their daughter. . . . Then they took that wooden image and set it up beside the road, calling out and weeping. . . .
>
> [Later] she descended together with three female companions and said to her mother: "Your daughter was originally a person of the Supreme Clear Realm. For a small transgression I was banished to live among humans. . . . When I leave here, I won't come back again." [She forecasts an epidemic and gives her parents the means to escape it.] [17]

In each of the eleven cases described above, Du tells us the auspicious circumstances of a Daoist saint's departure. Our single case of a nun who was no saint and comes to a bad end is recorded by Huangfu Mei in his *Sanshui xiaodu:*

> [In the spring of 868, suspecting her maid of a sexual relationship with one of her patrons,] Xuanji stripped Lüqiao naked and gave her a hundred lashes, but the latter still denied everything. . . . She said: "You seek the way of the Daoist triad, and of immortality, yet cannot forget the pleasures of the flesh." [Lüqiao vowed revenge after death if there were a heaven]. . . . Having spoken her mind, she expired on the floor. Frightened, Xuanji dug a pit in the backyard and buried her, assuring herself that no one would know of it. . . .
>
> A guest once dining in Xuanji's room happened to go urinate in the backyard on the spot of the burial. There he saw a swarm of black flies clustered over the earth. . . . Taking a closer look, he saw what seemed to be traces of blood. Besides, there was a stench. . . . [He told some others who] forced their way into Xuanji's house and uncovered the body. Lüqiao looked just as she had when alive. The watchman then reported Xuanji to the city authorities of the capital area. An official questioned her, and she wrote a confession. In court circles there were many who spoke on her behalf. The

city authorities reported the case to the emperor. In autumn, nonetheless, she was executed. While in prison she still wrote poetry. [18]

In all of these stories, the form of each woman's departure results from the life she lived. Fasting and meditation lead to transcendence; lasciviousness and violence lead to death and destruction. Both Du Guangting and Huangfu Mei use vivid physical descriptions of the end of their subjects' lives on earth to tell exemplary tales meant to instruct: to edify and warn. The following section considers what details of a subject's departure from this life can tell us about the verification and legitimization of her sanctity.

Verifying Sanctity

In his hagiographical accounts of saints' lives and departures, Du Guangting is deeply concerned with verification of their sanctity. His concern is comparable to that of a dynastic historian writing biographies of officials and emperors: he wants to assure us of the legitimacy of his subjects' claim to the positions they hold. In the case of the hagiographical accounts, verification comes from both form and content. Du uses the prestigious and familiar form of the dynastic biography, citing dates and giving familiar details that reflect positively upon his subject. In his *Little Tablets [By the Fellow] from Three Rivers,* Huangfu Mei, in contrast, uses an anecdotal and almost fictional form. The form itself heightens the emotional impact of his cautionary tale of Yu Xuanji, while marginalizing her and diminishing her stature. Huangfu pens an entertaining fable with plenty of voyeuristic details, rather than a reverent account of a figure he considers worthy of worship.

Further, within Du Guangting's accounts, the subjects' sainthood is verified by their accomplishments in life: fasting, meditating, teaching, saving, curing, defending, and restoring. Their magical attainments also attest to their sanctity: these were fruits of faith, visible proof that they had obtained the Dao. Special gifts include endless production of food and drink, celestial travel, communication with animals, deities' visits, and—most especially—youthful good looks and health. Compliance with holy texts included in the Daoist canon was also the mark of a saint: her teaching, behavior, and appearance must accord with scripture. In addition, her charisma might attract disciples or worshipers. During her life and after her death, she might be the center of a cult, and she might receive recognition by imperial authorities in the form of steles, records, shrines, and convents.

The most important verification occurs at her departure from this life; Du Guangting describes the manner and appearance of his subjects' "deaths" in great detail. He emphasizes each saint's beauty, vigor, and youthful appearance at the end. Her hair may suddenly grow, or her flesh glow. She invariably undergoes a swift death with dignity, a passage without pain, mess, or ritual pollution. (Ritual pollution refers to a state in which a person is unfit to be in the presence of the spirit or participate in the human community. In traditional Chinese society, women's bodies were believed to be great sources of ritual pollution.) The texts emphasize how her body does not rot or decay, no matter how long it is kept around. Not only does she not exude the stench of putrefaction, but her sweet-smelling body emits clouds of divine fragrance as she goes: the odor of sanctity. [19] She smells good. (This was in a religious context, in which meditating on decaying corpses was a regular part of religious training for dealing with transience.) She exerts control over death, predicting the time and circumstances of her own transformation and presiding over the ritual of her departure like a monarch. At her deathbed appear traditional auspicious omens, such as cranes and multicolored, fragrant clouds. Her life, crowned with the manner of her passing, makes the saint a good omen in herself, a spiritual ornament for the dynasty, and a sign of salvation in her time. Her passing may be marked by manifestations of spiritual power, such as lightning and thunder, divine music, or the appearance of deities. Her body may disappear or fly away, leaving behind only a husk, clothing, or accessories as evidence of her transformation. Reading these accounts, the modern reader may ask why they are so literal-minded? The details seem almost funny—and yet the physical details are the verification of transcendence that establishes the claim of legitimate sainthood for these women. For Daoists, the physical body is important; transcendence and immortality are individual and physical. The body is identified with the self. Without a body, there can be no transcendence. [20]

Lineage and Office

Striking continuities and shared values between this world and the next are demonstrated by the transformation narratives of the Tang Daoist holy women recorded by Du Guangting. Among the most important are lineage and bureaucracy. Once her sanctity is verified through her practices during life and the circumstances of her departure, the subject may be incorporated into a lineage. In medieval China, lineage normally meant family and clan and was designated by surname. Lineage provided the economic, social, and ritual units by which people identified themselves and represented themselves to others. A woman entered her husband's lineage at marriage. Nuns were outside the normal definition of lineage, but they created their own religious lineages and used them to identify themselves in this world and the hereafter. For a nun, her Daoist lineage would include her school, teacher, and heaven.

The whole text of Du Guangting's "Record of the Assembled Transcendents of the Fortified Walled City" can be read as a lineage register. The biographies are arranged in order of transmission of Shangqing Daoist doctrines and practices. The text opens with the life of the Queen Mother of the West, the highest goddess of the Shangqing school of Daoism. Du moves on to the lives of several divine teachers. After the teacher goddesses, he relates the biographies, in roughly chronological order, of great female saints from the Han (206 B.C.E. - 220 C.E.) through the Tang Dynasties. This last section makes up the bulk of his book. Each saint has embodied the Dao in an exemplary fashion and can serve as a model and a focus of worship. By including these women, Du claims their descent by way of textual and ritual transmission in a genealogy beginning with the highest deities in the highest heavens of his faith.

Not only does she have to smell good, the saint has to get a job. Daoist holy women, like holy men, obtain positions in the celestial imperium. In one of his accounts, Du Guangting generalizes about one group of female transcendents who fill official posts in the heavenly bureaucracy. He makes the startling claim that celestial posts are determined by merit rather than sex:

> All possess a heavenly appearance and the strictest beauty. In their proper ritual caps, they startle the masses. Their talents and knowledge shine forth heroically. All have attained the Celestial Office of Attendant Esquire of the Bright Chronograms and dwell in the grottoes. One is raised to the responsibility of Attendant Esquire according to virtue and talent, unrestricted by distinctions between male and female. [21]

In another context, the husband of the banished immortal Yang Pingzhi describes the bureaucracy of the grotto heavens. He asserts that the celestial imperium is much like that on earth:

> In the center of all of [the grotto heavens] are the sun and the moon and the flying essences, which we call the roots of concealed deities. The light they send down to illuminate the inside of the grottoes is no different from that in this world. Within them are transcendent kings, transcendent ministers, and transcendent officials who help and assist each other like officials in the world.
>
> People who have attained the Way and those who have accumulated virtue so as to transcend or become deities and return to life all dwell in

their midst as the population. Every year on the festivals of the three great primes, supreme realized beings from the various heavens descend and travel to the grotto heavens to observe how they regulate good and evil. In the human world, all such things as life and death, rise and fall, water and drought, wind and rain, are arranged in advance in the grottoes. Orders for sacrificial offerings at the shrines and ancestral temples of dragons and deities are all governed by the grotto bureaus. . . .

The transcendent officials in the grotto heavens are like the flock of governing agents among your commanderies and counties. One cannot record them one by one in detail. [22]

Female saints, like secular male officials who have contributed to the empire, receive posthumous titles. The difference is that Daoists believe their immortals actually take up these posts in the heavens after they leave this world. Their uncorrupted corpses verify their sanctity; the assignment of ranks signifies the legitimization of that sanctity.

Conclusion

Even such an apparently metaphysical and universal phenomenon as sainthood turns out to be, in significant part, culturally constructed, taking specific forms in different civilizations. Tang women saints stand between contemporary social values that emphasize loyalty to family and government, and Daoist values that stress individual salvation and religious communities. The female saints join and reconcile both aspects in their lives and transformations. Their transformation narratives verify and legitimatize their sanctity, linking lineage and bureaucracy on the one hand with the religious community and individual practice on the other.

These findings and other recent research in Daoist studies have rather broad implications for Chinese historical studies. It is becoming apparent that we need to redefine the part of Chinese tradition that we call Daoist, expanding it to include more elements of both elite and popular culture. For example, lineage and bureaucracy have always formed an important part of institutionalized religion. At the same time we must redefine the part that belongs to Confucianism, shrinking it so that we no longer lump everything that belongs to traditional China, such as bureaucracy or lineage, together as "Confucian." In addition, instead of seeing Confucianism and Daoism as two opponents competing for Chinese people's hearts and souls, we need to understand that the true rival of Daoism in the arena of religion is Buddhism. In China from medieval times, Daoism and Buddhism grew up together: sharing ideas, competing with each other, and addressing the same issues such as suffering, injustice, and death. We also need to study the women's poetry to hear what their own voices say about their experiences; compare transformation narratives of male and female Daoist saints; and compare Buddhist and Daoist saints. Looking outside China, we can begin to study Chinese and Western medieval women saints from a comparative perspective.

Notes

This paper is the most recent part of a larger study of the lives and practices of Tang Dynasty Daoist women saints. I outlined research on stages along female paths to immortality, according to the hagiographical record, in "Practice Makes Perfect: Paths to Transcendence for Women in Medieval China," *Taoist Resources* 2:2 (1990): 23–42; described women's physical practices in relation to notions of the female body, as part of a panel organized by Dorothy Ko on "The Mindful Body in China" for the Association for Asian Studies, 1994; and presented further developments in "Discipline and Transformation: Body and Practice in the Lives of Taoist Holy Women of the Tang Dynasty" at the First Japanese and American Taoist Studies Conference in Tokyo, 1995 (forthcoming in a conference volume in Japanese). I considered the process of sanctification in an early version of this paper, "Transformation and Sainthood: Records of Taoist Holy Women of the Tang Dynasty"; prepared for a panel on death narratives of Chinese women organized by Sherry Mou at the Thirty-First International Congress on Medieval Studies in 1996; and presented a later version at the Conference on Women in Confucian Cultures organized by Dorothy Ko and Susan Mann at University of California at San Diego in June, 1996. I would like to thank Professors Ko, Mann, and Mou and other participants for their comments on this work.

1. For the history of the Daoist religion, see Isabelle Robinet, *Histoire du taoisme: Des origines au XIVe siecle* (Paris: Cerf, 1991); and Stephen R. Bokenkamp, *Early Daoist Scriptures* (Berkeley: University of California, 1997).

2. For a discussion of the process of sanctification in the West, see Kenneth L. Woodward, *Making Saints* (New York: Simon and Schuster, 1990).

3. See Du Guangting, *Yongcheng jixian lu* [Records of the assembled transcendents of the fortified walled city], in *Yunji qiqian* [Seven slips from a bookbag of clouds], Weng Tu-chien, 1026, ch. 114. The text is found in the *Daozang,* the "Treasure-House of the Way," or "Daoist Canon." I use the *Zhengtong daozang* edition, reprinted (Taipei: Yiwen chubanshe, 1976), vol. 38, 30323–47. Hereafter this text is cited as DG, followed by page number. Texts in the Daoist canon are referred to here by Weng Tu-chien (Weng Dujian) followed by the number assigned to the text in Weng Tu-chien's *Tao tsang tzu mu yin te* [Combined indexes to authors and titles of books in two collections of Taoist (Daoist) literature], vol. 25 (Beijing: Harvard-Yenching Institute, 1935). Du Guangting is the subject of a study by Franciscus Verellen, *Du Guangting: Taoiste de cour a la fin de la Chine medievale* (Paris:

College de France, 1989). Portions of the *Yongcheng jixian lu* have been translated in Edward Schafer, "Three Divine Women of Ancient China," *Chinese Literature: Essays, Articles, and Reviews* 1 (1979): 31–42; in Livia Kohn, "The Mother of the Tao," *Taoist Resources,* 1.2 (1989): 37–119; in Suzanne E. Cahill, "Practice Makes Perfect: Paths to Transcendence for Women in Medieval China," *Taoist Resources,* 2.2 (1990): 23–42; and in Suzanne E. Cahill, *Transcendence and Divine Passion: The Queen Mother of the West in Medieval China* (Stanford: Stanford University Press, 1993). All translations from the works of Du Guangting in this paper are mine.

4. The *Sanshui xiaodu* [Little tablets (by the fellow) from three rivers] was written by Huangfu Mei, finished around 910, and preserved in several editions. I use the one collected in *Tangren xiaoshuo* [Tang fiction], compiled by Wang Guoyuan (Hong Kong: Zhonghua shuju, 1958): 293–7.

5. On liberation by means of the corpse, see Isabelle Robinet, "Metamorphoses and Deliverance from the Corpse in Taoism," *History of Religions* 19 (1979): 37–70.

6. DG, 30336.

7. Ibid., 30335.

8. Ibid., 30342.

9. Ibid., 30336.

10. Ibid., 30337. Hua Gu is the popular name of Huang Lingwei. See Russell Kirkland, "Huang Ling-wei," *Journal of Chinese Religions,* 20 (1992): 14–92.

11. DG, 30344.

12. Ibid., 30346.

13. Ibid., 30347.

14. Ibid., 30338.

15. Ibid., 30337.

16. Ibid., 30343.

17. Ibid., 30343.

18. This translation is adapted from that of Jeanne Kelly's "The Poetess Yu Hsuan-chi," in Y. W. Ma and Joseph S. M. Lau, *Traditional Chinese Stories: Themes and Variations* (New York: Columbia University Press, 1978): 306.

19. On women's bodies and pollution, see Emily Ahern, "The Power and Pollution of Chinese Women," in *Women in Chinese Society,* eds. Margery Wolf and Roxanne Witke (Stanford: Stanford University Press, 1975), pp. 193–214. On the odor of sanctity and the importance of the sense of smell in premodern times in the West, see Alan Corbin, *The Fragrant and the Foul* (Cambridge: Harvard University Press, 1986).

20. On the importance of the physical body for salvation in Christianity, see Caroline Walker Bynum, *Fragmentation and Redemption* (New York: Zone Books, 1992); and Caroline Walker Bynum, *The Resurrection of the Body* (New York: Columbia University Press, 1995).

21. DG, 30331.

22. Ibid., 30343.

CHAPTER SEVEN

FATHER IN HEAVEN, MOTHER IN HELL:
GENDER POLITICS IN THE CREATION AND
TRANSFORMATIONS OF MULIAN'S MOTHER

Sufen Sophia Lai
Grand Valley State University

> *The legacy of Mulian and his mother reflects the assimilation of Buddhism
> into the Confucian hierarchy and* yin-yang *dualism. The evolution of this
> legacy exemplifies a gender imposition in a patriarchal symbol system.*

Introduction

In the West, August is usually the month when Americans rush to the
beaches, national parks, art festivals, and camps, while urban Europeans
such as Parisians and Romans pack up and leave city bustle for weeks-long
ferro agosto (iron August) vacations in the rural South of Europe. For Chinese who observe the traditional celebration of the seventh lunar month
(late August to early September according to the solar calendar), this late
summer month is instead a month of extra caution and superstitious practices with which the living prudently cope with the potential menace of
the dead. Old Chinese myths and cosmology tell that the seventh lunar
month is when the gate to the Underworld opens and restless souls are released from their purgatorial realms to wander in the living world. In this
month of ghosts, old Chinese superstitions prohibit weddings, swimming,
and children's playing outside after nightfall. Besides the many taboos and
precautions, the culminating activity of this month-long observance is a
more-than-fourteen-hundred-year-old tradition called the Zhongyuan

(the Middle Primordial) Festival, more commonly known by the contemporary Chinese as the Ghost Festival (Gui jie) and by medieval Chinese as
the Yulanpen Feast. The exact meaning of *yulan* is not clear; however, most
scholars concede that *Yulanpen* is a foreign expression derived from the
Sanskrit word *ullambana,* meaning "hanging upside down" which describes
the deplorable state of subterranean souls; *pen* is a Chinese word designating "bowl" or "basin."[1] Placing offerings in the *yulan* bowl for the monks'
consumption is a symbolic gesture done in the hope of sparing one's ancestors the suffering of hanging upside down in the Underworld.

The earliest reference to the celebration of such a festival is found in
the sixth-century *Record of Seasonal Observances in Jingchu (Jingchu suishi ji)*
by Zong Lin (ca. 498–561).[2] The account relates the story of a Buddhist
monk called Mulian:[3]

> On the fifteenth day of the seventh month, monks, nuns, religious, and lay
> alike furnish bowls for offerings at the various temples and monasteries. The
> *[Yulanpen] Sutra* says that [these offerings] bring merit covering seven gen-
> erations, and the practice of sending them with banners and flowers, singing
> and drumming, and food probably derive from this.
>
> The sutra also says, "Mulian saw his departed mother reborn among the
> hungry ghosts. He filled his bowl with rice and sent it to his mother as an
> offering, but before the food entered her mouth it changed into flaming
> coals, so in the end she could not eat. Mulian let out a great cry and rushed
> back to tell the Buddha. The Buddha said, "Your mother's sins are so grave;
> there is nothing that you as a single individual can do about it. You must rely
> on the mighty spiritual power of the assembled monks of the ten directions:
> for the sake of the seven generations of ancestors and those in distress, you
> should gather [food] of the one hundred flavors and five kinds of fruit, place
> it in a bowl, and offer it to those of great virtue of the ten directions." The
> Buddha decreed that the assembly of monks should chant prayers on behalf
> of seven generations of ancestors of the donor, that they should practice
> meditation and concentrate their thoughts, and that they should then re-
> ceive the food. At this time Mulian's mother gained release from all of her
> sufferings as a hungry ghost. Mulian told the Buddha, "Future disciples of
> the Buddha who practice filial devotion must also carry out the [Yulanpen]
> offering." The Buddha said, "Wonderful."
>
> Based on this, later generations have expanded the ornamentation, push-
> ing their skillful artistry to the point of [offering] cut wood, carved bamboo,
> and pretty cuttings [of paper] patterned after flowers and leaves.[4]

It was from such a Buddhist context that the Yulanpen Festival was
linked to the legend of Mulian and the Ghost Festival. And since its inauguration in sixth-century China, the story behind the Buddhist Yulanpen

Feast—Mulian's legendary ordeal in saving his mother from Hell—has played an essential role in Chinese attitudes towards death and the dead. Yet, although basically a Buddhist festival, the Yulanpen Feast has incorporated Confucian values, Daoist cosmology, and folk customs for the release of the suffering hungry ghosts and for commemorating one's ancestors. Chinese folk beliefs and social customs have nurtured and been assimilated into the legend, so much so that Mulian's simple Buddhist episode has grown into an enormous body of literary and artistic expressions, festive customs, religious practices, and theatrical traditions. Since the Tang Dynasty (618–907), the Yulanpen Festival has been one of the few days when the treasures of the Buddhist monasteries are open to public viewing. Beginning in the Song Dynasty (960–1279), the fanfares of the festival would last for days, with Mulian's tours in Hell dramatized on stage.

It is impossible to discuss the Mulian legend without tracing the cultural roots and heritage of the Ghost Festival. Stephen F. Teiser has explored how the festival—with its Confucian, Daoist, and Buddhist cultural sources—has provided the Chinese with both resolution of their fear of the afterlife and reconciliation of the three ideologies. Looking at these three facets of the Ghost Festival provides the key to understanding the role of Mulian and his mother in Chinese cultural history. In tracing the development of the Chinese Ghost Festival, Teiser eloquently elucidates the "exceptional" aspect of Mulian's legend:

> The two major figures in the [Yulanpen] myth are a monk and a mother, neither of whom would appear to be very highly valued in a culture where the most pervasive social and religious institution is based on the principles of procreation and male descent. Even in its canonical versions, the story concerns [Mulian] saving his mother and not his father; rather than producing male descendants, [Mulian] attends to the salvation of his female ascendant. The myth of [Mulian] is quite exceptional in its preoccupation with the state of the mother after death, suggesting a course of action alternative to but not necessarily inimical to the ancestral patriliny.[5]

Mulian and his mother are indeed indelible cultural signs that not only crystallize the Chinese version of a Confucian-Daoist-Buddhist composite afterlife but also, more specifically, manifest the socioreligious contexts of gender in patriarchal China.

However, unlike Teiser, who approaches Mulian's rescuing ordeal from a less critical and perhaps a more forgiving gender perspective, I argue that the story's focus on Mulian saving his mother instead of his father from Hell, and its exceptional preoccupation with the state of the mother and her sinful nature, are a gender imposition of the feminine in patriarchal China. I contend that the story of the damnation of Mulian's mother shows how China accepted and assimilated Buddhism at the expense of the Chinese conception of the feminine. Mulian, as an agent of Buddha's almighty, heavenly, and redeeming patriarchy, is a composite of Buddhist virtues, Confucian filial piety, and Daoist shamanism in the form of yang. Mulian's mother, on the other side of this binary opposition, becomes the sinful, infernal "feminine other" imprisoned in "the realm of yin," as Chinese call Hell *diyu* (the underground realm) or *yin jian* (the space of the yin). The redemption of Mulian's mother from Hell through the paths of "hungry ghosts" *(pretas)* and "animals" to the "Human Realm" not only provides Chinese with vivid images of paths of reincarnation but also sets the stage for a gendered contrast between salvation and damnation: Buddha and Mulian are represented as heavenly males granting salvation and redemption, while Mulian's sinful mother is represented as the infernal female who symbolizes greed, selfishness, and ignorance.

With the above binary opposition in mind, this essay intends to explore the gender politics manifested through the roles of Mulian and his mother in the legacy of the Chinese Ghost Festival in three steps: (1) examining the Confucian and Daoist components, (2) mapping out the Buddhist context and the literary transformation of Mulian and his mother, and (3) investigating the Chinese conception of the feminine in the development of the yin-yang theory and the Chinese image of Hell.

The Ghost Festival in the Confucian Context

In the Chinese lunar calendar, the seventh month is traditionally a month of harvest and renewal that serves as a transition between summer and autumn. The "Monthly Ordinances" ("Yueling") section of the Confucian Classic *The Book of Rites (Li ji)* records imperial rituals for the seventh month:

> In this month there takes place the inauguration of autumn. Three days before the ceremony, the Grand Recorder informs the Son of Heaven, saying, "on such-and-such a day is the inauguration of autumn. The character of the season is fully seen in metal." On this the Son of Heaven devotes himself to self-adjustment; and on the day he leads in person the three ducal ministers, the nine high ministers, the princes of states [at court], and his great officers, to meet the autumn in the western suburb, and on their return he rewards the General-in-Chief, and the military officers in the court.[6]

As Teiser points out, "the 'Monthly Ordinances' was quite influential in the formation of Han rituals, and it provides a detailed and dependable picture of the rhythms of the seventh month prior to the development of Buddhist and Daoist services." Within the Confucian context, it was imperative that the imperial rulers follow the Monthly Ordinances in order "to link the Way of Heaven and the Way of Man" and also to oversee an agricultural society whose harvest was ultimately sanctioned by a feudal hierarchy. Consequently, in the seventh lunar month there was also a rite that, as described in *The Book of Rites,* involved the tasting *(chang)* of the first crop by the emperor and, symbolically, by his ancestors: "In this month the farmers present their grain. The Son of Heaven tastes it, while still new, first offering some in the apartment at the back of the ancestral temple."[7]

Teiser points out that two other important festivals in the seventh month also "used methods of purification and the joining of the sexes to bring about world renewal"—the Lustration *(xi)* and the Seventh Night *(qixi).* The Lustration is the semiannual exorcism performed at the water's edge on the fourteenth day of the seventh month, and the Seventh Night, called Chinese Valentine's Day by modern Chinese, observes the annual reunion of the constellations of the Cowherd and the Weaving Maiden (Altair and Vega in the West). In folk tradition, these two lovers were banished to opposite sides of the Silver River (Yinhe, or the Milky Way) and allowed to meet only on the seventh day of the seventh month of each year. Such Confucian cosmology and folk belief provide a compatible landscape for Mulian's cosmic journey through Heaven and Hell. As Teiser presents it:

> All of these festivals held during the seventh month exhibit a blending of polarities that we will see surface later, in a variety of forms, in the ghost festival. Communication between generations is evident in the offerings presented by the preeminent descendant, the emperor, to his exalted ancestors, just as the ghost festival joins the senior and junior members of the family through the exchange of gifts. The seventh month brings the Weaving Maiden her only chance to cross the celestial stream that separates her from the Cowherd, just as the ghost festival brings into being the bridge that allows the ghostly inhabitants of the *yin* world to return to their loved ones in the *yang* world.[8]

In such a cultural environment, it seems natural that Buddhist propaganda emphasizing Mulian's Confucian filiality would be set in a framework embodying gendered polarities. For Mulian to seek his father's redemption from Hell instead of his mother's would seem to disrupt the Confucian cosmic order.

The indigenous folk beliefs and various agrarian rituals have provided social contexts for the Confucian Monthly Ordinances in their many allusions to the seventh month as a season for inauguration, harvest, purgation, renewal, and communion with ancestors. These cultural elements underlying many social practices would later be incorporated into the ghost festivals of both Daoist and Buddhist characters. It was also this cultural background that allowed the Daoist Zhongyuan and the Buddhist Yulanpen Festivals to flourish.

The Daoist Zhongyuan (The Middle Primordial)

According to *The History of the Three Kingdoms (Sanguo zhi)*, the concept of Three Officers *(san guan)*—personified deities who are the officers of Heaven, of Earth, and of Water—was present in the very early stage of Daoism as three cosmic forces, the Three Primordials *(san yuan)*.[9] It was around 260 that the Three Primordials system evolved and was matched with the concept of the Three Officers.[10] The first full moon (around mid-February) was designated for the Upper Primordial (Shangyuan) celebration, on which day the Officer of Heaven bestows blessings on the human world; the seventh full moon (around late August) for the Middle Primordial (Zhongyuan), during which the Officer of Earth grants amnesty to sinners; and the tenth full moon (around late November) for the Lower Primordial (Xiayuan), whose Officer of Water expels misfortunes. In the undated "Jade Registrar" (Yuli, ca. eleventh century), the entire seventh month is further designated as the month for saving wandering ghosts and is customarily called the "month of ghosts" *(gui yue)*.[11] It is believed that on the first day of the month, the gate of the Underworld opens to set free all suffering ghosts to wander in the human world for a month. On the last day of the month—which is the assumed birthday of Dizang Bodhisattva ("Ksitigarbha" in Sanskrit)—the gate closes to confine the ghosts once again until the following year's month of ghosts.

This is how a Daoist Ghost Festival was described by the sixth-century *Classified Collection of Arts and Letters (Yiwen leiju)*:

> A Daoist scripture says, "The fifteenth day of the seventh month is the day of the Middle Primordial [Zhongyuan]. The Officer of Earth checks his figures, searching through the human world to distinguish good from evil. All of the gods and assembled sages arrive together at the palace to decide upon the length [of people's lives]. Ghosts from the human world summon the records, and hungry ghosts and prisoners all converge at once. On this day grand dark-metropolis offerings should be made to the Jade Capital Moun-

tain: select myriad flowers and fruits, precious gems and rare items, banners and jeweled vessels, delicacies and food, and offer them to all of the assembled sages. All day and all night Daoist masters should preach and chant this scripture, and great sages of the ten directions together should sing from its numinous pages. All of the prisoners and hungry ghosts can eat their fill, completely escape from suffering, and come back among humans.[12]

This depiction provides a clear picture of how the medieval Chinese celebrated this mid-year festival, which reflects the integration of the Confucian bureaucratic structure into Daoist cosmology. The presumed gathering of all the gods and sages at the palace evokes not only the imperial inauguration and tasting ceremonies prescribed in the Monthly Ordinances, but also the indigenous Lustration observance, requiring food, drink, and poetry as an integral part of the ceremony. Imbued with Daoist religious elements as well as Confucian ritualistic implications, the seventh month became a time when boundaries among the universes of celestial deities, human beings, and ghostly spirits were obscured. During this season, Chinese people are careful to avoid possible encounters with liberated ghosts and spirits, and they aspire to receive blessings from celestial spirits. We can read the Ghost Festival as the Chinese people's reconciliation of conflicting cultural elements: on the religious level, it is a sublimated gesture of benevolence and clemency to assuage the suffering of the dead in the Underworld; on the folkloric level, it represents a superstitious fear of the supernatural world and a need to appease wicked spirits and to bribe celestial spirits.

Mulian and His Mother in
Buddhist Literature and Folk Drama

As mentioned earlier, the Ghost Festival also has a Buddhist dimension, which is believed to have sprung from the Mulian legend. The imperial sponsorship of the Buddhist Ghost Festival dates as far back as 483,[13] but opinions vary as to whether the Daoist Zhongyuan or the Buddhist Yulanpen came first. From the Buddhist perspective, Mulian's adventure in the otherworld was the cause of the annual Yulanpen Festival; however, due to the multifaceted nature of the Ghost Festival, the legend of Mulian also evolved into a manifold legend that aspired to accommodate different practices of Chinese society. Therefore, the fundamentally Buddhist legend of Mulian's saving his mother from Hell underwent different phases of expansion and assimilation with indigenous Confucianism and Daoism. Such transformations of Mulian's legend are probably best traced through its literary forms.

The prototype of Mulian's life and deeds can be traced back to many Buddhist sutras, such as the variations of *The Yulanpen Sutra (Yulanpen jing)* and *The Sutra on Offering Bowls to Repay Kindness (Baoen fengpen jing)*, the earlier versions of them dated between 400 and 500.[14] *The Yulanpen Sutra* has been traditionally attributed to Dharmaraksa (ca. 265–313), but some Chinese and Japanese scholars argue for a later date and for a Chinese origin that probably resulted from the cooperative effort of both Indian and Chinese monks.[15] *The Yulanpen Sutra* is a very condensed scripture of about eight hundred words that preaches the Confucian values of filial piety and salvation of one's ancestors. Such a Chinese trait in a Buddhist text not only argues for its Chinese origins, but also makes clear how Buddhism, hitherto regarded in China as antithetical to the Confucian value system, was evolving. This brief scriptural narrative simply tells how Mulian attempted to feed and redeem his mother, who was suffering in the realm of hungry ghosts, this attempt becoming the inception of future Yulanpen Feasts. Put into dramatic form, the narrative can be divided into ten scenes:

    I.   Buddha resides in the kingdom of Sravasti, among the Jetavana trees in the garden of Anathapindika.

   II.   The Great Muqianlian (Mulian, or Maudgalyayana) begins to obtain the six penetrations.[16]

  III.   Mulian wants to redeem his parents and, therefore, uses his superpower to see his departed mother reborn among the hungry ghosts *(pretas)*.[17]

  IV.   Mulian provides a bowl of rice to his mother, who uses her left hand to guard the bowl and her right hand to gather up the rice; but before the food enters her mouth, it is changed into flaming coals.

   V.   Mulian cries out in grief.

  VI.   Mulian rushes back to report to the Buddha, who in return instructs Mulian on how to save his mother and prepare Yulanpen, which will also redeem seven generations of one's ancestors.

  VII.   With the help of monks from all directions, the Yulanpen Feast is performed and Mulian's mother saved.

 VIII.   Mulian proposes to the Buddha that the ritual of Yulanpen be established as an instrument for future disciples to redeem their ancestors.

  IX.   The Buddha rejoices in this proposal and gives further instructions for the practices of the Yulanpen.

   X.   The sutra ends with the remark that "Upon hearing what the Buddha preached, the *bhiksu* [monk] Mulian and the four classes of disciples rejoice and put it into practice."[18]

From this summary, it is obvious that *The Yulanpen Sutra* is a typical origin myth that explains and institutionalizes a religious practice. It seems that Mulian here was only a vehicle to carry out the teaching of the Buddha. The message was intended to reconcile the cherished Confucian ideal of filial piety and the Buddhist renunciation of secular human relations. As the title of the sutra suggests, this is more a story about how the Buddha ordained and sanctified Yulanpen, than about Mulian or his mother. The Buddha's clemency and preaching are the center of the story. Therefore, we are given only the hero's name and no other biographical information concerning him, and his mother is but a nameless character in the grand scope of the Buddha's omnipotent presence. The creator of Mulian's mother did not bother to name her or explain why she was damned to the realm of hungry ghosts.

Framing this narrative in terms of gender issues, one should point out that this prototypical discourse does not mention Mulian's father at all. In the later development of the Mulian legend, the father emerges as a key figure to contrast with the mother's greedy nature and to tell Mulian where his mother is. Also worth considering is the portrait of the mother in this sutra: her only sinful gesture was to use "her left hand to guard the bowl and her right hand to gather up the rice" when Mulian offers her the bowl of rice. Having been reborn among the hungry ghosts, the mother's instinct in protecting her precious food from the surrounding mob seems understandable, but in the Buddhist view, the roots of her sins are so deep and tenacious that no single individual can redeem her.

This particular legend entails the interaction of four symbolic orders represented by the Buddha, Mulian, his mother, and the Buddhist monastic community. Obviously, the Buddha is the omnipotent patriarch who dictates the course of human salvation. Mulian represents not only the mediation between Confucian values and Buddhist ideology but also the dilemma caused by the conflict of the two value systems. The mother represents the collective otherness (e.g., the otherworld and the other gender) that requires condemnation as well as reform. The monastic community represents the collective potency of Buddhism, projected as the necessary counterforce to solve Mulian's dilemma and the evil mother's otherness.

Whether *The Yulanpen Sutra* was an authentic Indian scripture or an apocryphal one created by Chinese Buddhists to promote Buddhism in China, the prototypical Mulian character was Chinese enough—in other words, Confucian and Daoist enough—that the Chinese readily integrated him into the Chinese religious family. In the sutras, Mulian was still identified as one of the Buddha's ten disciples by the name of an Indian, Maudgalyayana, famous for his miraculous powers. Beginning in the eighth century, the story of Mulian captured the Chinese imagination and proliferated into an enormous body of "transformation texts" *(bianwen)*, the literary corpus discovered in Dunhuang caves at the turn of the twentieth century.[19] As Victor H. Mair points out in *T'ang Transformation Texts,* the *bianwen,* dating from the eighth to the tenth centuries, refer in the broader sense to Chinese metrical prose literature, which has two oral components: "popular lectures" *(su jiang)* alternating with "sung texts" *(chang wen).*[20] In spite of many ambiguities and problems regarding the study of *bianwen,* most scholars agree that this literary form, popular in the Tang Dynasty, is so named because it "transforms" sutra texts into vernacular narratives in order to educate and probably entertain uninformed laymen. This transformation both popularized and secularized many Buddhist myths and hagiographies, thus making Buddhist teachings more accessible. In this Tang literary genre, we see the transmission of Buddhism and its assimilation into the Confucian and Daoist value systems. Therefore, in this new literary genre, just as Mulian and his mother are fleshed out with biographical details, so is the Chinese afterlife elaborated into a composite symbolic system incorporating Confucian bureaucracy, Daoist cosmology, and Buddhist theology. In the process of transformation, the original Mulian legend was embellished with poetic fancies by the transcriber, and at the same time merged with the transcriber's indigenous cultural values and ideologies.

In the transformation text "The Great Maudgalyayana Rescues His Mother from Hell" ("Damuqianlian mingjian jiumu bianwen"), we see the following new elements, which sketch a more complete and vivid narrative of Mulian's and his mother's ordeal:[21]

    I. Mulian (Mu-lien) is identified with a secular name, Luopu (Lopu), while his mother is known as Lady Qingti (Ch'ing-t'i).

    II. Lady Qingti's damnation is briefly explained as the result of her "stinginess and selfishness" and her deceiving both the secular and holy communities.

    III. Mulian's father is found and visited by Mulian in the "heavenly palace."

    IV. The father is enjoying the rewards of his virtue and favorable karma; by contrast, the evil mother is condemned to the Avichi Hell.[22]

    V. A detailed itinerary to different regions of Hell is ventured by Mulian.

    VI. The Underworld is "transcribed" as a bureaucratic structure mirroring the Confucian administrative system in the "living world."

VII.   Mulian's mother is saved from the Avichi Hell and purified through various stages: from the hungry ghosts through animals and humans and finally to the Land of the Buddha in the West.

VIII. Mulian's encounter in Hell is described as a regression to an infantile state in which he experiences "the maternal" and "the feminine" in negative ways.

Condemning Mulian's mother to the Avichi Hell, instead of to the realm of the hungry ghosts, marks a major departure from the original story of Mulian's mother. According to the *Sutra of the Remembrance of the True Law (Zhenfa nianchu jing)*, the primary cause for arriving in this deepest hell is committing one of the traditional Five Sins of Buddhism: (1) premeditated murder of one's natural mother; (2) premeditated murder of one's natural father; (3) premeditated intention to harm the Enlightened One and rejoicing in such an action; (4) premeditated evil intention to destroy the Buddhist community; and (5) premeditated murder of Arhats.[23] In this later text, however, the sins of greed, selfishness, and deception are imposed on the mother to justify her damnation to the Avichi Hell. As a result, she not only symbolizes a suffering soul in need of redemption but also embodies what the Buddhist establishment sees as a threat to the Buddhist holy community.

Through the secularization of the *bianwen* genre, the legendary Mulian was eventually detached from his Indian umbilical cord and transformed into a Chinese hero with appropriated historical acclamation. Under the Song Dynasty (960–1279), in the metrical prose literature called "precious scrolls" *(baojuan)*, which was derived from *bianwen* and usually chanted by nuns, the mother-son adventure turned into a sociohistorical drama recording the three incarnations of Mulian. Using the plot and the characterization of the *Great Maudgalyayana* text as a skeleton, *The Precious Scroll of Mulian's Three Incarnations (Mulian sanshi baojuan)* adds flesh and blood to the legend and makes it distinctively Chinese, full of ghostly aspects, spectacular deeds, and fantastic phenomena. Mulian's feats now span three lifetimes, and before he can redeem his mother from Hell, he is first reincarnated as the notorious ninth-century revolutionary Huang Chao, who rebelled against the Tang and occupied the capital on January 6, 881. The more than eight million deaths that resulted from the chaotic rebellion of this historical figure are explained as Mulian's karma, accumulated in his attempt to rescue his mother. The mother-son pair in this *Precious Scroll* version becomes the cause and effect of a catastrophe in Chinese history. It is only after three reincarnations that Mulian is able to plead for his mother's salvation and ascent to Paradise. Quite melodramatically, the story ends with the reunion of father, mother, and son in the Palace of Dizang Bodhisattva: "Three of them reunited, testifying the heavenly paradise together. The father and the son served as the left and right 'Steward of Law' [*hufa*] of Dizang Bodhisattva. Liu [Mulian's mother] enjoys a free and leisurely life. Fu Xiang [Mulian's father] and his family will never have to be reborn again in the Eastern Land [the human world] or be incarnated in the human body." [24] In this way, the three incarnations of Mulian draw to an end.

Through the medium of *baojuan* the legend of Mulian was further secularized and integrated into Chinese cultural and historical settings. The legend of Mulian evolved from a demonstrative Buddhist teaching of redemption in *The Yulanpen Sutra* into an epic family drama epitomizing the Chinese axiological system and history. In *The Eastern Capital: A Dream of Splendors Past (Dongjing menghua lu)*, completed in 1147, it is evident that— as early as the twelfth century—theatrical depictions of Mulian folklore played a vital role during the midyear Ghost Festival: "The fifteenth of the seventh lunar month is Zhongyuan festival . . . sutras regarding Mulian are printed for sale. . . . Beginning from *qixi* [the seventh night], the dramas of Mulian saving his mother [from Hell] are put on the stage until the fifteenth, and the audience doubles." [25] However, no texts of these dramas survive from the Song or Yuan (1279–1368) Dynasties; only titles such as *The Drama of Mulian Saving His Mother (Mulian jiumu zaju)*, *The Practice of Filial Piety in Mulian Saving His Mother (Mulian xingxiao xiwen)*, and *The Drama of Mulian's Entering the Dark Region (Mulian ruming zaju)* are recorded in various writings. [26] The most complete surviving script consists of one hundred scenes divided into three acts written (or most likely compiled and edited) by Zheng Zhizhen during the Ming Dynasty (1368–1644), called *A New Compilation of the Text to the Play About Mulian Rescuing His Mother and Exhorting Her to Goodness (Xinbian Mulian jiumu quanshan xiwen)*. [27] In the *Recollections of Taoan's Past Dreams (Taoan mengyi)*, Zhang Dai (1599-ca.1684, epithet: "Taoan") vibrantly depicted the pageantry of the Mulian drama:

> Yu Yunshu managed the stunt scenes. He set up a big platform, and selected actors from Jingyang township of Hui prefecture. There were about thirty or forty of them, all agile, fierce, and capable of wrestling with each other. They put the dramas of Mulian's ordeal on stage for three days and three nights. . . . On stage, the stunts performed were unnatural acts, such as passing cords, brandishing ropes, rotating tables, spinning ladders, turning somersaults, treading on jars and mortars, jumping ropes, escaping fires and swords, etc. There were grotesque characters and scenes such as heavenly and

chthonic deities, ox-heads, horse-faces, gates of ghosts, gates of death, rak-shas and yakshas [demons], saw-mortars, tripod-caldrons, knife-mountain, icicles, sword-trees, the court of Yama, iron city, and blood streams; all of these were as if they were the transformed images *(bian xiang)* of Hell painted by Wu Daozi. People traded many thousand coins for paper money [to burn as offerings to the dead]. The audience was anxious and afraid. Under the light, all the faces were like those of ghosts. During the scenes like "Lifting the Evil Ghosts of Five Directions," "Liu Fleeing the Tent," etc., thousands of people shouted in unison. Governor Xiong, who was startled, mistook it as the sudden arrival of pirates and sent out officers to investigate. Yu Yunshu himself went to explain the occurrence, and the Governor was finally at ease.[28]

There is no evidence as to whether this theatrical extravaganza observed by Zhang Dai was based on Zheng Zhizhen's three-act drama; however, this account of Ghost Festival celebrations provides evidence of the Chinese preoccupation with the Underworld. In Zheng Zhizhen's dramatic representation, there are three otherworld tours depicted on the stage:

   I.   Mulian's mother tours different regions of the otherworld (passing the Mountain of Broken Money, the Mountain of Slippery Oil, and the Platform for Observing the Homeland, crossing the River of Futility, and passing the Gate of Ascending to Heaven).
   II. Mulian journeys westward like a pilgrim through the Black Pine Forest, the Cold Ice Pond, the Flaming Fire Mountain, and the Quicksand River to the Land of the Buddha.
   III. Mulian trails behind his mother from court to court in the Earth Prison *(diyu,* Hell) until he finally meets his mother at the tenth court.

In this theatrical form, the Chinese Earth Prison is transported onto the stage, scene by scene, with thrilling and fearful yet entertaining effects. Such theatrical spectacles would inevitably conduct the audience on a visual and psychological journey like the tour of modern thrill-seekers through a haunted house in an amusement park. It seems that from the Song Dynasty onward, through a lively visual manner, the drama of Mulian's quest allowed the Chinese people to undertake an annual imaginary journey to the Underworld. This journey served a didactic purpose and also exorcised their fears of death and retribution.

   Given the previous brief review of the literary history of the Mulian legacy, we see that the creation and transformation of Mulian's mother is exploited to shape a Chinese axiological system that assimilates Confucian,

Daoist, Buddhist, and folk beliefs. As Daigan and Alicia Matsunaga point out, "in place of developing an interest in the nature of the exterior world, the early Buddhists were concerned with a spiritual cosmology that was used to serve two purposes: the first, as an *upaya* (skillful means) to induce the layman to practice virtue, and the second, as a representation of the various stages and potentials of human consciousness."[29] The spiritual cosmology is actually a psychological macrocosm of human nature. This psycho-cosmic universe projected by early Buddhism is divided into three worlds: the World of Desire, the World of Form, and the World of Nonform.[30]

However, in Buddhist cosmology, it is the *kama loka,* the World of Desire, that manifests most imminently the human psyche and psychological potentialities. The *kama loka* is further divided into five realms, or "Five Existences": (1) the realm of Hells; (2) the realm of unfulfilled desires or hungry ghosts; (3) the realm of animals; (4) the realm of humans; and (5) the realm of the Deva Heaven.[31] The story of the damnation and redemption of Mulian's evil mother is created and transformed within such a cosmological context. It is no coincidence that the series of sufferings that Mulian's mother undergoes is an evolutionary process by which she ascends step-by-step through these five existences. Due to the evil *karma* she accumulated during her lifetime, Mulian's mother was condemned to the lowest realm. It is through the mercy of the Buddha and through Mulian's strong desire to redeem her that her punishments are lessened and shortened so that she can ascend from one realm to another progressively. Thus, after being saved from the bed of nails in the Avichi Hell, Mulian's mother is elevated, but only to the realm of hungry ghosts, for, as explained both in *The Yulanpen Sutra* and the *Great Maudgalyayana* version, "her sin was too deeply rooted, and her *karma* was difficult to cast off." In the realm of hungry ghosts, according to the *Great Maudgalyayana* version, sinners suffer agony like that endured by Tantalus in Greek mythology:

> The throat feels like the tiny aperture of a needle, so small that water cannot drip through, while the head is like the [Tai] Mountain, which [the waters of] three rivers are not enough to cover. Without one's even hearing so much as a hint of water and drink, the months go by, the years pass, and the miseries of starvation must be endured. From a distance, pure, cool, refreshing waters can be seen, but up close, they turned into a pus flow. Delicious food, delectable meals, turn into blazing fire.[32]

Portrayed thus as hungry and thirsty among images of blood and fire, the mother symbolically embodies the dual qualities of Buddhist *kama* (desire) and *mara* (death or hostility) that correspond to the Freudian Eros-Thanatos

dualism of love and death. Mulian's quest for his mother's salvation is a confrontation with the two drives that are the sources of suffering according to
Buddhist ideology. Therefore, the water, mountain, and fire images in the
realm of hungry ghosts provide a psychological landscape of perverted appetites. The monumental Mount Tai symbolizes the magnitude of the sinner's insatiable gluttony and avarice that eventually defile true nourishment
and libation for redemption; "the tiny aperture of a needle" epitomizes how
hard it is for the sinner to pass through to deliverance.

In the case of Mulian's mother, her ordeals in the Avichi Hell have not
completely purged her evil nature. Thus, the food and water, once touched
by her, become horrible and inedible. Seeing her son coming with food,
"she succumbed to her miserliness and avarice":

> Mulian took the food and offered it to her in his begging bowl. But his
> mother was afraid that someone might snatch it from her; so glaring out at
> the companions all around her, she used her left hand to cover up the bowl,
> and scooped up the food with the right hand. Before the food reached her
> mouth, it turned into raging flame.[33]

When led to the Ganges to find relief, Mulian's mother is once again
scorched by fire:

> When people in the southern [continent] Jambudvipa saw this water, it was
> a pure, clear, refreshingly cool river; when the mortals of heaven saw this
> water, it was a crystal pond; when the fish and the tortoises saw it, it was a
> babbling brook; but when [Qingti] saw this water, it became a pus flow with
> fierce fire. She went to the water's edge and, without waiting for her son's
> blessings, out of greed supported herself on the shore with her left hand, and
> out of avarice dipped her right hand into the water, because her greed and
> avarice knew no bound. The water had not reached her lips when it turned
> into fire.[34]

In the Yulanpen ritual version of Mulian's quest, the quest for the salvation
of one individual soul is extended into a humanist fanfare for the entire as-
sembly in the realm of hungry ghosts. The Yulanpen Festival then evolves
into a symbolic communion for the living and the dead, as explained by
the Buddha to Mulian:

> It is not just for your mother that the Festival of Ullambana has been estab-
> lished on this day; it is also for meditative exercises, the day for the arhats to
> attain the Way, the day of absolution for Devadatta,[35] the day of rejoicing for
> the Yama King, the day when all the hungry ghosts eat their fill.[36]

Through the sacrament of Ullambana, once again Mulian's mother is elevated to a better existence—she is promoted to the realm of animals. In psychological terms, it seems that "once she was fed, mother [the id] and son [the ego] again lost sight of each other,"[37] and the suppressed id was no longer "nailed downed" in Hell but transformed into animal form in the conscious world. Subsequently, Lady Qingti is reincarnated as a black dog, which Mulian finds and takes to "the front of a Buddha stupa in Rajagriha, and for seven days and seven nights he chanted the Mahayana sutras, made his confessions, and recited the abstinences," so that Lady Qingti "was able to shed her dog skin and hang it up on a tree, once again assuming the body of a woman."[38] On the symbolic level, it seems that the id is the "hungry ghost" in the unconscious, and the "animal instinct" in the conscious world. Therefore, the questing ego has the urge to feed that hunger and to remove the animal skin of the id. As Joseph Campbell states, "the hero, whether god or goddess, man or woman, the figure in a myth or the dreamer of a dream, discovers and assimilates his opposites (his own unsuspected self) either by swallowing it or by being swallowed."[39] In Mulian's case, the ascetic monk is equipped with the emblem of the Buddha (the omnipotent superego), which prevents him from being swallowed by the devouring mother and instead transforms and assimilates her (the id) into the world of the superego and the ego: "Then, she felt herself spirited away by the *devas* and dragons and escorted by the Heavenly Maidens, and taken to the Trayastrinsha Heaven,[40] there to enjoy everlasting bliss."[41]

In the quest for his mother's redemption, Mulian himself also undergoes an evolutionary progression through the Five Existences in the World of Desire *(kama loka)*. Being a monk who has attained arhathood, Mulian has transcended human bondage in the World of Desire. His quest for his mother's salvation may therefore be seen as a final review of the World of Desire, allowing him symbolically to free himself once more by giving him a last exit before he ascends from the World of Form *(rupa loka)* into the World of Nonform *(arupa loka)*. Therefore, from a psychoanalytical perspective, Mulian's journey can be viewed as a rite of passage patterned in the separation–initiation–return formula. In Freudian terms, the ego (Mulian) has reconciled with the id (the mother) and is now ready to be with the superego, the Buddha. The suffering of Mulian's mother may be seen as a representation of the death and rebirth of the id, and the myth of Mulian's quest is eventually a unification myth projecting the collective id-ego-superego triad in the Chinese axiological system. In this Buddhist myth, human appetites and ignorance are represented through the mother, while enlightenment and wisdom are monopolized by the patriarchs, represented by the Buddha and Mulian's father. In Joseph Campbell's three-

stage departure-initiation-return journey pattern, an obvious gender inclination is projected: on the road of trial, as Campbell names it, the initiation process quite often takes the form of "meeting with the Goddess"
while a "woman [serves] as the Temptress." This is what he concludes about
the role of the feminine in the journey pattern:

> Woman, in the picture language of mythology, represents the totality of
> what can be known. The hero is the one who comes to know. As he pro-
> gresses in the slow initiation which is life, the form of the goddess under-
> goes for him a series of transfigurations: she can never be greater than
> himself, though she can always promise more than he is yet capable of com-
> prehending. She lures, she guides, she bids him burst his fetters. And if he
> can match her import, the two, the knower and the known, will be released
> from every limitation. Woman is the guide to the sublime acme of sensuous
> adventure. By deficient eyes she is reduced to inferior states; by the evil eye
> of ignorance she is spellbound to banality and ugliness. But she is redeemed
> by the eyes of understanding. The hero who can take her as she is, without
> undue commotion but with the kindness and assurance she requires, is po-
> tentially the king, the incarnate god, of her created world.[42]

Such observations no doubt describe the goddess-temptress tradition in
examples such as Dante's idealization of Beatrice, Emperor Mu's meeting
the Queen Mother of the West, the fantastic journey described in "You
xian ku," and Western knight-errantry themes.[43]

In Mulian's case, however, there is not a goddess for him to meet, but a
sinful and greedy mother for him to redeem. Quite contrary to Campbell's
assertion, Mulian's mother is not there to guide or initiate; rather, she is
there to facilitate Mulian's understanding of human nature, particularly the
infernal aspect. She represents human potential for either damnation or
salvation. In those mythological journeys, woman has been reduced to the
role of an instrument, a vessel, a symbolic other that needs to be redeemed
for the sake of the hero's initiation and salvation. Woman, under this patriarchal system, has become a signifier who has lost her true essential meaning but is manifested in accordance with what man wants her to be. By the
same token, we can also look at Mulian's cosmological journey from this
gender perspective.

It is my belief that the gender implications of Mulian's mythological
journey are not a mere accident, but rather reflect a Chinese cultural tendency to hierarchize and institutionalize genders, which we can see in
the development of the yin-yang belief system and in the evolution of
the Chinese conception of Heaven and Hell. It is also possible to see the
Yulanpen myth not just as a story used to fuse Buddhist and Confucian

values, but also a myth that further institutionalizes the Chinese conception of the feminine. In the following section, I will discuss the five phases of the yin-yang belief system and argue that the transformation of Mulian's mother from a nameless, insignificant hungry ghost in the early sutras to a greedy, selfish, deceiving sinner in the Avichi Hell in the Tang *Great Maudgalyayana* is the culminating stage of this belief system.

The Chinese Conception of the Feminine and the Yin-Yang System

One of the few remarks Confucius made concerning women has often been quoted to belittle them: "Women and people of low birth are very hard to deal with. If you are friendly with them, they get out of hand, and if you keep your distance, they resent it" (*Analects* 17:25).[44] Although scholars have different interpretations of this saying,[45] the misogynistic one is nonetheless the most prevalent and has helped to set a precedent for the ensuing Confucian doctrine that debased womanhood and prescribed a subservient role for woman in a patriarchal society. In later times, women were required to follow the so-called three obediences and four virtues *(sancong side),*[46] which oblige a woman to "obey her father before marriage, her husband after marriage, and her sons in widowhood" and to cultivate her "virtues, words, bearing, and work" *(de yan rong gong).*[47] Within such a Confucian context, woman has no other sociopolitical functions than those of daughter, wife, or mother.

Besides the Confucian subjugation of womanhood, the Chinese symbolic system entails an arbitrary alignment of the feminine and the masculine with the yin-yang binary and its correlation with the Underworld. As most people in the West understand it, the yin-yang is an inseparable duality designating binary pairs such as "dark versus bright," "negative versus positive," "conscious versus unconscious," "the feminine versus the masculine," and so on. According to Xu Fuguan, the yin-yang theory took more than a thousand years to form. Based on Xu Fuguan's study of the history of yin-yang theory, we may divide its development into four phases (the last of which is my own addition):[48] (1) pre-Confucian topography, in which the meanings of yin and yang are limited to weather conditions and topographical positions[49]; (2) the cosmological phase, in which yin-yang is incorporated into the *Book of Changes* and the "Five Elements" to form an intricate cosmological system advocated by a yin-yang school[50]; (3) the sociopolitical phase, generating yin-yang Confucianism; and (4) the theological phase, in which yin and yang are paired with Buddhist mythology to signify "the realms of the dead" *(yin jian)* and "the realm of the living" *(yang jian).*

The yin-yang theory in the first two phases asserts the balance and harmony of both aspects without the indication of their inferior-superior relationship. It was during the Han Dynasty that this inferior-superior relationship was advocated by Dong Zhongshu (179–104 B.C.E.) in *Luxuriant Dew from the Spring and Autumn Annals (Chunqiu fanlu)*, with a chapter entitled "Honoring yang and debasing yin" ("Yang zun yin bei"), which exclusively assigned superior qualities to yang and inferior ones to yin.[51] Here, yin and yang are two metaphorical disciplines that underlie sociopolitical strata. Further on, "all husbands, though lowly, are all yang, and all wives, though noble, are all yin,"[52] a clear hierarchy between male and female with a "gendered" bias towards the sociopolitical system and the inclination to suppress the social status of woman. It is probably not coincidental that two monumental works on women are produced during this time: Liu Xiang's *Biographies of Women (Lienü zhuan)* and Ban Zhao's "Admonitions for Women" ("Nü jie"), both of which hold up virtuous paragons for womanhood and impose social constraints on women's role in society. As Sherry Mou's essay in this collection points out, the *Biographies of Women* heralds the legacy of "chaste women," and "Admonitions for Women" becomes one of the basic readers for women's education. Furthermore, the binary opposition proposed by Dong Zhongshu's "yin-yang Confucianism" also anticipates the opposition between Mulian's mother, who is punished in Hell and the Buddha, who embodies the heavenly father and mercy. Given Dong Zhongshu's yin-yang system, Mulian's mother is in the realm of the inferior yin (the realm of punishment) and needs the mercy of the Buddha, in the realm of superior yang (the realm of virtue), to redeem her from her fallen state.

It is in the theological phase of yin-yang development that Mulian's mother becomes the ultimate symbol of female evil. Before the introduction of Buddhism into China, the Chinese had an indigenous concept of the Underworld as a "City of Darkness" *(you du)* vaguely located in the extreme North or as a realm underneath the Eastern Mountain Tai, governed by "the Imperial Lord of the Eastern Mountain" *(Dong yue di jun)* or "the Magistrate of Mt. Tai" *(Tai shan fu jun)*.[53] In Chinese Buddhist cosmology, the Sanskrit terms for Hell, *naraka* and *niraya*, were rendered in Chinese as "joyless" *(bu le)*, "disgusting/hateful" *(ke yan)*, "means or instruments of suffering" *(ku ju or ku qi)*, "earth prison"*(diyu)*, or "residence of darkness" *(ming fu)*. Among those terms, "earth prison" and "residence of shades" are probably most commonly used by laymen since the transmission of Buddhism into China during the second and the third centuries B.C.E. Though most of these Chinese translations are abstract terms denoting states of mind, in this Buddhist "earth prison" an obviously patriarchal propensity of the Underworld is clearly projected through the portrait of King Yama (Yanluo wang), the Judge of the dead, who presides over the imperial courts of the Underworld. With the influence of Buddhist cosmology, yin becomes a signifier for "the purgatorial hells," signifying a state opposite to living.

According to Japanese scholar Maeno Naoaki, the term *Yama* or *Yanluo wang* was first introduced to Chinese readers in *Luoyang qielan ji* (ca. 547). Yet the concept of a purgatorial "earth prison" as a place for meting out judgment and punishment became popular only in the Middle and Late Tang Dynasty (from the eighth to the tenth centuries), when *ming jian* (the realm of darkness) and *ming fu* (the mansion of darkness) were the most common words for the Buddhist Hell.[54] These terms are present in the Tang transformation texts, such as the *Great Maudgalyayana* and "Emperor Taizong's Ingression into the Dark Regions" ("Taizong ruming ji").[55] In his essay on the influence of Buddhism on Chinese classical literature, Tai Jingnong points out that when the Buddhist Hell eventually became a popular subject during the Tang Dynasty, Niu Sengru (779–847) was the first intellectual to deal with it in his *Records of the Mystical and the Supernatural (Xuanguai lu)*. Here, Hell has three names—"Earth Prison," "Yin Department" *(yin si)*, and "Dark Department" *(ming si)*—and King Yama is named "the Great King of the Yin Department" *(yin si dawang)*.[56] This text perfectly demonstrates the interaction of the indigenous Chinese conception of the Underworld with the Buddhist idea of Hell. Although after the importation of Buddhism, the term *you du* (the City of Darkness) was no longer used in literature, the conception of darkness was preserved by the terms *ming* and *yin*. With the addition to Hell of the idea of an earthly prison, the idea of a city of darkness is replaced by the image of a realm *(jian)*. While the word city evokes "human and living" sentiments, the term *jian* (realm, space, interval, room) evokes abstract, lifeless, claustrophobic, and confining images that connote the Buddhist conception of Hell as an Underworld prison with purgatorial punishments. The Tang Dynasty was an era of vigorous assimilation of Confucianism, Buddhism, and religious Daoism, which embraced and expanded the yin-yang theory and its practices, and thus obscured their boundary lines. The title "The Great King of the Yin Department" epitomizes this synthesis: "the Great King" is adapted from Yama (Yanluo wang), Yin resonates with Daoist sentiment, and "Department" evokes an administrative unit within the Confucian bureaucratic system.

It is evident that by the end of the tenth century, the conception of the Underworld was interwoven with the conception of yin. From the evolution of yin-yang symbolism and the development of the Chinese Hell, one can see that the creation and transformation of the filial Mulian and his depraved mother reflect not only a propagandist attempt to integrate Confucian values into the Buddhist doctrine but also the theological phase of the yin-yang evolution. Evidently, this mythology of Mulian and his mother also resulted from the synthesis of Confucianism, Daoism, and Buddhism that took place in the Early Tang Dynasty. As Shi Yongming points out in *Notions of Women in Buddhism (Fojiao de nüxing guan)*, mother figures (such as the Buddha's mother and his aunt who raised him) are highly regarded in early Buddhist scriptures, in which the virtues of several paragon mothers are praised and the Buddha's compassion for all living beings is compared to a mother's love for her child.[57] Using a depraved mother's damnation and redemption as a testimony of the Buddha's benevolence and authority seems incongruous with early Buddhist conventions.

Given such an incongruity, I would like to suggest that the creation of Mulian's mother is a result of a Chinese appropriation that not only generates a filial Buddhist son compatible with Confucian ideology but also posits a depraved mother compatible with yin-yang Confucianism. The addition of a father in the heavenly palace and the mother in the furthermost region of Hell clearly reflects a yin-yang opposition and hierarchization of the sexes. The conception of "the feminine" in the Tang transformation texts embodies all the features of yin that evolved over time: negativity, inferiority, the Underworld, the dark side of human nature, and punishment. Such a correlative symbolic system of "the feminine" versus "the masculine" is, as I have demonstrated, a result of cultural evolution, during which the attributes of the genders were institutionalized and hierarchized. Thus, in a sociopolitical context, the Underworld in the Chinese mind is an institutionalized symbolic system of masculine authority dictating the operation of justice and punishment. Such a masculine Underworld mirrors the bureaucratic upper world designated as the realm of yang *(yang jian)*. On the other hand, while the Underworld is expressed as the realm of yin *(yin jian)*, it is associated with femininity and sexuality to make it signify the symbolic other, the dark aspect of being, or the opposite of living. Hell in this context is not only female but also infused with sexual dynamics.

The cosmological journey undertaken by Mulian eventually can be boiled down to three interacting components: Hell (represented by the mother), the monk (Mulian), and the heavenly fathers (the Buddha and Mulian's father). Mulian's entire quest is indeed a manifestation of the correlations and interactions among these three components, which can be reduced to a structure of binary opposition. Hell, personified by the mother, has a negative female propensity that links the idea of Hell with the realm of yin. The Buddha and Mulian's father who are in the heavenly sphere overtly epitomize the patriarchal authority that corresponds to the yang order, and Mulian, the asexual monk, can be viewed as a neuter go-between who oscillates between the yin and yang realms.

NOTES

1. For more details on the etymology of *Yulanpen,* see Stephen F. Teiser, *The Ghost Festival in Medieval China* (Princeton: Princeton University Press, 1988), p. 21, n. 29.

2. Quoted in Chen Fangying, *Mulian jiumu gushi zhi yanjin ji qi youguan wenxue zhi yanjiu* [A study of the development of the tale of Mulian rescuing his mother and its related literature], History and Literature Series, No. 65 (Taipei: Taiwan National University, 1983), p. 61; and in Teiser, p. 28.

3. *Mulian* is the abbreviated Chinese transliteration of "Maudgalyayana," the name of one of the ten great disciples of the Buddha. He is frequently mentioned in the Mahayana sutras. He and Shariputra, a friend from his youth, constitute the most important pair of disciples in Mahayana Buddhism. Among the ten disciples, Maudgalyayana was distinguished for his supernatural abilities in clairvoyance and magic. His distinct ability to see through various realms of existence seems to make him a natural candidate for the Yulanpen myth. *Mulian* (literally "eye-connection") therefore seems to be quite an ingenious transliteration.

4. Quoted in Chen Fangying, p. 61; and in Teiser, pp. 56–7. For more about Zong Lin's account in early Chinese encyclopedias, see Teiser, p. 57, n. 13.

5. Teiser, p. 12.

6. *Li ji jinzhu jinyi* [The book of rites with annotations and modern translation], annotated and translated by Wang Mengou, 2 vols. (Taipei: Shangwu yinshuguan, 1984), pp. 285–6; the English translation is from James Legge, *Li Chi: The Book of Rites* (1899; repr. New York: University Books, 1967), vol 1, p. 284.

7. *Li ji jinzhu jinyi,* p. 287; see also Teiser, pp. 28–9.

8. Teiser, p. 30.

9. See *Sanguo zhi* [The history of the Three Kingdoms], by Chen Shou (233–97) (Beijing: Zhonghua shuju, 1959), ch. 8, "The Biography of Zhang Lu," in *Wei zhi,* pp. 263–6.

10. Chen Fangying, pp. 73 and 165.

11. Quoted in Teiser, p. 183, n. 27.

12. *Yiwen leiju* [A categorized collection of literary writing], comp. Ouyang Xun (557–641) (1965; repr. Shanghai: Zhonghua shuju, 1982), vol. 1, p. 80; quoted in and translated by Teiser, p. 36.

13. See *Fozu tongji* [The unified chronology of the Buddhist patriarchate], by Zhipan (fl. 1250–69), *Taishō shinshū daizōkyō,* no. 2035, ch. 37; and Chen Fangying, p. 166.

14. Chen Fangying, pp. 7–18; Teiser, p. 48, n. 3.

15. Chen Fangying, pp. 1–2; Teiser, p. 48, n. 5.

16. The six penetrations refer to Mulian's ability to see through the six "modes of existence" (*gati* in Sanskrit or in Chinese *liu dao*), which include three higher modes—celestial beings *(devas),* humans, and demons *(asuras)*—and three lower modes—animals, hungry ghosts *(pretas),* and hells *(naraka).* See *The Shambhala Dictionary of Buddhism and Zen* by Ingrid Fischer-Schreiber, Franz-Karl Ehrhard, and Michael S. Diener, trans. by Michael H. Kohn (Boston: Shambhala Publications, 1991), p. 76.

17. In Buddhist cosmology, *pretas* (literally "departed ones"), the hungry ghosts, constitute one of the three negative modes of existence: *sura* (evil spirits), *preta,* and *naraka* (hells). According to the traditional view, greed, envy, and jealousy are the causes for one's rebirth as a *preta.* See *The Shambhala Dictionary of Buddhism and Zen,* p.173.

18. [*Foshuo*] *Yulanpen jing* [The Yulanpen sutra], attributed to Dharmaraksa (ca. 265–313), in *Taishō shinshū daizōkyō sakuin,* no. 685; translation from Teiser, pp. 49–54.

19. Before Aurel Stein and Paul Pelliot, in separate expeditions, visited the Dunhuang caves and recovered thousands of manuscripts in 1907 and 1908, the *bianwen* writings had been sealed in the cave walls for almost a thousand years. Those manuscripts are now housed in the British Library and the Bibliothèque Nationale.

20. Victor Mair, *T'ang Transformation Texts* (Cambridge: Harvard University Press, 1989), pp. 9–10.

21. The discussion of Mulian in the transformation text here is based on Eugene Eoyang's translation of the Dunhuang *bianwen* Manuscript P2319, "The Great Maudgalyayana Rescues His Mother from Hell," collected in *Traditional Chinese Stories: Themes and Variations,* eds. Y. W. Ma and Joseph S. M. Lau (Boston: Cheng and Tsui Company, 1991), pp. 443–55 (this translation is hereafter cited as Eoyang).

22. The Avichi (or Avici) Hell is the "Hell of No-Interval" *(wu jian),* the last and deepest of the eight hot hells. According to Daigan and Alicia Matsunaga, the name is derived from how the Hell appears to sinners as they fall headfirst for two thousand years before arriving at its depths. Sufferings here are a thousand times worse than in the previous seven hells; the name also implies that the condemned go through an endless cycle of sufferings, death, and rebirth without intermission. For further details regarding the structure and punishments of the Avichi Hell, see Daigan Matsunaga and Alicia Matsunaga's *The Buddhist Concept of Hell* (New York: Philosophical Library, 1972), pp.99–103 and 131–6.

23. Matsunaga and Matsunaga, pp. 75–6 and 99–100.

24. Chen Fangying, p. 104.

25. *Dongjing menghua lu* [The eastern capital: a dream of splendors past], attributed to Meng Yuanlao (fl. 1110–60), in *Dongjing menghua lu wai sizhong* (Shanghai: Gudian wenxue chubanshe, 1957), ch. 8, p. 49; quoted in Chen Fangying, p. 122. The translation is my own.

26. Chen Fangying, p. 122

27. Zheng Zhizhen (fl. 1582), *Xinbian Mulian jiumu quanshan xiwen* [A new compilation of the text to the play about Mulian rescuing his mother and exhorting her to goodness], *Guben xiqu congkan* ed., Series 1, 67 (Taipei: Tianyi chubanshe, 1983).

28. Zhang Dai, *Taoan mengyi jinzhu jinyi* [Recollections of Taoan's past dreams with annotation and modern translation], trans. Zhou Xianqing (Taipei: Shangwu yinshuguan, 1984), ch. 6; also quoted in Chen Fangying, p. 123. The translation is my own.

29. Matsunaga and Matsunaga, p. 39.

30. Ibid., p.39.

31. Ibid., pp. 39–40; also see *The Shambhala Dictionary of Buddhism and Zen,* p. 230.

32. Eoyang, p. 452.

33. Ibid., p. 453.

34. Ibid., pp. 453–4.

35. Devadatta was Buddha Shakyamuni's cousin and enemy, who was swallowed up alive in Hell for his plot against the Buddha. See Eoyang, p. 454, n. 41.

36. Eoyang, p. 454.

37. Ibid., p. 454.

38. Ibid., p. 455.

39. Joseph Campbell, *The Hero with a Thousand Faces,* Bollingen Series XVII, 2d ed. (Princeton: Princeton University Press, 1968), p. 100.

40. Trayastrinsha is the heaven of Indra, one of the twelve spirits associated with the cult of the Master of Healing. The capital of his heaven is situated on Mount Sumeru, the central mountain of the nine mountain ranges of the universe. See Eoyang, p. 455, n. 42.

41. Eoyang, p. 455.

42. Campbell, p. 116.

43. In Dante's otherworld journey in the *Divine Comedy,* it is Beatrice who guides him through Paradiso and finally to God's presence. In *Mu tianzi zhuan* [An account (of the travels) of the son of heaven Mu], the restless King Mu of the Zhou Dynasty (Zhou Mu wang) also has a mythological death-rebirth quest that takes him to the Queen Mother of the West (Xiwangmu) in Mount Kunlun (the Chinese Olympus), where he is comforted by the goddess and taught a special song to carry home again in the dawn. "You xian ku" [The dwelling of playful goddesses] is about the narrator-scholar Zhang Wencheng, who on an official mission to Heyuan

seeks lodging one night in a large mansion with two beautiful and talented women, a young widow and her sister-in-law. They treat him to banquets, poetry, and sumptuous entertainment; the scholar spends the night in the widow's chamber and departs the next day. The encounter is described as if it is an otherworld journey in which the hero accidentally stumbles upon a goddess's dwelling. For brief discussions of editions and plots of *Mu tianzi zhuan* and "You xian ku," see *The Indiana Companion to Traditional Chinese Literature*, ed. William H. Nienhauser (Bloomington: Indiana University Press, 1986), pp. 632–3 *(Mu T'ien-tzu chuan [Mu tianzi zhuan])* and pp. 209–10 ("Yu-hsien k'u" ["You xian ku"] under "Chang Chao").

44. Arthur Waley, trans., *The Analects of Confucius* (New York: MacMillan, 1939), pp. 216–7.

45. See, for example, Li Chenyang, "The Confucian Concept of Jen [*ren*] and the Feminist Ethics of Care: A Comparative Study," *Hypatia* 9.1 (Winter 1994): 83.

46. The "three obediences" were originally a prescription for women's dress codes in mourning according to the rank of their male relatives, but later they were applied to other things as well. See *Yi li* [The book of ceremonies], in *Shisan jing zhushu* (1892; repr. Taipei: Yiwen yinshuguan, 1981), p. 359.

47. The term *four virtues* underwent similar transformation. Originally from *Li ji,* Ban Zhao's (49–120) explication of the four virtues in her "Admonitions for Women" ("Nü jie") is the best-known one. See *Hou Han shu* [History of the Latter Han Dynasty (25–220)], by Fan Ye (398–445) (Beijing: Zhonghua shuju, 1965), p. 2789.

48. See Xu Fuguan, *Zhongguo renxing lun shi* [Treatises on Chinese human nature] (Taizhong, Taiwan: Tunghai University Press, 1963), pp. 510–79; and Liang Qichao, "Yinyang wuxing shuo zhi laili" [The origin of *yinyang wuxing* theory], *Dongfeng zazhi* 20 (1923):70–9.

49. According to *An Explication of Written Characters (Shuowen jiezi),* the first complete and erudite lexicon and etymology of Chinese characters, *yin* means "dark, obscure, evening/night" and designates "the south bank of a river and the north side of a mountain" *(shui nan shan bei),* and *yang* signifies "height and brightness" and designates "the south side of a mountain" *(shan nan yue yang).* See *Shuowen jiezi zhu* [An explication of written characters with annotations], by Xu Shen (30–124) and annotated by Duan Yucai (1735–1815) (Shanghai: Shanghai guji chubanshe, 1981), 14B: 731. On the basis of *Shuowen jiezi zhu* and the *Book of Poetry (Shi jing),* Xu Fuguan concludes that yin-yang originally referred to the presence or absence of sunlight that signifies two kinds of weather conditions. This binary opposition not only has no gender implication but also has no specific value judgment.

50. Yin-yang never occurs in the original, pre-Confucian *Book of Changes (Yi jing).* The "Ten Wings" ("Shi yi") commentaries use it to interpret the bi-

nary concepts in the book, such as sky and earth, brightness and darkness, man and woman, and so on. See *Yi jing* [The book of changes] in *Shisan jing zhushu. Lü shi chunqiu* [The spring and autumn annals of Mr. Lü] and *Huainanzi* [Master Huainan] conceive of the human body as a microcosm of the cosmos; through such advocacy of human-cosmic correspondences ancient medical scholars understood and treated the human body as operating by yin and yang, and this system migrated further into alchemy, geomancy, astrology, sorcery, medical theory, and even the art of lovemaking *(fang zhong shu)* by way of esoteric Daoist practitioners aspiring to attain immortality. See Lü Buwei, *Lü shi chunqiu jiaoshi* [The spring and autumn annals of Mr. Lü with annotations], annotated by Chen Qiyou, 2 vols. (Taipei: Huazheng shuju, 1988) and *Huainan zi* [Master Huainan], by Liu An (d. 122 B.C.E.), *Sibu beiyao* edition (rept. Taipei: Zhonghua shuju, 1971). As a result, yin was understood not only to embody "darkness," "mother earth," and "femininity" but also to designate "female sexuality." That is why the vagina is "the path/way of yin" *(yin dao),* a synonym for *fang zhong shu,* while the penis is the "yang instrument" *(yang ju).* For believers, such *yin dao* (the art of lovemaking) is essential to the yang energy, or "original breath," in a man, and improper consorting with a woman might let the yang be consumed by the yin. Eventually superstitious and grotesque sexual practices were concocted, and female sexuality was regarded as a devouring, endangering, destructive, and fearful force, which society would try to control and suppress.

51. Dong Zhongshu, "Yang zun yin bei" (ch. 43) in *Chunqiu fanlu jinzhu jinyi* [Luxuriant dew from the *Spring and Autumn Annals*], annotated and translated by Lai Yanyuan (Taipei: Shangwu yinshuguan, 1984), pp. 289–91.

52. Dong Zhongshu, p. 290.

53. Prior to the influence of Buddhism, the Chinese indigenous terms for the land of the dead include: (1) "Yellow Spring" *(huang quan)* in the "Duke Yin First Year" (722 B.C.E.) account in *Zuo Commentary (Zuo zhuan,* the fourth to the third centuries B.C.E.); (2) "City of Darkness" *(you du)* in the "Yao dian" chapter of *The Book of Documents (Shangshu,* ca. 1122–551 B.C.E.), in the "Zhaohun" chapter of *Chuci* (the fourth to the third centuries B.C.E.), in *Lü shi chunqiu* (ca. 235 B.C.E.), in *Huainanzi* (ca. 122 B.C.E.), and in *Bowu zhi* (232–300 C.E.); and (3) "Mount Tai" and the "Magistrate of Mount Tai" *(Tai shan fu jun)* in the narratives of the supernatural *(zhiguai xiaoshuo)* written during the Wei, Jin, and Southern and Northern Dynasties (220–580).

54. Maeno Naoaki, "Mingjie youxing" [Tours in the dark regions] in *Zhongguo gudian xiaoshuo yanjiu zhuanji* 4 (Taipei: Lianjing chuban shiye gongsi, 1982), pp. 38–9.

55. See Wang Zhongming et al., *Dunhuang bianwen ji* [Collection of transformation texts from Dunhuang], 2 vols. (Beijing: Renmin wenxue chubanshe, 1957).

56. Tai Jingnong, "Fojiao gushi yu Zhongguo xiaoshuo" [Buddhist tales and Chinese fiction] in *Fojiao yu Zhongguo wenxue* [Buddhism and Chinese literature], ed. Zhang Mantao (Taipei: Dashen wenhua, 1978), pp. 73–5.

57. Shi Yongming, *Fojiao de nüxing guan* [Notions of women in Buddhism] (Gaoxiong, Taiwan: Foguang chubanshe, 1990), pp. 53–4.

CHAPTER EIGHT

BONDS OF CERTAIN CONSEQUENCE:
THE PERSONAL RESPONSES TO CONCUBINAGE
OF WANG ANSHI AND SIMA GUANG

Don J. Wyatt
Middlebury College

*Although surely not spurred by any regard for female equality, many Song-
period notables were nonetheless inclined toward circumspection in their dealings with women of every station.*

None of China's dynastic eras before the twentieth century afforded
particularly favorable circumstances for improving the status of
women, and we must view the Song—whether in its early (960–1126) or
its later (1127–1279) existence—as just as pernicious as any other period
in this regard. Although deserving of its place in history as the harbinger
of China's incipient transition to modern times, the Song represents an antithesis with regard to women—serving as a venue for the sudden (and
still-inexplicable) emergence of the cult of footbinding, the laying of the
definitive philosophical foundations for later prohibitions against widow
remarriage, and the spread and increased prominence of such conventions
as concubinage. Thus, despite its standing as a bellwether of modernity,
Chinese and Western observers must today also regard the Song as the
spawning ground for those traditional practices that were most indicative
of the physical torment and spiritual subjugation of Chinese women.

However, despite its novel features, the Song is again much like other
dynasties in that, for it, we can cull the record of women's conditions only
obliquely. In addition to the handicap of being modern scholars at some

remove, we must rely almost exclusively on the writings of Song men to find out about the circumstances of Song women because—like their counterparts in other traditional eras and certainly when contrasted with their male contemporaries—they produced so few writings that have survived. Relying on Song men for commentary on the situations of the very women whose oppression they were inclined to perpetuate might at first seem wholly disadvantageous. We could expect the writings of Song men concerning women to be little more than rationalizations of or condolences for their deplorable state. The truth, however, is not even this climactic, for most surviving records by Song authors are singularly uninformative with reference to the conditions of women as such. The plight of women in general and their concerns were hardly ever more than an incidental topic in these writings.

Nevertheless, some Song records, sometimes written by noteworthy literati scholars, were produced, and consequently these are of inestimable value to our understanding. These records fall generally into two types. The first are third-person records mainly detailing interactions between wives (or often anonymous women, such as concubines) and certain men of prominence. These records—despite their usually deprecatory tone and fragmentary nature—at least provide narratives, even if they only rarely provide evidence of the motivations behind the actions of the male elites depicted in them. The second type—which is rare indeed and thus all the more valuable—consists of first-person deliberations on women themselves or some specific aspect of their situation. This latter type doubtless affords us direct, if measured, insight into the beliefs and values of the male authors.

The following essay, which integrates both types of records, examines the attitudes exhibited and conduct displayed by perhaps the two most famed Song statesmen—Sima Guang (1019–86)[1] and Wang Anshi (1021–86)[2]—with respect to concubinage and the importance of securing descendants. Both men wrote either extensively or in a dispersed manner about both subjects, but the more explicit was Sima Guang, especially on concubinage. Shao Bowen (1057–1134)[3] is the provider of two revealing accounts of Sima and Wang in action. My aim here is not to offer a radically revisionist conclusion on these individuals or the subjects of concubinage or ensuring progeny, for, from my assessment of the relevant evidence, one is not forthcoming. But I do hope to show that the relationships among at least two Song men, their wives, and their potential concubines were on several levels intellectually significant—intriguing much beyond the restrictive arena of the purely procreative or the limited realm of sexual gratification and its denial.

The Principals

Sima Guang and Wang Anshi were famous political rivals, and the broad outlines of their ideological struggle are well known and often told. Both men, at different times, served emperor and empire in the highest bureaucratic capacities. Sima, proud of his long tenure of service at Kaifeng,[4] was philosophically much older than his mere two years' seniority over Wang might suggest. History has correctly made Sima the conservative, largely because of his staunch defense of the northern landed elite interests of his day. Wang Anshi, an upstart "technocrat" from the South, gained the ear of the youthful and impressionable Emperor Shenzong (reigned 1067–85) upon the latter's accession to power, and Wang thereby was able to position himself as the agent of change. Wang conceived and implemented a controversial series of "new policies" *(xinfa)* with which he sought to redirect the course of the empire entirely; Sima vehemently resisted him at every turn. The saga of their struggle is copiously preserved in their extensive biographies in the *Song shi* [The history of the Song Dynasty].[5]

But acknowledging the many differences between Sima Guang and Wang Anshi does not diminish the fact that they were products of a culture increasingly edging toward profound coalescence and convergence. Even though they were archantagonists, because of their movements in identical circles of power and because of the exalted but roughly equal political standing that they both enjoyed by the end of their lives, Sima and Wang must have had certain common core experiences. Among the least known and yet most revealing of these experiences was at least one momentous personal brush with (and almost identical response to) the institution of concubinage.[6]

Wang Anshi

In the *He'nan Shaoshi wenjian qianlu* [Former record of things heard and seen by Mr. Shao of He'nan]—his important unofficial history of the Song Dynasty up to his time[7]—Shao Bowen offers the following accounts of Sima's and Wang's separate reactions to the unsolicited intrusion of concubinage into their personal lives. Although it occurred slightly later than Sima Guang's, Wang Anshi's encounter with concubinage in 1061 merits initial treatment because it is the first to appear of Shao Bowen's two accounts:

> When Wang [Anshi] Jinggong became responsible for drafting imperial pronouncements, his wife [surnamed] Wu purchased a concubine *(qie)* [for

him]. When he encountered the woman, Jinggong said: "What kind of woman are you?" She responded: "Your wife has ordered me to do your bidding." [Wang] said: "Of whose family are you?" [The woman] said: "While serving in the army, my husband was blamed for the loss of the grain transport ship of a division under a general-in-chief. Our family holdings were completely confiscated [as punishment]. But, still, this was not enough; [it was ordered that] I be sold as a concubine to make compensation." Lord [Wang] piteously asked: "How much did my wife pay to purchase you?" [The woman] replied: "Nine hundred thousand [copper cash]." Lord [Wang] summoned forth his wife, ordered that the woman and her mate be allowed to become husband and wife as before, and made a gift of the sum paid [for the woman] to them.[8]

This passage, although brief, graphically informs us of at least three facets of the making of Song-period concubines and their procurement. First, as historian Patricia Ebrey has pointed out, it was not irregular for wives— either at the request of their husbands or, as in this case, on their own initiative—to purchase concubines.[9] Second, the above passage indicates that concubinage could easily result as a condition of punishment. In this case, much as in a form of indentured servitude without foreseeable prospect of liberation,[10] the woman's lost freedom is a part of the penalty exacted against her husband. Third, whereas Ebrey has suggested that the primary determinants in the price paid for a concubine were factors like talent or training,[11] the foregoing passage indicates that women like Wang Anshi's potential concubine could command considerable sums of money either by virtue of their own status at birth or through marriage or perhaps simply by virtue of the ability to pay of the families they entered as concubines. Moreover, in addition to what it reveals about the Song institution of concubinage in practice, the above passage also exposes us to a stock psychological feature of Chinese marital practice that not only spans the entire traditional era but, arguably, persists to this day. When asked by Wang, "Of whose family are you?" (or, perhaps more literally, "To whose clan do you belong?"), the woman omits any mention of her natal or "birth" family. In conformance to the convention of the male authors of such anecdotes, she almost instinctively identifies herself with the lineage of her husband—the one into which she has married and the one that, by association, has also jeopardized her freedom.

Yet, despite the substantive information it provides as a simple and straightforward chronicle, the foregoing account of Wang Anshi's encounter with a concubine is not without some significant interpretive difficulties. Chief among these is the question of what prompted Wang's wife, Lady Wu, to obtain a concubine for him in the first place. One immediately plausible explanation would be the condition of childlessness—or, more properly, the condition of the family being without male offspring who might serve as heirs. During the Song generally and especially among the families of Wang Anshi's "gentleman-officials'" *(shidaifu)* class background, the acquisition of a concubine was a conventional solution to the anxiety-provoking situation of a family's failure to produce a male descendant.[12] Despite the already-codified nature of the concubinage system,[13] there was no legal expectation that men take concubines in the Song period; yet, given the fact that the all-important continuation of the descent line was at stake, the social pressures—in the face of the threat of heirlessness—must have been enormous. This situation led to increased proliferation and codification of the system. Historian Ann Waltner, chiefly addressing the later periods of the Ming (1368–1644) and Qing (1644–1911), in which concubinage had become a much more common and codified practice than in the Song period, writes that "the Ming code stipulated that a man who had reached the age of forty and had no sons by his wife could take a concubine."[14] But she also adds that, even in eras such as the Song, long before concubinage achieved official sanction, there was little to obstruct a man of means from taking a concubine apart from his wife's jealousy.[15] In Wang Anshi's case, jealousy does not appear to have been a problem.[16]

The necessity of a concubine to provide offspring would supply a tidy-enough explanation for the actions of Wang's wife had she not already—seventeen years prior to the event in question—presented her husband with his son Wang Pang (1044–76). Pang was Anshi's only son to survive to maturity,[17] but he would die while only in his thirties[18]—thus causing his father much personal grief as well as depriving him, under bizarre circumstances,[19] of the continued descent line so necessary for conducting the rites of ancestor worship.[20]

To suggest that Wang Anshi's wife sought to supply her husband with a concubine because she had some uncanny premonition of their son Pang's untimely death fifteen years later stretches credulity. Nevertheless, Song Chinese attitudes toward sexual relations, because they were so extremely procreative, were largely consonant with those that had prevailed throughout the bulk of China's traditional history, and therefore the possibility remains both plausible and not so easily discounted that Anshi's wife intended that her husband should avail himself of the concubine as further insurance against the lack of progeny.[21] Still more likely, however, is the possibility that Wang's wife procured the concubine as a token of her esteem for her husband; in all likelihood, her presentation of this "bought woman" was orchestrated to coincide with the occasion of his most recent career advancement.[22] Wang was appointed secretary to the Proclamation Drafting Section (Zhigao'an)—the post referred to in the passage—in the sixth moon of 1061, when he was forty-one years old by Chinese reckoning. This was hardly one of his more prestigious Kaifeng posts, and, in this light, Wang's wife's gift to her husband at this time of a woman who would become a permanent fixture of their household might seem gratuitous, if not shortsighted. Nonetheless, no matter how much of an alien impulse it might constitute for us as modern Western observers, such gestures by a wife as the gift of a concubine were relatively common within a subset of the elite classes in the Song world, especially when the wife herself was beyond childbearing age.

But Wang Anshi's response to a situation in which he could see no justifiable compromise is at least as important as his wife's motives, and his immediate actions are also explained with comparable ease. Wang's rejection of the concubine should not be taken as an indication of a concern of his for the oppression of women in general, if he even perceived this as their general plight. Instead, his concern was evidently that a *shidaifu* woman— a woman of his class—might fall into concubinage. Patricia Ebrey has pointed out that this was a concern held in common among elite men of the time, for whom the prospect of female members of their class falling into servitude and poverty was a cause for genuine worry.[23]

Thus, we may be quite justified in taking Wang's case as just one instance of one elite man's protection of a woman of his class. However, this does not entirely supply us with the motives behind his evasiveness toward concubines over the long term. In other words, accepting Wang's aversion to this concubine as a single and isolated instance—one in which her attributes as a fallen but still married, elite woman prevented him from pressing his advantage—is easy. But it does little to account for or explain why Wang never subsequently availed himself of a more suitable concubine of nonelite status. One plausible explanation, at least in Wang's particular case, is commitment to the ideal of a monogamous marriage, for we know that his devotion to his wife, Lady Wu—a woman of considerable literary refinement—was extreme.[24] However, we cannot really know whether it was ultimately Wang's affection for her or some other factor that prevented him from ever availing himself of a concubine. He appears never to have commented directly on the subject.

Sima Guang

Sima Guang's encounter with concubinage was a product of very different circumstances than Wang Anshi's, and, while it was more explicitly conventional, Sima's response to it also appears more complex. Like Wang's, Sima's encounter also occurred early in his career, during the time when he was associated with his patron and mentor Pang Ji (988–1063).[25] But Sima was clearly not presented with a concubine as a sexual favor betokening his growing status as an official. Instead, as Shao Bowen informs us, his encounter resulted directly from the serious situation of his having failed to produce a male heir. Shao states that

> When he accompanied Pang [Ji] Yinggong upon his summons to serve as controller-general *(tongpan)* of Taiyuan prefecture [Shanxi], Sima [Guang] Wengong had yet to have any sons. Yinggong's wife spoke to [her husband] about this [situation] and she purchased a concubine for Sima. [But] Lord [Sima] took pains not to [even] gaze upon her and [Pang's] wife suspected that Sima had some reason that made him apprehensive.
>
> One day, [Pang's wife] instructed the concubine, saying: "Wait until we leave [the premises] and then enter the study from the boudoir. Hope that he will give you a glance." The concubine did as she was told [but] Lord [Sima], expressing shock [at her arrival], said: "Why do you come here when [my] wife—your mistress—is out!" and hurriedly sent her away. When [Pang] Yinggong was informed of this, he advised his subordinates of [Sima's] worthiness.[26]

This encounter occurred sometime between 1054 and 1057—during the early years of his career and during his only prolonged stint of service in the provinces.[27] Although already married, Sima, unlike Wang Anshi at the same time, was without sons. Pang Ji's wife—Lady Liu—held no greater fears about Sima's heirless state than others did; it is merely that she felt more compelled, out of the convention of "face" or *mianzi,* to attempt to change it. Pang Ji's wife doubtless thought that her securing a concubine for Sima was a fitting way to honor the essentially disciple-master relationship that existed between the childless man and her husband. After all, Sima had followed Pang Ji into the provinces at substantial risk to his own future career track. Pang, formerly a grand councilor,[28] was the political loser in a factional struggle of the sort that had become typical at the imperial court. As a result of his defeat in this imbroglio, Pang relinquished his capital appointment and withdrew temporarily to the provinces. Pang's wife no doubt factored Sima Guang's loyalty to her husband into her decision to procure a concubine for him.

Explaining why Sima received the unsolicited assistance of Pang Ji's wife, Lady Liu, is thus less complicated than explaining how her proposed solution could have been so much at odds with Sima's wishes and sensibilities.[29] At least part of the answer for the actions of Pang's wife is to be found in the intensely public-minded and tradition-directed nature of Song social order. Song society was one in which the collective insistence on adherence to convention, even in such seemingly personal matters as barrenness, was allowed to override the expressed preferences of individuals, especially if those preferences varied at all with convention. Whether widely known or not, Sima's aversion to availing himself of a concubine could have easily become downplayed largely because his predicament was not viewed as the plight of an individual. In the spirit of collectivity, Sima could not be left to grapple with his childlessness alone. Especially due to his high standing within their circumscribed and elite circle, close friends and even casual acquaintances saw Sima's problem as a community problem requiring, if necessary, a group strategy.

Therefore, we cannot expect Sima's disinclination to avail himself of a concubine—even if it was overtly known to his associates[30]—to have drawn the same kind of noninterventionist response that is characteristically expected and universally recognized, especially among Western social intimates, today. This fact perhaps best accounts for how both Lady Liu and Wang Anshi's own wife, Lady Wu, could proceed to make arrangements that neither Sima nor Wang would accept. The constrictive Song rites of social interaction between men and women (and, evidently, as the case of Pang Ji and Sima Guang indicates, between men and other men[31]) were pervasive and dictated by a formalism hard for us to reconstruct or even imagine today. This is perhaps best illustrated by the fact that Pang Ji's wife, despite her consultation with her husband, was no more privy to how young Sima might react to a concubine than Wang Anshi's wife was. The profound ignorance of these women about the scruples of men so well known to them suggests that, during and certainly before the Song period, there was no premium placed on cross-gender communication in these matters, which were perhaps considered taboo or, at least, indelicate. Although this failure to communicate could lead to some embarrassing results, Song men and women's discussions of issues like concubinage seem to have continued to shrink from treading deeply beneath the emotional surface until the actual physical presence of a concubine made such discussion—as well as a possible clash—unavoidable.

But, despite the well-intentioned plotting of his friend's wife, Sima Guang found it no easier to bend the constraints of propriety than Wang Anshi. Sima's primary reasons for this were, however, different from Wang's and rooted in his vision of proper relationships within the social hierarchy. Sima, in his own manual on rituals, the *Simashi shuyi* [Mr. Sima's notes on the Ceremonies and Rites canon],[32] does discuss concubines, taking them to be a natural and assumed fixture of the cultural landscape. His remarks here are brief, and, as Ebrey points out, they mainly address issues of what concubines' appropriate conduct should be toward their masters and mistresses.[33] According to Sima, concubines should, for instance, "obey their master's or mistress's orders promptly"[34]—an expectation that, given Shao Bowen's anecdote describing Sima's own experience, should not surprise us. In the section of the final chapter of his *Jiafan* [Family norms] devoted to concubine *(qie)* relations, Sima argues strenuously for rigid distinctions between concubines and their "masters"—specifically, the legal wives of the men they serve. The relationship of a concubine to the mistress of the house was to be, at all times, a subordinate one that neither threatened nor undermined the legal wife's authority. Sima states that: "In the inner [quarters], although maidservants and concubines don clothing and consume food, it should be the case that they do so only after their superiors"[35] and "concubines serve [their] mistresses in the same manner as ministers serve [their] rulers."[36]

Choice or Ambivalence

Anthropologist Jack Goody has remarked on the enduring "multi-functional" quality of concubinage as well as many other Chinese social institutions, stating that "Concubines, often taken to provide heirs in a barren marriage, may be acquired for other, more immediate gratification."[37] But Sima's reaction suggests that, at least for him, if the solemn drive to secure progeny could not justify such action, it would be even less justified by the pursuit of sexual gratification. A similar case can be made in connection with Wang Anshi's late-life situation. After the untimely death of his adult son Pang, Wang Anshi might well have felt compelled to compensate with additional offspring (inasmuch as he, but probably not his wife, was still able). To do so was the only means of ensuring that his own spirit would be properly venerated upon his death. For this all-important purpose, the services of a concubine were the normative solution, and, despite all of his earlier aversions, Wang, at that time and under those circumstances, might well have availed himself of a concubine's services with overwhelming social approval. Still, he refused.

Unlike Wang Anshi, Sima Guang eventually succeeded in remedying his situation through the reliable alternative of adoption. Still, a supreme irony attends Sima's arrangement because his condition of being heirless would ultimately never change. Unbeknownst to him and much to the regret of many of his contemporaries, when Sima died so did his descent line. Shao Bowen provides us with a poignant narrative of how this occurred:

I was [personally] extremely sympathetic with regard to [Sima's] being without heirs. Having no sons, he took his clansman's son [Sima] Kang [1050–90] to be his heir. Kang was styled Gongxiu; in his worthiness, he was similar to Master [Sima]; those who knew him said, "Heaven gave birth to him with a purpose."

Gongxiu and I interacted with increasing familiarity. When Master [Sima] died, Gongxiu mourned him by means of the white ribbon binding the hair [that signifies the death of a parent]. By Yuanyou [1086–94], Sima Kang was verging on becoming greatly utilized [by the state], but he also, unfortunately, died; he was specially canonized as a grand master of remonstrance.

Gongxiu had one son [Sima] Zhi [died 1100?]. When [Zhi] was only a few years old, Gongxiu wrote to me of the lad. As everyone of the Fan Chunfu generation then serving as members the Hanlin Academy said, "[Now,] in the future, [Sima Guang] Wengong's progeny will be extended [through Zhi]." This was not something that I [also] could resist saying.

The [imperial] court knew of [Zhi] and when I was transferred from serving as county defender in Zhangzi to the western capital [Luoyang] to serve as director of education instructor, I made sure that Zhi obtained his course of study. He continued to chronicle the [activities of the] Sima clan.

Zhi was styled Zili and, when he matured, he resembled [his father] Gongxiu in worthiness. [All in] the empire spoke of him as a man genuinely emerging from [his adopted grandfather] Wengong's gate. [But,] he also died young and without sons; thus, Wengong's line of descent was terminated.[38]

Sima Kang himself—the father of Zhi—appears to have mourned his adopted father Guang (upon his death in 1086) deliberately and with all of the earnest fervor that Shao Bowen suggests. In fact, the literalness of Kang's conformance to mourning protocol is thought to have directly precipitated his own death, thus preventing him from producing any subsequent heirs. According to the *Song shi,* Kang commemorated Sima Guang's passing traditionally—by indulging in the ritually prescribed practice of building a vigil hut at the burial site in which he, as primary descendant, temporarily dwelt and survived only on coarse foods.[39] During this time, Kang contracted a stomach illness, supposedly from sleeping on the ground, and this malady developed, in short order, into a chronic life-threatening sickness to which he eventually succumbed.[40]

However, beneath the crucial details (many of which are to be found nowhere else) that Shao Bowen's moving account provides is the implicit evidence that Sima Guang's contemporaries ultimately perceived his attempts to ensure a legacy of descent as ill-fated and futile. On the one hand, Shao and the other well-wishers could take solace in the fact that the perpetuation of Sima Guang's lineage was in force at the time of his death and that, through death, Sima himself was spared the agony of witnessing its sad termination. On the other hand, Shao's account—albeit the product of hindsight—is eerily fatalistic. Its tone leads us to infer that, despite the heartfelt hopes and expectations of his sympathizers, Sima's attempt to fashion a descent line through adoption was—from the outset—somehow predestined to fail. This result, in itself, was tragic enough. But, for Shao Bowen and virtually all his contemporaries, constrained as they were by the normative cultural expectation that offspring should be produced directly through either wife or concubine, the greatest pity was that a man of such eminence as Sima Guang should have had to resort to adoption in the first place—that he had been cursed with having no natural sons.

Consequential Matters

Shao Bowen's intimate reflections on the cruel fate dealt to Sima Guang's fabricated descent line elicit certain critical questions about the collective response of these two Song intellectuals to concubinage. Given the cultural sanction enjoyed by concubinage and its entrenchment in society, was there a shared set of ethical considerations that guided men like Sima Guang and Wang Anshi in their disinclination to avail themselves of concubines? Did their personal aversions to making use of the practice have a common root? As already established, Sima and Wang almost certainly operated according to a uniform code pertaining to Song elites concerning relations with concubines. But should their reluctance to exploit the women in question be used to suggest that they maintained any particular empathy for their plights or perhaps for those of women in general?

To claim that the reactions of Sima Guang and Wang Anshi were initiated and conditioned by their conformance to a single, elevated, and humane principle of respect for women is a tempting hypothesis. However, I would argue against it by first observing that the reasons for rejecting concubines among Song men were probably as numerous and individual as the reasons for procuring them. We should no more accept Sima's and Wang's separate responses as generating from a single source or code or ethos than we should accept them as enlightened. Neither Sima nor Wang demonstrated any particular concern for the oppression of women in general, even if we assume they regarded women as oppressed. Nor did either man ever question concubinage as an institution. In fact, both men accepted concubinage as a natural and assumed fixture of the cultural landscape, and we might go so far as to take Sima's adjurations on mistress-concubine relations as not merely a defense of hierarchical values but also as a defense of the institution itself.

Nevertheless, as damning as a defense of concubinage may seem to us today, we do Sima Guang and Wang Anshi a severe disservice if we choose to hold their attitudes up to a modern Western moral yardstick. Sima and Wang inhabited a world very different from our own, one in which our conception of monogamy,[41] though obviously not valueless, was hardly viewed as the definitive condition of marital life. Rather, Sima and Wang moved in an arena in which the variety of accepted relations—both within and without the bonds of formal marriage[42]—was, if not more diverse, less stigmatized than our own. Moreover, we should be mindful that this variety—again, unlike our own—was spawned more out of necessity than gratuitousness. In the Chinese view, the primary rationale for concubinage was identical with that for marriage itself because, whether in the Song or in later periods, the chief purpose underlying both institutions was procreative. Thus, it is misguided and unfair for us today to fault Sima and Wang for viewing the institution of concubinage in the same manner as did the bulk of their contemporaries. Concubinage was normally a secondary remedy (after marriage) for the same undesirable situation—being without heirs.

Although history has shown an antiquarian outlook to have probably been truer for Sima Guang than for Wang Anshi,[43] the age—whether actual or alleged—of most customs was, in itself, the prime litmus test of their validity and purposefulness. Regardless of how they might have felt about the impingement of concubinage on their personal lives, cultural preservationists like Sima and Wang saw its continuance, like that of any other time-honored custom, as, to one degree or another, self-validating. From the Song Confucianist perspective, a custom could and should be expected to enjoy continued longevity only if it was seen as efficacious and, perhaps even more importantly, salubrious—not morally damaging. Only if it met these criteria could it be seen as serving a useful (i.e., social) purpose for most of the members of the culture. Such customs were by definition good ones, and they rightfully deserved their places within the culture. According to the frames of mind exhibited by men like Sima Guang and, perhaps to a lesser extent, Wang Anshi, concubinage fit this mold; otherwise, like any other morally vacuous or debilitating practice, it would have died out long ago. After all, Sima and Wang both viewed concubinage as a social resource; as such, it was nothing less than an age-old cultural "given," sanctioned in the classics and designed to fill for others, if not for Sima and Wang themselves, an unbearable human void—the lack of an heir. Thus, for Song men, and untold numbers of Song women, concubinage—as an institution—was less a reflection of the cruelties of class than a product of the necessity of culture, and, from a purely culturalist perspective, Sima and Wang were no more "right" in refusing to accept concubines than their wives and associates were in seeking to provide the two men with them.

In the end, I am convinced that we can never hope to know exactly why both Sima Guang and Wang Anshi refused to avail themselves of concubines, though we possibly come as close to knowing as we ever will by observing a final comment of Shao Bowen's. Shao offers that "[Wang] Jinggong and [Sima] Wengong pursued neither song nor sex; they were neither covetous of position nor profit-seeking. They were entirely alike [in these respects]."[44] But Bowen's statement is more of a description than an explanation; it sheds little light on what inspired or motivated the exemplary conduct of its subjects. The questions remain: What—if anything—is exceptional about these acts of Sima and Wang? Is there any common denominator—aside from their individual responses to concubinage having been recorded by the same man—that links Sima and Wang?

Having deduced that we cannot ever really know what moved Sima Guang and Wang Anshi to reject the concubines presented to them, but having also determined that a noble or enlightened regard for women was almost certainly not a factor, we might legitimately question whether there is any more to be said about these interactions. If our own motives are strictly explanatory, much is to be said for regarding the episodes chronicled as hopelessly opaque. But our inability to ascertain either Sima's or Wang's motives for rejection neither robs their acts of historical significance nor prevents us from commenting productively on them from this valuable perspective.

Sima Guang's and Wang Anshi's rejections of the concubines are significant because, while uniquely and distinctively personal, their responses were not really private. By virtue of their unassailable positions as men of political eminence, Sima and Wang were necessarily seen by their contemporaries and especially their supporters as exhibiting virtuous behavior, even if this behavior was the product of motives that we today would not recognize as completely virtuous. The very actions themselves of distinguished men like Sima Guang and Wang Anshi were held to be as exemplary as the actors responsible for them. Even the most purely domestic behavior—even that touching on the intimacies of the inner chamber—was naturally elevated as a standard for others and erected as a model for emulation. This is the one pivotal reason why such delicate matters as the rejection of the concubines by Sima and Wang were ever recorded and preserved for posterity. For the most exalted members of Song political culture, much as for the most prominent wielders of political power in our time, there was no facet of their lives that was truly trivial.

But the cultural necessity for the public framing of Sima Guang's and Wang Anshi's personal responses to concubinage cannot fully account for Shao Bowen's decision to record them, and to suggest so would obscure a final, crucial layer of significance. Even while we have little choice but to view their attitudes toward concubinage as probably highly representative of their time, there can be little doubt that the actions of Sima Guang and Wang Anshi were more than empty gestures and, to an imprecise degree, exceptional—not commonly in evidence throughout society. Such, after all, was a signature feature of the great man: his every action—including the acceptance or the refusal of a concubine—was exceptional because it was seen as originating from a level of moral insight several rungs above that possessed by most other men.

We can never know whether Sima Guang and Wang Anshi intended for their behavior with respect to the concubines to be didactic or in any way cautionary. Cultural necessity for public scrutiny notwithstanding, they had no advance assurances that anyone would bother to record and preserve the conduct ascribed to them. To attribute to Sima and Wang such intentionality and such a level of self-consciousness would be to exceed what we can historically verify. But it is clear that the behavior of these two exemplars, which was deemed as categorically "worthy," had both a didactic and a cautionary effect upon Shao Bowen (and very likely throngs of others). Nevertheless, what Shao Bowen's record most clearly reveals is that, like the weightiest matter of statecraft, an encounter with a concubine could be a matter of consequence, too. Only understanding these episodes drawn from their interior lives in this light allows us to place them rightfully alongside the more celebrated public achievements for which Wang Anshi and Sima Guang have become forever enshrined in their culture's history.

Notes

Earlier versions of this essay were presented as part of the special session on "Women and Chinese Classics" at the twenty-seventh International Congress on Medieval Studies, Western Michigan University, Kalamazoo, Michigan, May 7–10, 1992, and as part of the panel "Interdisciplinary Perspectives on Women and Confucian Tradition" at the twenty-second annual meeting of the New England Conference of the Association for Asian Studies, University of Vermont, Burlington, Vermont, October 19, 1996. I thank the participants in both forums who made helpful suggestions for revision, especially Sherry J. Mou, Anne Behnke Kinney, Ping Ping Lee, and Sin yee Chan. I also thank Patricia Buckley Ebrey, John Chaffee, Linda Walton, Paul Ropp, James Hargett, and Paula Schwartz for their useful comments and assistance.

1. Sima Guang of Xia County in Shaan prefecture (extreme northern modern Shaanxi, just within the Great Wall) was granted official rank as an adolescent through the "shadow" or yin privilege that was the prerogative of his bureaucrat father, Sima Chi (980–1041). Guang, however, chose to compete through the examination system anyway and acquired the doctorate or *jinshi* degree in 1038. His political career was very circumscribed geographically, with nearly all of his posts being elevated ones situated at or near the national capital. But Sima Guang is probably better remembered as a political theorist and writer of history than as a bureaucrat. His work *Zizhi tong jian* [Comprehensive mirror for aid in government] is a panoramic history of China from the beginning of the Warring States era (403 B.C.E.) to the year before the Song founding (959). It required a quarter-century to complete, much of which Guang spent out of office. Upon returning to office in 1086, following fifteen years of exile in Luoyang after his displacement by Wang Anshi, Sima Guang was appointed vice director of the left and concurrent vice director of the chancellery *(zuopuye jian menxia shilang),* then the highest civilian office in the empire. For more on his bureaucratic assumptions and ideals, see Anthony William Sariti, "Monarchy, Bureaucracy, and Absolutism in the Political Thought of Ssu-Ma Kuang," *Journal of Asian Studies* 32.1 (1972): 53–76. In all cases, the bulk of the biographical information I have supplied in the notes is drawn from Ch'ang Pi-te et al., eds., *Songren zhuanji ziliao suoyin* [Index to biographical materials of Song figures] (Taipei: Dingwen shuju, 1976). I have, for the most part, followed the translations of official titles provided by Charles O. Hucker in *A Dictionary of Official Titles in Imperial China* (Stanford: Stanford University Press, 1985).

2. Wang Anshi's life and activities are among the best known, in China and the West, of any Song-period figure. Wang was an obscure southerner from the remote area of Fuzhou's Linchuan County (modern eastern Jiangxi). After he had earned the *jinshi* in 1042, Wang's career proceeded uneventfully; he served in minor provincial posts (mainly around present-day Nanjing) until 1060, when he secured his first capital appointment in the State Finance Commission *(Sansi).* Thereafter, Wang was rapidly promoted until he took effective ministerial control of the government early in 1069, when Emperor Shenzong summoned him from the Jinling (modern Nanjing) area (where he was serving as governor) to take up the post of participant in determining government matters *(canzhi zhengshi).* His assumption of this post was historically significant because it, for the first time, led to the tipping (and, in the minds of some, skewing) of the regional and class balance of the entire Song bureaucratic system. For more on his goals through the reforms, see James T. C. Liu, *Reform in Sung China: Wang An-shih (1021–1086) and his New Policies* (Cambridge, Mass.: Harvard University Press, 1959), pp. 1–4, 7–10, 27–30.

3. Shao Bowen not only produced a substantial body of scholarship but also had an extremely active and occasionally difficult political career. During

the Yuanyou period (1086–1094), on the basis of recommendation rather than by passing the examinations, he was appointed to serve as an assistant instructor *(zhujiao)* in Confucianism at the subsidiary northern dynastic capital, Daming (presently in the extreme southeastern corner of Hebei province). Subsequently, he was transferred to serve as commandant of Zhangzi County in Luzhou (in modern southeastern Shanxi province). When Emperor Huizong (reigned 1100–25) assumed the throne and employed daily feasts in order to solicit the opinions of his ministers, Shao wrote memorializing the emperor and stating that the laws and regulations of the dynastic founder—Emperor Taizu (r. 960–76)—should be restored and that benevolence should be promoted and mendacity condemned. He further argued that the residual factionalism of the Yuanyou period should be terminated by distinguishing between superior and inferior individuals. He also called for a moratorium on using indigent peasants as soldiers. Shao's demands increasingly drew the ire of many less visionary members of the bureaucracy, however, and he soon found himself in a remote provincial appointment overseeing the three hundred drainage canals and other such public works at Yaozhou (now part of the Xi'an region in Shaanxi province). He was later transferred to serve as prefect of Guozhou (in the northern part of today's Nanchong County in eastern Sichuan province) and eventually managed to secure a position in Chengdu circuit (central Sichuan), serving out the remainder of his career there as a penal officer. For additional information on Shao Bowen's life in English, see Julia Ching, "Shao Po-wen," in *Sung Biographies,* ed. Herbert Franke (Weisbaden: Franz Steiner Verlag, 1976), pp. 846–9. See also James T. C. Liu, *China Turning Inward: Intellectual-Political Changes in the Early Twelfth Century* (Cambridge, Mass.: Council on East Asian Studies, Harvard University Press, 1988), p. 107.

4. This was the He'nan site of the eastern and primary Song capital; the secondary capital, also in He'nan, was located 150 miles to the west at Luoyang. Sima was already serving directly under his third emperor by the time that Wang had amassed enough power to begin challenging him for his position.

5. For Sima Guang and Wang Anshi, respectively, see *Song shi* [The history of the Song Dynasty], eds. Toghto et al. (Beijing: Zhonghua shuju, 1977), 16: 10757–72 and 15: 10541–53. The late Robert M. Hartwell contended that, despite embracing the same historical analogisms, Sima's and Wang's differences developed primarily from their different attitudes toward the past. For his substantive comparisons of the sources of Sima's and Wang's distinct political philosophies, see "Historical Analogism, Public Policy, and Social Science in Eleventh- and Twelfth-Century China," *American Historical Review* 76.3 (1971): 690–727. See also Peter K. Bol, "Rulership and Sagehood, Bureaucracy and Society: An Historical Inquiry into the Political Visions of Ssu-ma Kuang and Wang An-shih," ACLS Workshop on Sung

Dynasty Statecraft in Thought and Action, Scottsdale, Arizona, January 1986 (unpublished). See also Peter K. Bol, *"This Culture of Ours": Intellectual Transitions in T'ang and Sung China* (Stanford: Stanford University Press, 1992), chap. 7, in which many of the same arguments contained in "Rulership and Sagehood, Bureaucracy and Society" are advanced.

6. To date, the most thorough discussion of concubinage as a Late-Song-period institution is provided by Patricia Buckley Ebrey. See her "Concubines in Sung China," *Journal of Family History* 11 (1986): 1–24.

7. This work covers the entire early Song period, but the author concentrates on the moments of political personages active during the reigns of Emperors Shenzong, Zhezong (r. 1085–1100), and Huizong.

8. Shao Bowen, *He'nan Shaoshi wenjian qianlu* [Former record of things heard and seen by Mr. Shao of He'nan] (Taipei: Guangwen shuju, 1970), 11.12a-b. This is a reprint of the *Hanfenlou* 1132 prefaced edition.

9. Ebrey, "Concubines in Sung China," p. 13. See also Patricia Buckley Ebrey, *The Inner Quarters: Marriage and the Lives of Chinese Women in the Sung Period* (Berkeley: University of California Press, 1993), pp. 220–1.

10. Though they were not the norm, limited-term concubinage contracts were not unknown under the Song. See Ebrey, "Concubines in Sung China," pp. 11–2. See also Ebrey, *The Inner Quarters,* pp. 220, 222, and 226.

11. Ebrey, "Concubines in Sung China," p. 8. See also Ebrey, *The Inner Quarters,* pp. 220–2.

12. Although it constituted a miniscule portion of the overall Song population, Ebrey offers the estimate that about one-third of this class, at one time or another, had concubines. See, Ebrey, "Concubines in Sung China," p. 2.

13. The legal statutes on the position of Song concubines were inherited, like most other Song laws, from the legal code of the Tang (618–906) Dynasty. See Ebrey, "Concubines in Sung China," pp. 5–7. See also Ebrey, *The Inner Quarters,* pp. 218–9.

14. See Ann Waltner, *Getting an Heir: Adoption and the Construction of Kinship in Late Imperial China* (Honolulu: University of Hawai'i Press, 1990), p. 23. The quotation is from p. 22.

15. Waltner, p. 23. The late Lloyd E. Eastman, also writing primarily with reference to the later traditional era, confirmed Waltner's opinion, stating in his *Family, Fields, and Ancestors: Constancy and Change in China's Social and Economic History, 1550–1949,* (Oxford: Oxford University Press, 1988), p. 32, that "Decisive for the concubine's status in the household, in many cases, was the attitude of the first wife." For a discussion of strategies employed during the Song to reduce the wife's jealousy toward her husband's concubine or, at least, to minimize the concubine's mistreatment at the hands of the wife, see Ebrey, "Concubines in Sung China," pp. 12–4. See also Ebrey, *The Inner Quarters,* pp. 228–9.

16. Apart from chastity, lack of jealousy was considered the highest of female virtues. Together with the fact that she was Wang Anshi's wife, Lady Wu's

conformance to this standard no doubt partly explains her inclusion among the paragons of Song Confucian womanhood and her enfeoffment as duchess of the state of Yue. For more on wifely jealousy and other divisive aspects of Song marital life, see Ebrey, *The Inner Quarters*, pp. 165–70.

17. Although conventionally accepted as the first of two, Pang was evidently Anshi's second of apparently three sons. See note 19. Anshi also had three daughters, one of whom died in infancy in 1048. See Wang Anshi's "Yinnü, muzhiming" [Funeral inscription of a girl of Yin (County)], in his *Linchuan wenji, Liuhutang* 1884 ed., 63.1. See also H. R. Williamson, *Wang An Shih: A Chinese Statesman and Educationalist of the Sung Dynasty*, 2 vols. (London: Arthur Probsthain, 1935), 2: 250.

18. The details of Wang Pang's death (which occurred during the time of his father's nominal service in Jiangsu) are provided, somewhat derisively, by his contemporary Wei Tai (ca. 1050–1110). In Wei Tai, ed., *Dongxuan bilu* [East Pavilion notes], *Hubei xianzheng yishu*, 10.12b, Wei informs us that

Wang Pang was already sick at the time when he was transferred from serving as a lecturer at the Hall for the Veneration of Governance to serving as an edict attendant. Feeling inadequate in expressing his gratitude [for his new appointment], he escorted his father, Wang [Anshi] Jinggong, out to Jinling [where he went to serve as military commissioner-councilor].

As the next year approached, [Anshi] again assumed control of the government and returned via Zhenjiang by boat. Pang was forced to travel ahead on horseback and, arriving early, entered the East Administration. That same day, his illness recurred and, in a little more than a year, he was dead. In the end, [Pang] was one who, feeling inadequate in expressing his gratitude, ended up astride a yellow-haired monkey seat. He arrived at his destination in one day.

The sardonic tone of Wei Tai's account is curious because he is known to have been an admirer of Wang Anshi and to have "had a taste for the reforms." See Etienne Balazs, *A Sung Bibliography*, ed. Yves Hervouet (Hong Kong: Chinese University Press, 1978), p. 102. We can surmise that, for whatever reason, Wei Tai did not view Wang Pang—whom he possibly knew personally—in a similarly favorable light. The foregoing account notwithstanding, there is evidence elsewhere that Wei regarded Pang as at least something of a philosopher, who was adept in the traditional Five Elements (or Phases) theory *(wuxing)*. In his *Dongxuan bilu*, 15.7, he notes: "Wang Pang always said: 'The superior man greatly delights in consuming sour things; the inferior man greatly delights in consuming salty things.' It appears that sourness is superior, deriving its nature from wood, and saltiness is subordinate, deriving its nature from water."

19. Although it doubtless conformed with established mores, Wang Anshi's relationship with his son Wang Pang was also strife ridden, with their con-

flict culminating over Pang's role in cutting off the Wang descent line. Wang Pang, before his own early death, had cruelly intimidated his own young son to death, thus savagely and perhaps willfully predetermining his father's heirless condition. This event not only informs us of the kinds of clashes that could arise between a Song-period father and son, but also indicates the freakish manner in which Anshi's descent line was eventually terminated. Wei Tai again, in *Dongxuan bilu,* 7.2b, supplies a frank rendition of this unfortunate occurrence, which he attributes mainly to Pang's mental derangement:

> Wang Jinggong's second son was named Pang; when he served as Great Supplicator at the Court of Imperial Sacrifices, he clearly suffered from a mental disorder. Pang took a woman surnamed Pang as his wife and, within a year, she gave birth to a son.
>
> Pang thought that this son [was not his because the infant] did not resemble him. He hatched numerous schemes out of his desire to kill the boy; ultimately, the child died from fear and, subsequently, Pang and his wife began to fight.
>
> [Wang] Jinggong knew that his son had lost his faculties and he [also] felt that his daughter-in-law was blameless. While he wished to divorce her [from his son], he feared that such an egregious act might precipitate harmful rumors. In the end, he selected a son-in-law, to whom he remarried her.

Viewed from a modern standpoint, Wang Anshi's solution of remarrying this particular daughter-in-law to the husband of one of his own daughters might seem like an unsatisfactory solution. However, within the context of Song times, when a divorced upper-class woman could possibly face economic destitution, Wang's solution was seen as humane and magnanimous.

20. Interestingly, although ancestor worship had already become a large and diffuse popular tradition by the eleventh century, the prescriptions for its practice throughout the Song period were predominantly dictated by the philosophers—men like Zhang Zai (1020–77) and Cheng Yi (1033–1107) and, eventually, during the twelfth century, Zhu Xi (1130–1200). For brief discussions of the prescriptions that these early Song thinkers established, see Patricia Buckley Ebrey, "The Early Stages in the Development of Descent Group Organization," in *Kinship Organization in Late Imperial China, 1000–1940,* eds. Patricia Buckley Ebrey and James L. Watson (Berkeley: University of California Press, 1986), pp. 37–9; as well as Patricia Buckley Ebrey, *Confucianism and Family Rituals in Imperial China: A Social History of Writing about Rites* (Princeton: Princeton University Press, 1991), pp. 50–3, 57–67. For more-extensive discussions of Zhu Xi's later contributions, see Ebrey, *Confucianism and Family Rituals,* chaps. 5–6. See also Chu Hsi [Zhu Xi], *Chu Hsi's Family Rituals: A Twelfth-Century Chinese Manual*

for the Performance of Cappings, Weddings, Funerals, and Ancestral Rites, trans. Patricia Buckley Ebrey (Princeton: Princeton University Press, 1991).

21. Sociologist Judith Stacey states that the demands for lineal descendants are primarily what led to the eventual state sanctioning of concubinage. See her *Patriarchy and Socialist Revolution in China* (Berkeley: University of California Press, 1983), p. 32.

22. For more on prestige as an impetus for a wife's purchase of a concubine for her husband, see Ebrey, *The Inner Quarters,* p. 220.

23. Ibid., p. 218.

24. Williamson, *Wang An Shih,* 2: 256.

25. Pang Ji of Chengwu County in Shanzhou (extreme southwestern modern Shandong) served variously and ably at the court of Emperor Renzong (reigned 1022–63), who, near the end of their lives, enfeoffed Pang as duke of the state of Ying (Yingguogong). See Pang's biography in *Song shi,* 15:10198–202.

26. Shao Bowen, *He'nan Shaoshi wenjian qianlu,* 11.12b. An account of this episode survives in at least one other strikingly similar but even more embellished version. Zhang Shunmin (ca. 1034–ca. 1110), in his *Huamanlu* [Painted plaster record], *Tang Song congshu* ed., 1.29a–b, states:

Sima Wengong and [Pang Ji's eldest son] Pang Yuanlu [1015–47] were both sons-in-law of Dragon Diagram Chamber Academician Zhang Cun [984–1071]; the Zhang sisters were virtuous and kind. [When] Pang Yinggong was dispatched to serve as a commander at Taiyuan, [Sima] Wengong accompanied him on this transferal. At this time, [Sima] was more than thirty years old [but] he had yet to have any sons.

Lord Pang and his wife, who was surnamed Liu, wished to procure someone [for Sima] and [Lady] Liu disclosed this to [Lady] Zhang, who was happily unopposed because she [herself] had never thought of doing it. [But this was also something that] Wengong [himself] had never once desired, and Pang [Ji] and [Lady] Liu knew this—that [Sima] would surely be suspicious of a concubine.

[So] one day, [Pang and his wife Liu] invited [Sima's] wife Zhang to survey flowers and Wengong did not go along. When his meal was already prepared, this young, all-dolled-up maid entered the study, carrying tea. Lord [Sima] irritably said: "[Now] this [is becoming of a] servant! Today the mistress of the house is not at home and [yet] you come and go, doing whatever [you please]!"

The next day, at his office, Yinggong extolled Sima to his aides as someone who still maintained the comportment of the ancestors—saying to them that he appeared to be peerless. District Mistress Sun Zhao said: "It is a shame that Aide Sima was unable to pluck the zither, and yet able to force servants to flee." All who heard this laughed aloud.

The honorary title district mistress *(xianjun)* was conferred only upon virtuous women who, during the Song period, were usually the wives of chief secretaries *(shuji)* serving in the household of the imperial heir-apparent. Apart from the fact that she held this title, nothing more is known about either Sun Zhao herself or whose wife she might have been.

27. This is, of course, notwithstanding the fifteen-year period of Sima's Luoyang exile, when he was, at least technically, not in service.

28. Pang Ji became a grand councilor *(chengxiang* or *zaixiang)* in the tenth moon of 1051 and served just over a year and a half before resigning in the seventh moon of 1053. See Xu Ziming, *Song zaifu biannianlu* [Arranged chronological record of Song Stewards-Bulwark of State] (Taipei: Wenhai chubanshe, 1929), 5.36b–9b.

29. Corroboration of this hypothesis is contained in yet another record that describes Sima's failure to exploit the presence of the potential concubine. Although he lived much too late for his account to have had any basis in anything but secondhand information, Zhou Hui (1126–ca. 1198), in his *Qingbo biezhi* [Complementary notes by one living near Qingbo (gate)], *Zhibuzuzhai congshu* ed., 3.21a-b, colorfully depicts the curious combination of discomfort and disapproval that supposedly typified Sima's behavior when he was confronted with the prospective concubine and what he considered to be her overtly lurid displays of sexual behavior. Zhou begins his description by conveying the alleged substance of an exchange of letters between Sima and a younger contemporary:

Recommendee Liu Meng [1040–79], in a letter to Sima Wengong, stated: "I entreat you to allow me to supply you with a sum of 500,000 [copper cash] for the purpose of relieving this deficiency [of your lack of sons] through the purchase of a lowly maid . . ." Lord [Sima], in a letter of reply, stated: "As for [my way of] family life, when eating one does not often dare to eat meat; when clothing one's self, one does not dare to wear only silk. How dare I use 500,000 [cash] to purchase a maid . . . ?"

Lord [Sima's] being without sons was a long-standing predicament and a man of Qinghe commandery prefecture [southern Hebei] bought a concubine for him. One day, a maid, arriving in a carriage and sumptuously dressed, entered the study chamber and cast [Sima] a glance. He, however, hardly took notice of her. The concubine, thinking this to be a cause for testing him [further], grasped a book box and asked: "Vice Censor-in-chief, what book is this?" Lord [Sima], assuming a solemn face and folding his hands in a bow [of farewell], said: "This is the *Documents* [classic]," and the concubine, shrinking back [from this], retreated.

Zhou's account—because it dictates a much later time of occurrence and because it, while lacking the same specifics, so uniquely embellishes the already-established narrative—may well be legendary. Nevertheless, its existence attests to the durability of Sima's image as a man who had absolutely no inclinations toward concubinage.

30. Zhang Shunmin seems to be the only one of the chroniclers to insist unequivocally that Pang Ji and his wife Lady Liu were both completely aware of Sima's disinclination *before* the concubine was procured. See note 26.

31. For an elucidating discussion—based on the examination of earlier letter-writing etiquette manuals *(shuyi)*—of what Song male-to-male verbal interactions might have been like, see Patricia Buckley Ebrey, "T'ang Guides to Verbal Etiquette," *Harvard Journal of Asiatic Studies* 45.2 (1985): 581–613.

32. This work, in ten *juan*, represents Sima's individual glosses on each item in the *Yi li* [Book of ceremonies] section of the *Li jing* [Classic of rites]. However, it also incorporates Sima's commentaries on numerous practices that had become current only during his own time. See Balazs, p. 183.

33. Ebrey, "Concubines in Sung China," p. 3.

34. Sima Guang, *Simashi shuyi* [Mr. Sima's notes on the Ceremonies and Rites canon], *Congshu jicheng* ed., 4.46. See also Ebrey, "Concubines in Sung China," p. 3.

35. Sima Guang, *Wengong jiafan* [Wengong's family norms], *Cangshu shisanzhong* ed., 10.5b. Interestingly, appended to this statement is the cautionary annotation: "Whether one is [of] high or low [status], a person must not be without rites."

36. Ibid.

37. Jack Goody, *The Oriental, the Ancient, and the Primitive: Systems of Marriage and the Family in the Pre-Industrial Societies of Eurasia* (Cambridge: Cambridge University Press, 1990), p. 135.

38. Shao Bowen, *He'nan Shaoshi wenjian qianlu*, 18.13b–4. For a description of Sima Guang's funeral, see Ebrey, *Confucianism and Family Rituals*, pp. 73–5, in which Ebrey refers to Sima Kang as Guang's "only son" rather than the *adopted* only son that he was. For more on adoption as a traditional Chinese progeny-securing strategy and the mutual ritual obligations that came to apply to adopter and adoptee under late traditional law, see Waltner, *Getting an Heir*, pp. 48–71. See also Goody, *The Oriental, the Ancient, and the Primitive*, pp. 119–21. The Fan Chunfu generation refers specifically to the second, third, and fourth sons of the famed scholar-statesman Fan Zhongyan (989–1050)—Fan Chunren (1027–1101), Fan Chunli (1031–1106), and Fan Chuncui (1032–1101)—each of whom served for a time in the Hanlin Academy (Hanlin yuan) as "palace writers" *(neihan)* responsible for offering special counsel, contributing to the drafting of imperial pronouncements, and undertaking official compilation projects.

39. *Song shi*, 16:10771.

40. Ibid.

41. Interestingly, Goody, in *The Oriental, the Ancient, and the Primitive,* p. 50, states that marriage in traditional Chinese society "was basically monogamous in the sense that a man contracted a full marital union with only one fertile wife."

42. Ebrey's main argument is that concubines were *not* the secondary wives that they have so often been interpreted as having been by modern scholars. See, for example, the presentation of concubinage proffered by Richard J. Smith in his *China's Cultural Heritage: The Qing Dynasty, 1644–1912,* 2d ed. (Boulder: Westview Press, 1994), p. 254, in which the status of concubines is contrasted with that of the "principal wife." Ebrey establishes—convincingly—that, at least under the Song, concubines should not be classed as "wives" because they enjoyed neither the same ritual, legal, nor social standing as Song-period wives. See Ebrey, "Concubines in Sung China," p. 1.

43. One of the most visceral criticisms leveled against Wang by his opponents in his time was that he had scant appreciation for customs, especially as they varied from region to region. Shao Bowen inherited this view; in *He'-nan Shaoshi wenjian qianlu,* 11.8b, with hostile reference to Wang's administration in general, he states: "It seemed as though the laws of the ancestors had been entirely changed." See, however, the defense of Wang Anshi as a defender of antiquity posed in Bol, *"This Culture of Ours,"* pp. 217–8.

44. Shao Bowen, *He'nan Shaoshi wenjian qianlu,* 11.12b. This equation is unexpected and all the more interesting because Sima Guang, as principal Luoyang opposition leader against the infamous New Policies of Wang Anshi, invariably enjoys a far more favorable portrayal in Shao Bowen's writings.

BIBLIOGRAPHY

Ahern, Emily. "The Power and Pollution of Chinese Women." In *Women in Chinese Society,* edited by Margery Wolf and Roxanne Witke, 193-214. Stanford: Stanford University Press, 1975.

Armstrong, Nancy. "Postface, Chinese Women in a Comparative Perspective: A Response." In *Writing Women in Late Imperial China.* See Widmer and Chang, 397-422.

Balazs, Etienne. *A Sung Bibliography,* edited by Yves Hervouet. Hong Kong: Chinese University Press, 1978.

Ban Zhao [Pan Chao] (45-ca. 120). "Lessons for Women" (or "Admonitions for Women"). In *Pan Chao* [Ban Zhao]: *Foremost Woman Scholar of China,* 82-90. See Swann.

Ban Zhao 班昭. "Nü jie" 女誡 [Admonitions for women]. In *Hou Han shu* 後漢書, 2786-92.

[*Foshuo*] *Baoen fengpen jing* [佛說] 報恩奉盆經 [The sutra on offering bowls to repay kindness]. Anonymous (317-420). In *Taishō shinshū daizōkyō sakuin* 大正新修大藏經索引, no. 686.

Barfield, Thomas J. *The Perilous Frontier: Nomadic Empires and China.* Cambridge: Basil Blackwell, 1989.

Barraclough, Geoffrey. *The Medieval Papacy.* New York: W. W. Norton & Company, 1979.

Beckwith, Christopher I. *The Tibetan Empire in Central Asia: A History of the Struggle for Great Power among Tibetans, Turks, Arabs, and Chinese During the Early Middle Ages.* Princeton: Princeton University Press, 1987.

Beili zhi 北里志 [Record of the Northern Quarters], by Sun Qi 孫棨 (Tang Dynasty). In *Beili zhi, Jiaofang ji, Qinglou ji* 北里志, 教坊記, 青樓記. Shanghai: Gudian wenxue chubanshe, 1957.

Bei Qi shu 北齊書 [The history of the Northern Qi Dynasty], by Li Baiyao 李百藥 (565-648). Beijing: Zhonghua shuju, 1972.

Bei shi 北史 [The history of the Northern Dynasties], by Li Yanshou 李延壽 (seventh century). Beijing: Zhonghua shuju, 1974.

Blamires, Alcuin. *The Case for Women in Medieval Culture.*

Oxford: Clarendon Press, 1997.

Bozhou zhi 亳州志 [The gazetteers of Bozhou]. Compiled by Ren Shoushi 任壽世. N.p.: n.p., 1825.

Bokenkamp, Stephen R. *Early Daoist Scriptures.* Berkeley: University of California, 1997.

Bol, Peter K. "Rulership and Sagehood, Bureaucracy and Society: An Historical Inquiry into the Political Visions of Ssu-ma Kuang and Wang An-shih." Paper presented at ACLS Workshop on Sung Dynasty Statecraft in Thought and Action. Scottsdale, Arizona. January 1986 (unpublished).

------. *"This Culture of Ours": Intellectual Transitions in T'ang and Sung China.* Stanford: Stanford University Press, 1992.

Brooke, Christopher. *The Medieval Idea of Marriage.* Oxford: Oxford University Press, 1989.

Buck, Pearl S., trans. *All Men Are Brothers.* New York: John Day Company, 1968.

Bynum, Caroline Walker. *Fragmentation and Redemption.* New York: Zone Books, 1992.

------. *The Resurrection of the Body.* New York: Columbia University Press, 1995.

Cahill, Suzanne E. "Practice Makes Perfect: Paths to Transcendence for Women in Medieval China." *Taoist Resources* 2.2 (1990): 2342.

------. *Transcendence and Divine Passion: The Queen Mother of the West in Medieval China.* Stanford: Stanford University Press, 1993.

Cambridge History of China. Volume 6, *Alien Regimes and Border States,* edited by Herbert Franke and Denis Twitchett. Cambridge: Cambridge University Press, 1994.

Campbell, Joseph. *The Hero with A Thousand Faces.* Bolligen Series XVII. 2d ed. Princeton: Princeton University Press, 1968.

Cao Zhengwen 曹正文. *Zhongguo xia wenhua shi* 中國俠文化史 [The history of the Chinese knight-errant]. Taipei: Yunlong chubanshe, 1997.

Ch'ang Pi-te 昌彼德 et al., eds. *Songren zhuanji ziliao suoyin* 宋人傳記資料索引 [Index to biographical materials of Song figures]. Taipei: Dingwen shuju, 1976.

Chen   Fangying   陳芳英. *Mulian jiumu gushi zhi yanjin ji qi youguan wenxue zhi yanjiu* 目連救母故事之演進及其有關文學之研究 [A study of the development of the tale of Mulian rescuing his mother and its related literature]. History and Literature Series, no. 65. Taipei: Taiwan National University, 1983.

Chen   Jo-shui. "Empress Wu and Proto-Feminist Sentiments in Tang China." In *Imperial Rulership and Cultural Change in Traditional China*, edited by Frederick Brandauer and Chun-chieh Huang. Seattle: University of Washington Press, 1995.

Chen   Peng   陳鵬. *Zhongguo hunyin shigao* 中國婚姻史稿 [Manuscript of the history of marriage in China]. Beijing: Zhonghua shuju, 1990.

Chen   Yinke   陳寅恪. "Sui Tang zhidu yuanyuan luelun gao" 隋唐制度淵源略論稿 [On the origins of the institutions in the Sui and Tang Dynasties]. In *Chen Yinke xiansheng lunwen ji* 陳寅恪先生論文集 [Collected essays of Mr. Chen Yinke]. 1944. Reprint. Taipei: Jiusi chubanshe, 1977.

------. *Tangdai zhengzhi shi shulun gao* 唐代政治史述論稿 [A preliminary study of the political history of the Tang Dynasty]. 1957. Reprint. Shanghai: Shanghai guji chubanshe, 1982.

Chen   Yingxian   陳迎憲. "Minzu tuanjie de dongren shipian" 民族團結的動人詩篇 [A poem for national unity]. *Renmin ribao* 人民日報 March 25, 1992, p. 7.

Chen   Yongling,   陳永齡,   ed.   *Minzu   cidian*   民族詞典 [Encyclopedia of Chinese minorities]. Shanghai: Cishu chubanshe, 1987.

Cheng   Shude   程樹德. *Jiu chao lü kao* 九朝律考 [A study of Chinese law of nine dynasties (from the Han to the Sui)]. Shanghai: The Commercial Press, 1927.

Ching,   Julia. "Shao Po-wen." In *Sung Biographies*, edited by Herbert Franke. Weisbaden: Franz Steiner Verlag, 1976.

Chodorow,   Nancy. *The Reproduction of Mothering Psychoanalysis and the Sociology of Gender*. Berkeley: University of California Press, 1978.

Chow,   Rey. *Women and Chinese Modernity: The Politics of*

Reading Between West and East. Minneapolis: University of Minnesota, 1991.

Chu Hsi [Zhu Xi]. *Chu Hsi's Family Rituals: A Twelfth-Century Chinese Manual for the Performance of Cappings, Weddings, Funerals, and Ancestral Rites*. Translated by Patricia Buckley Ebrey. Princeton: Princeton University Press, 1991.

Ch'ü T'ung-tsu. *Law and Society in Traditional China*. 1961. Reprint. Paris: Mouton, 1965.

Ci yuan 辭源 [The origins of words]. 4 vols. Beijing: Shangwu yinshuguan, 1984.

Collier, Jane F., and Michelle Z. Rosaldo. "Politics and Gender in Simple Societies." In *Sexual Meanings: The Culture Construction of Gender and Sexuality*. See Ortner and Whitehead, 275-358.

Corbin, Alan. *The Fragrant and the Foul*. Cambridge: Harvard University Press, 1986.

"Damuqianlian mingjian jiumu bianwen" 大目乾連冥間救母變文 [The great Maudgalyayana rescues his mother from hell]. In *Zhongguo chuantong duanpian xiaoshuo xuanji* 中國傳統短篇小說選集 [*Traditional Chinese stories: themes and variations*], edited by Ma Youhuan, Liu Shaomin (Joseph S. M. Lau), and Hu Wanchuan, 639-61. Taipei: Lianjing, 1979.

Daozang 道藏. (See *Zhengtong Daozang* and Weng Tu-chien.)

Davis, Natalie Zemon. "Women's History in Transition: The European Case." *Feminist Studies* 3, nos. 3-4 (Spring/Summer 1976): 83-103.

De Beauvoir, Simone. *The Second Sex*. 1949. New York: Vintage Books, 1974.

des Rotours, Robert, trans. *Courtisanes chinoises à la fin des T'ang* [Chinese courtesans at the end of the Tang]. Bibliothèque de l'Institut des Hautes Etudes Chinoises, vol. 22. Paris: Presses Universitaires de France, 1968.

Dien, Albert E. *State and Society in Early Medieval China*. Stanford: Stanford University Press, 1990.

Donahue, Charles, Jr. "The Canon Law on the Formation of Marriage and Social Practice in the Later Middle Ages."

Journal of Family History (Summer 1983): 144-58.

Dong Jiazun 董家遵. "Cong Han dao Song guafu zaijia xisu kao" 從漢到宋寡婦再嫁習俗考 [A study on widow remarriage from the Han to the Song Dynasties]. In *Zhongguo funü shi lunji*, 139-64. See Pao Chia-lin.

Dong jing menghua lu 東京夢華錄 [The eastern capital: a dream of splendors past] (1147), attributed to Meng Yuanlao 孟元老 (flourished 1110-1160). In *Dong jing menghua lu wai sizhong* 東京夢華錄外四種. Shanghai: Gudian wenxue chubanshe, 1957.

Dong Zhongshu 董仲舒 (ca. 179-104 B.C.E.). *Chunqiu fanlu jinzhu jinyi* 春秋繁露今註今譯 [Luxuriant dew from the *Spring and Autumn Annals*]. Annotations and modern translation by Lai Yanyuan 賴炎元. Taipei: Shangwu yinshuguan, 1984.

Du Guangting 杜光庭 (850-933). *Yongcheng jixian lu* 墉城集仙錄 [Records of the assembled transcendents of the fortified walled city]. In *Yunji qiqian* 雲笈七籤 [Seven slips from a bookbag of clouds], Weng Tu-chien, 1026, ch. 114.

Duby, Georges. *The Knight, the Lady and the Priest*. Translated by Barbara Bray. New York: Pantheon Books, 1983.

Dudbridge, Glen. *The Tale of Li Wa, Study and Critical Edition of a Chinese Story from the Ninth Century*. London: Ithaca Press, 1983.

Dull, Jack. "Marriage and Divorce in Han China: A Glimpse at 'Pre-Confucian' Society." In *Chinese Family Law and Social Change*, edited by David C. Buxbaum. Seattle: University of Washington Press, 1978.

Eastman, Lloyd E. *Family, Fields, and Ancestors: Constancy and Change in China's Social and Economic History, 1550-1949*. Oxford: Oxford University Press, 1988.

Ebrey, Patricia Buckley. *Aristocratic Families of Early Imperial China: A Case Study of the Po-ling Tsóui Family*. Cambridge: Cambridge University Press, 1978.

------. "Concubines in Sung China." *Journal of Family History* 11 (1986): 1-24.

------. *Confucianism and Family Rituals in Imperial China: A Social History of Writing about Rites*. Princeton: Princeton

University Press, 1991.

------. "The Early Stages in the Development of Descent Group Organization." In *Kinship Organization in Late Imperial China, 1000-1940*, edited by Patricia Buckley Ebrey and James L. Watson. Berkeley: University of California Press, 1986.

------. *The Inner Quarters: Marriage and the Lives of Chinese Women in the Sung Period.* Berkeley: University of California Press, 1993.

------. "T'ang Guides to Verbal Etiquette." *Harvard Journal of Asiatic Studies* 45.2 (1985): 581-613.

Edwards, Louise. "Women Warriors and Amazons of the Mid-Qing Texts *Jinghua yuan* and *Honglou meng.*" *Modern Asian Studies* 29.2 (1995): 225-55.

Eoyang, Eugene, trans. "The Great Maudgalyayana Rescues His Mother from Hell" (Dunhuang *bianwen* Manuscript P2319). In *Traditional Chinese Stories: Themes and Variations*, edited by Y. W. Ma and Joseph S. M. Lau. Boston: Cheng and Tsui Company, 1991.

Fairbank, John K., ed. *The Chinese World Order: Traditional China's Foreign Relations.* Cambridge: Harvard University Press, 1970.

------. "A Preliminary Framework." In his *The Chinese World Order*. 1-5.

Fei Xiaotong 費孝通. *Shengyu zhidu* 生育制度 [The reproductive system]. Tianjin, China: Tianjin renmin chubanshe, 1981.

Fozu tongji 佛祖統紀 [The unified chronology of the Buddhist patriachate], by Zhipan 志磐 (fl. 1250-69). In *Taishō shinshū daizōkyō sakuin* 大正新修大藏經, no. 2035.

Foucault, Michel. *The History of Sexuality.* Vol. 1. New York: Pantheon Books, 1978.

Fu Lecheng 傅樂成. "Tangren de shenghuo" 唐人的生活 [Life under the Tang]. In his *Han-Tang shi lunji* 漢唐史論集, 114-41. Taipei: Lianjing chuban shiye gongsi, 1977.

Gan Bao 干寶 (Jin Dynasty). *Sou shen ji* 搜神記 [In search of deities]. Taipei: Hongshi chubanshe, 1982.

Ge Liang 葛亮. "Han yu Xiongnu diyige heqinyue kaoshu" 漢與匈

奴第一個和親約考述 [The textual research of the first *heqin* agreement between the Han and the Xiongnu]. *Zhongguo bianjiang shidi yanjiu* 中國邊疆史地研究 2 (1995): 94-9.

Gilmartin, Christina K., et al., eds. *Engendering China: Women, Culture, and the State*. Cambridge: Harvard University Press, 1994.

Godley, Michael R. "The End of the Queue: Hair as Symbol in Chinese History." *East Asian History* 8 (December 1994): 53-72.

Goody, Jack. *The Oriental, the Ancient, and the Primitive: Systems of Marriage and the Family in the Pre-Industrial Societies of Eurasia*. Cambridge: Cambridge University Press, 1990.

Gu Jiegang 顧頡剛. "Wushi yu wenshi zhi tuihua" 武士與文士之蛻化 [The metamorphosis of the knight-errant and the literati]. In *Shilin zashi chu bian* 史林雜識初編 [The first compilation of miscellaneous topics on history]. Beijing: Zhonghua shuju, 1963.

Gujin tushu jicheng 古今圖書集成 [Synthesis of books and illustrations of ancient and modern times]. Compiled by Chen Menglei 陳夢雷 (1651- ca. 1723) et al. 1725. Reprinted. Beijing: Zhonghua shuju, 1934.

Han Fei zi 韓非子 (ca. 280-233 B.C.E.). *Han Fei zi xuan* 韓非子選 [Selections from *Han fei zi*], edited by Wang Huanbiao 王煥鑣. Shanghai: Shanghai renmin chubanshe, 1974.

Han shu 漢書 [The history of the Former Han Dynasty], by Ban Gu 班固 (32-92). Beijing: Zhonghua shuju, 1962.

Harris, Olivia. "The Power of Signs: Gender, Culture and the Wild in the Bolivian Andes." In *Nature, Culture, and Gender*, 70-93. See MacCormack and Strathern.

Hartwell, Robert M. "Historical Analogism, Public Policy, and Social Science in Eleventh- and Twelfth-Century China." *American Historical Review* 76.3 (1971): 690-727.

Hisayuki Miyakawa. "An Outline of the Naitō Hypothesis and Its Effects on Japanese Studies." *The Far Eastern Quarterly* 14.4 (August 1993): 533-52.

Holmgren, Jennifer. "Imperial Marriage in the Native Chinese and Non-Han State, Han to Ming." In *Marriages and Inequality in Chinese Society*, 58-96. See Watson and Ebrey.

------. *Marriage, Kinship and Power in Northern China*. Norfork, England: Ashgate Publishing, 1995.

------. "Observations on Marriage and Inheritance Practices in Early Mongol and Yuan Society, with Particular Reference to the Levirate." *Journal of Asian History* 20.2 (1986): 127-92.

------. "Women's Biographies in the *Wei-shu*: A Study of the Moral Attitudes and Social Background Found in Women's Biographies in the Dynastic History of the Northern Wei." Ph.D. diss., Australian National University, Canberra, 1979.

Honig, Emily, and Gail Hershatter. *Personal Voices: Chinese Women in the 1980s*. Stanford: Stanford University Press, 1988.

Hou Han shu 後漢書 [The history of the Later Han Dynasty], by Fan Ye 范曄 (398-445). Beijing: Zhonghua shuju, 1965.

Hou, Sharon S. "Women's Literature." In *The Indiana Companion to Traditional Chinese Literature*, 175-94.

Hsia, C. T. *The Classic Chinese Novel*. New York: Columbia University Press, 1968.

Hsing Yi-tien 邢義田. "Qin Han de lüling xue--jian lun Cao-Wei lü boshi de chuxian" 秦漢的律令學一兼論曹魏律博士的出現 [The rise and decline of law-learning in Qin Han officialdom--an explanation of the emergence of the erudites of law in the early third century]. *The Bulletin of the Institute of History and Philology, Academia Sinica* 54.4 (1983): 51-101.

Hsu, Cho-yun. *Ancient China in Transition: An Analysis of Social Mobility, 722-222 B.C.* Stanford: Stanford University Press, 1965.

Hu Shi 胡適. "Shuo Ru" 說儒 [On Ru]. 1934. In *Hu Shi wencun* 胡適文存 [Collected writings of Hu Shi]. Taipei: Yuandong tushu gongsi, 1968. 1-82.

Huainan zi 淮南子 [Master Huainan], by Liu An 劉安 (d. 122 B.C.E.). *Sibu beiyao* 四部備要 ed. Reprint. Taipei: Zhonghua shuju, 1971.

Huangfu Mei 皇甫枚 (fl. 880). *Sanshui xiaodu* 三水小牘 [Little tablets (by the fellow) from three rivers]. Collected in Wang Guoyuan 汪國垣 *Tangren xiaoshuo* 唐人小說 [Tang fiction]. Hong Kong: Zhonghua shuju, 1958. 293-7.

Huang Jiuru 黃九如. *Zhongguo nümingren liezhuan* 中國女名人列傳 [Biographies of famous Chinese women]. Shanghai: Zhonghua shuju, 1937.

Hucker, Charles O. *China's Imperial Past*. Stanford: Stanford University Press, 1975.

------. *A Dictionary of Official Titles in Imperial China*. Stanford: Stanford University Press, 1985.

Hulsewé, A. F. P. *Remnants of Qin Law*. Leiden: E. J. Brill, 1985.

The Indiana Companion to Traditional Chinese Literature. Edited and compiled by William H. Nienhauser, Jr. 2d ed. Taipei: SMC Publishing, 1986.

Ishida Mikinosuke 石田幹之助. *Zōtei Chōan no haru* 增訂長安の春 [Spring of Chang'an, the revised and enlarged edition]. Tokyo: Heibonsha, 1967.

Jagchid, Sechin 扎奇斯欽. *Menggushi luncong* 蒙古史論叢 [Theses on the history of Mongolia]. Taipei: Xuehai chubanshe, 1981.

Jagchid, Sechin, and Van Jay Symons. *Peace, War, and Trade Along the Great Wall: Nomadic-Chinese Interaction through Two Millennia*. Bloomington: Indiana University Press, 1989.

Jiaofang ji 教坊記 [Record of the Department of Stage Performances], by Cui Lingqin 崔令欽 (Tang Dynasty). *Jiaofang ji qianding* 教坊記僉訂, edited by Ren Bantang 任半塘. Shanghai: Shanghai Zhonghua shuju, 1962.

Jin shu 晉書 [The history of the Jin Dynasty], by Fang Xuanling 房玄齡 (578-648). Beijing: Zhonghua shuju, 1974.

Jiu Tang shu. See *Xinjiaoben jiu Tang shu fu suoyin*.

Jiu Tang shu 舊唐書 [The old history of the Tang Dynasty], by Liu Xu 劉昫 (888-947) et al. Beijing: Zhonghua shuju, 1975.

Jiu Wudai shi 舊五代史 [The old history of the Five Dynasties], by Xue Juzheng 薛居正 (912-81) et al. Beijing: Zhonghua shuju, 1976.

Johnson, Wallace, trans. *The T'ang Code*. Vol. 1, *General Principles*. Princeton: Princeton University Press, 1979.

------, trans. *The T'ang Code*. Vol. 2, *Specific Articles*. Princeton: Princeton University Press, 1997.

Kaiyuan Tianbao yishi 開元天寶遺事 [Anecdotes of the Kaiyuan and Tianbao eras], by Wang Renyu 王仁裕 (Five Dynasties). *Congshu jicheng* 叢書集成 edition.

Kang Le 康樂. *Cong xijiao dao nanjiao* 從西郊到南郊 [From the west suburb to the south suburb]. Taipei: Daohe chubanshe, 1995.

Katō Shigeshi 加藤繁. *Tang-Song shidai zhi jinyin yanjiu* 唐宋時代之金銀研究 [Studies of Tang-Song gold and silver]. Translation of his *Tō-Sō jidai no kingin no kenkyū* 唐宋時代金銀の研究. 1924. Taipei: Xinwenfeng chubanshe, 1974.

Kelly, Jeanne, trans. "The Poetess Yu Hsuan-chi." In *Traditional Chinese Stories: Themes and Variations*, edited by Y. W. Ma and Joseph S. M. Lau, 305-6. New York: Columbia University Press, 1978.

Kingston, Maxine Hong. *The Woman Warrior, Memoirs of a Girlhood among Ghosts*. New York: Vintage Books, 1975.

Kinney, Anne Behnke. "Dyed Silk: Han Notions of the Moral Development of Children." In *Chinese Views of Childhood*, edited by Anne Behnke Kinney, 17-56. Honolulu: University of Hawai'i Press, 1995.

Kirkland, Russell. "Huang Ling-wei." *Journal of Chinese Religions* 20 (1992): 14-92.

Kishibe Shigeo 岸邊成雄. "Chōan hokuri no seikaku to katsudō" 長安北里の性格と活動 [Character and activity of the Northern Quarters in Chang'an]. *Rekishi to bunka* 歴史と文化 4, *Rekishigaku kenkyū hōkoku* 歴史學研究報告 7 (1959).

------. "Tōdai gikan no soshiki" 唐代妓館の組織 [Organization of brothels in the Tang dynasty]. In *Tōkyō daigaku kyōyō gakubu jinbun kagakuka kiyo* 東京大學教養學部人文科學科紀要 5, *Kodai kenkyū* 古代研究 2 (1955).

Ko, Dorothy. "The Body as Attire: The Shifting Meanings of Footbinding in Seventeenth-Century China." *Journal of Women's History* 8.4 (Winter 1997): 8-27.

------. *Teachers of the Inner Chambers: Women and Culture in*

Seventeenth-Century China. Stanford: Stanford University Press, 1994.

Kohn, Livia. "The Mother of the Tao." *Taoist Resources* 1.2 (1989): 37-119.

Lau, D. C., trans. *The Analects*. 1979. New York: Dorset, 1986.

------, trans. *Mencius*. 1970. Reprint. New York: Penguin, 1984.

Lau, Joseph S. M. 劉紹銘. "Tangren xiaoshuo zhong de aiqing yu youqing" 唐人小說中的愛情與友情 [Love and friendship in Tang fiction]. *Youshi wenyi* 幼獅文藝 39.3 (March 1974): 80-90.

Lee, Jen-der 李貞德. "Conflicts and Compromise between Legal Authority and Ethical Ideas: From the Perspectives of Revenge in Han Times." *Journal of Social Sciences and Philosophy* 1.1 (1988): 359-408.

------. "Family Execution and Collective Responsibilities in Han Law: Its Change of Nature and Significance." Unpublished manuscript.

------. "Han Sui zhijian de 'shengzi buju' wenti" 漢隋之間的「生子不舉」問題 [Infanticide and child abandonment from Han to Sui]. *The Bulletin of the Institute of History and Philology, Academia Sinica* 中央研究院歷史語言研究所集刊 66.3 (1995): 747-812.

------. "Jealousy in the Six Dynasties: Crime in the South and Virtue in the North." Unpublished manuscript.

------. "The Life of Women in the Six Dynasties." *Journal of Women and Gender Studies* 4 (1993): 47-80.

------. "Women and Marriage in China during the Period of Disunion." Ph.D. diss., University of Washington, 1992.

------. "Xi Han lüling zhong de jiating lunli guan" 西漢律令中的家庭倫理觀 [Ethical ideas in law of the Western Han Dynasty]. *Zhongguo lishi xuehui shixue jikan* 中國歷史學會史學集刊 19 (1987): 1-54.

Lee, Lily Xiao Hong. *The Virtue of Yin: Studies on Chinese Women*. Canberra: Wild Peony, 1994.

Legge, James, trans. *Li Chi: The Book of Rites*. 2 vols. 1899. Reprint. New York: University Books, 1967.

Levy, Dore J. "Transforming Archetypes in Chinese Poetry and Painting: The Case of Ts'ai Yen." *Asia Major*, 3d series,

6.2 (1993): 147-68.

Levy, Howard. "The Gay Quarters of Chang'an." *Orient/West* 7.9 (1962): 93-105; 7.10 (1962): 121-8; 8.6 (1963): 115-22; 9.1 (1964): 103-10.

Lévi-Strauss, Claude. *Structural Anthropology*. New York: Basic Books, 1963.

Li Chenyang. "The Confucian Concept of Jen and the Feminist Ethics of Care: A Comparative Study." *Hypatia* 9.1 (Winter 1994): 70-89.

Li ji 禮記 [The book of rites]. In *Shisan jing zhushu* 十三經注疏.

Li ji jinzhu jinyi 禮記今註今譯 [The book of rites with annotations and modern translation]. Annotated and translated by Wang Mengou 王夢鷗. 2 vols. Taipei: Shangwu yinshuguan, 1984.

Li Ruzhen 李汝珍 (1763-1830). *Jinghua yuan* 鏡花緣 [Romance of the mirrored flowers]. Taipei: Zhiyang chubanshe, 1988.

Li Xiaolin. "Chinese Women Soldiers: A History of 5,000 Years." *Social Education* 58 (February 1994): 67-71.

Li Yu-ning, ed. *Chinese Women Through Chinese Eyes*. Armonk, New York: M.E. Sharpe, 1992.

Liang Qichao 梁啟超. "Yinyang wuxing shuo zhi laili" 陰陽五行說之來歷 [The origin of *yinyang wuxing* theory]. *Dongfang zazhi* 東方雜誌 20 (1923): 70-79.

Liao Meiyun 廖美雲. *Tang ji yanjiu* 唐伎研究 [A study of Tang *ji*-entertainers]. Taipei: Xuesheng shuju, 1995.

Lin Enxian 林恩顯. "Cong minzu zhuyi guandian kan Han-Tang zhi heqin zhengce" 從民族主義觀點看漢唐之和親政策 [Examining the *heqin* policy of the Han and the Tang from the perspective of nationalism]. *Zhongguo bianzheng* 中國邊政 95.10 (October 1987): 10-21.

------. *Tujue yanjiu* 突厥研究 [Study of the Turks]. Taipei: Shangwu yinshuguan, 1989.

Lin Gan 林幹. *Tujue yu Huihe lishi lunwen xuanji* 突厥與回紇歷史論文選集 [Selected theses on the history of the Turkic and Huihe peoples]. 2 vols. Beijing: Zhonghua shuju, 1985.

------, ed. *Xiongnu shiliao huibian* 匈奴史料彙編 [Collected historical materials on the Huns]. 2 vols. Beijing: Zhonghua shuju, 1988.

------. *Zhongguo gudai beifang minzushi xinlun* 中國古代北方民族史新論 [New discussions on China's northern minority history during ancient times]. Hohhut, Mongolia: Nei Menggu renmin chubanshe, 1993.

Liu, James J. Y. *The Chinese Knight-Errant*. Chicago: University of Chicago Press, 1967.

Liu, James T. C. *China Turning Inward: Intellectual-Political Changes in the Early Twelfth Century*. Cambridge, Mass.: Council on East Asian Studies, Harvard University Press, 1988.

------. *Reform in Sung China: Wang An-shih (1021-1086) and his New Policies*. Cambridge, Mass.: Harvard University Press, 1959.

Liu Xianzhao 劉先照 and Wei Shiming 韋世明. "Lun lishi shang he lishi wenxue zhong de Zhaojun heqin" 論歷史上和歷史文學中的昭君和親 [The discussion of the Zhaojun *heqin* in history and historical literature]. In *Minzu wenshi lunji* 民族文史論集. Beijing: Minzu chubanshe, 1985. 202-22.

Liu Xiang 劉向 (77-6 B.C.E.). *Lienü zhuan* 列女傳 [The biographies of women]. *Sibu beiyao* 四部備要 ed. Reprint. Taipei: Zhonghua shuju, 1983.

Liu Zhiji 劉知幾 (661-721). *Shitong tongshi* 史通通釋 [Comprehensive explanations of the historical perspectives]. Annotated by Pu Qilong 蒲起龍 (1679-1761). Taipei: Shijie shuju, 1980.

Lü Buwei 呂不韋 (d. 235 B.C.E.). *Lü shi chun qiu jiaoshi* 呂氏春秋校釋 [The spring and autumn annals of Mr. Lü with annotations]. Edited and annotated by Chen Qiyou 陳奇猷. 2 vols. Taipei: Huazheng shuju, 1988.

Lun yu 論語 [The analects]. In *Shisan jing zhushu* 十三經注疏.

Luo Genze 羅根澤. *Yuefu wenxueshi* 樂府文學史 [The history of *yuefu* literature]. Taipei: Wenzhe chubanshe, 1972.

Luoyang qielan ji. See *Xinyi Luoyang qielan ji*.

Ma Dazheng 馬大正 and Hua Li 華麗. *Gudai zhongguo de beibu bianjiang* 古代中國的北部邊疆 [The northern frontiers in ancient Chinese history]. Hohhut, Mongolia: Nei Menggu renmin chubanshe, 1993.

MacCormack, Carol P. "Nature, Culture and Gender: a Critique." In MacCormack and Strathern. 1-21.

------, and Marilyn Strathern, eds. *Nature, Culture and Gender*. New York: Cambridge University Press, 1980.

MacKinnon, Catharine A. "Feminism, Marxism, Method, and the State: An Agenda for Theory." In *The Signs Reader: Women, Gender & Scholarship*, edited by Elizabeth Abel and Emily K. Abel. Chicago: University of Chicago Press, 1983.

Maeno Naoaki 前野直彬. "Mingjie youxing" 冥界遊行 [Tours in the dark regions]. *Zhongguo gudian xiaoshuo yanjiu zhuanji (4)* 中國古典小說研究專集 (四). Taipei: Lianjing chuban shiye gongsi, 1982.

Mair, Victor, ed. *The Columbia Anthology of Traditional Chinese Literature*. New York: Columbia University Press, 1994.

------. *T'ang Transformation Texts*. Cambridge: Harvard University Press, 1989.

Mann, Susan. "What Can Feminist Theory Do for the Study of Chinese History? A Brief Review of Scholarship in the U.S." *Jindai Zhongguo funü shi yanjiu* 近代中國婦女史研究 [Research on women in modern Chinese history] 1 (June 1993): 241-60.

Mao Han-guang 毛漢光. *Zhongguo zhonggu shehui shi lun* 中國中古社會史論 [A discussion of Chinese medieval social history]. Taipei: Lianjing chuban shiye gongsi, 1988.

Martin-Liao, Tienchi. "Traditional Handbooks of Women's Education." In *Women and Literature in China*, edited by Anna Gerstlacher et al, 165-89. Bochum, Germany: Studienverlag Brockmeyer, 1985.

Matsunaga, Daigan, and Alicia Matsunaga. *The Buddhist Concept of Hell*. New York: Philosophical Library, 1972.

McMahon, Keith. *Misers, Shrews, and Polygamists: Sexuality and Male-Female Relations in Eighteenth-Century Chinese Fiction*. Durham: Duke University Press, 1995.

Meng Yue 孟悅 and Dai Jinhua 戴錦華. *Fu chu lishi dibiao: Zhongguo xiandai nüxing wenxue yanjiu* 浮出歷史地表: 中國現代女性文學研究 [Voices emerging into the foreground of history: a study of contemporary Chinese women's literature]. Taipei: Shibao wenhua, 1993.

Mengzi 孟子 [Mencius]. In *Shisan jing zhushu* 十三經注疏.

Mou, Sherry J. "Gentlemen's Prescriptions for Women's Lives: Liu Hsiang's [Liu Xiang] *The Biographies of Women* and Its Influence on the 'Biographies of Women' Chapters in Early Chinese Dynastic Histories." Ph.D. diss., The Ohio State University, 1994.

Nan shi 南史 [The history of the Southern Dynasties], by Li Yanshou 李延壽 (seventh century). Beijing: Zhonghua shuju, 1975.

Nian'ershi zhaji 廿二史劄記 [Notes on the twenty-two histories], by Zhao Yi 趙翼 (1727-1814). *Congshu jicheng* 叢書集成 edition.

Nie Chongqi 聶崇岐. "Nüzi zaijia wenti zhi lishi de yanbian" 女子再嫁問題之歷史的演變 [The historical evolution of women's remarriage]. In *Zhongguo funü shi lunji*, 128-38. See Pao Chia-lin.

Ning Faxin 寧法新. *Yidai mingyuan Wang Zhaojun* 一代名媛王昭君 [A heroine of her time: Wang Zhaojun]. Taipei: Hanxin wenhua shiye, 1995.

Niu Zhiping 牛志平. "Tangdai hunyin de kaifang fengqi" 唐代婚姻的開放風氣 [The flexibility in marriage during the Tang Dynasty]. *Lishi yanjiu* 歷史研究 4 (1984): 80-6.

Oba Osamu 大庭脩. *Shin Kan hōseishi no kenkyū* 秦漢法制史研究 [Study on the legal history of the Qin and Han Dynasties]. Tokyo: Sobunsha, 1982.

O'Hara, Albert Richard, trans. *The Position of Woman in Early China According to the Lieh Nü Chuan "The Biographies of Chinese Women."* Taipei: Mei Ya Publications, 1971.

Ortner, Sherry B., and Harriet Whitehead, eds. *Sexual Meanings: The Cultural Construction of Gender and Sexuality*. New York: Cambridge University Press, 1991.

Paderni, Paola. "I Thought I Would Have Some Happy Days: Women Eloping in Eighteenth-Century China." *Late Imperial China* 16.1 (1995): 1-32.

Pan Chao. (See Ban Zhao.)

Pao Chia-lin 鮑家麟. "Yin-yang xueshuo yu funü diwei" 陰陽學說與婦女地位 [The yin-yang theory and the position of women]. In *Zhongguo funü shi lunji, xuji* 中國婦女史論集續集, edited by Pao Chia-lin, 37-54.

------, ed. *Zhongguo funü shi lunji* 中國婦女史論集 [Collection of Chinese women's history]. Taipei: Daoxiang chubanshe, 1979.

Parsons, John Carmi, and Bonnie Wheeler, eds. *Medieval Mothering*. New York: Garland Publishing, 1996.

Peiwen yunfu 佩文韻府 [A comprehensive rhyming dictionary]. Compiled by Zhang Yushu 張玉書 (1642-1711) et al. Shanghai: Shanghai guji chubanshe, 1983.

Phillips, E. D. *The Mongols*. New York: Frederick A. Praeger, 1969.

Pu Songling 蒲松齡 (1640-1715). *Liaozhai zhiyi* 聊齋誌異 [Strange stories from the Leisure Studio]. 1886. Reprint. Beijing: Zhongguo shudian, 1981.

Qiu Yongsheng 邱永生. "Gong si Zhaojun de Xieyou gongzhu" 功似昭君的解憂公主 [Princess Xieyou, who has the same merit as Zhaojun]. *Renmin ribao* 人民日報 [People's Daily] October 9, 1987, p. 8.

Qiu Zhonglin 邱仲麟. "Bu xiao zhi xiao Tang yilai gegu liaoqin xianxiang de shehui shi chutan" 不孝之孝唐以來割骨療親現象的社會史初探 [The unfilial filiality, a preliminary investigation into the social history of the phenomena of 'cutting a piece of flesh to heal one's parents' since the Tang Dynasty]. *Xin shixue* 6.1 (March 1995): 49-94.

Quan shanggu sandai Qin-Han Sanguo liuchao wen 全上古三代秦漢三國六朝文 [Comprehensive collection of literature from ancient times to the Six Dynasties]. Compiled by Yan Kejun 嚴可均 (1762-1843). 1894. Reprint. Beijing: Zhonghua shuju, 1958.

Quan Tang Shi 全唐詩 [Complete Tang poetry]. Compiled by Peng Dingqiu 彭定求 (1645-1719) et al. 25 vols. Beijing: Zhonghua shuju, 1960.

Quan Tang wen 全唐文 [Complete Tang prose], 1,000 ch. Compiled by Dong Gao 董誥 (1740-1818) et al. 11 vols. 1814. Reprint. Beijing: Zhonghua shuju, 1982.

Rawski, Evelyn S. "Ch'ing [Qing] Imperial Marriage and Problems of Rulership." In *Marriage and Inequality in Chinese*

Society, 170-203. *See* Watson and Ebrey.

Ren Bantang 任半塘. *Tang xinong* 唐戲弄 [Tang theater], 2 vols. Shanghai: Shanghai guji chubanshe, 1984.

Richardson, Hugh E. *Tibet and Its History.* 2d ed. Boston: Shambhala, 1984.

Riley, Denise. *"Am I That Name?" Feminism and the Category of "Women" in History.* Minneapolis: University of Minnesota, 1988.

Robinet, Isabelle. *Histoire du Taoisme: Des origines au XIVe siecle.* Paris: Cerf, 1991.

------. "Metamorphoses and Deliverance from the Corpse in Taoism." *History of Religions* 19 (1979): 37-70.

Ropp, Paul S. "The Status of Women in Late Imperial China: Evidence from Letters, Laws and Literature." Paper presented at the American Historical Association. Washington D.C., 1987.

Rossabi, Morris, ed. *China Among Equals.* Berkeley: University of California Press, 1983.

Rubin, Gayle. "The Traffic in Women: Notes on the 'Political Economy' of Sex." In *Toward an Anthropology of Women,* edited by Rayna R. Reiter. New York: Monthly Review Press, 1975.

Sanguo zhi 三國志 [The history of the Three Kingdoms], by Chen Shou 陳壽 (233-97). Beijing: Zhonghua shuju, 1959.

Sariti, Anthony William. "Monarchy, Bureaucracy, and Absolutism in the Political Thought of Ssu-Ma Kuang." *Journal of Asian Studies* 32.1 (1972): 53-76.

Schafer, Edward. *The Divine Woman.* San Francisco: North Point Press, 1980.

------. *The Golden Peaches of Samarkand: A Study of T'ang Exotics.* Berkeley: University of California Press, 1963.

------. "Notes on T'ang Geisha," Parts 1-4:1. "Typology"; 2. "The Masks and Arts of T'ang Courtesans"; 3. "Yang-chou in T'ang Times"; and 4. "Pleasure Boats." *Schafer Sinological Papers,* Issues 2, 4, 6, 7. 1984.

------. "Three Divine Women of Ancient China." *Chinese Literature: Essays, Articles, Reviews* 1 (1979): 31-42.

Scott, Joan. *Gender and the Politics of History.* New York:

Columbia University Press, 1988.

Seo Tatsuhiko. "Tōdai Chōan no sakariba [chū]" 唐代長安の盛り場（中）[Downtown area of Tang Chang'an, 2]. *Shiryū* 史流 30 (1989): 37-91.

------. "Tōdai Chōan no sakariba [shō]" 唐代長安の盛り場（上）[Downtown area of Tang Chang'an, 1]. *Shiryū* 史流 27 (1986): 1-59.

------. "Tōdai kōhanki no Chōan to denki shōsetsu" 唐代後半期の長安と伝奇小說 [Chang'an in the latter half of the Tang and *chuanqi* tales]. In *Hino Kaisaburō hakushi shōju kinen ronshū* 日野開三郎博士頌壽記念論集. Fukuoka, Japan: Chūgoku shoten, 1987.

Serruys, Henry. *Sino-Mongol Relations During the Ming: The Tribute System and Diplomatic Missions (1400-1600).* Bruxelles: Insititut belge des hautes etudes chinoises, 1967.

The Shambhala Dictionary of Buddhism and Zen. Ingrid Fischer-Schreiber (Buddhism), Farnz-Karl Ehrhard (Tibetan Buddhism), and Michael S. Diener. Translated by Michael H. Kohn. Boston: Shambhala Publications, 1991.

Shangqiu xian zhi 商丘縣志 [Gazetteer of Shangqiu County]. Compiled by Liu Dechang 劉德昌. 1705. Reprint from the 1932 lithographed *Zhongguo fangzhi congshu* 中國方志叢書 [Collectanea of Chinese gazetteers]. Taipei: Chengwen chubanshe, 1968.

Shao Bowen 邵伯温 (1057-1134). *He'nan Shaoshi wenjian qianlu* 河南邵氏聞見前錄 [Former record of things heard and seen by Mr. Shao of He'nan]. Taipei: Guangwen shuju, 1970. *Hanfenlou* 涵芬樓 1132 prefaced edition.

Shi ji 史記 [Records of the Grand Historian], by Sima Qian 司馬遷 (145-ca. 86 B.C.E.). Beijing: Zhonghua shuju, 1959.

Shi jing 詩經 [The book of poetry]. In *Shisan jing zhushu* 十三經注疏.

Shisan jing zhushu 十三經注疏 [The thirteen classics with annotations and notes]. 1821 ed. 8 vols. Reprint. Taipei: Yiwen yinshuguan, 1981.

Shi Yongming 釋永明. *Fojiao de nüxing guan* 佛教的女性觀 [Notions of women in Buddhism]. Gaoxiong, Taiwan: Foguang chubanshe, 1990.

Shuihu zhuan 水滸傳 [Water margin, or all men are brothers], by Shi Nai'an 施耐庵 (1296-1370) and Luo Guanzhong 羅貫中 (Ming Dynasty). Introduction by Miao Tianhua 繆天華. Taipei: Sanmin shuju, 1981.

Shuowen jiezi zhu 說文解字注 [An explication of written characters with annotations (by Duan Yucai)], by Xu Shen 許慎 (30-124). Annotated by Duan Yucai 段玉裁 (1735-1815). Shanghai: Guji chubanshe, 1981.

Sima Guang 司馬光 (1019-86). *Simashi shuyi* 司馬氏書儀 [Mr. Sima's notes on the Ceremonies and Rites canon]. *Congshu jicheng* 叢書集成 edition.

------. *Wengong jiafan* 溫公家範 [Wengong's family norms]. *Cangshu shisanzhong* 藏書十三種 edition.

------. *Zizhi tong jian* 資治通鑒 [Comprehensive mirror for aid in government]. Vol. 3. Jiulong, Hong Kong: Zhonghua shuju, 1956.

Smith, Richard J. *China's Cultural Heritage: The Qing Dynasty, 1644-1912*. 2d edition. Boulder: Westview Press, 1994.

Song Dexi 宋德熹. "Tangdai de jinü" 唐代的妓女 [Prostitutes of the Tang dynasty]. In *Zhongguo funü shi lunji, xuji* 中國婦女史論集續集, edited by Pao Chia-lin 鮑家麟. Taipei: Daoxiang chubanshe, 1991.

Song shi 宋史 [The history of the Song Dynasty], edited by Toghto 脫脫 (1314-55) et al. Beijing: Zhonghua shuju, 1977.

Song shu 宋書 [The history of the (Liu) Song Dynasty], by Shen Yue 沈約 (441-513). Beijing: Zhonghua shuju, 1974.

Song Yun 松筠. *Weizang tongzhi* 衛藏通治 [The chronicle gazetteer of Tibet]. Lhasa: Xizang yanjiu bianjibu, 1982.

Spivak, Gayatri Chakravorty. *In Other Worlds: Essays in Cultural Politics*. New York: Routledge, 1988.

Stacey, Judith. *Patriarchy and Socialist Revolution in China*. Berkeley: University of California Press, 1983.

Su Bing 蘇冰 and Wei Lin 魏林. *Zhongguo hunyin shi* 中國婚姻史 [History of marriage in China]. Taipei: Wenjin chubanshe, 1994.

Sui shu 隋書 [The history of the Sui Dynasty], by Wei Zheng 魏徵 (580-643) et al. Beijing: Zhonghua shuju, 1973.

Sun Shuyu 孫述宇. *Shuihu zhuan de laili xintai yu yishu* 水滸傳

的來歷心態與藝術 [The origin, psychology, and art of
        Shuihu zhuan]. Taipei: Shibao chubanshe, 1983.

Sun Xiao 孫曉. *Zhongguo hunyin xiaoshi* 中國婚姻小史 [A
        brief history of Chinese marriage]. Beijing: Guangming
        ribao chubanshe, 1994.

Sung, Marina H. "The Chinese Lieh-nü Tradition." In *Women in
        China*, edited by Richard W. Guisso and Stanley
        Johannesen, 63-74. Lewiston, NY: Philo, 1981.

Swann, Nancy Lee, trans. "Lessons for Women." In her *Pan Chao*
        [Ban Zhao]: *Foremost Woman Scholar of China*, 82-90.
        New York: The Century, 1932.

Tai Jingnong 臺靜農. "Fojiao gushi yu Zhongguo xiaoshuo" 佛教
        故實與中國小說 [Buddhist tales and Chinese fiction]. In
        Fojiao yu Zhongguo wenxue 佛教與中國文學
        [Buddhism and Chinese literature], edited by Zhang Mantao
        章曼濤. Taipei: Dashen wenhua, 1978.

Taiping guangji 太平廣記 [Extensive gleanings of the reign of
        Great Tranquillity]. Compiled by Li Fang 李昉 (925-96) et
        al. 3 vols. 1755. Reprint. Taipei: Xinxing shuju, 1973.

Taishō shinshū daizōkyō sakuin 大正新修大藏經索引. 30 vols.
        Tokyo: Taishō shinshū daizōkyō kankōkai, 1940-.

Tan Qixiang 譚其驤. *Zhongguo lishi ditu ji* 中國歷史地圖集
        [The historical atlas of China]. Vol. 4. Shanghai:
        Cartographic Publishing House, 1982.

Tang liangjing chengfang kao 唐兩京城坊考 [A study of the two
        Tang capitals, their cities and wards], by Xu Song 徐松
        (Qing Dynasty). Beijing: Zhonghua shuju, 1985.

Tang lü shuyi 唐律疏議 [Annotations of the Tang code], by
        Zhangsun Wuji 長孫無忌 (d. 689). Taipei: Hongwenguan
        chubanshe, 1986.

Tang zhiyan 唐摭言 [Tidbits from the Tang], by Wang Dingbao
        王定保 (Five Dynasties). Shanghai: Shanghai guji
        chubanshe, 1978.

Teiser, Stephen F. *The Ghost Festival in Medieval China*.
        Princeton: Princeton University Press, 1988.

T'ien Ju-k'ang. *Male Anxiety and Female Chastity: A Comparative
        Study of Chinese Ethical Values in Ming-Ch'ing Times*.
        Leiden: E. J. Brill, 1988.

Tierney, Brian. *The Crisis of Church and State 1150-1300.* Toronto: University of Toronto Press, 1988.

Tu Cheng-sheng 杜正勝. *Gudai shehui yu guojia* 古代社會與國家 [Society and state in ancient China]. Taipei: Yunchen wenhua chubanshe, 1992.

Verellen, Franciscus. *Du Guangting: Taoiste de cour a la fin de la Chine medievale.* Paris: College de France, 1989.

Waley, Arthur, trans. *The Analects of Confucius.* New York: MacMillan, 1939.

------, trans. "The Ballad of Mulan." In *The Columbia Anthology of Traditional Chinese Literature,* 474-76. See Mair.

Wallacker, Benjamin E. "Chang Fei's [Zhang Fei's] Preface to the Chin Code of Law." *T'oung Pao* 72.4-5 (1986): 229-68.

Waltner, Ann. *Getting an Heir: Adoption and the Construction of Kinship in Late Imperial China.* Honolulu: University of Hawai'i Press, 1990.

Wang Anshi 王安石 (1021-86). "Yinnü muzhiming" 鄞女墓誌銘 [Funeral inscription of a girl of Yin (County)]. In his *Linchuan wenji* 臨川文集 [Literary collection of (Master) Linchuan]. *Liuhutang* 六瑚堂 1884 edition.

Wang Chien-wen 王健文. "Xi Han lüling yu guojia zhengdang xing--yi lüling zhong de 'budao' wei zhongxin" 西漢律令與國家正當性--以律令中的﹁不道﹂為中心 [Western Han law codes and the legitimacy of the state--a study of the "crimes of depravity"]. *Xin shixue* 新史學 3.3 (1992): 1-36.

Wang Furen 王輔仁 and Suo Wenqing 索文清. *Zangzu shiyao* 藏族史要 [A brief history of Tibet]. Chengdu, China: Sichuan renmin chubanshe, 1982.

Wang Gungwu. "Some Comments on the Later Standard Histories." In *Essays on the Sources for Chinese History,* edited by Donald D. Leslie, Colin Mackerras, and Wang Gungwu. Columbia: University of South Carolina Press, 1973.

Wang Mingsheng 王鳴盛 (1722-98). *Shiqi shi shangque* 十七史商榷 [A critical study of the seventeen dynastic histories]. 2 vols. Beijing: Shangwu yinshuguan, 1964.

Wang Shounan 王壽南. "Tangdai gongzhu zhi hunyin" 唐代公主之婚姻 [The marriage of Tang princesses]. In *Zhongguo funü shi lunwen ji, di er ji* 中國婦女史論文集, 第二輯 [Collection on Chinese women's history], edited by Li Yu-ning 李又寧 and Zhang Yufa 張玉法, 90-144. Vol. 2. Taipei: Shangwu yinshuguan, 1988.

Wang Shunu 王書奴. *Zhongguo changji shi* 中國娼妓史 [A history of prostitutes in China]. 1934. Reprint. Shanghai: Shanghai shudian, 1992.

Wang Tongling 王桐齡. "Tang-Song shidai jinü kao" 唐宋時代妓女考 [An examination of Tang-Song prostitutes]. *Shixue nianbao* 史學年報 1 (1929): 21-31.

Wang Zhonghan 王鐘翰, ed. *Zhongguo minzu shi* 中國民族史 [History of Chinese nationalities]. Beijing: Shehui kexueyuan chubanshe, 1994.

Wang Zhongming 王重民 et al. *Dunhuang bianwen ji* 敦煌變文集 [Collection of "transformation texts" from Dunhuang]. 2 Vols. Beijing: Renmin wenxue chubanshe, 1957.

Watson, Burton. *Basic Writings of Mo Tzu, Hsün Tzu, and Han Fei Tzu.* New York: Columbia University Press, 1967.

Watson, Rubie S., and Patricia Buckley Ebrey, eds. *Marriage and Inequality in Chinese Society.* Los Angeles: University of California Press, 1991.

Wei shu 魏書 [The history of the (Northern) Wei Dynasty], by Wei Shou 魏收 (506-72). Beijing: Zhonghua shuju, 1974.

Wei Tai 魏泰 (ca. 1050-1110). *Dongxuan bilu* 東軒筆錄 [East Pavilion notes]. *Hubei xianzheng yishu* 湖北先正遺書 edition.

Wen Kang 文康 (Qing Dynasty). *Xianü qiyuan* 俠女奇緣 [The lady knight-errant's fantastical adventures]; original title *Ernü yingxiong zhuan* 兒女英雄傳 [A tale of heroic lovers]. Guangxi, China: Renmin chubanshe, 1980.

Weng Tu-chien (Weng Dujian) 翁獨健. *Tao tsang tzu mu yin te* 道藏子目引得 [Combined indexes to authors and titles of books in two collections of Taoist (Daoist) literature]. Vol. 25. Beijing: Harvard-Yenching Institute, 1935.

Widmer, Ellen, and Kang-I Sun Chang, eds. *Writing Women in Late Imperial China.* Stanford: Stanford University Press, 1997.

Williamson, H. R. *Wang An Shih: A Chinese Statesman and*

Educationalist of the Sung Dynasty. Vol. 2. London: Arthur Probsthain, 1935.

Winthrop, Robert H. *Dictionary of Concepts in Cultural Anthropology*. New York: Greenwood Press, 1991.

Wolf, Margery. *Women and the Family in Rural Taiwan*. Stanford: Stanford University Press, 1972.

Wong, Sun-ming. "Confucian Ideal and Reality: Transformation of the Institution of Marriage in T'ang China (A.D. 618-907)." Ph.D. diss., University of Washington, 1979.

Woodward, Kenneth L. *Making Saints*. New York: Simon and Schuster, 1990.

Wu Fengpei 吳豐培, ed. *Xizang zhi* 西藏志 [Gazetteers of Tibet]. Lhasa: Xizang yanjiu bianjibu, 1982.

Wu Qingxian 吳慶顯. "Qian Han dui xiyu guojia de heqin zhengce" 前漢對西域國家的和親政策 [The *heqin* policy toward the western territory in the Former Han Dynasty]. *Zhongguo bianzheng* 中國邊政 114.12 (December 1992): 13-7.

Wu, Yenna. *The Chinese Virago, A Literary Theme*. Cambridge: Council for East Asian Studies, Harvard University, 1995.

Xiang Shuyun 向淑雲. *Tang dai hunyin fa yu hunyin shitai* 唐代婚姻法與婚姻實態 [The marriage law and reality of marriage of the Tang Dynasty]. Taipei: Shangwu yinshuguan, 1991.

Xiao jing 孝經 [The classic of filiality]. In *Shisan jing zhushu* 十三經注疏.

Xinjiaoben jiu Tang shu fu suoyin 新校本舊唐書附索引 [The new annotated edition of the history of the Tang Dynasty with index], by Liu Xu 劉昫 (888-947) et al. Taipei: Dingwen shuju, 1979.

Xin Tang shu 新唐書 [The new history of the Tang Dynasty], by Ouyang Xiu 歐陽修 (1007-72), Song Qi 宋祁 (996-1061), et al. Beijing: Zhonghua shuju, 1975.

Xin Wudai shi 新五代史 [The new history of the Five Dynasties], by Ouyang Xiu 歐陽修 (1007-72) et al. Beijing: Zhonghua shuju, 1974.

Xinyi Luoyang qielan ji 新譯洛陽伽藍記 [Record of the monasteries of Luoyang with a new translation], by Yang

Xuanzhi 楊衒之 (fl. 528). Translated by Liu Jiuzhou 劉九洲. Taipei: Sanmin shuju, 1994.

Xu Fuguan 徐復觀. *Zhongguo renxing lun shi* 中國人性論史 [Treatises on Chinese human nature]. Taizhong, Taiwan: Tunghai University Press, 1963.

Xu Shen 許慎 (30-124). *Shuowen jiezi* 說文解字 [Explicating the written characters]. Shanghai: Shanghai guji chubanshe, 1981.

Xu Wei 徐渭 (1521-93). *Si sheng yuan* 四聲猿 [The four shrieks of the monkey]. Prefaced by Zhou Zhongming 周中明. Shanghai: Shanghai guji chubanshe, 1984.

Xu Xueqing 徐學清. "You zao xinqu yong Zhaojun" 又造新曲詠昭君 [Making another new song for Zhaojun]. *Renmin ribao* 人民日報 October 22, 1987, p. 7.

Xu Ziming 徐自明. *Song zaifu biannianlu* 宋宰輔編年錄 [Arranged chronological record of Song stewards-bulwark of state]. Taipei: Wenhai chubanshe, 1929.

Yangjiafu shidai zhongyong yanyi zhizhuan 楊家府世代忠勇演義志傳 [The heroic lives of Yang family generals]. Prefaced by Yuan Shishuo 袁世碩. Vol. 539 of *Guben xiaoshuo jicheng* 古本小說集成, edited by Qinhuai moke 秦淮墨客. Shanghai: Shanghai guji chubanshe, 1990.

Yang Lien-Sheng. "Historical Notes on the Chinese World Order." In *The Chinese World Order*, 20-33. See Fairbank.

Yang Mu (Wang Jingxian) 楊牧 (王靖獻). "Lun yizhong yingxiong zhuyi" [On a kind of heroism], in his *Wenxue zhishi* 文學知識 [Literary knowledge]. Taipei: Hongfan shuju, 1979.

Yen Keng-wang 嚴耕望. "Bei Wei shangshu zhidu kao" 北魏尚書制度考 [On the system of Shangshu of the Northern Wei]. *The Bulletin of the Institute of History and Philology, Academia Sinica* 中央研究院歷史語言研究所集刊 18 (1948): 252-360.

Yi jing 易經 [The book of changes]. In *Shisan jing zhushu* 十三經注疏.

Yi Junzuo 易君左. *Zhongguo baimeiren tuyong* 中國百美人圖詠 [Book of a hundred Chinese beauties]. Hong Kong: Tianfeng yinshuachang, 1958.

Yi li 儀禮 [The book of ceremonies]. In *Shisan jing zhushu* 十三經注疏.

"Yi Qian Geng shaqi shi" 議錢耿殺妻事 [On Qian Geng's killing his wife], in *Quan Jin wen* 全晉文 [Comprehensive collection of literature from the Jin Dynasty], by Zu Taizhi 祖台之. In *Quan shanggu sandai Qin-Han Sanguo liuchao wen*, ch. 138, p. 12a.

Yiwen leiju 藝文類聚 [A categorized collection of literary writing]. Compiled by Ouyang Xun 歐陽詢 (557-641). 1965. Reprint. Shanghai: Shanghai guji chubanshe, 1982.

Yü Ying-shih. "Han Foreign Relations." In *The Cambridge History of China, Volume 1: The Chin and Han Empires, 221 B. C. -A. D. 220*, edited by Denis Twitchett and Michael Loewe, 377-462. Cambridge: Cambridge University Press, 1986.

------. "Intellectual Breakthroughs in the T'ang-Sung Transition." In *The Power of Culture, Studies in Chinese Cultural History*, edited by Willard J. Peterson, Andrew H. Plaks, and Ying-shih Yü, 158-71. Hong Kong: The Chinese University Press, 1994.

------ 余英時. *Shi yu Zhongguo wenhua* 士與中國文化 [Literati and Chinese culture]. Shanghai: Shanghai renmin chubanshe, 1987.

[*Foshuo*] *Yulanpen jing* [佛說] 盂蘭盆經 [The *Yulanpen* sutra]. Attributed to Dharmaraksa (ca. 265-313). In *Taishō shinshū daizōkyō sakuin* 大正新修大藏經索引. no. 685.

Yuli 玉曆 [The jade calendar]. Attributed to Danchi 淡癡 (fl. 1030). Taipei: Ruicheng shuju, n.d.

Yuan Xingpei 袁行霈. *Baiwange weishenmo: Zhongguo wenxue* 百萬個為甚麼: 中國文學 [Millions of why: Chinese literature]. Taipei: Xiapu chubanshe, 1994.

Yuefu shiji yibaijuan 樂府詩集一百卷 [Yuefu poetry in 100 chapters], edited by Guo Maoqian 郭茂倩 (twelfth century). *Sibu congkan* 四部叢刊 (集部) ed.

Yue Qingping 樂清平. *Zhongguo de jia yu guo* 中國的家與國 [Chinese concepts of family and country]. Changchun, China: Jilin wenshi chubanshe, 1990.

Zhang Dai 張岱 (1599-ca. 1684). *Taoan mengyi jinzhu jinyi* 陶庵

夢憶今註今譯 [Recollections of Taoan's past dreams with annotation and modern translation]. Translated by Zhou Xianqing 周咸清. Taipei: Shangwu yinshuguan, 1984.

Zhang Jing 張敬. *"Lie^a nü zhuan yu qi zuozhe"* 列女傳與其作者 [*The Biographies of Women* and its author]. In *Zhongguo funü shi lunwen ji* 中國婦女史論文集 [Collection of Chinese women's history], edited by Li Yu-ning 李又寧 and Zhang Yufa 張玉法, 50-60. Taipei: Shangwu yinshuguan, 1981.

Zhang Shunmin 張舜民 (ca. 1034-ca. 1110). *Huamanlu* 畫墁錄 [Painted plaster record]. *Tang Song congshu* 唐宋叢書 edition.

Zhao Ye 趙曄. *Xinyi Wu-Yue chunqiu* 新譯吳越春秋 [A new translation of the spring and autumn annals of the kingdoms of Wu and Yue]. Annotated by Huang Rensheng. Taipei: Sanmin shuju, 1996.

Zheng Qinren 鄭欽仁. *Bei Wei guanliao jigou yanjiu xubian* 北魏官僚機構研究續編 [Second study on the bureaucratic system of the Northern Wei]. Taipei: Daohe chubanshe, 1995.

Zhengtong Daozang 正統道藏 [Zhengtong edition of the treasure house of the way]. 1444. Reprint. Taipei: Yiwen chubanshe, 1976.

Zheng Zhizhen 鄭之珍 (fl. 1582). *Xinbian Mulian jiumu quanshan xiwen* 新編目連救母勸善戲文 [A new compilation of the text to the play about Mulian rescuing his mother and exhorting her to goodness]. *Guben xiqu congkan* 古本戲曲叢刊 ed. Series 1, 67. Taipei: Tianyi chubanshe, 1983.

Zhongguo lidai mingren shengji dacidian 中國歷代名人勝跡大字典 [Dictionary of famous Chinese people and places]. Hong Kong: Sanlian shuju, 1994.

Zhou Hui 周煇 (1126-ca. 1198). *Qingbo biezhi* 清波別志 [Complementary notes by one living near Qingbo (gate)]. *Zhibuzuzhai congshu* 知不足齋叢書 edition.

Zhou li 周禮 [The book of rites of the Zhou Dynasty]. In *Shisan jing zhushu* 十三經注疏.

Zhu Zongbin 祝總斌. "Luelun Jin lü rujia hua" 略論晉律儒家

化 [On the Confucianization of the Jin law]. *Zhongguo shi yanjiu* 中國史研究 2.26 (1985): 101-24.

GLOSSARY

"Ai jiefu fu" 〈哀節婦賦〉

An Ji 安驥

An Lushan 安祿山

Anping 安平

Anyang 安陽

Anyi (Princess) 安義 (公主)

Bai (Ms.) 白 (氏)

Bai Xingjian 白行簡

Ban Gu 班固

Ban Zhao 班昭

bao 報

bao chou 報仇

bao en 報恩

baogu 保辜

baojuan 寶卷

Baotang si 保唐寺

"Bei di" 北狄

Beili 北里

Beiliji[a] 北里妓

Beili zhi ji[a] 北里之妓

"Bei ruo" 卑弱

"Ben sang" 〈奔喪〉

biji 筆記

Bian Dongxuan 邊洞玄

bian tong 辯通

bianwen 變文

bian xiang 變相

bo[a] 博

bo[b] 駁

Bohai Feng 渤海封 (氏)

Bo Juyi 白居易

Boling Cui (Po-ling Ts'ui) 博陵崔 (氏)

boshi 博士

Bowu zhi 《博物志》

buce zhi di 不測之地

budao 不道

bujing 不敬

bu le 不樂

butiao zhi tu 不調之徒

buxiao 不孝

bu xiao zhi xiao 不孝之孝

buzei guan 捕賊官

Cai Yan 蔡琰

Cai Yong 蔡邕

canzhi zhengshi 參知政事

Cao Cao 曹操

"Cehe Huihe gongzhu wen" 〈冊賀回紇公主文〉

Chanyu 單于

chang 嚐

chang[a] 娼 (prostitute)

chang[b] 倡 (entertainer)

Chang'an 長安

Changle fang 長樂坊

changshi 常侍

chang wen 唱文

Changyun 長雲

"Chezhong nüzi" 〈車中女子〉

Chen 陳

Chen Huimeng 陳慧猛

Chen Miao 陳邈

Chen Ping 陳平

cheng 丞

chengchen 稱臣

chengdi 稱弟

Chengdu 成都

Chengwu 成武

Cheng Xian 程咸

chengxiang 丞相

chengxu 稱胥

Cheng Yi 程頤

Chengzu (Emperor) 成祖 (r. 1403-24)

chi 笞

chongbo feimao zhe, dan fu liupin 充博非貌者、但負流品

Chongren fang 崇仁坊

Chongyi furen 崇義夫人
Chu 朱
Chuci 《楚辭》
Chu'er 楚兒
chūko 中古
chuanqi 傳奇
Chunqiu 《春秋》
ci 賜 (granting)
ci 詞 (literary genre)
ci 慈 (kind)
ci hui 慈惠
cike 刺客
cimu 慈母
Ci Mulan ti fu congjun 《雌木蘭替父從軍》
Cixi (Empress Dowager) 慈禧(太后) (1834-1908)
cong ren zhi yi 從人之義
Congshu jicheng 《叢書集成》
cuyou rongse 粗有容色
Cui Hao 崔浩
Cui Hong 崔宏
Cui Shensi 崔慎思
Cui Ting 崔挺
Cui Xiaofen 崔孝芬
Cui Yin 崔胤
Cui Zhen 崔振
Cui Zuan 崔纂
Da Ji 妲己
da jingyin 大京尹
Daming 大名
dani 大逆
dani budao 大逆不道
"Dawan liezhuan" 〈大宛列傳〉
Dayi (Princess) 大義 (公主)
Dazhao (Temple) 大昭(寺)
Dazhong 大中
dan 石
dao 盜
Dao (Tao) 道

"Daode jing" 〈道德經〉
Daowu (Emperor) 道武帝 (r. 386-409)
de yan rong gong 德言容功
Dezong (Emperor) 德宗 (r. 780-804)
Dengli Khaghan 登里可汗 (r. 759-80)
di 帝
Di 狄
dimu 嫡母
diyu 地獄
Dizang 地藏
dian 奠
"Dianlue" 〈典略〉
Dong Changling 董昌齡
Dongguang 東光
dongtian 洞天
Dongwei (Village of) 東魏(村)
"Dongyi, fuyu" 〈東夷夫餘〉
Dong yue di jun 東嶽帝君
"Doulü" 〈鬥律〉
Dou Sengyan 竇僧演
"Dousong" 〈鬥訟〉
Dou Yuan 竇瑗
Dugu Shiren 獨孤師仁
Du Xing 杜興
Dunhuang 敦煌
ernü 兒女
Fajia 法家
Fan Chuncui 范純粹
Fan Chunfu 范純夫
Fan Chunli 范純禮
Fan Chunren 范純仁
Fan Li 范蠡
Fan Su 樊素
Fan Tai 范泰
Fan Zhongyan 范仲淹
fang 坊
Fang Qianli 房千里
Fang Xuanling 房玄齡

fang zhong shu 房中術

Feng (Ms.) 封 (氏)

Feng Hui 封回

Feng Junyi 封君義

Feng Liao 馮嫽

Fengxian 逢僊

fu 婦 (a married woman; wife)

fu 賦 (a poetic genre)

fudao muyi 婦道母儀

fude 婦德

fugong 婦工

Fuhao 婦好

Funiang 福娘

furen bu ju lu 婦人不居廬

furong 婦容

fu tian ye ke bei hu yuan si wu ta 夫天也可背乎願死無他

Fuxiang 輔相

fu xiao de zhi ben ye jiao zhi suo you sheng ye 夫孝德之本也教
之所由生也

fuxiu er qu 拂袖而去

fuxun 婦訓

fuyan 婦言

fuyi er qu 拂衣而去

Fuzhou 福州

gaiyu 丐育

"Gaodi ji" 〈高帝紀〉

Gao Meimei 高妹妹

"Gao Min nü bei" 〈高愍女碑〉

Gaozu (Han emperor) (漢) 高祖 (r. 206-195 B.C.E.)

Gaozu (Tang emperor) (唐) 高祖 (r. 618-26)

ge 歌

gegu 割股

Gobi (Gebi) 戈壁

gong'an 公案

gongcheng 宮城

gongji[a] 宮妓

Gong Jiang 恭姜

gongren 宮人

Gongsun Sheng 公孫勝
Gongxiu 公休
Gou Jian 勾踐
Gou Xiangu 緱仙姑
"Gudai zhishi jieceng de xingqi yu fazhan" 〈古代知識階層的興
　　起與發展〉
Gu Jiegang 顧頡剛
Gujin shuohai 《古今說海》
"Guren qi" 〈賈人妻〉
guanji[a] 官妓
"Guan ju" 關雎
Guanqui Dian 毋丘點
Guanqiu Jian 毋丘儉
Guanqiu Zhi 毋丘芝
Guanxi zhenlienü Huguo Ma furen 關西貞烈女護國馬夫人
Guangping You 廣平游 (氏)
Guangzhai fang 光宅坊
Gui'er 桂兒
Gui jie 鬼節
gui yue 鬼月
Guizi 龜茲
Guo Duan 郭鍛
guo furen 國夫人
Guozhou 果州
Guo Ziyi 郭子儀
"Handai xunli yu wenhua chuanbo" 〈漢代循吏與文化傳播〉
Handan 邯鄲
"Han Ji qi" 〈韓覬妻〉
Hanlin yuan 翰林院
Han shu 《漢書》
Hangzhou 杭州
"Haoxia" 豪俠
Hebei 河北
He'nan 河南
heqin 和親
He Yufeng 何玉鳳
Heyuan 河源
He Zeng 何曾

Hongfu 紅拂

Honghua (Princess) 弘化 (公主)

Honglou meng《紅樓夢》

Hongxian 紅線

"Hou fei zhuan"〈后妃傳〉

Hou Meng 侯蒙

hu 斛

Hu (Ms.) 胡 (氏)

Hubei 湖北

Hu Changcan 胡長粲

hufa 護法

Huhanye 呼韓邪

"Hu hun"〈戶婚〉

husu 胡俗

Hu Zheng 胡證

Hua 花

hua 化

Hua Gu 花姑

"Huayang wang Kai fei"〈華陽王楷妃〉

Huazhou 滑州

Huai'en 淮恩

Huang Chao 黃巢

huangcheng 皇城

Huang Chonggu 黃崇嘏

Huang Guanfu 黃觀福

Huang Lingwei 黃靈微

Huangpo 黃陂

huang quan 黃泉

Hui (prefecture) 徽(州)

Huihe 迴紇

"Huihe" 迴紇

Huizong (Emperor) 徽宗 (r. 1101-25)

"huo meng ye" 火猛也

ji[a] 妓 (entertainer)

ji[b] 姬 (courtesan)

ji ji 及笄

jimu 繼母

Ji'nan (Grand Princess) 濟南 (長公主)

jiqin 期親
ji shu jiaofang 籍屬教坊
jiafu 假父
jiaji[a] 家妓
Jia Miao 賈邈
jiamu 假母
jian 漸 (gradual)
jian 間 (space)
Jian'an 建安
jianli 賤隸
"Jianzhen jiefu Li" 〈堅貞節婦李〉
jianghu yiqi 江湖義氣
Jiang Qing 江青
Jiangsu 江蘇
Jiangxi 江西
Jiangzhen 祥真
jiang zi yi er zhong sui bugan qiang 將自劓刵眾遂不敢彊
jiaofang 教坊
jie 節
jie yi 節義
jin 金
Jincheng (Princess) 金成 (公主)
jinguo yingxiong 愧國英雄
Jinling 金陵
jinshi 進士
jinwu 金吾
jinyuan 禁苑
Jingchu suishi ji 《荊楚歲時記》
Jingfeng (Gate) 景風(門)
Jinggong 荊公
Jinghua yuan 《鏡花緣》
"Jing shisan niang" 〈荊十三娘〉
jing shi zi ji 經史子集
Jingyang 旌陽
jingzhao 京兆
jiupin zhengyuan guan 九品正員官
jōko 上古
ju jiang dao jiebi ge'er yi zi shi. . . xun zu 遽將刀截鼻割耳以

自誓…尋卒
juan 卷
Junchen 軍臣
junzi 君子
Kaifeng 開封
ke yan 可厭
Khan 可汗
kinsei 近世
ku 苦
ku ju 苦具
"Kuli liezhuan [Zhang Tang]" 〈酷吏列傳 (張湯)〉
ku qi 苦器
kunbian fugong 髡鞭付宮
Kunlun 崑崙
K'ung Fu-tzu (Kong fuzi) 孔夫子
kyōbō to iu no ga gikan no kashō de atte 教坊と云うのが, 妓館
　　　の華稱であつて
Lai'er 萊兒
Lanling (Grand Princess) 蘭陵 (長公主)
Laoshang 老上
li 吏 (subofficial clerk)
li 禮 (propriety)
li 里 (quarter)
Li (Ms.) 李 (氏)
Li Ao 李翱
libu 吏部
Li Chong 李沖
Li Fengji 李逢吉
Li Gongzuo 李公佐
Li Hua 李華
lijie 禮節
Li Jing 李靖
Li jing 《禮經》
Li Kui 李逵
Li Qingzhao 李清照
Li Wa 李娃
liyuan 梨園
Li Zhen 李貞

lianzuo 連坐

liang 兩

Liang Hong 梁鴻

Liang Hongyu 梁紅玉

lie^a 列

lie^b 烈

lie^bfu 烈婦

lie^bhuo 烈火

lienü 烈女

lie^a nü 列女

lie^bnü 烈女

Lienü zhuan 《列女傳》

Lie^a nü zhuan 列女傳

Lie^bnü zhuan 烈女傳

lie^bri 烈日

lie^bshi 烈士

lie zhuan 列傳

Lin Chong 林沖

Linchuan 臨川

Linqing 臨清

Ling (Empress Dowager) 靈 (太后) (r. 516-28)

Lingbao 靈寶

Linghu Gao 令狐滈

Liu 劉

Liu Bang 劉邦

liu dao 六道

"Liu fan" 六反

Liu Hui 劉輝

Liu Ji 劉寂

Liu Jing 劉敬

"Liu Jing zhuan" 〈劉敬傳〉

Liu Meng 劉蒙

Liu Rong 劉肜

Liu Tainiang 劉泰娘

Liu Xiang 劉向

Liu Xin 劉歆

Liu Yan 劉琰

Liu Yuxi 劉禹錫

Liu Zongyuan 柳宗元
Lu Daoqian 盧道虔
"Lu Fang zhuan" 〈盧芳傳〉
Lu Meiniang 盧眉娘
lumu 盧墓
lushi canjun 錄事參軍
Lu Yu 盧毓
Lu Zhaolin 盧照鄰
Lu Zhengsi 盧正思
Luzhou 潞州
Lü (Empress) 呂 (后)
lü boshi 律博士
Lüqiao 綠翹
luan 鸞
luanfeng 鸞鳳
"Luanniao shi xu" 〈鸞鳥詩序〉
Luo (Ms.) 羅 (氏)
Luo Binwang 駱賓王
Luopu 羅卜
Luoyang 洛陽
Ma Nie 馬臬
maiduan 買斷
Medu 冒頓
menfang zhi zhu 門房之誅
menxia 門下
mianzi 面子
miao 妙
*minji*ᵃ 民妓
Ming (Emperor) 明帝 (r. 466-72)
Ming-chun (Mingjun) 明君
ming fu 冥府
ming jian 冥間
"Mingli" 名例
ming si 冥司
Mu dachong Gu Dasao 母大蟲顧大嫂
Mu Guiying 穆桂英
Mulan 木蘭
"Mulan ci" 〈木蘭辭〉

Mulan shan 木蘭山

"Mulan shi" 〈木蘭詩〉

Mulian 目連

Mulian jiumu zaju 《目連救母雜劇》

Mulian ruming zaju 《目連入冥雜劇》

Mulian sanshi baojuan 《目連三世寶卷》

Mulian xingxiao xiwen 《目連行孝戲文》

Muqianlian 目乾連

Mutianzi zhuan 《穆天子傳》

Mu yecha Sun Erniang 母夜叉孫二娘

"mu ye yi er ci" 母也義而慈

"Mu yi" 母儀

mu yi 母儀

Muzong (Emperor) 穆宗 (r. 821-4)

na 納

naqie 納妾

nai bu ren jia 乃不忍嫁

"Nan-Bei chao zhu lü kao xu" 南北朝諸律考序

Nanchong 南充

Nanjing 南京

"Nan Xiongnu zhuan" 〈南匈奴傳〉

Nanyuan 南院

neifu 內附

neihan 內翰

neiren 內人

Nei xun 《內訓》

"Nei ze" 〈內則〉

Nengzhi 能之

nijie jueli 逆節絕理

nilian ji mo 泥蓮既沒

"Nie bi zhuan" 〈聶嬖傳〉

Nie Feng 聶鋒

Nie Rong 聶榮

"Nie Yinniang" 聶隱娘

Nie Zheng 聶政

Ningguo (Princess) 寧國 (公主)

Ningyuanguo 寧遠國

Niu Sengru 牛僧儒

"Nü jie" 〈女誡〉
Nü lunyu 《女論語》
nüren shi huoshui 女人是禍水
Nü sishu 《女四書》
nü xia 女俠
Nü xiaojing 《女孝經》
nü zhuangyuan 女狀元
Nü zhuangyuan ci huang de feng 《女狀元辭凰得鳳》
Pan Jinlian 潘金蓮
Pang 龐
Pang Ji 龐籍
Pang Yuanlu 龐元魯
Pei 裴
Pei Du 裴度
Pei Xing 裴鉶
Pei Xun 裴詢
pen 盆
"Peng Chong zhuan" 〈彭寵傳〉
Pi Rixiu 皮日休
Pingkang li (fang) 平康里(坊)
qi 棄
Qi lue 《七略》
Qiqing 齊青
qi san chu yu gaiyang 其三出于丐養
qishi 棄市
Qian guo furen 汧國夫人
Qianjin (Princess) 千金 (公主)
Qianqing 千頃
Qiang 羌
Qiao Zhizhi 喬知之
qie 妾
Qinren fang 親仁坊
Qinren zhu yisun 親仁諸裔孫
qinxiang zhi xia 卿相之俠
Qinghe 清河
Qinghe Cui 清河崔 (氏)
Qingti 青提
Qiuran ke 虯髯客

qu 娶

Qujiang　曲江

Qujiang (Park)　曲江(園)

"Rao E bei"　〈饒娥碑〉

ren 仁

ren zhi 仁智

Renzong (Emperor)　仁宗 (r. 1022-63)

Ru　儒

Rujia　儒家

rushi 儒士

ruanyu 軟玉

Runan (Prince)　汝南 (王)

Runniang　潤娘

ruo 若

sancong 三從

sancong side 三從四德

sangong langzhong 三公郎中

san guan 三官

Sanqu　三曲

Sansi　三司

san yuan 三元

"Sang da ji"　〈喪大記〉

"Sangfu"　〈喪服〉

"Sangfu sizhi"　〈喪服四制〉

"Sangfu xiao ji"　〈喪服小記〉

Shaan　陝

Shaanxi　陝西

Shandong　山東

"Shan furen"　〈陝婦人〉

shan nan yue yang 山南曰陽

Shanshan　鄯善

Shanxi　山西

Shanzhou　單州

Shang　商

Shangde (Princess)　尚德 (公主)

Shangqing　上清

shangshu 尚書

shangshu sheng 尚書省

Shangyuan 上元
Shao Bowen 邵伯溫
She Saihua 佘賽花
Shengui 神龜
shenti fa fu shou zhi fumu, bugan huishang, xiao zhi shi ye 身體
　　髮膚受之父母不敢毀傷孝之始也
Shenzong (Emperor) 神宗 (r. 1067-85)
shi 士 (literati)
shi 詩 (poetry)
Shi Chaoyi 史朝義
Shi Chong 石崇
shidaifu 士大夫
"Shi fu shidai" 〈弒父時代〉
shijia 十家
shijie 尸解
Shi jing 《詩經》
shi nong gong shang 士農工商
Shisan mei 十三妹
shi shen 失身
shi si ru gui 視死如歸
shi song bo 蒔松柏
shi song shu bai 蒔松數百
"Shi yi" 〈十翼〉
shi zu 士族
shou jie 守節
shou shu song bo cheng lin 手樹松柏成林
shou zhi song bo 手植松柏
shuji 書記
shuyi 書儀
shui nan shan bei 水南山北
shun 順
Shuofu 《說郛》
Sibu beiyao 《四部備要》
Sichuan 四川
sili jiaowei 司隸校尉
Sima Chi 司馬池
Sima Guang 司馬光
Sima Kang 司馬康

Sima Shi 司馬師
Sima Xiangru 司馬相如
Sima Zhi 司馬植
situ 司徒
Song Jiang 宋江
Song shi 宋史
Song Yue 嵩嶽
su jiang 俗講
Suzong (Emperor) 肅宗 (r. 756-61)
Sun neihan Beili zhi 《孫內翰北里志》
Sun Zhao 孫兆
Sun Zi (SunWu) 孫子 (孫武)
Tai (Mount) 太(山)
Taihe 大(太)和
Taihe (Princess) 太和 (公主)
taijiao 胎教
Taiqing 太清
Tairen 太妊
Tai shan fu jun 太(泰)山府君
Taiwu (Emperor) 太武帝 (r. 424-51)
Taiyuan 太原
Taiyuan (Grand Princess) 太原 (長公主)
Taizong (Emperor) 太宗 (r. 627-49)
"Taizong ruming ji" 〈太宗入冥集〉
Taizu (Emperor) 太祖 (r. 960-76)
Tang Ci 唐賜
Tang Fu 唐副
Tang lü 《唐律》
Tangren shuohui 《唐人說薈》
Tao (Dao) 道
Tianbao 天寶
Tianshui Xian'ge 天水僊哥
Tianyou 天祐
tingwei 廷尉
tingwei shaoqing 廷尉少卿
tongji 同籍
tongpan 通判
"Tongque ji'" 〈銅雀妓〉

Tou Ngo (Dou E) 竇娥

Tsu (zu) 族

"Tufan, shang" 〈吐番 (上)〉

"Tufan, xia" 〈吐番 (下)〉

Tujue 突厥

"Tujue, shang" 〈突厥 (上)〉

Tuyuhun 吐谷渾

Tuoba 拓跋

Wanli 萬曆

Wannian (County) 萬年(縣)

Wang (Ms.) 王 (氏)

Wang Anshi 王安石

Wang Fajin 王法進

Wang Fengxian 王奉仙

Wang Jian 王建

Wang Lianlian 王蓮蓮

Wang Mang 王莽

"Wang Mang zhuan" 〈王莽傳〉

Wang Pang 王雱

Wang Shi 王式

Wang Susu 王蘇蘇

Wang Tuan'er 王團兒

Wang Ying 王英

Wang Zhaojun 王昭君

Wei 魏

Weibo (General) 魏博 (大將)

Wei Huacun 魏華存

Wei lue 魏略

"Wei Pu qi Fang shi" 〈魏溥妻房氏〉

Wei Rong 韋融

Wei Tai 魏泰

wei Wannian xian buzei guan Guo Duan suo na 為萬年縣捕賊官郭鍛所納

wei xi jiaofang ji 未係教坊籍

weiyou fengmao 微有風貌

Wei Yuanfu 韋元甫

Wei Zeng 衛增

Wei zhi 魏志

Wei Zhou 韋宙

Wencheng (Princess) 文成 (公主)

wenci youyu jie gai buzu 文詞有餘節概不足

Wendi (Emperor) 文帝 (r. 179-157 B.C.E.)

"Wendi ji" 〈文帝紀〉

Wengong 溫公

wenjia lingxing 聞家令姓

Wenming (Empress Dowager) 文明太后 (r. 466-7, 476-90)

"Wen sang" 〈問喪〉

wenshi 文士

Wenzong (Emperor) 文宗 (r. 827-40)

wo jia yi zhongyi zhu 我家以忠義誅

Wu 吳

Wu (King) (r. 841-28 B.C.E) 武王

Wuchang xianjun 武昌縣君

Wu Daozi 吳道子

Wudi (Emperor) 武帝 (r. 140-87 B.C.E.)

"Wudi ji" 〈武帝紀〉

Wuding 武丁

"Wu du" 〈五蠹〉

wufu 五服

wu jian 無間

wulun 五倫

wushi 武士

Wusun Kunmi 烏孫昆彌

wuxia xiaoshuo 武俠小說

wuxing 五行

Wu Yansi 武延嗣

Wu Yuanji 吳元濟

Wu Zetian (Emperor) 武則天 (r. 684-705)

xi 褉

Xi'an 西安

Xijing zaji 《西京雜記》

Xijun (Princess) 細君 (公主)

Xiwangmu 西王母

Xiyu duhufu 西域都護府

"Xiyu zhuan" 〈西域傳〉

"Xiyu zhuan, xia" 〈西域傳 (下)〉

Xizong (Emperor) 僖宗 (r. 873-88)

xia 下 (subsequent)

Xia 夏

xia 俠 (knight-errant)

xianü 俠女

Xiayuan 下元

xian 仙

Xian'an (Princess) 咸安 (公主)

Xianbei 鮮卑

xianjun 縣君

xian ming 賢明

"Xianming zhuan" 〈賢明傳〉

"Xianzhi" 〈纖指〉

Xianzong (Emperor) 憲宗 (r. 806-20)

xianghuo xiongdi 香火兄弟

xiao 孝

Xiaofu 小福

Xiao Gou 蕭遘

Xiaojing (Emperor) 孝靜帝 (r. 534-50)

xiao lie 孝烈

Xiaoman 小蠻

Xiaoming (Emperor) 孝明帝 (r. 516-28)

Xiaorun 小潤

xiaoshuo 小說

"Xiao Wangzhi zhuan" 〈蕭望之傳〉

Xiaowen (Emperor) 孝文帝 (r. 471-99)

Xie (Miss) 解 (氏)

Xie Jie 解結

"Xie Xiao'e" 〈謝小娥〉

Xieyou (Princess) 解憂 (公主)

xinfa 新法

Xinjiang 新疆

Xinxing (Princess) 新興 (公主)

xing 刑

"Xinglü" 〈刑律〉

xingshi 行尸

Xiong 熊

Xiongnu 匈奴

"Xiongnu liezhuan" 〈匈奴列傳〉
"Xiongnu zhuan, shang" 〈匈奴傳 (上)〉
"Xiongnu zhuan, xia" 〈匈奴傳 (下)〉
xu 序
Xu (Empress) 許 (皇后)
Xu Xiangu 徐仙姑
Xuandi (Emperor) 宣帝 (r. 73-49 B.C.E.)
Xuanguai lu 《玄怪錄》
Xuanwu (Emperor) 宣武帝 (r. 500-15)
Xuan[a]zong (Emperor) 宣宗 (r. 846-59)
Xuan[b]zong (Emperor) 玄宗 (r. 712-56)
Xue Xuantong 薛玄同
Xueyantuo 薛延陀
Xun (Ms.) 荀 (氏)
Xun Yi 荀顗
ya 雅
Yaniang 牙娘
Yancheng 鹽城
Yan Lingbin 顏令賓
yanlü 燕侶
Yanluo wang 閻羅王
yang 陽
Yang Chang[a] 楊娼
Yangdi (Emperor) 煬帝 (r. 581-604)
yang jian 陽間
yang ju 陽具
"Yang liefu zhuan" 〈楊烈婦傳〉
yangliu 楊柳
Yang Miao'er 楊妙兒
Yang Pingzhi 陽平治
Yang Weizhen 楊維楨
Yang Ye 楊業
"Yang zun yin bei" 〈陽尊陰卑〉
yao 妖
"Yao dian" 〈堯典〉
Yaoniang 窈娘
yaotiao shunü 窈窕淑女
Yaozhou 耀州

yi 意 (intent)
yi 義 (righteousness)
yi 儀 (rites; ceremonies; exemplars)
Yi 夷
Yicheng (Princess) 義成 (公主)
yi er bai jin 一二百金
Yi li 儀禮
yixia 義俠
Yizhang qing Hu sanniang 一丈青扈三娘
Yizhi 宜之
Yizong (Emperor) 懿宗 (r. 859-73)
yin 陰 (opposite of *yang*)
yin 蔭 ("shadow" privilege)
yin dao 陰道
Yinhe 銀河
yinji[a] 飲妓
yin jian 陰間
yin si 陰司
yin si dawang 陰司大王
ying 媵 (concubine)
Ying'er 迎兒
Yinggong 穎公
Yingguo 營郭
Yingguogong 穎國公
yingji[a] 營妓
yingxiong 英雄
Yong'er 永兒
Yongzhou 邕州
you du 幽都
You Minggen 游明根
you puye 右僕射
youshi 游士
youxia 游俠
"Youxia liezhuan" 〈游俠列傳〉
"You xian ku" 〈游仙窟〉
You Ya 游雅
you yintai 右銀臺
You Zhao 游肇

Youzhou 幽州
yu 玉
Yu (Ms.) 于 (氏)
Yu Cong 于琮
yudai 魚袋
yufu 魚符
Yu Huan 魚豢
Yulanpen 盂蘭盆
Yu Luozhen 俞洛真
Yuqing 玉清
yushi tai 御史台
Yu Xianye 尉顯業
Yu Xuanji 魚玄機
Yu Yan 尉彥
Yu Yunshu 余蘊叔
Yu Zhuo 于梲
Yuan 袁
yuan 猿
Yuandi (Emperor) 元帝 (r. 48-33 B.C.E.)
"Yuandi ji" 〈元帝紀〉
Yuan Gan 元幹
Yuan Hui (Prince of Chengyang) (城陽王) 元徽
Yuan Jingzhe (Prince of Zhangwu) (章武王) 元景哲
Yuan Qin 元欽
Yuan Shen (Prince of Guangyang) (廣陽王) 元深
yuan shi 淵識
Yuan Xiang 元詳
Yuan Xiuyi 元脩義
Yuanyou 元祐
Yue 越
Yue (Prince) 越(王)
yuefu 樂府
"Yueling" 〈月令〉
zaju 雜劇
"Zalü" 〈雜律〉
zaixiang 宰相
zan 贊
Zhang 張

Zhang (Ms.) 張 (氏)
Zhang Cun 張存
Zhang Fei (Chang Fei) 張斐
Zhang Jinfeng 張金鳳
Zhang Lu 張魯
"Zhang Qian zhuan" 〈張騫傳〉
Zhang Rongfei 張容妃
zhang shi 長史
Zhang Shuye 張叔夜
Zhang Shunmin 張舜民
Zhangsun Lü 長孫慮
Zhangsun Sheng 長孫晟
Zhangsun Zhi 長孫稚
Zhang Wencheng 張文成
Zhang Yong 張用
Zhang Zai 張載
Zhang Zhuzhu 張住住
Zhangzi 長子
Zhaodi (Emperor) 昭帝 (r. 86-74 B.C.E.)
"Zhaodi ji" 〈昭帝紀〉
Zhao Guangyuan 趙光遠
"Zhaohun" 〈招魂〉
Zhao Luanluan 趙鸞鸞
"Zhao nü zhuan" 〈趙女傳〉
Zhaorong 沼容
zhaotao shi 招討使
Zhezong (Emperor) 哲宗 (r. 1085-1100)
zhen 貞
Zhenjiang 鎮江
zhen shun 貞順
Zhenyuan 貞元
Zheng (Ms.) 鄭 (氏)
Zhengguang 正光
Zheng Guangye 鄭光業
Zheng Juju 鄭舉舉
Zheng Yanzu 鄭嚴祖
zhi 志 (gazetteer)
zhi 智 (wisdom)

Zhigao'an 制誥案

zhiguai xiaoshuo 志怪小說

zhi song bo 植松柏

zhi yi 止矣

zhong 中 (middle)

zhong 忠 (loyalty)

zhonggu 中古

"Zhongguo jinshi zongjiao lunli yu shangren jingshen" 〈中國近世 宗教倫理與商人精神〉

zhongshu sheng 中書省

zhong xiao jie yi 忠孝節義

Zhong Xingshuo 中行說

Zhongyuan 中元

Zhou (King) (帝)紂

Zhou Hui 周輝

Zhou Mu wang 周穆王

Zhu (Village of) 祝(家莊)

zhubu 主簿

zhujiao 助教

Zhu Shuzhen 朱淑真

Zhu Xi 朱熹

Zhuzi yulei 《朱子語類》

zhuan 傳

zhuangyuan 狀元

Zhuangzi 《莊子》

zi 字

Zili 子立

Zimei 子美

Zizhi tongjian 《資治通鑑》

Zong Lin 宗懍

zun 尊

Zuocheng 胙城

zuokui 左揆

zuo puye 左僕射

zuopuye jian menxia shilang 左僕射兼門下侍郎

zuosi langzhong 左司郎中

zuoyou jiaofang 左右教坊

Zuo zhuan 《左傳》

ABOUT THE CONTRIBUTORS

Suzanne Cahill is working on a manuscript about medieval Chinese Daoist holy women: their lives, physical practices, poetry, work, and associated material culture. Her last book, *Transcendence and Divine Passion: the Queen Mother of the West in Medieval China* (Stanford UP, 1993), concerned cultural images of the highest goddess of Daoism. She teaches Chinese History at the University of California at San Diego.

Ning Chia, from Beijing, China, received her Ph. D. from The Johns Hopkins University in 1992 and is Associate Professor of History at Central College, Iowa. Her specialty is China's Inner Asian frontiers, and her major publications concern the early Qing Dynasty, especially the Lifanyuan (Court of Colonial Affairs), in administrating the multiethnic empire. Her current Lifanyuan research, based on Manchu archives, focuses on the royal female hierarchy of the Manchu court of the early Qing.

Sufen Sophia Lai teaches English and East Asian Studies at Grand Valley State University in Michigan. She has published comparative literary studies on utopias and love suicides, and she has translated works into Chinese and English. She is completing a book on the history of Chinese ideas of the afterlife and funerary practices, and is translating a collection of poems by the Taiwanese-Mongolian poet Hsi Murong.

Jen-der Lee is Associate Research Fellow in the Institute of History and Philology at the Academia Sinica, Taipei, Taiwan. She has published several articles on women's lives and childbirth customs in early medieval China, and is now finishing two articles on women's professions in early medieval China, one on wet nurses and the other on female healers. She also teaches women's history at both National Taiwan University (Taipei) and National Tsinhua University (Hsinchu).

Sherry J. Mou is Assistant Professor in the Department of Chinese at Wellesley College, MA. She is the editor for the Chinese entries in *Military Women Worldwide: A Biographical Dictionary,* forthcoming from Greenwood Press. She has published on the fiction writer Zhang Ailing, has translated literary criticism by modern Chinese writers, and is working on a book on the tradition of biographies of women in the official histories before the Song Dynasty.

Don J. Wyatt is Professor in the Department of History and in the Program in International Studies at Middlebury College, VT. He is the author of *The Recluse of Loyang: Shao Yung and the Moral Evolution of Early Sung Thought* (U of Hawai'i Press, 1996) and numerous essays on the history of Chinese philosophical and political thought. He is now completing a book on the cultural influence of Chinese ideas of prescience before and during the Song Dynasty.

Victor Xiong, Associate Professor of Chinese History and Chair of Asian Studies at Western Michigan University, has written *Sui-Tang Chang'an* (Ann Arbor: Center for Chinese Studies Publications, the U of Michigan Press, forthcoming 1999). He has published numerous articles in English and Chinese in such academic journals as *T'oung Pao, Journal of Asian Studies, Bulletin of the Asian Institute, Papers on Far Eastern History,* and *Wenwu.* He has also edited *Early Medieval China* (vols. 1–3) and *Chinese Historians* (vols. 7–9).

INDEX

Romanized Chinese titles are placed alphabetically, letter by letter, regardless of word divisions.

adultery, 4, 16
    Liu Hui's case with Zhang Rongfei and Chen Huimeng, 4–6
    penalty under Han, 9–10, 11, 16
    penalty under Northern Wei, 9, 10–11, 12
    penalty under Tang, 28n. 27
Analects, see Lun yu
ancestor worship, 119, 188–9, 219, 233n. 20
An Lushan Rebellion, 118
Anyi (Princess), 63
Armstrong, Nancy, xx

Bai (Ms.), 34n. 86
Bai Xingjian (d. 826), 160
"The Ballad of Mulan" ("Mulan ci"), *see under* Mulan
Ban Zhao (Pan Chao, d. 116), *see* "Nü jie"
bao (reciprocation), 79, 90, 93–6 *passim*
    bao chou (repaying someone as revenge), 90, 96
    bao en (repaying someone for mercy received), 90, 96
Baoen fengpen jing (The Sutra on Offering Bowls to Repay Kindness), 194
baogu (protecting the innocent), 12, 31nn. 59, 60
baojuan (precious scroll), xxiv, 197–8
Baotang Monastery, 154, 163
Barfield, Thomas, 43, 48, 70n. 42
Beili (Northern Quarters or Pingkang li), 152–54, 156, 157, 159–62
    red-light district, 152, 153, 161–2

Beili zhi (Record of the Northern Quarters), 149, 153–60, 163n. 1, 166n. 39
Bei shi (The History of the Northern Dynasties), 15
Bian Dongxuan, 176–7
bianwen (transformation texts), xxiv, 196, 197
bian xiang (transformed images), 199
Bible, 172
Blamires, Alcuin, xix, xxi
Bohai Feng, 20, 30n. 49, 36n. 97
Bo Juyi (772–846), 151, 156
Boling Cui (Po-ling Ts'ui), 19–20, 36n. 92
boshi (erudite), 36n. 96, 159
Bozhou zhi (Gazetteers of Bo County), 87
budao (immoral), 13–14, 32n. 65
Buddhism, xv, xvii, 119, 120, 175, 184, 188–90, 193–7, 200–2, 206–7
    assimilated with Confucianism and Daoism, 190, 194, 206, 207
    Avichi Hell (Hell of No-Interval), 196, 197, 200, 201, 204, 209n. 22
    Buddha in the legend of Mulan, 188, 194, 197, 200, 201, 208, 208n. 3
    Buddhist, xviii
    in competition with Daoism, 171
    pretas ("departed ones"), 190, 209n. 17
    spiritual cosmology, 200, 205–6
        arupa loka (World of Nonform), 202
        kama loka (World of Desire), 200
        liu dao (six modes of existence), 209n. 16
        mara (death or hostility), 200
        rupa loka (World of Form), 202
    see also Mulian, the legend of
bujing (disrespect), 32n. 65
buxiao (not being filial), 13

bu xiao zhi xiao (unfilial piety), 133
buzei guan (metropolitan police officer), 157

Cahill, Suzanne, xxiv
Cai Yan, 139n. 8
Cai Yong (132–92), 139n. 8
Campbell, Joseph, 202–3
canzhi zhengshi (participant in determining government matters), 229n. 2
Cao Cao (155–220), 139n. 8
Cao Zhengwen, 90
Catholic Church, xxvii, 1, 2, 172
chang (tasting), 191
chang[a] (prostitute), 150, 164 n.6
chang[b] (entertainer), 150
Chang'an, 149, 150, 152, 153, 158, 161
Changle fang, 150
changshi (attendant-in-ordinary), 159, 168n. 72
chang wen (sung texts), 196
chanyu (shanyu), *see under* heqin
chastity, *see under* virtues, womanly (feminine)
chengxiang (*zaixiang,* a grand councilor), 221, 235n. 28
Cheng Yi (1033–1107), 233n. 20
Chengzu (Emperor) (r. 1403–24), 81
Chen Huimeng, 4, 5, 8, 21
Chen Miao, 81
Chen Yinke, 22, 37n. 99
Chia, Ning, xxiii, 107n. 49
Chodorow, Nancy *(The Reproduction of Mothering),* 51, 140n. 18
Chongren fang, 162, 169n. 81
Chongyi furen (Consort of Righteousness Upholding), 124
Chow, Rey, xxxixn. 26
chuanqi (fantastic tale), 78, 79, 88, 90–1, 94, 95, 104, 120, 160
Chu'er, 154, 157–8
Chunqiu (Spring and Autumn Annals), 7
Chunqiu fan lu (Luxuriant dew from the *Spring and Autumn Annals*), *see* Dong Zhongshu
Ch'ü T'ung-tsu *(Law and Society in Traditional China),* 22, 30n. 50, 120, 121
ci (maternal love), *see* Confucian motherhood
cimu (foster mother), 15

Cixi (Empress Dowager) (1834–1908), 139n. 6
collective responsibility, *see lianzuo*
Collier, Jane F. (and Michelle Z. Rosaldo), 52, 66
concealment, *see under* law
concubinage, xvi, xxii, xxvi–xxviin. 4, 160, 167n. 60, 220, 231nn. 6, 10, 237n. 42
    goals and functioning of, 216, 218, 223, 225–7, 231–2n. 16, 234n. 22
    in late imperial times, 219
    Sima Guang's views of, 222–3, 236n. 30
    in Song times, 215, 217–8, 231nn. 10, 13, 237n. 42
    and Wang Anshi, 218, 219–20, 223
    and wife-husband relations, 218–9, 22, 225, 231n. 15
Confucianism, xv, xvii, 42, 66, 78, 89, 102, 113, 128, 132, 134, 184, 204, 226, 234n. 21
    assimilation with Buddhism, 189–92, 193–6, 203–7
    Confucian classics, xix, 1, 5, 18–20 *passim,* 133
    Confucianists, xviii, 123
        attitude towards law, 172
    Confucian virtues and chivalrous ladies in Tang tales, 92–6
    in *Ernü yingxiong zhuan (A Tale of Heroic Lovers),* 102–3
    family ethics, 3, 6, 8, 13, 15, 17–23 *passim,* 46–7, 119
    in Mulan, 84, 86
    neo-Confucianism, xvii, xxviin. 2, 110
    the Southern and Northern Dynasties' different interpretations of, 13
    and wives, 13
    and women warriors, 78, 95, 103–4
    and *xia* (knights-errant), 88–90
    see also under literati tradition, Chinese
Confucianization, 1, 2, 3, 20, 22–3, 104
    of the Northern Wei Dynasty, 20
Confucius, xxviin. 9, 173, 204
courtesan, *see* female entertainers; *chang*[a] (prostitute); *ji*[a] (entertainer)
cross-dressing women, xxi, xxv
    in *Ernü yingxiong zhuan*

Cui Hao, 34n. 82, 36n. 97
Cui Hong, 36n. 97
Cui Shensi, 91–2, 94–5
Cui Ting, 35 n. 92
Cui Xiaofen, 35–6n. 92
Cui Zhen, 35n. 92
Cui Zuan, 16–18 *passim,* 19–20, 22, 28n.
    15, 29n. 32, 34n. 86, 36n. 92
    on the case of Liu Hui, 3–11
    versus Empress Dowager Ling, 18

daifu, xvii
Dai Jinhua, xvi
da jingyin (prefect of the metropolitan area),
    159
*Damuqianlian mingjian jiumu bianwen (The
    Great Maudgalyayana Rescues His Mother
    from Hell),* 196–8, 200, 206
dani budao (high treason and crimes of
    depravity), 33n. 73
Dante, 203, 210n. 43
Dao (Tao), 181
"Daode jing" ("Scripture of the Way and Its
    Power"), 171
Daoism, xv, xvii, 96, 102, 119, 180, 184,
    206–7
    Daoists, xviii, xxii, xxiv, 192–3
        bureaucracy, 182–4
        the goal of medieval Chinese, 172
        lineage, 182–3
        sainthood, 172–3, 174–5
            female saints, 173–4, 180, 183–5
            transformation of, 175–8
        integration of Confucianism, 193
        in the Mulan legend, 189–90
        and *xia,* 89, 90, 93, 94
Daowu (Emperor) (r. 386–409), 36n. 97
Davis, Natalie Zemon, 110
Dayi (Princess), 48, 49, 58, 62–3
Dazhao (Temple), 50
de Beauvoir, Simon *(The Second Sex),* 140n.
    18, 146n. 74
des Rotours, Robert, 154, 164n. 1, 165n.
    27, 166nn. 34, 38, 167nn. 45, 46
de yan rong gong (virtues, words, bearings,
    and work), *see* virtues, womanly: four
    virtues
Dezong (Emperor) (r. 780–804), 61, 81
Dien, Albert E., xxvin. 2

dimu (legal wife), 15
diyu (the underground realm), 190, 199,
    205
Dizang Bodhisattva, 192, 198
Dong Changling, 127, 129–30, 146n. 73
*Dongjing menhua lu (The Eastern Capital: A
    Dream of Splendors Past),* 198
dongtian (grotto heavens), 174, 180, 183–84
Dongxuan bilu (East Pavilion Notes), see Wei
    Tai
Dong Zhongshu (ca. 179–104 B.C.E.,
    Chunqiu fan lu), 112, 123, 205
Dou Sengyan, 29n. 38
Dou Yuan, 14–15, 16, 20, 23
Du Guangting (850–933), 172–80, 181–3
Dunhuang, 28n. 15, 196, 209n. 19

Easterman, Lloyd E., 231n. 15
Eastern Market (Tang, Chang=an), 152, 162
Eastern Zhou Dynasty (770–256 B.C.E.),
    xvii
Ebrey, Patricia Buckley, 218, 220, 223,
    231nn. 9–13, 237n. 42
education of women, xix
    see also women's roles: "learned
        instructresses"
Edwards, Louise, 78–9
*Ernü yingxiong zhuan (A Tale of Heroic
    Lovers,* by Wen Kang, flourished
    1821–60), 94, 95, 101–3, 104
        An Ji, 101–3
        Thirteenth Sister (*Shisan mei,* He
            Yufeng, or Jade Phoenix), 77, 79,
            93, 101–3, 104
        Zhang Jinfeng (Golden Phoenix),
            101–2
Evans-Prichard, E. E., 52
Eve and Original Sin, xxii

Fajia (legalist school), 89, 173
families
    definition of family hierarchy, 5,
        15–16
    formed through *heqin,* 46–7
    powerful clans *(shi zu)* of the Tang
        Dynasty, 115, 141n. 26
    uterine family, xx
Fan Chunfu, 224, 236n. 38
fang (ward), 150, 165 n. 14

Fang Qianli ("Story of Yang Chang^a"), 150

Fang Xuanling, 42, 125

Fan Su, 151, 156

Fan Ye (398–445), *see Hou Han shu*

Fan Zhongyan (989–1050)
    sons: Fan Chunren (1027–1101),
        236n. 38; Fan Chunli
        (1031–1106), 236n. 38; Fan
        Chuncui (1032–1101), 236n. 38

Fei Xiaotong, 51

Feng (Ms.), 36 n. 97

Feng Hui, 30 n. 49, 36n. 97

Feng Junyi, 14–15, 20, 37 n. 98

Feng Liao, 60

ferro agosto (iron August), 187

filiality, *see* filial piety

filial piety (filial duty, filiality, *xiao*), 47, 77,
    79, 84, 86, 92, 101, 114, 121, 130,
    131–2, 134, 141n. 28
      and the Mulan legend, 82, 188, 191,
        194, 195
      unfilial filiality, 133
      and women warriors, 78–9

footbinding, xvi, 215

fornication, penalty for, 9, 28n. 27

Foucault, Michel, 51

Freud, Sigmund, 51, 200–2 *passim*

fu (a married woman; wife), 34 n. 86, 115,
    141n. 24

fu (entering a spirit into the ancestral
    temple of a dead person), 142n. 43

fudao (the way of married women), 122

Fuhao, 80, 104

Fu Xiang (Mulian's father), 198

fuxun (the teaching of married women),
    122

gaiyu (*ji^a*-entertainer adopted in childhood),
    153

Gan Bao, *see Sou shen ji*

Ganges, 201

Gaozu (Han emperor) (r. 206–195 B.C.E.),
    41, 46, 48–9, 55, 56–7

Gaozu (Tang emperor) (r. 618–26), 42, 124,
    129

geisha, 149, 164n. 5
    see also ji^a (entertainer)

gender (as a critical category), xviii, xix, 39,
    189–90

Gilmartin, Christina K., et al., 54

Gobi (Gebi), 42

Golden Lotus, *see* Pan Jinlian

gong'an (detective work), 120

gongcheng (Palace City), 150

Gong Jiang, 112, 113, 140n. 14

Gongsun Sheng, 96

Goody, Jack, 223, 237n. 41

Gou Xiangu, 179

Grand Supreme One, 176

Guangping You, 19–20

Guangzhai fang, 150

Guanqiu Dian, 33n. 74

Guanqiu Jian, 16–17, 19, 23, 33n. 74

Guanqiu Zhi, 33 n. 74

Gui jie (Ghost Festival), *see* Yulanpen
    Festival

gui yue (month of ghosts), 192

Gu Jiegang, xviiin. 11

Gujin tushu jicheng (*Synthesis of Books and
    Illustrations of Ancient and Modern Times*),
    87

Guo Duan, 157–8, 167nn. 60, 61

Guo Ziyi, 157

Han (ethnic people or culture), 6, 8, 20, 44,
    81–2, 99–100, 104

Han code, 16

Han Dynasty (206 B.C.E.–220 C.E.), xv, xvii,
    2, 3, 9, 10, 18, 20, 22, 67, 151, 183, 205
    heqin policy, 39, 41, 53, 44–5, 46–49
        passim, 51, 55–57, 58–62 *passim,*
        107n. 49
    yin-yang theory, 112, 122–3, 205

Han Fei zi zhuan (*Biography of Han Fei zi,*
    by Han Fei, ca. 280–33 B.C.E.), 88–9

Hanlin yuan (Hanlin academy), 224, 236n.
    38

Han shu (*History of the Former Han Dynasty*),
    42, 44, 56, 64, 81

Hartwell, Robert M., 230n. 5

He'nan Shaoshi wenjian qianlu (*Former Record
    of Things Heard and Seen by Mr. Shao of
    He'nan,* by Shao Bowen), *see* Shao
    Bowen

heqin (marriage between Chinese imperial
    princesses and nomadic rulers of Inner
    Asia), xxi, xxii, xxv, 39–41, 43–54, 107n.
    49

and China's frontier policies, 48–9, 55,
    65–7 *passim*
  chengchen (submitting oneself as a
      Han vassals), 49
  chengdi (submitting oneself as a
      younger brother-in-law), 49
  chengxu (submitting oneself as a son-
      in-law), 49
  see also neifu
  and the empowerment of women,
      52–3
  literature, 61–3, 64–5
  sources of women in, 44
  with Tujue *khaghan*, 42–3, 45, 48–50
      passim, 56–8, 60–3 *passim*, 65
  with Tujuhun, 43, 45, 50, 57, 61
  with Uyghur *khaghan*, 43, 49, 57,
      60–1, 65 *passim*
  with Wusun *kunmi*, 44, 47–9, 57,
      59–61, 69n. 23
  with Xiongnu *chanyu*, 41, 43–9, 51,
      53–7, 58–61 *passim*, 64, 68n. 6,
      69n. 26, 70n. 42, 100
He Zeng, 33n. 74
Hippolyta, 99
Holmgren, Jennifer, 59, 120–1, 123, 128,
    144n. 64
Honghua (Princess), 61
Honglou meng (Dream of the Red Mansions),
    xx, 79
*Hou Han shu (The History of the Later Han
    Dynasty*, Fan Ye, 398–445), 49, 64, 109,
    110, 139n. 8
Hsia, Chih-tsing, 96–7
Hu (Ms.), 31n. 62
Hua Gu (Flower Maiden, Huang Lingwei),
    177–8, 186n. 10
Huai'en, 43
Huainanzi (Master Huainan), 212n. 50
Huamanlu (Painted Plaster Record), see Zhang
    Shunmin
Huang Chao, 197
huangcheng (Imperial City), 152, 165n. 14
Huangfu Mei (fl. 880, *Shanshui xiadu*), 172,
    174, 176, 180–1, 186n. 4
Huang Guanfu, 180
Huang Lingwei, *see* Hua Gu
huangquan (Yellow Spring), 212n. 53
Hu Changcan, 32n. 62

hufa (steward of law), 198
Huhanye, *see heqin:* with Xiongnu *chanyu*
Huihe, *see* Uyghur
Huizong (Emperor) (r. 1101–25), 96, 230n.
    3, 231n. 7
Hu Shi, xvii, xxviin. 9

Inner Asia, 39, 40, 43–4
    definition of, 67n. 1
    heqin women's view of, 57
    Manchuria, 67n. 1
    Mongolia, 67n. 1
    Xinjiang (Central Asia), 67n. 1
    see also heqin
Ishida Mikinosuke, 153, 163n. 1

Jade Capital, 176
Jagchid, Sechin (and Van Jay Symons), 55,
    56, 63
jealousy, 4, 13, 21, 32n. 62, 37n. 102, 219,
    231n. 15
ji^a (entertainer), xxii, xxiv, 149–54, 156–61,
    163n. 2
    functionality of, 150–2
    Beiliji^a (Northern-Quarters
        entertainer), 150, 152, 156,
        160–1
    Chu'er (Runniang), 154, 155,
        157–8
    clientele, 156–7
    Funiang (Yizhi), 153, 155, 156,
        158–60 *passim*, 166 n. 39
    Gui'er, 155
    Lai'er (Fengxian), 155, 156, 157
    Liu Tainiang, 155
    precarious life of, 157–9
    Tianshui Xian'ge (Jiangzhen),
        155, 156, 167n. 46
    Wang Lianlian (Zhaorong), 155
    Wang Susu, 155
    Wang Tuan'er, 153–4
    Xiaofu (Nengzhi), 155
    Xiaorun (Zimei), 155
    Yang Miao'er, 153, 157
    Yaniang, 155, 157
    Yan Lingbin, 155, 158
    Ying'er, 155
    Yong'er (Qiqing), 155
    Yu Luozhen, 155, 160

Zhang Zhuzhu, 155
Zheng Juju, 155, 156, 167n. 46
gongji[a] (court entertainer), 150, 160
gongren (court persons), 150
  neiren (insiders), 150, 165n. 15
  shijia ("the ten"), 150
guanji[a] (official entertainer), 150–51,
  160
jiaji[a] (home entertainer), 150–1, 160
minji[a] (unofficial entertainer), 164n.
  11
yingji[a] (army entertainers), 150–1,
  160, 166n. 40
yinji[a] (beverage entertainer), 150–1,
  160
in literary works, 151, 156–7, 158–9
redemption, 159–60
see also chang[a]*, chang*[b]*, ji*[b]
jiafu (adoptive father), 153
Jia Miao, 29n. 38
jiamu (adoptive mother) (madam), 153, 160
jian (space, realm), 206
jianghu yiqi (vagrant spirit of justice), 96
Jiang Qing, 139n. 6
jianli (bond servant), 150
jiaofang (Department of Stage Performances),
  154, 159–60, 166n. 39
Jiaofang ji, 165n. 15
ji[b] (courtesan), 150
jie (integrity), 102–3, 134
jimu (stepmother), 15
Ji'nan (Grand Princess), 21, 30n. 45
Jincheng (Princess), 50
*Jingchu suishi ji (Record of Seasonal
  Observances in Jingchu),* 188
*Jinghua yuan (Romance of the Mirrored
  Flowers),* 78, 79
jinguo yingxiong (headdressed hero), 81
jinshi (presented scholar), 150, 152, 154,
  156, 157, 229nn. 1, 2
jinwu (imperial insignia guard), 159
jiqin (relatives with a one-year mourning
  obligation), 6, 16, 22, 35n. 87
*Jiu Tang shu (The Old History of the Tang
  Dynasty),* 42, 110–34 *passim*
  cases on daughter-in-law, 123
  cases on mourning, 117–18, 119
  cases on revenge, 120
  "Eulogy" *(zan)* to the biographies of
    women, 113–14, 125

"Introduction" *(xu)* to the biographies
  of women, 111–13, 114
Joan of Arc, 77
Junchen, 44
junzi (Confucian gentlemen), 122

Kaifeng, 217, 220
*Kaiyuan Tianbao yishi (Anecdotes of the
  Kaiyuan and Tianbao eras),* 152
Kang Le, 37n, 100
Kat? Shigeshi, 166n. 38
khatun, 49
Khitan, 45, 57
Kingston, Maxine Hong *(The Woman
  Warrior),* 78, 79
Kinney, Anne Behnke *(Chinese Views of
  Childhood),* 145n. 67
Kishibe Shigeo, 156, 166n. 39
knight-errant, *see xia*
Ko, Dorothy, xix, xxviin. 4
kunbian fugong (penalty of beating and
  head-shaving), 4
K'ung Fu-tzu (Kong fuzi), xxviin. 9

lady knights-errant *(nü xia and xianü),* xxi,
  78, 79, 81
  autonomy in marriage of the, 94,
    103
  basic elements of, 91
  in *Ernü yingxiong zhuan,* 101–3
  in *Shuihu zhuan,* 97–9
  in *Taiping guangji,* 91–5
  in *Yangjiafu shidai zhongyong yanyi
    zhizhuan,* 100–1
  in Zhao Ye's *Wu-Yue chunqiu,* 90–1
  see also women warriors
Lai, Sufen, xxiii, xxiv, 112
Lanling (Grand Princess), 3, 4, 7, 13, 21,
  27–8 n. 9
  marital relationships with Liu Hui,
    4–5, 7–8
Lau, Joseph S. M., 91
law
  changes in, 32n. 66
  in interpreting *budao,* 32n. 65
  during the Han Dynasty, 33n. 73
  during the Xianbei rule, 29n. 37
  concealment, 18
  and collective responsibility, 15–16
  in Tang code, 15

Confucianist and Legalist views of, 172–3

establishment of crimes, 12–13

penalties by family relations, 11, 14–15, 30n. 50, 31n. 52

learned instructress, *see* women's roles

Lee, Jen-der, xxii–xxiii, 142n. 37

Legalist, *see* Fajia

levirate, *see under* marriage

Lévi-Strauss, Claude, 51, 53

Levy, Howard, 163–4n. 1

Lhasa, 50

li (*lijie,* propriety), 104n. 1, 113–14, 115, 121, 141nn. 22, 28, 165n. 13

li (subofficial clerk), 18

Li (Ms.), 10

Liang Hong, 112, 113, 140n. 13

Liang Hongyu, 77

lianzuo (collective responsibility), 3, 6–8, 15–18, 22, 33n. 73, 34n. 79, 35n. 87 of wives, 18

Liaozhai zhiyi (*Strange Stories from the Leisure Studio,* by Pu Songling), 95, 101

Li Chong, 35n. 92

lie[a] *nü* (women), 109–10, 138n. 4

lie[b] *nü* (righteous woman with integrity and principles), 87, 103, 110, 138n. 4

Lie[a] *nü zhuan, see Lienü zhuan*

Lie[b]*nü zhuan* (biographies of chaste women), 110

Lienü zhuan (*The Biographies of Women,* by Liu Xiang), 81, 87, 104n. 1, 109–10, 122–3, 128, 131, 138n. 1, 145nn. 66, 67, 205

"Mu yi" ("Correct Deportment of Mothers"), 104n. 1

"Nie bi zhuan" ("Biographies of the Pernicious and the Depraved"), 105n. 7, 139n. 6

prenatal instruction, 145n. 67

"Xianming zhuan" ("Biographies of the Capable and Intelligent"), 145n. 66

lienü zhuan (biographies of women sections in official histories), 109–10

in the two Tang histories, 110–34

lie zhuan (biography), 88

Li Fengji, 151

Li ji (*The Book of Rites*), 117–18, 122–3, 141n. 20, 143n. 55, 190, 191

chapters on mourning, 142n. 34

"Nei ze" ("Regulations of the Interior"), 123, 143n. 55

"Yueling" ("Monthly Ordinances"), 190–1

Li jing (*Classic of Rites*), xviii, 236n. 32

Li Kui, 96–7

lineage, Daoist, 182–4

Lin Enxian, 44

Ling (Empress Dowager) (r. 516–28), 4, 7, 10, 11, 21, 27–8n. 9, 35n. 88, 36n. 97

Lin Gan, 42

Lingbao (Numinous Treasure), 172

Linghu Gao, 159

Li Qingzhao, xix

Li Ruzhen (1763–1830, *Jinghua yuan*), 78

literati tradition, Chinese, xvi–xix, xx, xxi, xxii–xxiv *passim,* xxviiin. 11

literati, xvii, 156

origin of *shi,* xvii, xxviiin. 11

ru (Confucianists), xvii, xxviin. 9

wenshi (literati), xxviiin. 11

wushi (knights-errant), xxviiin. 11

Yin shi (*ru,* Confucianists), xvii

youshi (errant-gentlemen), xvii

Zhou shi, xvii

shidaifu (literati or gentleman-officials), xvii, 219, 220

women's position in, xviii–xix

see also Confucianism

Liu Bang, 56

Liu Hui, 3–8, 11, 13, 18–23, 28n. 11, 29n. 32, 35n. 88

marital relationships with Grand Princess Lanling, 4–5, 7–8

see also under Weishu; Lanling (Grand Princess)

Liu, James J.Y., 89–90, 91, 96, 102

Liu Ji, 117

Liu Jing, 46

Liu, Lady (wife of Pang Ji), 221–2, 234n. 26, 236n. 30

Liu Meng (1040–79), 235n. 29

Liu Rong, 31n. 57

Liu Song Dynasty (420–79), 35n. 87, 37n. 102

Liu Xiang (77–6 B.C.E.), *see Lienü zhuan*

Liu Yan, 31n. 56

Liu Yuxi, 151

Liu Zhiji (661–721, *Shitong*), 139n. 8

Li Wa, 160

Li Xiaolin, 80

liyuan (Pear Gardens), 150
 and the divorce case of Grand Princess
  Lanling and Liu Hui, 4, 7
 and other legal cases, 31n. 53
 versus the legal bureaucrats, 18–19, 21

loyalty (*zhong*), 79, 86, 92, 102–3, 113, 116,
 124
 see also virtues, womanly

Lü, Empress, 56

lü boshi (erudite for legal learning), 36n. 96

Lu Daoqian, 30n. 45

Lu Meiniang (Divine Maiden), 178

lumu (the mourning ritual of building a hut
 next to a tomb), 117–18

Lun yu (Analects), 141n. 22

Luo (Ms.), 32n. 62

Luo Binwang (d. 684), 153

Luopu, 196

Luoyang, 224, 237n. 44

*Luoyang qielan ji (Record of the Monasteries of
 Luoyang)*, 206

Lü qiao, 180

*Lü shi chunqiu (The Spring and Autumn
 Annals of Mr. Lü)*, 212n. 50

Lu Yu, 34n. 86

Lu Zhengsi, 29n. 39

MacCormack, Carol P., 46–7, 53

MacKinnon, Catherine A., 121–2

Maeno Naoaki, 206

maiduan (exclusive purchase), 154, 161

Mair, Victor H., 196

Ma Nie, 98

Mann, Susan, xix, xxviiin. 21

Mao Han-guang, xxvin. 2

marital violence, 11–16, 23
 and *baogu* (protecting the innocent), 12
 case of Grand Princess Lanling and
  Liu Hui, 4
 implication for verdicts of, 11

marriage
 and Confucian family ethics, 1, 2, 6,
  10, 11, 13, 18, 21, 22, 23
 intermarriage between races, 8
 levirate, 59–61, 62
 see also heqin

Martin-Liao, Tienchi, xvi

Matsunaga, Daigan and Alicia, 200, 209n.
 22

Maudgalyayana, *see* Mulian

May Fourth Movement, xvi, xix

medieval China, *see* periodization, Chinese

Medu (Maodun), 41, 44, 46, 56–7, 68n. 6

Mencius (or Mengzi, *Mencius*), xxviiin. 15,
 112, 114, 141n. 23

Meng Yue, xvi

menxia (Department of Chancellery), 4,
 6–8, 19

mianzi ("face"), 221

Middle Ages (European), 1, 21–2

Ming (Emperor) (r. 466–72), 21, 37n. 102,
 81

Ming-chun (Mingjun), *see* Wang Zhaojun

Ming Dynasty (1368–1644 C.E.), xvi, 41,
 79, 87, 91, 96, 97, 103, 198, 219
 heqin policy, 44
 women warriors in novels of the,
  100–1

ming fu (residence of darkness), 205, 206

ming jian (the realm of darkness), 206

ming si (Dark of Department), 206

Moist, 89, 90

Mongols, 41, 44, 59, 67, 67n. 1, 99

motherhood, Confucian, 113, 128, 130, 131
 maternal love (*ci*), 116
 mothering, 128–9
 sagacity, 129–30
 taijiao (fetal instruction), 145n. 67

Mou, Sherry, xxiii, 205

mourning obligations (ceremonies or
 rituals), 21, 142n. 36

Mulan, 77–9, 81–8, 92–4 *passim,* 100, 103
 in local histories, 86–7
 in "Mulan ci" ("The Ballad of
  Mulan"), 81–6
 in Xu Wei's *Si sheng yuan (The Four
  Shrieks of the Monkey)*, 87–8

"Mulan ci" ("The Poem of Mulan," by
 Yang Weizhen), 86

Mulan shan (Mount Mulan), 86–7

"Mulan shi" ("The Poem of Mulan," by
 Wei Yuanfu), 86, 105n. 9

Mulian ("eye-connection," Muqianlian,
 Maudgalyayana, or Luopu), the legend
 of, 193–205, 207–8, 208n. 3
 as a composite of Confucianism,
  Buddhism, and Daoism, 189–90
 earliest reference of, 188
 Freudian interpretation of, 200–1, 202

in Joseph Campbell's terms, 202–3
in *Yulanpen Sutra,* 194–5
see also Qingti, Lady; Yulanpen Festival
Mulian jiumu zaju (The Drama of Mulian Saving His Mother), 198
Mulian ruming zaju (The Drama of Mulian Saving His Mother), 198
Mulian sanshi baojuan (The Precious Scroll of Mulian's Three Incarnations), 197
Mulian xingxiao xiwen (The Practice of Filial Piety in Mulian Saving His Mother), 198
Muqianlian, *see* Mulian
Mutianzi zhuan (An Account [of the travels] of the Son of Heaven Mu), 203, 210–11n. 43
mutilation, bodily, xxii, 4
   gegu (cutting a piece of flesh), 147n. 78
   of self, 119 (the case of Li Miaofa), 125–6 (the case of Ms. Lu, wife of Fang Xuanling), 127 (the case of Ms. Cheng), 133–4
   and sexuality, 126, 127, 131–2
   and women's subjectivity, 134

Naitō Konan (1866–1934), xv
   Naitō hypothesis, xxviin. 2
Nanyuan (Southern Office), 157, 167n. 56
neifu (being a subordinate part of China), 49, 50
neihan (palace writers), 236n. 38
Nei xun (Instructions of the Interior, by Empress Xu), 81
neo-Confucianism, *see under* Confucianism
Nie Feng, 93
Nie Rong, 110
Nie Zheng, 110
nijie jueli (to go against moderation and rupture reason), 32n. 65
Ningguo (Princess), 48, 49, 60–1, 65
Ningguo, Little (Princess), 48, 51
Ningyuanguo, 45
Niu Sengru (779–847, *Xuanguai lu*), 206
"Nü jie" ("Admonitions for Women," by Ban Zhao), xix, 81, 83, 104n. 1, 122–3, 205
Nü lunyu (The Female Analects), 81
Nü sishu (The Four Books for Women), 81
nü xia, see lady knight-errant
Nü xiaojing (Book of Filial Piety for Women), 81
Nü xun (Instructions of the Interior), 81

Pang Ji (Yinggong, 988–1063), 221–2, 234n. 25, 234–5n. 26, 235n. 28, 236n. 30
   Pang Yuanlu (1015–47, son)
Pan Jinlian (Golden Lotus), 77, 97
Parsons, John Carmi, 128–9
Pei Xun, 29n. 39, 30n. 43
periodization, Chinese
   "high antiquity" (*jōko*), xv
   medieval age, China's, xv, xviin. 2, 1–3, 8, 13, 22
   "medieval Chinese" (*zhonggu*), xv
   "middle antiquity" (*chūko*), xv
   "modern times" (*kinsei*), xv
Phillips, E.D., 59
Pingkang li (fang), *see* Beili
prostitution, 149, 161, 168n. 77
   see also female entertainers; *chang^a* (prostitute); *ji^a* (entertainer)
Pu Songling (1640–1715), *see Liaozhai zhiyi*

Qian guo furen (Duchess of Qian), 160
Qianjin (Princess), 56, 58
Qiao Zhizhi, 151–2
Qi Dynasty, Northern (550–77), 32n. 66, 37n. 98
qie (concubine), *see* concubinage
Qin Dynasty (221 B.C.E.–207 B.C.E.), xvii, 13, 41
Qingbo biezhi (Complementary Notes by One Living Near Qingbo), see Zhou Hui
Qing Dynasty (1644–1911 C.E.), xvi, 41, 46, 65–6, 79, 81, 91, 93, 95, 100–1, 103, 122, 219
Qinghe Cui, 20, 36n. 97
Qingti, Lady, 195, 196, 201–2
   and the tradition of goddess-temptress, 202–3
qishi (execution in the marketplace), 9, 13, 34n. 86
Qiu Zhonglin, 133
qixi (Seventh Night), the legend of, 191, 198
Queen Mother of the West, 183, 203, 210n. 43
Qujiang, 155

red-light districts, *see under* Beili
Ren Bantang, 165n. 13
Renzong (Emperor) (r. 1022–63), 234n. 25

righteousness (*yi*), 113–14, 116
Riley, Denise, xx
ritual pollution, 182
Rosaldo, Michelle Z., 52
Rubin, Gayle, 51, 52, 57
Rujia (Confucius school), xxviin. 9, 173
    see also under Confucianism
Runan (Prince), 21, 31n. 53
Runniang, 154

sainthood, *see* Daoist sainthood
sancong (three obediences or three
    followings), 18, 34n. 75, 35n. 87, 104n.
    1, 140n. 20, 211n. 46
sancong side (three obediences and four
    virtues), 78, 204
sangong langzhong (Director of Three
    Dukes), 4, 19
san guan (three officers), 192
Sanguo zhi (*The History of the Three
    Kingdoms*), 192
Sanqu, 154
Sanshui xiaodu (*Little Tablets [By the Fellow]
    from Three Rivers* by Huangfu Mei), 174,
    180–1
Sansi (State Finance Commission), 229n. 2
san yuan (Three Primordials), 192
Schafer, Edward, 156, 164nn. 5, 6
Serruys, Henry, 44, 70n. 42
sex crimes, *see* adultery; fornication
sexuality, woman's, 112–4, 115, 121–2, 126,
    127, 130, 132, 134
    degenderization, 125–6, 130
    see also womanly virtues: chastity
Shangde (Princess), 155
Shang Dynasty (sixteenth to eleventh
    centuries B.C.E.), xvii, 80, 152
Shangqing (Supreme Clear Realm), 171,
    173, 174, 176–7, 180, 183
shangshu (imperial secretary), 6
shangshu sheng (Department of State
    Affairs), 4, 6, 7, 14–5, 19
Shangyuan (Upper Primordial), 192
Shanshan, 44
Shanxi, 100, 221
Shao Bowen (1021–86, *He'nan Shaoshi
    wenjian qianlu*), 216, 225, 228, 229–30n.
    3, 237n. 43
    account on Wang Anshi and Sima
        Guang, 217–8, 227

Shenzong (Emperor) (r. 1067–85), 217,
    231n. 7
shi (literati), *see under* literati
Shi Chaoyi, 43
Shi Chong, 64
shidaifu (literati or gentleman-officials), *see
    under* literati
Shi ji (*Records of the Grand Historian*, Sima
    Qian, 145-ca. 86), 41, 42, 88, 90, 110,
    152,
    "Youxia liezhuan" ("Biographies of
        Wandering Knights"), 88, 90
shijie (liberation by means of the corpse),
    175
Shi jing (The book of poetry), xviii, 113–14
Shitong (*Historical Perspectives*), *see* Liu Zhiji
Shi Yongming, 207
shi zu (powerful clans), 115
Shu Han period (222–80), 31n. 56
Shuihu zhuan (*Water Margin*), 79, 88, 96–9,
    104
    Lin Chong, 99
    Madame Ma, as possible model for
        Ten-feet Green, 98–9
    Song Jiang, 96–9
    Yizhang qing Hu sanniang (Ten-feet
        Green), 97–9 *passim*
Shu jing (Book of Documents), xviii, 114, 235
shun (obedient), 132
Shuowen jiezi (*Explicating the Written
    Characters*, by Xu Shen, 30–124), 110,
    138n. 4
shuyi (etiquette manuals), 236n. 31
sili jiaowei (metropolitan commandant), 33n.
    74
Sima Guang (Wengong, 1019–86), xxiv, 44,
    216, 217, 229n. 1, 234n. 26, 235n. 29,
    235nn. 32, 35, 237n. 44
    concubines, 220–1
        Lady Liu's possible motives, 221–2
        refusal, 225–8
        views on, 222–3
    Jiafan (Family Norms), 223
    relatives: Sima Chi (980–1041,
        father), 229n. 1; Sima Kang
        (Gongxiu, adopted son), 224,
        236n. 38; Sima Zhi (Zili, Sima
        Kang's son), 224
    Simashi shuyi (Mr. Sima's notes on the
        Ceremonies and Rites canon), 222–3

Zizhi tongjian (*Comprehensive Mirror for Aid in Government*), 42, 43, 229n. 1
Sima Qian, *see Shi ji*
Sima Shi, 33n. 74
Sinocentrism, 40, 48
Si sheng yuan (*The Four Shrieks of the Monkey*), 87–88
Smith, Richard J., 237n. 42
Song Dexi, 164n. 11
Song Dynasty (960–1279), xvii, 41, 86, 91, 96, 110, 115, 215–20, 222, 225–6
    Mulian legend in *baojuan* of the, 197–8
    sources for *Shuihu zhuan,* 98–9
    sources for *Yangjiafu shidai zhongyong yanji zhizhuan,* 100–1
    spirit of collectivity, 222
    types of writings on women, 216
    Yulanpen Festival in, 189
Song Ruohua, 81
Song shi (*The History of the Song Dynasty*), 96, 100, 101, 217, 224
Sou shen ji (*In Search of Deities,* by Gan Bao, ca. 320), 83–4, 90
Southern Dynasties (420–598), 9
Spivak, Gayatri Chakravorty, 132, 134, 146n. 75
Stacey, Judith, 234n. 21
"Story of Yang Chang[a]," 150
Subaltern consciousness, 132, 134, 146n. 75
subjectivity of women, 113, 134
suicide, 126, 131
Sui Dynasty (581–618), xviii, 41, 129
    heqin practice, 45, 48, 49, 56, 58, 61
Sui shu (*The History of the Sui Dynasty*), 48, 56
su jiang (popular lectures), 196
Sun Qi (Tang Dynasty, *Beili zhi*), 152, 153, 155, 156, 158–60, 163–4n. 1
Sun Shuyu, 96, 97, 98
Sun Zhao, 234–5n. 26
Sun Zi (Sun Wu), 80
Suzong (Emperor) (r. 756–61), 43, 49, 60, 65

Tai (Mount), 201, 205
Taihe (Princess), 57
Taihe period (827–35), 127
Tai Jingnong, 206

Taiping guangji (*Extensive Gleanings of the Reign of Great Tranquillity,* by Li Fang), 91–5, 142–3n. 45
    "Chezhong nüzi" ("The Woman Inside a Carriage"), 91
    "Cui Shensi" ("Cui Shensi['s wife]"), 91, 9294–5
    "Guren qi" ("The Merchant's Wife"), 91, 94
    "Haoxia" ("Gallant Knights"), 92
    "Hongxian" ("Red Thread"), 91, 92, 94
    "Jing shisan niang" ("Lady Jing the Thirteenth"), 91, 92
    "Nie Yinniang" ("The Mysterious Girl of the Nie Family," by Pei Xing), 91–5
    "Qiuran ke" ("The Curly-Bearded Stranger"), 91–2, 94
    Hongfu, 92, 94
    "Xie Xiao'e" ("Story of Xie Xiao'e," by Li Gongzuo), 92–3, 142n. 45
Taiqing (Grand Clear Realm), 174
Tai shan fu jun (the Magistrate of Mt. Tai), 205, 212n. 53
Taiwu (Emperor) (r. 424–51), 34n. 82, 36n. 94
Taiyuan (Grand Princess), 29n. 39, 30n. 43
Taiyuan (Prefecture), 221
Taizong (Emperor) (r. 627–49), 42, 57, 119
"Taizong ruming ji" (Emperor Taizong's Ingression into the Dark Regions"), 206
Taizu (Emperor) (r. 960–76), 230n. 3
Tang Ci, 13
Tang Dynasty (618–907), xv, xviii, 11, 20, 22, 59, 81, 86, 103, 104, 134, 196, 197, 204, 206–7
    Buddhism in, xvii, xxiv, 206–7
    Daoism in, xvii, 171–4
    heqin policy, 39–45 *passim,* 48, 49–50, 56, 57, 61
    ji[a]-entertainers in Chang'an of the, 149–53
    official histories' biographies of women, 110–33
    see also Jiu Tang shu; Xin Tang shu
    transformation narratives, 175–81
    Yulanpen Festival in, 189
Tang Fu, 13–4

Tang lü (Tang code), 144n. 63
    penalty difference for a wife and a
        husband, 31n. 52
        *Tang lü shuyi (Annotations of the Tang
            code)*
            "Dousong" ("Assault and
                Accusations"), 29n. 31
            "Miscellaneous Articles," 29n. 31
*Taoan mengyi (Recollections of Taoan's Past
    Dreams)*, 198
Teiser, Stephen F., 189, 191
Ten Commandments, 172
Tibet, 43, 50, 57, 61, 67, 67n. 1
T'ien Ju-k'ang *(Male Anxiety and Female
    Chastity)*, 143n. 52
tingwei (chamberlain for law enforcement),
    35n. 92
tingwei shaoqing (chief minister of law
    enforcement), 19
tongji (family members registered in the
    same household), 18
tongpan (controller-general), 221
Tou Ngo (Dou E), 100
Tujue, *see under heqin*
Tuoba, 3, 18, 20
Türgis, 43
Tuyuhun, *see under heqin*

ullambana (hanging upside down), 188, 201–2
Uyghur (Huihe), 43, 48, 67

virtues, womanly (feminine), 122, 134
    (fudao)
        chastity *(zhen)*, 77, 113, 115, 116,
            121–2, 124, 125–6, 127, 131–2,
            147n. 85
        four virtues *(fude,* womanly virtue;
            fugong, womanly work; *furong,*
            womanly bearing; *fuyan,* womanly
            words), 104n. 1, 204
        see also loyalty; motherhood,
            Confucian; righteousness; *sancong;
            shun*

Waltner, Ann, 219
Wang, Mrs. (Daoist adept), 177
Wang Anshi (Jinggong, 1021–86), xxiv, 216,
    223, 225–8, 229n. 2; 232n. 18
    concubines, 217–8
    his wife's possible motives, 118–20

refusal, 225–8
    Wang Pang (1044–76, son), 219, 223,
        232–3nn. 17–9
Wang Fajin, 176
Wang Fengxian, 178
Wang Gongwu, 110
Wang Jian, 174–5
Wang Mang, 44, 51
Wang Shi, 159
Wang Ying, 97, 99
Wang Zhaojun, 45, 51, 54, 58, 60, 62, 63,
    64–5, 100
    in history, 45, 51, 60, 64
    in literary creation, 54, 62, 63, 64–5
Wannian (County), 157–8
Water Margin, see Shuihu zhuan
Wei Dynasty, Northern (386–534), 20
    see also under Confucianization
Wei Huacun (Lady), 177–8
Wei Rong, 10, 30n. 44
*Wei shu (The History of the (Northern) Wei
    Dynasty)*
        "Biography of Liu Hui" *(Liu Hui
            zhuan)*, 3, 28n. 16
        "Doulü" ("Law of Assault"), 5, 8
        "Dousong" ("Assault and
            Accusations"), 29n. 31
        "Monograph of Law," 3
Wei Tai (ca. 1050–1110, *Dongxuan bilu*),
    232n. 18
Wei Yuanfu, 86
Wei Zeng, 159
Wei Zhou, 159
Wencheng (Princess), 50
Wendi (Emperor) (r. 179–157 B.C.E.), 49,
    59
Wenming (Empress Dowager) (r. 466–7,
    476–90), 35n. 92, 37n. 100
Wenzong (Emperor) (r. 827–40), 127
Wheeler, Bonnie, 128–9
widowhood, 113, 130
    widow chastity, 126
    widow remarriage, 126, 128, 144nn.
        63, 64, 145n. 70
    widow suicide, 122
Wolf, Margery ("uterine family"), xx
womanhood, Chinese, xvi, 111, 122, 133,
    134, 146n. 74, 231–2n. 16
    in Confucian tradition, 78, 82, 83,
        85–6, 87, 92, 95, 122–3, 134, 204

and sexuality, 112–3
see also sexuality, women's; virtue, womanly
The Woman Warrior: Memoirs of a Girlhood Among Ghosts, 78
white tigers, 78–9, 105n. 2, 139n. 8
see also Maxine Hong Kingston
women
in Chinese medieval times, xv, xx
and family, xxi–xxii
in medieval Europe, xix
see also under literati tradition
women's bodies, xxii
women's education, *see* education of women
women's roles, xxi
as daughters-in-law, 123–4, 145n. 67
as devoted widows (in biographies of women), 111, 116, 126–8, 130, 131, 137
as dutiful wives (in biographies of women), 111, 116, 122–6, 130, 131, 137
relationship with husbands, 132
as exemplary mothers (in biographies of women), 111, 116, 128–30, 131, 137
in family, xxi
in literature, xxi
as filial daughters (in biographies of women), 111, 116, 117–22, 130, 137
as learned instructresses (as a motif in biographies of women), 123, 128–9, 144n. 65, 146n. 71
see also heqin; motherhood; widowhood
women warriors, Chinese, xxi, 77–80 *passim*
in *The Woman Warrior,* 78
see also Fuhao; Mulan; lady knight-errant
"women worthies," 110, 139n. 8
Wong, Sun-ming, 122–3
Wu (King) (r. 841–28 B.C.E), 80
Wu, Lady (wife of Wang An-shi), 217–20, 222, 231–2n. 16
Wuchang xianjun (District Mistress of Wuchang), 127
Wu Daozi, 199

Wudi (Emperor) (r. 140–87 B.C.E.), 43–4, 49
Wuding (Shang king, 1324–1265 B.C.E.), 80
wufu (the five degrees of mourning), 2
wulun (five human relationships), 143n. 49
Wusun *kunmi, see under heqin*
wuxia xiaoshuo (knight-errant romances), 93, 100, 101
wuxing (five elements), 204, 232n. 18
Wu Yansi, 151–2
Wu Yuanji, 124
Wu Yue chunqiu (Spring and Autumn Annals of the Kingdom of Wu and the Yue, by Zhao ye, first century), 90–1
Wu Zetian (Emperor) (r. 684–705), 20–1, 151–2
Wyatt, Don J., xxiv–xxv, xxviin. 4

Xi (people), 45
xi (lustration), 191
xia (knight-errant), xxviii, 88–90, 92, 95
five categories of, 90
Xi'an, 149
Xian'an (Princess), 61
Xianbei, 3, 6, 8–9, 20, 22, 29n. 37, 35n. 88, 37n. 100
xianü, see lady knight-errant
Xianü qiyuan, see Ernü yingxiong zhuan
Xianzong (Emperor) (r. 806–20), 57
Xiao jing (The Classic of Filiality), 117, 133
Xiaojing (Emperor) (r. 534–50), 30n. 43
Xiaoman, 151
Xiaoming (Emperor) (r. 516–28), 35n. 92
Xiaowen (Emperor) (r. 471–99), 12, 20, 34n. 83, 35n. 92, 36n. 94, 37n. 100
Xiaowu (Emperor) (r. 500–15), 35n. 92
Xiayuan (Lower Primordial), 192
Xie (Ms.), 17, 34n. 79
Xie Xiao'e, 92–3, 120–1, 127, 142n. 45
see also under Taiping guangji
Xieyou (Princess), 47, 60, 61
Xijun (Princess), 57–60 *passim,* 61–2
xinfa ("new policies"), 217
xing (banishment and execution), 5, 28n. 21
xingshi (walking corpse), 175
Xin Tang shu (The New History of the Tang Dynasty), 110–34 *passim*
cases on daughter-in-law, 123–4
cases on mourning, 117–19
cases on revenge, 120–1

"Introduction" *(xu)* to the biographies of women, 114–15

Xinxing (Princess), 42

Xiongnu, *see under heqin*

Xiong, Victor, xxiv

Xiubian Mulian jiumu quanshan xiwen (A New Compilation of the Text to the Play About Mulian Rescuing His Mother and Exhorting Her to Goodness), 198, 199

Xiyu duhufu (the military office in western territory), 60

Xizong (Emperor) (r. 873–88), 149

xu (Introduction), 111, 113–16, 122, 126, 128

Xuandi (Emperor) (r. 73–49 B.C.E.), 16, 47

Xuanguai lu (Records of the Mystical and the Supernatural), see Niu Sengru

Xuanwu (Emperor) (r. 500–15), 19, 21

Xuanᵃzong (Emperor) (r. 846–59), 149, 160

Xuanzong (Emperor) (r. 712–56), 48, 150

Xue Xuantong, 179

Xueyantuo, 42–3

Xu Fuguan, 204

Xun (Ms.), 33n. 74

Xun Yi, 33n. 74

Xu Shen, *see Shuowen jiezi*

Xu Wei (1521–93), 87–8, 94
  see also Si sheng yuan

Xu Xiangu, 179

Yama (Yanluo wang), 201, 206

Yancheng, 117

yang (opposite of yin), 190, 191, 207–8, 211n. 49
  see also yin (opposite of yang); yin-yang theory

Yangdi (Emperor) (r. 581–604), 58

Yangjiafu shidai zhongyong yanyi zhizhuan (The Heroic Lives of the Yang Family Generals), 100–1, 103, 104
  Mu Guiying, 77, 100–1
  She Saihua, 77, 100–1
  Yang Ye, 100–1

yang jian (the realm of the living), 204, 207

Yang Mu, 84

Yang Pingzhi, 179

Yang Weizhen, 86

Yaoniang, 151–2

yi (intent), 26, 29n. 32

yi (righteousness), 79, 94, 96, 102–3, 113–14

Yicheng (Princess), 60, 61

Yi jing (The Book of Changes), 204, 211–2n. 50

Yi li (The Book of Ceremonies), 2, 5–6, 14, 15, 25, 35n. 87, 140n. 20, 141n. 28, 236n. 32
  "Sangfu" ("Mourning") chapter, 2, 25, 27n. 5, 34n. 75, 35n. 75

yin (opposite of yang), 111, 140nn.16, 17, 191, 211n. 49, 211–2n. 50
  association with hell, 190, 205–7
  see also yin-yang theory

yin ("shadow" privilege), 206

ying (concubine), 160

yin jian, 190, 204, 207

yin si (Yin Department), 206

yin si dawang (the Great King of the Yin Department), 206

yin-yang theory, 140nn. 16, 17, 112, 122–3, 140n. 17, 190, 203, 204–8, 211–2n. 50
  yang zun yin bei (yang is dominating and yin is submissive), 112, 205

Yiwen leiju (Classified Collection of Arts and Letters), 192–3

Yizong (Emperor) (r. 859–73), 149

"Yongcheng jixian lu" (Records of the Assembled Transcendents of the Fortified Walled City), 173, 183

you du (City of Darkness), 205–6

You Minggen, 36n. 94

youxia (knight-errant), 79, 90, 91
  see also under literati

"You xian ku" ("The Dwelling of Playful Goddesses"), 203, 210–1n. 43

You Ya, 36n. 94

You Zhao, 5, 7, 10, 19–20, 36n. 94, 177

Yuandi (Emperor) (r. 48–33 B.C.E.), 44, 58, 64

Yuan Dynasty (1271–1368), 59, 65, 91, 99–100, 128, 198

Yuan Hui (Prince of Chengyang), 29n. 38

Yuan Jingzhe (Prince of Zhangwu), 30n. 44

Yuan Qin, 30n. 49, 36n. 97

Yuan Shen (Prince of Guangyang), 29n. 38

Yuan Xiuyi, 6, 20

Yuanyou, 224

Yu Cong, 155, 160

Yuefu Collection (Yuefu shiji), 82, 86
Yulanpen Festival, 188–9, 192–5, 198, 200–1
    Confucian influence of the, 190–2
    the origin of, 187–9
    The Yulanpen Sutra (Yulanpen jing), 188, 194–6, 198, 200
Yuli (Jade Registrar), 192
Yuqing (Jade of Clear Realm), 174
yushi tai (censorate), 127
Yu Xianye, 30n. 43
Yu Xuanji (844–68), 174, 175, 176, 180–1
Yü Ying-shih, xxvin. 3, xxviiinn. 11, 12
Yu Yunshu, 198–9
Yu Zhuo, 155, 160

zaixiang, see chengxiang
zaju (variety plays), 87, 99
zan (eulogy), 111, 113–14, 122, 125
Zhang (Ms.), 13–4, 32n. 65
Zhang, Lady (wife of Sima Guang), 234n. 26
Zhang Cun (984–1071), 234n. 26
Zhang Dai (1599–ca. 1684), 198–9
Zhang Fei (Chang Fei), 32n. 65
Zhang Rongfei, 4–6 *passim*, 8, 21
Zhang Shunmin (ca. 1034–ca. 1110, *Huamanlu*), 234n. 26, 236n. 30
Zhangsun Lü, 31n. 55
Zhangsun Sheng, 49
Zhangsun Zhi, 32n. 62
Zhang Yong, 98
Zhang Zai (1020–77), 198–9, 233n. 20
Zhaodi (Emperor) (r. 86–74 B.C.E.), 33n. 73
Zhao Guanyuan, 157
Zhao Luanluan, 156
Zhao Ye, *see Wu Yue chunqiu*
Zhao Yi (1727–1814), 161
zhen (devotion or virtue), 113, 134, 147n. 85
    see also under womanly virtue

Zhenfa nianchu jing (Sutra of the Remembrance of True Law), 197
Zheng (Ms.), 10, 30n. 42
Zheng Guangye, 158
Zheng Yanzu, 30n. 39
Zheng Zhizhen (fl. 1582), 198–9
Zhezong (Emperor) (r. 1085–1100), 44
Zhigao'an (Proclamation Drafting Session), 220
zhongshu sheng (Secretariat), 19
zhong xiao jie yi (loyalty, filial piety, integrity, and righteousness), xxiii, 78, 102, 103
Zhong Xingshuo, 59
Zhongyuan (Middle Primordial), 176, 187–8, 192–3, 198
    see also san yuan; Shangyuan; Xiayuan; Yulanpen Festival
Zhou (King), 152
Zhou Dynasty (eleventh century–256 B.C.E.), xvii, 58
Zhou Dynasty, Northern (557–81), 58
Zhou Hui (1126–ca. 1198, *Qingbo biezhi*), 235–6n. 29
Zhou li (The Book of Rites of the Zhou Dynasty), 141n. 28
zhuangyuan (champion of the imperial examination), 88
Zhuangzi, 171
zhubu (assistant magistrate), 33n. 74
zhujiao (an assistant instructor), 230n. 3
Zhu Shuzhen, xix
Zhu Xi (1130–1200), 161, 233n. 20
Zizhi tong jian, see under Sima Guang
Zong Lin (ca. 498–561, *Jingchu suishi ji*), 188
zuopuye jian menxia shilang (vice director of the left and concurrent vice director of the chancellery), 229n. 1
zuosi langzhong (left bureau director), 151
zuoyou jiaofang (Departments of Stage Performances), 150, 159–60